DISCARDED

Hegel

and the *Philosophy of Right*

'Dudley Knowles writes clearly, engagingly, and with evident enthusiasm for his topic, in a way that retains the reader's interest throughout . . . [his] open approach and pedagogic style will make the book extremely popular with students and teachers alike.'

Robert Stern, *Sheffield University*

'The Routledge Philosophy GuideBook to *Hegel and the Philosophy of Right* will be a welcome addition, and beneficial to students of Hegel's *Philosophy of Right* . . . The writing is lively and engaging, and Knowles relates many of Hegel's arguments to contemporary debates in political philosophy.'

Mark Tunick, *Florida Atlantic University, USA*

Hegel's *Philosophy of Right* is recognized as one of the great works of political philosophy. His place in the history of ideas is significant and he can be seen as a precursor of Marx, a critic of Kant, and the target of anti-Enlightenment irrationalism. Until now there has never been a secondary text that deals solely with this influential work and Dudley Knowles's careful exposition will be a welcome aid to anyone studying the *Philosophy of Right*, or indeed Hegel's wider writings.

This book contains broad discussions of such topics as persons and rights, property, punishment, moral psychology, civil society, freedom and war. Knowles also reviews the background to the *Philosophy of Right* and explains the key concepts of Hegel's thought.

Dudley Knowles is Senior Lecturer in Philosophy at the University of Glasgow. He is author of *Political Philosophy* (London: Routledge, 2001), and editor of *Explanation and its Limits* (1990) and (with John Skorupski) *Virtue and Taste* (1993).

Routledge Philosophy GuideBooks

Edited by Tim Crane and Jonathan Wolff
University College London

LONDON AND NEW YORK

Routledge Philosophy GuideBook to

Hegel
and the
Philosophy
of Right

ROUTLEDGE

■ Dudley Knowles

First published 2002
by Routledge
11 New Fetter Lane,
London EC4P 4EE

Simultaneously published in
the USA and Canada
by Routledge
29 West 35th Street,
New York, NY 10001

*Routledge is an imprint of
the Taylor & Francis Group*

© 2002 Dudley Knowles

Typeset in Times by Florence
Production Ltd, Stoodleigh, Devon
Printed and bound in Great Britain
by TJ International Ltd,
Padstow, Cornwall

*British Library Cataloguing in
Publication Data*
A catalogue record for this book is
available from the British Library

*Library of Congress Cataloging
in Publication Data*
A catalog record for this book has
been requested

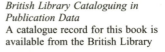

ISBN 0–415–16577–6 (hbk)
ISBN 0–415–16578–4 (pbk)

To Anne, Katy and Helen, with love

Contents

Preface

Strangely, I can still remember the first time I read any Hegel. I was returning from the Natural History Museum in Kensington, in a good mood because I had just been told that the rock which my father-in-law used as a doorstop was in fact the fossilized vertebra of a plesiosaur. (I have it still.) And being so cheerful, I nipped into a second-hand bookshop on my way home. The philosophy shelves were spare, but they had a copy of Walter Kaufmann's *Hegel*, which I bought to celebrate serendipity. On the Underground I had a shot at reading his translation of the formidable Preface to the *Phenomenology of Spirit*.

There is a philosophers' version of an urban myth which records that a famous artist had the most erotic weekend of his life, unable to get out of bed, transfixed by his reading of the *Phenomenology*, all at one go! I cannot record an erotic experience on the Underground train, but I do remember the experience of being desperately perplexed by the text, yet having confidence in Kaufmann's evidently sincere belief that

anyone can understand (even the darkest passages in) Hegel if they study him closely. In any event the book was so interesting, with its letters and stories, that I went back to the start and read it from cover to cover.

In this book I have tried to rediscover and communicate this confidence. Throughout my teaching of Hegel I have maintained, as a first objective, the belief that all students (optimistically says he: all 'general readers') can understand Hegel if they work hard enough at the texts. This belief has been my guiding principle as I have struggled to write this book. Friends of mine have found the project comical. The late Flint Schier used to josh my efforts at 'picking apart the pellets of the Owl of Minerva', and Stanley Kleinberg still does, in his uniquely pedantic fashion. If I had the cheek to preface it with a slogan of my own composition it would be 'You, too, can understand Hegel', and Flint would, and Stanley will, guffaw.

Even if my publishers were to write this slogan on buses, I don't expect it would sell more copies. But my experience is that more and more students are interested in Hegel's writings, especially his ethics and political philosophy. And this interest is well judged. Hegel's historical importance is firmly established. His stance as an opponent of liberal theory, notably the social contract theory of Rousseau, his status as a critic of Kant's project in ethics (and much else), his standing as both a source and a target for Marx's doctrines: these standard positionings of Hegel's social thought require that we bring the original into clear view.

Just as important, Hegel is notable for the quality of his contribution to philosophical problems which perplex us still. It's *not wise* to think about freedom of action and social freedom, the nature of human rights, the justification of private property, the practice of punishment, the attribution of agency and responsibility, the quality of moral motivation, the possibilty of deducing moral duties, or the modern opposition of liberalism and communitarianism, without investigating what Hegel has to say on the topic. And if one wishes to investigate the credentials of social institutions, from the family to the predominant form of economic activity (capitalism), to the state, Hegel's reflections offer a sensible place to begin, or a sensible target to attack, not least because his stance is so different from those most commonly encountered nowadays. The study of any of the great dead philosophers takes us out of the parochialism of the present, but in many ways, as you will discover, Hegel offers a unique challenge.

So I offer this book as a companion to anyone who wishes to advance their studies in any of these areas by reading Hegel. My intention, to repeat, has been to clarify his arguments. But clarification and commentary are not docile tasks; they have to be engaged in a critical spirit in order to unearth the most plausible reading or the strongest position to challenge. I'm not unsympathetic to Hegel's positions, but I'm not sympathetic either. I'm not concerned to blacken his reputation amongst philosophers, nor to enhance it. I want to make his work more available by making it more accessible – and that's it. Most definitely, I'm not a hostile or a fan with a typewriter. My interest in the history of political philosophy and its great practitioners is maintained by my enthusiasm for advancing our present understanding of the problems they discuss.

I've been studying and teaching the *Philosophy of Right* on and off for many years. So it is proper that I acknowledge my debts, most of all to other scholars. If the quality of secondary work is an oblique measure of the greatness of a philosopher, as I suspect it is, Hegel has been fortunate in modern times, and I have been a co-beneficiary. In order of reading, I record as the books from which I learnt most: Raymond Plant (*Hegel*), Charles Taylor (*Hegel*), Shlomo Avineri (*Hegel's Theory of the Modern State*), Eric Weil (*Hegel et l'État*), Allen W. Wood (*Hegel's Ethical Thought*), Michael Hardimon (*Hegel's Social Philosophy*) and lately, and not fully digested, Frederick Neuhouser's splendid *Foundations of Hegel's Social Theory*.

This is but a small portion of my debt to other scholars. I've read other books, and articles galore. I've learned much from meetings with other students of Hegel, at the Hegel Society of Great Britain, in 1998 at the meeting of the Hegel Society of America in Athens, Georgia, and in 2000, at a Liberty Fund colloquium in Cambridge, led by Iain Hampsher-Monk and Noel O'Sullivan. I've been lucky, too, in the quality of the students I've taught, undergraduates and graduates in Glasgow, and latterly postgraduates of the St Andrews and Stirling Graduate Programme. By chance, a good number of these have been native German speakers who have responded patiently to questions arising from my slow reading of the German texts. I should mention particularly Stephen Drost and Dagmar Wilhelm. I've discussed much of this material with two doctoral students, Steve Marriott and David Rose, both happily successful, and have been forced to think through my ideas more carefully in their company. I'm grateful to the University of Glasgow for giving me study leave to advance this project, but, most of all, for the use of its library.

My greatest debt is to my friend, John Skorupski, who knows more about Hegel than he lets on. Years and years ago he attended classes I gave in Glasgow on the *Phenomenology*, and over the last few years we have taught together a course in St Andrews which has concentrated on the *Philosophy of Right*. The style of the classes has been that I have spoken for a while, and then John has pinned me to the wall, asking me to clarify, explain more fully, or justify positions I have taken, and making me reply to objections he has put. And the students have then joined in. This has been a regular and salutary experience. I have taken the lessons home, and worked many of them into this book. My work has been much the better for it and it has sustained my enthusiasm for this project. I guess this sort of (costly) joint teaching is rare in universities. It's a pleasure to report my experience that it works, with, I trust, great benefits to all concerned.

Other debts should be recorded. I am grateful to Jo Wolff for agreeing that I present my work on the *Philosophy of Right* in this form, to Tony Bruce and especially Muna Khogali at Routledge for pressing me to get it finished in the kindest possible way, to Siobhan Pattinson for helping me through the final stages to publication, and to Anne Southall for helping with all sorts of secretarial assistance. Two referees for Routledge, Mark Tunick and Bob Stern, commented on the manuscript with a care and detailed attention that go far beyond a reader's duty. I am very grateful to them for helping me to improve the book.

This book has achieved mythical status in my family, yet another source of domestic comedy as I have stopped and started it, written up bits and pieces in articles and reviews associated with it, over far too many years. But this is one of the few occasions when I have the last laugh, as I dedicate it, with love, to Anne, Katy and Helen.

A note on the texts

My study of the *Philosophy of Right* in English translation began with
T. M. Knox's *Hegel's Philosophy of Right* (Oxford: Clarendon Press,
1952) and I find that I still have many sections (inaccurately)
committed to memory. Whilst working on this book, however, I have
chiefly used the Cambridge translation, *Elements of the Philosophy of
Right*, translated by H. B. Nisbet and edited by Allen W. Wood
(Cambridge: Cambridge University Press, 1991). I am grateful to the
publishers and to Professor Nisbet for their kind permission to quote
extensively from this translation. I have selected this translation
because it is more accurate, notably in placing in parentheses German
terms which bear multiple translations according to context, and terms
which German readers can identify as having a technical (philosophical) usage together with colloquial implications. (Likewise, in my
discussion of the text, I sometimes signal the technical usage of a term
by placing the German word in parentheses, sometimes by using capital
letters that are generally inappropriate in English, as for example,
Abstract Right or Ethical Life (*Sittlichkeit*).) Since the selection of
an English term in translation often represents an interpretative or
editorial decision, it is important that these are signalled in the text. In
this respect, as in the provision of a helpful glossary, Nisbet's practice is exemplary.

The German texts I have made most use of are K.-H. Ilting's
four-volume G. W. F. Hegel, *Vorlesungen über Rechtsphilosophie
1818–31* (Stuttgart–Bad Cannstatt: Frommann Verlag, 1974), notably
volume 2, which contains the 1820 published edition together
with Hegel's handwritten notes, and the Suhrkamp edition: G. W. F.
Hegel, *Grundlinien der Philosophie des Rechts oder Naturrecht and
Staatswissenschaft im Grundrisse*, volume 7 (1986) of Hegel, *Werke*,
eds Eva Moldenhauer and Karl Markus Michel (Frankfurt: Suhrkamp
Verlag, 1970). For other writings of Hegel, I have most frequently used
the Glockner edition: G. W. F. Hegel, *Sämtliche Werke*, 20 volumes
plus *Hegel-Lexikon*, Auflage der Jubiläumsausgabe, ed. H. Glockner
(Stuttgart–Bad Cannstatt: Frommann Verlag, 1965), because that is the
edition I have beside my desk.

Refences to main paragraphs of the text of the *Philosophy of Right* are given by number as, e.g., §111. Hegel frequently supplements this material in remarks, which are indented in the text. These are referred to as *Remarks*, e.g. §111R. in English editions; in German editions as, e.g., §111B (*Bemerkungen* or *Anmerkungen*). E. Gans's 1833 edition of the *Philosophy of Right* also included edited selections from the verbatim lecture notes of students who attended Hegel's classes in 1821–2 and 1822–3 (Hotho) and 1824–5 (v. Griesheim). These have been included, and translated, in subsequent editions and are referred to as *Additions*, e.g. §111A in English editions, in German editions as §111Z (*Zusätze*). The complete text of these lecture notes is published in Ilting's edition. Other manuscript lecture notes have been discovered. References to these are to be found in the bibliography at the end of this book. To my knowledge, no-one has demonstrated that these secondary sources are unreliable (which says something about Hegel's style of lecturing as well as testifying to the assiduity of his students). I refer to the Preface of the *Philosophy of Right* by citing the page numbers of the Wood/Nisbet and *Werke* editions in sequence: thus PR 20/24 will take you to one of Hegel's most famous sayings. If I cite Wood's notes to the Cambridge edition, I do this by page number. Abbreviations used when citing other works by Hegel are given in the list of abbreviations.

Abbreviations

The following abbreviations are used for references to works by Hegel and Kant. For full details of works cited, and methods of citation, see the bibliography at the end of the volume.

Works by Hegel

EL	*Hegel's Logic*
ES	*Hegel's Philosophy of Mind*
ETW	*Early Theological Writings*
ILPWH	*Lectures on the Philosophy of World History: Introduction*
JR	*Jenaer Realphilosophie*
Knox	*Hegel's Philosophy of Right*
LPH	*The Philosophy of History*
PP	*The Philosophical Propaedeutic*
PR	*Philosophy of Right*
PS	*Hegel's Phenomenology of Spirit*
PW	*Political Writings*
SL	*Hegel's Science of Logic*
SW	*Sämtliche Werke*, plus *Hegel-Lexikon*

VNS	*Vorlesungen über Naturrecht und Staatswissenschaft*
VPR	*Vorlesungen über Rechtsphilosophie*
VPR17	*Hegel's Lectures on Natural Right and Political Science: The First Philosophy of Right (Heidelberg 1817–1818)*
VPR19	*Philosophie des Rechts: Die Vorlesung von 1819/20 in einer Nachschrift*
Werke	*G. W. F. Hegel: Werke*

Works by Kant

| GMM | 'Groundwork of the Metaphysics of Morals' |
| MM | 'The Metaphysics of Morals' |

Chapter 1

Hegel's life, work and influence

Life

Georg Wilhelm Friedrich Hegel was born in Stuttgart in August 1770, the eldest of three surviving children. His father, Georg Ludwig Hegel, was a minor civil servant at the court of the Duchy of Württemberg. He was an intelligent and studious child, but never docile. At 14 he went to the Stuttgarter Gymnasium, where he encountered Enlightenment ideas, reading Rousseau (at first or second hand), Adam Smith (in translation), and Lessing, who influenced his recorded aspiration to become a man of letters, a popular educator. From the Gymnasium he advanced in 1788 to the Tübingen Stift, a Protestant seminary designed to qualify students as pastors in the Lutheran Church. By an extraordinary coincidence he found himself in the same class as Friedrich Hölderlin, who would become one of the finest German poets. In 1790 these two close friends found another fellow philosophical spirit in the person of Friedrich Wilhelm Joseph von Schelling, all three sharing a room and nursing disgruntlements against the

old-fashioned studies and regime of the Stift, which they believed to embody the reactionary, claustrophobic spirit of old-fashioned Württemberg. Jointly they followed the events of the French Revolution and enthused over the victories of the revolutionary army against the forces of the Hapsburg Empire.

The three friends had plenty to talk about other than their studies. Believing as so many great thinkers have done that they lived in an age of transition, they speculated on what form the new world should take. In particular, they derived from Rousseau and Lessing a concern to identify the spiritual contours of the society that would emerge from the revolutionary turmoil, and under the influence of Hölderlin in particular, they looked backwards to an idealized conception of ancient Greece as a world of beauty and harmony and forward to a society that could accommodate the revolutionary aspiration to freedom. Hostile to the orthodox Christianity drummed into them at the Seminary (and no doubt regurgitated in their successful examination performances) the three friends were entranced by Jacobi's critical revelation of Lessing's alleged Spinozistic pantheism. From these controversies Hegel was to develop an early preoccupation with the form of religion or spirituality that would serve as the lifeblood of the emergent new civilization. Though fascinated by the political developments of their age, their response was that of rarefied spiritual analysis as much as close political study and debate.

The group split at the end of their studies in Tübingen. In 1793 both Hegel and Hölderlin took up positions as house tutors, Hegel moving to Berne, Hölderlin moving to Waltershausen, Jena and Weimar before settling in Frankfurt where Hegel was to join him in 1797. By the time Hegel arrived in Frankfurt his ambitions had crystallized. He no longer aspired to be a man of letters, influencing events through the plausibility and cogency of his understanding of modern religion and current affairs, and by writing articles and pamphlets. He had decided to be an academic philosopher (and unfortunately took this to mean that henceforth he had to speak a different language in his writing from that which he used with his wine-merchants and whist partners). Prompted by Hölderlin, who in these early years was approaching the height of his poetical achievement, Hegel perceived, but darkly, the truth of a variety of absolute idealism, which for the while aligned itself with the work of Schelling, but in historical terms advanced the trajectory of Kant's and Fichte's idealism.

In 1801 this strong commitment to academia induced him to follow Schelling (already an established professor) to Jena, to a post as *Privatdozent*, a (virtually unpaid) tutorial assistant – *plus ça change*. Jena at that time must have been a dazzling university community, strongly research orientated, with celebrity professors, and in consequence, students flocking in. Unfortunately, shortly after or just before Hegel arrived most of Jena's academic stars left. Schelling, his youthful friend, and latterly patron, departed for Würzburg in 1803 in the wake of a sex scandal. So Hegel found himself as isolated as before. Hegel stayed in Jena until 1807 – never finding a fully paid, permanent position – spinning out a legacy and applying for jobs all over the place, even claiming the ability to teach botany when a job turned up. He did good philosophical work, first in Schelling's orbit as author of a text describing *The Difference between Fichte's and Schelling's Systems of Philosophy* (1801), next as co-editor of, and contributor to, the *Critical Journal of Philosophy* (1802–3). In these capacities Hegel published in 1802–3 his essay on Natural Law – 'On the Scientific Ways of Treating Natural Law, on its Place in Practical Philosophy, and its Relation to the Positive Sciences of Right' (PW: 102–80 / SW 1: 435–537). In this important early work Hegel introduces criticisms of 'individualist' normative ethics, notably social contract theories of the state and Kantian ethics, which he kept in place for the rest of his intellectual life, and which he would redeploy in the *Philosophy of Right*. Then, wonderfully, following Schelling's departure, he completed *The Phenomenology of Spirit* (1806–7).

Hegel's commitment to an academic career had not diminished his interest in ethical and political affairs and in the *Phenomenology* he introduced readers to the domain of *Geist* or spirit, encountered first in the chapter on self-consciousness as the development of social-cum-psychological structures which enhance self-understanding through creating the necessity for mutual recognition. This process, partly historical, partly analytical, includes the celebrated section on 'Master and Slave'. Two further quasi-narratives follow. In the chapter on 'Reason' Hegel explores man's attempt to employ reason in the quest to understand both the natural world and the moral rules governing our behaviour. In so far as this is a project engaged by individual seekers after truth, epitomized in Kant's attempt to display how a conception of one's own rational agency can be quarried to yield the truths of morality, it must fail. Self-consciousness is shown to be an intersubjective phenomenon in the chapter on 'Spirit' and again it is explained as a historical formation. Beginning with the tragic conflict of family, religious and political allegiances revealed in Sophocles's *Antigone*, Hegel quickly traverses the Roman world and pre-Reformation Christianity to take up the story of the development of spirit in modern Europe. Once again it is a story of conflict and failure as forms of social life are shown to be inadequately structured to permit modern persons to feel at home in their ethical surroundings. Political absolutism corrupts those who collude in its aristocratic rigmaroles. The opposing eighteenth-century projects of 'Enlightenment' and 'Faith' ensure that neither the party of scepticism nor the proponents of genuine religious feeling can give a satisfying account of the modern temper. The revolutionary aspiration to freedom ends in the horror of the Terror period of the French Revolution. Neither Romanticism, nor Kantian moral self-legislation, nor the Rousseauian retreat of the conscientious 'beautiful soul' can heal the divisions in the modern soul and the modern nation-state.

Having disclosed the disastrous spiritual condition of the modern world, Hegel identifies religion and philosophy as the successively more adequate resources to reintegrate our fragmented personalities and shattered social structures. They offer first a glimpse, then a certainty, that man's attempt to comprehend himself, the natural world in which he is located, and the social world to which he must accommodate himself, can finally be successful.

Hegel could not have been satisfied with many elements of the *Phenomenology*.[1] It was a major victory that, after years of intellectual struggle, it finally saw the light of day in print. It provided the opportunity for him to map out the contours of his mature philosophical doctrines, but in the books to follow, many of these would have to be reworked. In the particular sphere of social and political philosophy it is primarily a critical text. History has bequeathed us a legacy of muddled insight and partial truth which reveal that we are living on the cusp of a new rational world. Hegel clearly needed to take himself back to the drawing board before he could portray the modern state as a rational structure which permits self-identification and mutual recognition, which does justice to man's aspiration to freedom in a social world from which there is no escape.

In March 1807, a month after his landlady in Jena had given birth to his illegitimate child and a month before publication of the *Phenomenology*, Hegel took up a post in Bamberg as editor of a daily newspaper, the *Bamberger Zeitung*. He clearly enjoyed the immersion in current affairs, but after less than two years in the post he chose to return to education, not as a university teacher, but as rector of the Gymnasium in Nuremberg. His friend Niethammer, the commissioner for education in Bavaria, engaged Hegel as a pioneering educationalist, trusting him to deliver the reforms he had been devising. In addition to general administration, Hegel was to be principal teacher of philosophy, charged with introducing pupils to speculative philosophy (a subject he was later to judge to be too difficult for schoolchildren). In this role he prepared for his pupils *The Philosophical Propaedeutik* designed to cover in elementary fashion central doctrines in his philosophy (PP). In Nuremberg Hegel married and settled down to a stable, well-respected position in the community. He took his professional duties seriously and found time to carry forward his philosophical work, publishing the *Science of Logic* in three volumes (1812–16).

He stayed nearly eight years in Nuremberg, gaining his first fully professional university post as professor in Heidelberg in 1816. A year later he published the *Encyclopaedia of the Philosophical Sciences* as a handbook to accompany his lectures. Following the format he had introduced for his teaching materials in Nuremberg, this book is a series of numbered paragraphs, often expanded with exegetical notes (Remarks), which he spoke about in his lectures. (Given his lame, stumbling performances in the lecture theatre, these must have been of considerable assistance to his students. More useful still must have been his extempore comments, which were written up by the students and are nowadays published alongside the text.) Hegel was to retain this format three years later in the *Philosophy of Right*.

It makes for an astonishing stylistic performance. In the main paragraphs Hegel demonstrates that he has mastered the canonical professional voice of the philosopher, first sanctified by Kant, then developed by Fichte and Schelling. This requires that argument be radically compressed, the chief instrument of compression being the severe weight of jargon introduced into the discipline. This makes for density and obscurity. It gives the appearance of science and systematicity, whilst fostering ambiguity and equivocation. In suggesting that true philosophy needs to speak in its own voice, it has been a professional disaster in eliciting the complicity of readers in a love of arcana. Mercifully, and contrary to the implicit judgement that this severe and forbidding voice is absolutely necessary for *obiter dicta* at the cutting edge of philosophy, the Remarks (and in most editions, the interpolated lecture notes compiled by students – *Zusätze*: Additions) amplify and clarify the main text. The effect is to give the *Encyclopaedia* and the *Philosophy of Right* a multiple stylistic personality, reading sometimes as impenetrable cant, sometimes as careful philosophical argumentation, and sometimes even as crisp journalistic prose.

Hegel moved on quickly from Heidelberg to the philosophy chair in Berlin (1818), though not before he had given the first version of the lectures that were to be written up as the *Philosophy of Right* (VPR 17). Arguably, for the first time in Hegel's writings, questions of life and work get entangled in the specific sense that scholars have forced us to take a view on how far Hegel's responses to the immediate political issues of his day dictated the content (and hence settle the interpretation) of his published writings. In a broad sense, this was always true. Hegel was proud to be identified as one of the generation of the French Revolution, in much the same sentimental way that I might claim to be a child of the 1960s. Hegel remembered (and celebrated) the fall of the Bastille in 1789 just as I bore my children with tales of Grosvenor Square and demonstrations against the US war in Vietnam. He was appalled by Robespierre's Terror (1792–3), but for years had a rose-tinted view of Napoleon as the sweeper-clean of anachronistic institutions, imposing rational norms on the antiquated social and political structures of those portions of Europe that had the good fortune to be conquered by the French armies.

Prussia was one of the German states that had been set on the track of reform during the Napoleonic era. Ancient privileges were to be swept away in the service of administrative and economic efficiency. Bowing to the spirit of the times, the king, in 1812, had promised a constitution which, though neither democratic nor republican, would acknowledge and regulate competing claims to power in a manner that, he and his ministers trusted, would enlist the willing allegiance of all sectors of the community to the central authority. Hegel was naturally sympathetic to these reformist aspirations as the legacy of Napoleonic rationality. Following the final defeat of Napoleon in 1815, the programme of reform slowed down. Metternich's influence at the Congress of Vienna sanctioned the assertion of the old particular interests of *ancien régime* German states which would be compromised by any explicit constitution. Nonetheless the times were not right for a forceful reclamation of any ancient local privileges which would disempower those elements of the middle classes who were attracted by the Napoleonic ideal of the career open to talents in business or in government.

Repression needed the excuse of an incipient breakdown of law and order before it could take off the velvet gloves. As ever, the occasion was provided by the spectacular revolutionary act of a soft-brained youth. In March 1819 a radical student, Karl Sand, assassinated the reactionary playwright August von Kotzebue. The spectre of revolutionary anarchy was raised. Sand was convicted and executed, and the hunt was on for revolutionary 'demagogues'. (Plato's equation of democracy and demagoguery has been a constant of anti-democratic political rhetoric since fourth-century BCE Athens.) In the second half of the twentieth century mankind became used to student revolt. This has been the inevitable result of structural confrontations within modern states that both require a cadre of educated specialists, motivated by the ideal of the career open to talents, if they are to keep up with the technological advances of economic competitors, and which yet retain a regime of inherited privilege wishing to reserve the political fruit of any technological and administrative advances for themselves. I guess (not being a historian) that Prussia, just at the time that Hegel arrived in Berlin to advance his academic career in the glow of unpressured success, was the *first* nation to identify the modern university as a crucial site of social instability. This was most unfortunate.

That Sand was a student, that 'Jacobin' students were organizing their subversive activities in *Burschenschaften* (student societies

7

distinguished for their drinking exploits as much as for their political agendas), focussed the attention of the political authorities on the universities as the source of political turmoil. Reaction throughout Germany was swift. The Carlsbad decrees of 1819, devised by Metternich and accepted by the King of Prussia with little reluctance, struck directly at the universities of Germany as the sources of subversion. Amongst other measures, they made direct provision for the dismissal of any university teachers who engaged in subversive activities and forbad their reinstatement in other universities.

Hegel was undoubtedly very anxious. A student of his (Asverus) was arrested, fellow-teachers in Berlin were under suspicion, one of them (the theologian de Wette) was dismissed. Hegel himself was having difficulty appointing a teaching assistant, since his nominee (Carové) was ideologically suspect. Hegel could have taken the view that the government repression was excessive, serving to thwart justified reform in the interest of reactionary forces. But it seems he did not. Instead he held Fries and his acolytes (including de Wette) responsible for stirring up student passions and provoking the severe reaction of the state. Jacob Friedrich Fries (1773–1843) was an old philosophical rival, a critic of Hegel's work and previously a (successful) competitor for academic jobs. Hegel attacks him directly in the Preface to the *Philosophy of Right* and concludes that the government is quite right to investigate the content of these subversive philosophical doctrines.

> These principles identify what is right with *subjective ends and opinions*, with *subjective feeling and particular conviction*, and they lead to the destruction of inner ethics and the upright conscience, of love and right among private persons, as well as the destruction of public order and the laws of the state.
>
> (PR: 17/21–2)

If a philosophy leads in this direction – the destruction of public order – no wonder that the state will suppress it.

The explicitness of Hegel's attacks on his contemporaries (who were being investigated and fired from their posts), together with fawning remarks about the patronage of the state for philosophy, led many contemporary readers of the *Philosophy of Right* to denounce it as a reactionary tract, serving the private ends of its author and the public policy of a reactionary regime. Hegel's denunciations in the Preface are clear and explicit to the point that no-one should suppose that the rational state will provide any protection for academic freedom. Any self-respecting philosopher will shiver at Hegel's defence of a close state scrutiny of the philosophical doctrines taught in the university. Whatever his private views of Fries or his professional views of Fries's work in philosophy, nothing can excuse this self-serving public comment. And note: it is written in the lively, direct prose of the engaged journalist; it is not concealed in the jargon of technical philosophy. It is *up front*, making Hegel's allegiances clear to the censor who will not read beyond the first pages of the book. It is exactly what it was intended to be: a statement that makes clear Hegel's position on the burning political issue of the day, a statement which tells readers what view those who share his philosophical commitments should take on the state repression which was being conducted as the *Philosophy of Right* was being seen through the press.[2]

How do these dismal facts affect our reading of the *Philosophy of Right*? The crucial questions concern the charges of conservatism and authoritarianism that have been brought against it. The doctrine of the *Philosophy of Right* is *conservative* if it ascribes normative force to the *status quo*, if the fact that certain institutions are in place serves to justify those institutions and derogate prescriptions for reform and commands as to how things 'ought to be'. Conservatism of this stripe is a philosophical position; it is conservatism with a small 'c' and it has nothing to do with the doctrines of the Conservative Party or any such political allegiance. As we shall see in Chapter 3, there are good reasons for ascribing this variety of conservatism to Hegel and there are also good reasons for rejecting the imputation.[3]

The charge of authoritarianism is different. The jargon is not precise, but I deem it to denote the opposite of liberalism. This term, too, is imprecise, but I judge liberalism to be the political doctrine that emphasizes the freedom and equality of individual citizens and insists that these values constrain the legitimate powers of the state in its dealings with citizens. The terms 'freedom' and 'equality' are also imprecise. But it is appropriate for an evaluation of Hegel's views to mention one peripheral issue in the literature on freedom (or liberty) which the preceding discussion has brought to prominence: are citizens free if philosophy teachers in the universities are subject to the scrutiny of the state with respect to the content of their teachings, and subject to dismissal if their teaching and published works meet with the disapproval of the state's inspectors? Hegel is an authoritarian to the degree that he rejects or is prepared to compromise standard liberal freedoms; and, with respect to the specific issue raised, his views are clearly authoritarian. On other issues, as we shall see, his stance is recognizably liberal. I see little point in coming to an overall judgement.

As we shall see later, the separate charges of conservatism and authoritarianism which critics have brought against Hegel require careful review in light of a reading of the whole text of the *Philosophy of Right* (and a reading of that in the context of the whole of his work). At this time, Hegel's loyalties to his students, his university colleagues and his state employers stretched him in all directions. And this shows in his work. As, probably (the author says ruefully) does the fact that he was growing older, both more settled and more anxious, and certainly more distant from his youthful enthusiasms. It is extremely difficult to locate the temper of Hegel's *Philosophy of Right* along the liberal–authoritarian spectrum on the basis of internal evidence within the book. Authoritarian sentiments are expressed directly, but Hegel's commitment to freedom as the greatest of values is articulated in ways that the philosophical liberal will endorse (and, indeed, cheer) and the detail of life in the rational state requires that specific liberal freedoms (freedom of conscience, freedom of the press, notably) be recognized. One conclusion, however, that it is absolutely safe to draw is that Hegel is not writing as the recruiting sergeant of Prussian militarism nor as the tame courtier of Hohenzollern absolutism. He was an insecure professor, nervous, resentful and consequently bad tempered in private and public debate. But he was kindly and openly helpful to students and junior colleagues who were experiencing political difficulties.

It was unfortunate for Hegel (if a boon for Hegel scholarship) that the *Philosophy of Right* was approaching publication at a time of such severe public and personal difficulties. Hegel was never again put under the same professional pressure. The rest of his time in Berlin was spent in comparative calm, although he continued to have academic enemies, in particular Schleiermacher, who blackballed his membership of the Prussian Academy. He continued to lecture on the *Philosophy of Right* up to 1825. He twice prepared new editions of the *Encyclopaedia of the Philosophical Sciences* (1827 and 1830), but the sections on objective mind which briefly recapitulate the substance of the *Philosophy of Right* were not revised in a fashion which prompted him to revise the latter. He lectured on aesthetics, on the philosophy of religion, on the philosophy of history, and the history of philosophy, a subject which he can fairly be considered to have invented. His professional career prospered, culminating in his appointment as rector of the university from 1829–30.

He began to enjoy travel, visiting Prague and Vienna, and in 1827 spending a month in Paris. Whilst there, in fashionable homage to Rousseau, he travelled out to Montmorency to see the Hermitage where Rousseau composed his greatest works. No doubt this kindled the memory of his youthful enthusiasms, but it did not lead him to revise the critical readings of Rousseau published in the *Philosophy of Right*. Until his death he took an active interest in current affairs, not only in Germany but in France and Britain, too. His last publication was a severely critical study of the proposals for parliamentary reform in Britain, an essay 'On the English Reform Bill' (1831) (PW: 234–70). Hegel died in Berlin on 14 November 1831, during a cholera epidemic in the city, although his death may have been due to other causes (Pinkard 2000: 652–3).

Work

Hegel's writings on moral and political philosophy are nested within his overall philosophical system. This is an attempt, perhaps the last serious attempt by a philosopher of the first rank, to articulate the meaning of life, the universe and everything. We best read him as the last (and in his view, the culmination) of a quartet of German idealists, his predecessors in point of publication being Immanuel Kant (1724–1804), Johann Gottlieb Fichte (1762–1814), and F. W. J. von Schelling (1775–1854). The key principle of his system is that of reason. The core insight of his idealism is the thought that reason can grant us knowledge of the world only if that world is itself rational, which is to say literally constituted by reason. Thus reason discloses the rational in the real. This insight can seem banal; we can only understand what is in principle intelligible. But as worked out by Hegel it has astonishing implications.

Reason, we might say, is familiar to us as the faculty of thought, more particularly, of disciplined thought. If that is right, we can investigate the disciplines which structure our thinking. A narrow view of these disciplines is that they comprise the subject of formal logic, the study of patterns of valid inference. A wider view identifies these disciplines as the structure of the conceptual scheme we employ when we think about anything. So we start by thinking about our most basic thoughts about things, that they exist, are beings or have being. Once entertained and examined, these first thoughts about our conceptual scheme are discerned to have their own dynamic. Their evident contradictions and incompletenesses force the thinker to unravel the totality of the logical structure of thought. In the first part of the *Encyclopaedia* this exercise comprises the 'Science of Logic'. To summarize crudely (and in a fashion that I trust may stimulate in some a desire for further reading), it articulates the doctrine of being, the doctrine of essence and the doctrine of the concept. If Hegel is right, this philosophical enquiry will explain what we think about, how we think about it, and how thought grants us knowledge. Metaphysics and epistemology meet in the ancient thought that knowledge cannot be explained as a relation between one kind of thing (human subjects) and another (the world), that is, the knowledge subjects have of objects. Rather it must be a relation of self-knowledge: reason's recognition of itself. As they say in trendy and most non-Hegelian language, real knowledge requires the denial or obliteration or sublimation or deconstruction of the subject–object dichotomy. Hegel's intention is most plausibly characterized as an attempt to render the distinction of subject and object 'safe and unproblematic, by showing that there is unity *as well as* difference here'.[4]

This thought is not silly; indeed, it is familiar. The very model of knowledge for Descartes is the thinker's thought of himself that he exists as a thinking thing. In Christian theology, God's omniscience, His complete knowledge of the world (e.g. that a sparrow falls) derives from His knowledge of His own creation. That I know that I exist and what I am (a thinking thing), and that makers have knowledge of what they have fashioned or created: such claims have served for many as incontrovertible premises of philosophical argument (which is not to say that these thoughts are uncontentious).

Let us conclude, for the sake of argument but not irresponsibly, that all knowledge is basically self-knowledge. This entails that reason grants us knowledge of the world just in case the structures of the world (which our claims to knowledge describe) actually exemplify the way we think about it. This looks sensible from one point of view: how could we have knowledge of a world which was recalcitrant to our ways of thinking about it? But the answer might be: we can't; it is so recalcitrant, so we can't claim knowledge of it. Hegel cannot understand how anyone might advance this sceptical option, since he thinks it so obviously false. He thinks that he can determine, seemingly a priori, the structure of how the natural world must be and hence on 'logical' grounds alone, can evaluate the claims of what is taken as the best science. This is the drift of the 'Philosophy of Nature' which takes up the second part of the *Encyclopaedia*. It would have been more persuasive had he not been so desperate to savage the reputation of Newton. It is a lovely open question how far the structures of human reasoning constrain the content of scientific hypotheses, how far philosophical considerations can lead to the rejection of scientific theories. There are still plenty of philosophers (and scientists) who think that the standard interpretation of quantum mechanics cannot be right, believing perhaps, as Einstein is reported, that 'God doesn't play dice'.

So: Hegel has articulated the only way thought can be rationally structured, and he has defended this account by describing the patterns of reason in the world studied by natural science and by repudiating scientific theories which (he thinks) violate the constraints of rationality. His investigation of reason proceeds by turning inwards to an examination of the mind of the thinker. The third part of the *Encyclopaedia* is the 'Philosophy of Mind' ('Mind' translating *Geist*, alternatively translated as 'spirit'). The first element of the study of mind is the study of human nature, the domain of psychology broadly understood. This is the province of 'Subjective Mind', of universal *individual natures*, of what is true of each of us taken as individuals, examining ourselves subjectively as specimens of humanity. But this is not the whole story about mind. Mind, or 'spirit' as it is more commonly translated in this context, has an objective dimension in *social* structures. The (almost) final element of Hegel's *Encyclopaedia*, the System of Philosophy, is 'Objective Mind'. This is a summary version of the *Philosophy of Right*.

The underlying claim is that the social world is a structure of mind. This thought should have enormous plausibility. Prior to (and after) careful philosophical investigation, one might jib at metaphysical idealism, at the thought that the natural world is basically mental, because its basic structures are rational. Most philosophers and common folk alike take the natural world to be a material world, contrasting mind and matter as distinct kinds of substance in Cartesian vein, or insisting that the mind itself is material. When we study the social world, it is hard to think of such distinctive features of it as religions, economies, systems of morality, laws and states as anything other than interpersonal structures of understandings, intentions and expectations objectified systematically in patterns of behaviour. A law, for example, is not an inscription on a tablet of stone or a signed piece of paper lodged in a parliamentary vault, or a simple conformity amongst citizens' actions. It is a social rule, where a rule itself is an interpersonal mental phenomenon, its specific content constituted by understandings, intuitions, expectations and the like. However we understand Marx's ambition, expressed in the 1872 Preface of *Capital*, to turn Hegel 'right side up again', taking him to have stood the proper relation between the ideal and the real world 'on its head' (Marx 1977: 420), we should not attempt to understand the social world merely as a structure of material objects. Hegel's idealism finds its most persuasive site, its most comfortable habitat, in his study of the social world. Critics of Hegel have found his particular metaphysics of absolute idealism crazy and fantastic. (For some reason, idealism seems to attract this species of unhealthily unphilosophical criticism.) Whatever one's attitude to idealism in metaphysics, this should not contaminate one's reading of Hegel's study of the social world, which can be no other than a structure of objective mind.

Having introduced the subject matter of the *Philosophy of Right* as a study of the structures of mind objectified in the social world, I want to comment now on three aspects of it. First, I have been speaking of social phenomena as structures of intentions, expectations and the like. The list of mental functions could be expanded, those cited being explained in terms of desires and beliefs, feelings and distinctive character traits being added. For Hegel, the element of mind which is constitutive of the social order is the will (§4). Hegel has a very complex story to tell about the will. At this stage we should expect him to articulate the will in terms of the whole range of beliefs and motives which are engaged in social interactions, in particular in rule-governed behaviour, and we shall see in the next chapter how he does this. But we can emphasize now his insistence that the will is free, and hence, by implication, the principle that the structures of the social world are structures of freedom: '[T]he system of right is the realm of actualized freedom . . .' (§4). In the *Philosophy of Right* the social structures that are foregrounded are normative systems, systems of rules concerning personal rights, the pursuit of the good, and social duties arising from family life, civil society and membership of the state. To use once again the example of law, laws are coercive prohibitions which protect the rights of citizens as they go about the business of making a living. As structures of will, coercive laws are, *ipso facto,* structures of freedom. This is the sort of surprising, if not quite paradoxical, view that can signal good philosophy and yet ought to ring alarm bells for politically alert readers. These alarm bells, or rather the critical disposition they prompt, should be a constant accompaniment to students of the *Philosophy of Right*.

Second, the structure of norms ('the system of right') which is studied in the *Philosophy of Right* is a *rational* structure. This follows from the fundamental presuppositions of Hegel's system, as I have presented it. This should strike us initially as another surprising claim. After all, we might look around us to the political community we inhabit and (in the UK) find integral elements of the constitution (the monarchy, the House of Lords), not to say deeply embedded elements of social life (the Church of England), which seem conspicuously irrational. If we look back to Germany c. 1820, as we are doing when we inspect Hegel's account of ethical life in Part 3 of the *Philosophy of Right*, we shall find the institutions even more quaint, and probably deeply wrong in respect of the prescriptions they encode, which Hegel evidently endorses. This suggests that we should examine carefully the canons of reason that are employed to display the rationality of life in Hegel's modern state.

I should emphasize now that this question encroaches on a vexed interpretative and philosophical issue. Earlier, when I stated that reason was the key principle of Hegel's system, I did not signal that his conception of reason was at all idiosyncratic, although I did say that he was employing principles of reason that were wider in scope than the rules of deductive (and, let's say too, inductive) inference. Whatever Hegel's rules of reason amount to, and however they are grounded, or in whatever way they emerge and operate, autonomously, freely, from our engagement in the activity of philosophy, they must be explicit, statable and hence inspectable. The simple-minded way of characterizing the distinctive operation of reason in the Hegelian system is to say that, rather than obeying the rules of formal logic, it follows its own dialectical logic.

I expect readers to perk up at the mention of dialectic. Formal logic is limited in its application. Most philosophers employ arguments beyond its reach and it can be a dreary subject to study. The formalization of arguments can display the advantages of theft over honest toil. The thought that we might disobey its canons in pursuit of the deeper reaches of philosophical thought is seductive. One might be excited, therefore, at the prospect of dialectical reason carrying us from the initial intuitions of the *Philosophy of Right* to its (thereby defensible) conclusions. It promises to have dialectical credibility – and this should sound impressive. The credentials of reason are unimpugnable; its form (or content, or both) as dialectic sounds right. Carry on!

The difficulty of this programme is easy to specify: what is dialectical reason? In §31R Hegel tells us that it is 'the moving principle of the concept, which not only dissolves the particularizations of the universal, but also produces them'. This tells us that dialectic both provides the argumentative dynamic of the book as the conceptual structures of the social world are articulated and constitutes the rationality of the existent social world which actualizes the concept. We can in fact recite a formula for the logic of the concept which structures the whole book: the sequence of universal, particular and individual, this last being a particular instantiation of the universal. This structure is exemplified in the sequence of parts. Part 1, 'Abstract

Right', is the domain of universality; Part 2, 'Morality' is the domain of particularity; Part 3, 'Ethical Life' (*Sittlichkeit*) is the domain of individuality. The structure is recapitulated, too, within 'Ethical Life': section one, the 'Family', is the sphere of universality; section two, 'Civil Society', is the sphere of particularity; and section three, the 'State' is the sphere of individuality which integrates the first two within the political order.

This structure has a distinctive elegance, but we must ask what work it does. Since I think this question can only be tackled by looking at the detail of the argument as it proceeds, we are mercifully spared a deeper treatment of these basic categories.

There is another way of specifying dialectic reason which is less formulaic and mysterious. On this account, dialectic is an approach to a subject matter, here the social world and the way that we think about it, which that subject matter itself prompts, as it were autonomously or freely. Generally this will involve a series of steps requiring first of all the identification of constituent elements or categories which are then aporetically examined for contradictions, tensions and incompletenesses. Finally, a higher-level concept is introduced which resolves the problematic structure (whereupon the cycle may be recapitulated at a higher level still). Dialectic is thus a way of thinking appropriate to a world which incorporates conflicts and tensions between disparate elements and resolves these by introducing hierarchical structures within which they are integrated. Characterized informally, dialectic is the attempt to resolve otherwise intractable dichotomies by reviewing them in a wider context.[5] Taking these matters at a high level of generality, this looks to be a promising approach to the social world, so long as we do not expect it to constitute a rigorous methodology. And again, if dialectic has anything to offer as a process of reason, that should come out in the wash as the book is examined in detail.

There is yet a third understanding of dialectic that connects it to the final aspect of reason which we should consider – the dialectic which is revealed in history. Hegel tells us, in the *Introduction to the Lectures on the Philosophy of World History*, that 'the only thought that philosophy brings with it is the simple idea of reason – the idea that reason governs the world and that world history is therefore a rational process' (ILPWH: 27; SW 11: 34). The history of mankind is the history of spirit. Spirit (think here of 'the human spirit', though the term has strong religious connotations for Hegel) realizes itself in history, which is to say that the human spirit has developed to a point where humans (at least in the voice of Hegel) fully understand their nature and the social world they inhabit. This point is sometimes put by saying that spirit knows itself, or spirit is conscious of spirit. And spirit's self-knowledge is freedom: 'for freedom, by definition, is self-knowledge' (ILPWH: 55; SW 11: 47). The self-knowledge in which the freedom of spirit consists is not the product of an act of immediate introspection by a solitary thinker, as it is for Descartes. It is rather the achievement of mankind working through history to gain a proper understanding of its developing nature and how best it can live, and struggling to put these insights into effect. If there has been a basic mechanism at work it has been one of forms of social life first of all collapsing because they failed to give adequate recognition to the way mankind was coming to understand itself, then reconstructing themselves on a more adequate basis, then collapsing again before being reconstituted in a more satisfactory manner. In history the dialectical processes of reason have generated a succession of forms of social life which failed because they were able to recognize only a contradictory or one-sided conception of human spirit. We might think of the human spirit as a space–time worm which freely transforms its own nature throughout the course of its life cycle. Transections taken at different stages of its history will reveal a changing pattern of ill-assorted elements, but at the present, as Hegel understands things, it is revealed as a coherent and satisfying, fully developed, whole. By the time the *Philosophy of Right* is written, this life history is over. Indeed were it not over, had the human spirit not attained full knowledge of itself, the *Philosophy of Right* could not have been written.

I shudder at the number of grandiose and contentious claims which have been summarized brutally in the last paragraph. Some of them will be taken up in Chapter 3 when we discuss the Preface to the *Philosophy of Right*. We shall return to others briefly in the last chapter for we shall discover that the book ends with an account of the history of the world in eight pages! And to make matters worse, my reading is very controversial (McCarney 2000: 169–94). For the moment it is enough that we take Hegel to be using the powers of reason to articulate the structures of reason as these have developed into, and are exhibited within, the social world in which he is fully at home.

Hegel after Hegel

For the moment, I want to say no more about Hegel's philosophical system and the method of doing philosophy which it entails. We shall return to the topic later. A few very brief words about Hegel's intellectual legacy are in order. During his lifetime, particularly after he arrived in Berlin, Hegel was a philosopher who attracted disciples. Both the oracular style of his writing and the ambitious content, promising a rational grasp of the whole modern world, elevated him to a curious stature, probably best described in modern terms as *guru*. (This is a dangerous standing; it invites the charge of charlatanry. Schopenhauer (1788–1860), in Hegel's lifetime, denounced him as a charlatan, as did others. Hegel has never escaped the charge altogether, notwithstanding his eminence.) Some of Hegel's followers (Right Hegelians) welcomed his display of rationality in the ramshackle institutions of contemporary Prussia. Others (Centre Hegelians, notably Eduard Gans, the editor of the 1833 version of the *Philosophy of Right*) welcomed what they saw as Hegel's invitation to the reconstruction and reform of political institutions. Still others, the Left or Young Hegelians, found in Hegel's corpus material that could be employed in a radical critique of modern life.

Their initial focus was on the understanding of the role played by religion in modern life, intriguingly recapitulating Hegel's own youthful preoccupation. This group of writers, including Ludwig Feuerbach (1804–72), David Friedrich Strauss (1808–74), Bruno Bauer (1809–82) and August von Cieszkowski (1814–94), purged Hegel's concept of spirit (*Geist*) of its religious connotations and developed a secular teleology which identified God as a distinctively human projection fashioned in order to reconcile humankind to the miserable facts of its alienated existence in a corrupt social world.[6] Demystifying Hegel, these writers concluded that the subject of history was not spirit, but man, and their project modulated from a critique of metaphysics and religion into social criticism. (For a full account of these developments, see Toews 1980, summarized in Toews 1993.)

With hindsight, it is evident that the most radical and most influential of the Left Hegelians were Karl Marx (1818–83) and Friedrich Engels (1820–95). Much ink has been spilled in the investigation of the intellectual relationships between Marx and Engels and Hegel and most of it has been devoted to investigating Marx's 'inversion' of the Hegelian system. We shall discuss some of the detail of Marx's critique in Chapter 12, but since I think that technical elaborations of Hegel's dialectic are fanciful, and find the dialectical elements of Marx's historical materialism unintelligible, readers will have to look elsewhere for an account of this episode of intellectual history. What should be of enormous interest to students of these thinkers is an account of the similarities and differences in their substantial doctrines, as against their methodological pronouncements (Wood 1993). Both of them are fascinated by the detailed study of the modern social world and the interrelatedness of the institutions within it – religion, political organization, and crucially, the form of economic life. The fundamental difference between them is that whereas Hegel sought to explain why citizens should feel at home in a social world which is essentially rational, Marx saw these institutions as fundamentally alienating, as the source of conflicts and tensions which will rip modern society apart and pave the way for the revolutionary transformation of capitalism into socialism and communism. In the twentieth century this battleground has been revisited as scholars have rediscovered the Hegelian origins of Marx's doctrines (Georg Lukács (1885–1971)), and as Marxism itself has been transformed through the reintegration of key Hegelian themes. At the heart of the neo-Marxist project of the Frankfurt school of Critical Theory (Max Horkheimer (1895–1973), Theodor Adorno (1903–69), Herbert Marcuse (1898–1979), and others, including latterly Jürgen Habermas (1929–)) is a (non-idealist) conception of a rational life for humans that can serve as the basis for the immanent critique of society.

The Hegelian system has been kept alive by a different kind of opponent. Søren Kierkegaard (1813–55) developed his radically individualistic ethics in conscious hostility to what he identified as Hegel's deliberate engulfment of persons within a social system which stifled their freedom to create their own authentic life trajectories. Other recognizably existentialist philosophers can profitably be read as advancing their positions against the Hegelian salient as well as recording surprising and significant debts. Jean-Paul Sartre (1905–80) is a notable example, and Georges Bataille (1897–1962) is a more surprising one. (Dilettante, iconoclast, pornographer, philosophical näif: I find Bataille's references to Hegel (the enemy, the opposition), genuinely trustworthy, and this not simply because he reproduced the substance of Kojève's Paris lectures: Kojève 1969.)

Hegel's social philosophy was revivified in Italy in the work of Benedetto Croce (1866–1952) and there, too, it had probably its most embarrassing endorsement – in the work of Giovanni Gentile (1875–1944) who argued that Hegel's concept of the rational state could be fruitfully employed to display the ethical credentials of Mussolini's Fascist regime.

Neither dull, empiricist Britain nor robust, pragmatist America have been immune to the tides of Hegelianism. In Britain, a remarkable school of social philosophers centred on the Universities of Glasgow and Oxford rediscovered Hegel's ideas. Major luminaries include Edward Caird (1835–1908), T. H. Green (1836–82), F. H. Bradley (1846–1924), Bernard Bosanquet (1848–1923), and Sir Henry Jones (1852–1922). These philosophers, in part through an identification of freedom with active citizenship, were notable for applying their philosophical stance to problems of practical politics – a communitarian style of applied ethics one hundred years before either of these genres became influential amongst contemporary philosophers.[7] Buy good clothes, keep them in the cupboard long enough: sooner or later, you'll be fashionable once again. This appears to be the story of Hegelian ethics as well as devious, long-sighted, consumerism.

A dialectical transition?

More important, to my mind, than either further background study of Hegel's system or scholarly reflection on the Hegelian ancestry of later or modern philosophical movements, is that the reader buckle down to the study of the text of the *Philosophy of Right* and try to work out the content of his argument as he elaborates it in that text. To this end I shall postpone a discussion of the Preface of the book until after we have studied the Introduction (and mention later appropriations of

Hegel's ideas as these are prompted in the course of our study). At first this might seem a cock-eyed procedure. But the Introduction to the *Philosophy of Right* is a genuine introduction which sets out the apparatus he will use in the argument that follows. A careful reading and clear understanding of the Introduction will shape one's approach to the rest of the book. Indeed, it will give us a sight of the thesis of the book in miniature. Having achieved this prospect, we can return to grapple with the methodological puzzles thrown up by the Preface, but by this time we shall have something concrete and specific in view.

In teaching Hegel, I have always tried to avoid presenting excessive introductory material. One learns most about Hegel when wrestling directly with the difficulties of the texts. More general wisdom dawns with the light cast by these exegetical and critical studies. One can't first unravel, or be told, the secrets or the mysteries and then confidently advance towards the subject matter. And crucial issues should not be identified anachronistically in light of controversies engaged long after Hegel was dead.

Hegel writes obscurely, and this can make him a hard philosopher to grapple with. But it is a mistake to believe that one can find a key to tackling his system which can open all doors. Instead, one must rattle and shake the arguments as one finds them, and the doors open slowly. The 'labour of the concept' is hard labour, but as Hegel's doctrines become clearer readers will encounter a distinctive and original philosophical voice, with good and interesting things to say on philosophical problems that still require careful attention. This voice has been obscured by his own peculiar fashion of utterance as well as by the clamour of fans and hostiles who would puff him up or shout him down. But since you will find the effort rewarding, I suggest we get down to studying the Introduction.

Chapter 2

The Introduction to the *Philosophy of Right*

Preliminaries

On my reading of the Introduction to the *Philosophy of Right*, it offers the key to an interpretation of the book as a whole. In it we find a sequence of arguments which lead us to the conclusion that the normative life of a society is a complex structure of will. In speaking of the normative life of a society I mean to include the range of moral beliefs attributable to members of that society together with the characteristic temper or cast of mind associated with the holding of these beliefs. These in turn will include emotions and feelings, as well as the settled habits of moral sensitivity we judge to be virtues. I mean to include, too, the range of actions deemed to be expressive of these beliefs, feelings and virtues as well as, most importantly, the institutions which permit, form and guide their expression. Such institutions will include private property and contract, punishment, domestic associations, structures of economic life, the law and the state.

All these together I described as a structure of will. What does this mean? The most straightforward response is: Wait and see! The defence of the claim will be in the detail. But some prefatory remarks are in order, not least so that the following discussion can be orientated *vis-à-vis* other positions with which the reader may be familiar.

Modern political philosophy has been marked by the opposition of two camps – individualists (or liberals) versus communitarians. Individualists are the inheritors of the traditions of Locke and Mill (and many, many others). They speak to values of individual liberty and equality of moral status. In recent times, the most influential spokesmen for this tradition have been John Rawls and Robert Nozick. Contemporary communitarianism has developed as a response to these philosophers. In such writers as Charles Taylor, Alasdair MacIntyre and Michael Sandel, we encounter what may be described as 'metaphysical' objections to individualist political theories. Though I don't want to pin names on any of the specific theses that follow, I believe them to be illustrative of a broadly characterizable philosophical position. In the first place, this amounts to a denial that the premises of individualism, the ideals of liberty and equal moral status as I have glossed them, are rich enough to yield conclusions about how our communal life shall be lived. In particular, it is urged that we cannot disassociate ourselves in thought from the concrete ties which bind us in actual relationships to others in order to investigate the legitimacy of the duties they impose. Such ties, we are told, are *constitutive* of our *moral identities*. We just cannot, as a matter of fact, attain a theoretical perspective from which we can evaluate their propriety without losing the moral gravity with which their obligations press upon us. The family gives us a plausible example. We just find ourselves with the moral obligations of parents or children, obligations of care and sustenance or obedience and respect. We can't step out of these domestic roles to appraise the moral norms of domesticity. To do so would be to detach ourselves just one step too far, to ask one question too many, for already we would have lost that immediacy which is distinctive of natural social relationships. And the same thought can be taken to apply in respect of our political obligations: we just find ourselves, willy-nilly, to be citizens of our respective nation-states, which claim our allegiance on the basis of our contingent membership, subject to laws which frame at least the broadest contours of our duties.

Even those who sympathize with the tenor of such theories will want to know more. Especially, they will enquire about the metaphysics of social membership. The communitarian can expand eloquently and luxuriously on the distinctive mindset of children, parents and spouses who feel 'at home' with the demands of their domesticity, but once the hard question is put – What is it for one's identity to be constituted by one's membership of a community? – an answer cannot be dodged or clouded by rhetoric. It is fair to say that communitarian writers have been more persuasive as critics of individualism than they have been as constructors of a theory of social identity. No better start can be made in this enterprise than by studying the central doctrines of the most explicit of social metaphysicians – Hegel. And an understanding of Hegel's position in these disputes requires that we come to grips with the Introduction to the *Philosophy of Right* – with Hegel's social metaphysics of freedom.

Second, a study of the Introduction to the *Philosophy of Right* illuminates the character of Hegel's social idealism. The simplest way of grasping this is as a thesis to the effect that social institutions, understood quite broadly to include political establishments (states, legislatures, laws), economic organizations (firms, factories, unions, markets), domestic arrangements (patterns of family life and the education of children), religious movements and social units (everything from churches to football clubs), are to be understood as structures of thought and will. Thus, to rehearse an example discussed previously, laws are not pieces of paper with Her Majesty's signature appended, nor yet the the observed regularities of behaviour within human communities. They are to be understood in terms of the related intentions, generally expressed as desires, values and principles, of legislators, court officials and subjects who identify themselves as the occupants of these roles – which are not, of course, exclusive. Likewise, commodity production is not to be understood in terms of the physical mix of human and non-human energy and capital with the raw materials of production. Rather, this productive enterprise is itself to be explained in terms of the needs and purposes of initially self-interested agents who educate themselves to devise technologies and work patterns geared to satisfy their increasingly social, increasingly artificial needs. Mind, Hegel would have us believe, is objectified in social institutions. Again there are other candidates in the field. Marxists, famously, counterpose to Hegelian idealism a materialist analysis of the social world. I leave them to explain what this distinctive 'materialism' might amount to.

Third, since, as we shall see, the will is free, the structures of will which comprise the normative life of a community are structures of freedom. This is a difficult and controversial claim which will be subjected to the closest examination in what follows. For the moment we should notice one striking implication of it: Hegel will expound a theory of freedom which integrates our thinking about what some have held to be discrete philosophical problems.

John Stuart Mill opens his essay *On Liberty* with the announcement that

> The subject of this Essay is not the so-called Liberty of the Will, so unfortunately opposed to the mis-named doctrine of Philosophical Necessity; but Civil, or Social Liberty: the nature and limits of the power which can be legitimately exercised by society over the individual.

> (Mill 1910: 65)

Divide and rule is probably the most distinctive philosophical strategy, but we should not assume that it is always appropriate. It is an important feature of Hegel's discussion of freedom that philosophical puzzles concerning freedom of the will, freedom of action, the nature of free agency, are tackled alongside problems concerning social freedom. For some, this conflation of philosophical topics heralds confusion. It may turn out to be so – but if it does, the confusion will not be the product of a sloppy inadvertence. It is distinctive of Hegel's thought in these areas that we can act freely only in the context of a form of social life that sustains and protects that freedom; a free society is necessary if freedom of the will is to be a real feature of citizens' lives.

We should now proceed to the text. And once again, we shall not begin at the beginning, we shall move directly to §4. When Hegel announces that the 'basis of right is the *realm of spirit*, and its precise location and point of departure is the *will*' he expresses the kind of idealism I have hastily sketched. Since, as he insists 'the will is *free*', the system of right – what I called above the normative life of a society – is 'the realm of actualized freedom' (§4). It is the programme of the book to explain this system of right, this realm of actualized freedom.

We should examine a couple of implications of this brief announcement, since they are both reported in the Addition to §4. First, Hegel defends his insistence at §4 that the will is free. He argues that this is an analytic truth on a par with 'all bodies have weight' and claims to have proved this. Readers who follow his references to the *Encyclopaedia* are likely to return disappointed. It would be entirely wrong, though, to think that Hegel begs the question of the will's freedom at this very early stage and erects his entire theory of freedom on shaky, unexamined foundations. On the contrary, since we have no conception of what a strict proof that the will is free would be like anyway, what we need is an articulation of the concept of the free will which meets some of the pre-theoretical constraints which one might place on such an account (e.g. that the concept of will thus articulated shall serve to explain, in whole or in part, human action), which refutes standard objections to the concept and which rejects inadequate formulations of it. This, as we shall see, is the sort of account Hegel provides. In fact, we shouldn't regard Hegel as just another great dead philosopher who had something to say about free agency. We should regard him as the greatest and most sophisticated of philosophers of freedom.[1]

Second, Hegel rejects a straightforward distinction between mind and will, between theoretical or cognitive activity on the one hand and practical activity on the other. As ever, he is hostile to the thought that these might be discrete faculties of the mind. His arguments for this are complex, but again the thought is reasonably straightforward. He claims that cognition is essentially active, that the pursuit of knowledge is itself an intentional activity and may often be motivated by the need to seek efficient means to explicit ends, and that, on the other side, operations of the will require conceptualizations of ourselves and our experience: to act successfully we have to understand the world in which we live and to describe it truthfully. The different directions of fit – thought seeking to represent the world as it is and will seeking to change the world, to make it how we want it to be – do not license the conclusion that thought and will are two different mental faculties, operating independently of each other. 'These different attitudes are therefore inseparable' (§4A).[2] As we have seen, at a deeper metaphysical level this is underpinned by a rejection of all subject–object models of knowledge. These are replaced by a conception of knowledge as self-knowledge, as the maker's knowledge available to spirit, an active and self-directing creator of the conditions of its own intelligibility.

§§5–7. The Structure of the Will

The will is analysed as having two elements which, though incomplete and one-sided, complement each other so as to engender a concept of the will which is properly conceived as the unity of both. The first element of the will that Hegel discusses is

> the element of *pure indeterminacy* or of the 'I's pure reflection into itself, in which every limitation, every content, whether present immediately through nature, through needs, desires and drives, or given and determined in some other way, is dissolved; this is the limitless infinity of *absolute abstraction* or *universality*, the pure thinking of oneself.
>
> (§5)

Hegel's thought is that the thinking or willing subject can abstract the content from its mental activity and focus its attention, reflexively, on the form that such activity takes. We can think about our thinking, become conscious of our consciousness. Such abstraction has in the past been motivated by philosophical scepticism and religious feeling. When the drive to clear our consciousness of all content, except bare consciousness itself, is completed, achieving a pure consciousness of consciousness, the abstraction has been claimed to have a further dimension. Since the entire content has been eliminated in thought, all particularity attaching to the subject, the thinker, likewise vanishes. Hegel is best represented here as reaching for that point of self-eclipse which Descartes's critics, from Leibniz and Lichtenberg to Russell and Geach in more recent times, have urged as the proper conclusion of the *cogito*. Even the 'I' of the 'I think, therefore I am' formula should be abstracted, since my knowledge of *who* I am can be subjected to doubt. On this account 'there is some thinking going on' is the knowledge which scepticism cannot challenge. This is 'the unrestricted infinity of absolute abstraction or universality' but not so much 'the pure thought of oneself' (in Knox's translation) or 'the pure thinking of oneself' (as Nisbet translates) as 'pure thought thinking itself' or 'the pure thinking of itself [*Das reine Denken seiner selbst*]' (§5). That is to say: thought which is as abstracted, as pure as this, will not have any identifiable subject (as its content); it will not be recognizably *my* thought or *yours*. Since we have used our thought to reach beyond the self that thinks, we touch infinity. (If you think this sounds like the purveyor of philosophical snake oil, you may well be right. Folks advertise this stuff on the London Underground – £100 for a 12-week course, which is not much to pay for the ability to achieve occasional self-eclipse if you are a miserable soul.) The will so characterized is universal in all respects.

This first, one-sided element of the will is no more than a *component* of the will; better, perhaps, a capacity for abstraction which is required for the possibility of free action. Interestingly, Hegel believes that the belief that this capacity for abstraction is the whole truth about freedom has been exemplified in a variety of cultural forms which he presents (plausibly) as distinctively pathological. If we seek a self which flies 'from every limitation, every content' as a restriction, seeking to obliterate the mundane self through the chanting of mantras, we may overcome the differences between man and man, self and other, but this may blind us, as Hegel believes is the case with the Hindu fanaticism of pure contemplation, to wicked and despotic forms of social life (as innocents may judge that they haven't got their £100 worth). The evils of Brahminism,[3] however, do not compare with the destructive forces unleashed when the drive for negative freedom seeks open political expression. Then we witness 'the fanaticism of destruction, demolishing the whole existing social order, eliminating all individuals regarded as suspect by a given order, and annihilating any organization which attempts to rise up anew' (§5R). This negative freedom[4] is characterized as 'absolute' and 'universal freedom' in the *Phenomenology* where 'its sole work and deed . . . is therefore death . . . the coldest and meanest of all deaths, with no more significance than cutting off a head of cabbage or swallowing a mouthful of water' (PS ¶590; SW 2: 454).

Of course, the example of political nihilism which Hegel has in mind here is the period of the Terror in the French Revolution, although he mentions the dreadful massacres, the 'Revolution of the Hooligans' (my liberal translation) in Münster, in this context, too.[5] We are equally familiar with the power of nihilism in episodes of permanent or cultural revolution, in the Khmer Rouge assault on the Cambodian people and in the frenzy of rootless international terrorism; all these attest the continuing force of the will without content, the negative will, the will to destruction. If one finds it hard to work out exactly the connection between the will thus conceived and these examples, one could think of the matter this way: will may fairly be described as having no content when the ideals which motivate action are so far distanced from the possibility of achievement that no constructive effort is likely to be rewarded, when 'the *fury* of destruction', a strictly mindless thrashing about, seems the only form of engagement available. (It is, of course, a controversial political claim that some, or all, terrorist behaviour exhibits this radical dislocation between ends and means.)[6]

The second element of the will, introduced in §6, is the will of a particular subject with a determinate object. When I desire a drink, it is I who am the desiring subject and a drink is the object or 'content' of my desire – the sort of content that the abstract will of §5 abstracts *from*. Where the first element of will is abstract, the second is concrete; where the first is indeterminate the second posits a determinacy; the first is universal, the second particular; the first is infinite – reaching beyond an empirically identified self – and the second finite. But the incompleteness of this second element of will is evident too, although this point is not stressed in the *Philosophy of Right*. The self cannot be identical with an episodic, desiring consciousness, otherwise it would vanish in the moment of satisfaction, consumed in its consummation of desire (PS ¶¶ 174–7; SW 2: 145–8). Further, the self so identified would be chained to a desire which operates as a limit to its freedom. The desiring self is transient and bounded, neither enduring nor free.

Section 7 represents the will proper as the unity of these elements, a unity which is expressed in the thought that the essence of freedom of the will is self-determination. The notion of self-determination is deeply puzzling. How can I make something of myself that I am not? If I have to hand a piece of wood and a knife, within practical limits set by the material and my skill, I can make of it what I like – a spinning top, a clothes peg, a doll. I can approach the material with a range of options and employ it as I choose to fulfil any of a number of projects. Can I choose what to make of *myself* in this way? Suppose we say this: self-determination is the activity of the will in determining the self. The will is the maker and the self its creation. But if we put the matter this way, we distinguish the will and the self; understanding self-determination on the model of other-determination, as when I make a toy, forces us to prise apart elements (will and self) which, if not identical, are related as part to whole. We seem to lose the essence of self-determination if we view the self as other to be operated on by the will. Yet surely some such account of the self as *other* is necessary if self-determination is to be seen as integral to freedom.

The alternative image to that of creation is one of development or growth. But if we conceive of self-determination as akin to biological development, if the matured self is the *telos* of a process of life history, then the freedom which is constitutive of the idea of self-determination has vanished.

Somehow the two models of self-determination, the models of self-creation and self-development, have to be combined. Freedom seems to require that the self is not constrained by its materials in the process of creation. But then the self is regarded as a plastic other, constituted as a range of possible futures into which the self-chooser can project himself by existential quantum leaps. If, on the other hand, we stick fast to the idea of a constituted self, the only determination that is possible has to be explained by a teleological principle of development that belies freedom; we 'speak as if the will were already assumed to be a *subject* or *substratum* . . . But', Hegel continues, 'the will is not complete and universal until it is determined, and until this determination is superseded and idealized; it does not become will until it is this self-mediating activity and this return into itself' (§7R).

I have framed as a puzzle about self-determination what is more readily seen as a puzzle about freedom. Hegel tells us that the understanding can easily grasp the first two moments of the will and we must take it that he has two things in mind: first, the Kantian conclusion that we regard ourselves as autonomous beings with freedom rooted in a noumenal self beyond the reach of natural determination. At the same time we are unable to escape the sense of our placement in a natural world which causes us to respond to its causal inputs. As noumenal selves we resist the shadow of determinism, insisting that our selves are independent of desires from which we may abstract ourselves. As phenomenal selves we recognize the specific pull of desire. For the Kantian, movement beyond this radical duality of the self is inconceivable.

The same philosophical agenda may be written in a different fashion: arguably, the simplest, most straightforward way of thinking about freedom is found in Hobbes. We act freely when nothing stops us doing what we want to do.[7] Kant, following Rousseau's account of free will and moral liberty, tells us that our freedom resides in the distinctively human capacity to resist the promptings of our desires, our ability to reject what seems most desirable, what we feel to be our greatest temptation. The Hobbesian and Kantian accounts, as so wickedly condensed, can't both be right, yet both are plausible, and both find support in our philosophically untutored intuitions. A good way of characterizing the task Hegel sets himself in the Introduction to the *Philosophy of Right* is to portray him as extracting the truth from these contending positions. We may then find a way of accepting both of them without contradiction – as good an example as any of dialectic at work.

What some see as a contradiction – two opposing positions; only one can be right – Hegel sees as a challenge of constructive alignment. Perhaps we can do justice to both traditions of thinking. Since they both incorporate valuable insights, surely we must do so. For Hegel, what for others may be a dilemma sets the task of philosophy. What conception of the self can reveal 'this innermost insight of speculation ... this ultimate source of all activity, life and consciousness?' (§7R). There is no point in holding on to these two independent conceptions of the self, since, taken by themselves, they are both false, or at best, incomplete. They must be united, not as the horns of a dilemma, but within a unifying theory which makes sense of the oppositions.

Don't read §7 as an argument; it expresses a desideratum. Once again, it is programmatic. It heralds, in the most cryptic fashion, the arguments which are to follow. As so often, Hegel prefaces his argument with an opaque formulation of his conclusion, as though he challenges himself to make sense of conflicting intuitions, of standpoints which are obviously true (or obviously contain some measure of truth), yet can't both be true as stated, since they clearly contradict each other. We have to see how the argument develops to gauge whether this ambition can be fulfilled.

§§8–9. The Particular, Desiring, Self

Hegel often parades his arguments in a distinctive form which he believes captures the structures of speculative reason in the subject matter. This is the sequence, or triad: Universal, Particular, Individual.[8] We have seen how Hegel's initial portrayal of the structure of the will follows this pattern. He discusses first the elements of universality (§5), then the elements of particularity (§6), then states that will proper is the unity of these moments, individuality (§7). We might expect him to follow this sequence in his elaboration of the free will. But he doesn't. He begins at §§8–9 with a further characterization of the particular will. This suggests that he is employing a different strategy: his study will begin with an account of the simplest (most 'immediate') conception of the will and then this simple conception will be filled out as successive weaknesses in the account are diagnosed. As they appear, increasingly more sophisticated analyses are corrected as their inadequacies are charted. The end point of this development will be a complete theory of the free will which incorporates all the insights of the partial accounts whilst eliminating their inadequacies. Or so Hegel hopes.

Particularization is characterized in terms of its *form* and its *content*. The first of these, the form of the particular will, is described in §8, the second, the content of the particular will, in §9. We saw earlier in our discussion of §6 that the particular will is particular along two dimensions. If I desire an apple the will is particular as the will of a determinate subject (in this case, me, Dudley Knowles), and it is particular as a specific content is determined (that apple or its consumption). The first form of the will, elaborated as (a) in §8, concerns the willing subject as this is determined in the light of the will's objectivity.

The argument here was first published in the *Phenomenology* (PS ¶¶166–8; SW 2: 139–42) and developed further in the *Encyclopaedia* (ES §§424–5). The most primitive form of self-consciousness is that achieved by the subject of desire when that subject reflects back upon itself in the light of its focus upon an object in the external world which it desires. It is implicit in the phenomenology of the desiring subject that he identifies himself through his desiring consciousness. If I desire an apple, this brings with it a sense of myself as the 'that-apple-desirer'. This is 'the *formal* will as self-consciousness, which *finds* an external world outside itself' (§8). If my purpose is to eat the apple, I identify myself in the activity required to achieve this purpose successfully, 'in the process of translating the subjective end into objectivity through the mediation of activity' (§8).

At the point where mind is fully self-conscious, this self-consciousness will not be furnished mediately through some external object of desire. Its determinate character will be 'its own'. At the present stage, where the will is that of a particular desiring consciousness, will is considered an 'appearance' only since it is defined and understood entirely in terms of the object which prompts the desire and (as Hegel points out in the *Phenomenology*) this sense of self is no more stable or enduring than the object of present consumption. Still, the overall point is clear. The desiring consciousness of the particular will introduces the moment of self-consciousness. It is the most primitive sense of ourselves that we have acquired. Perhaps, speculating about the emerging self-consciousness of babies, it represents the first glimmerings of self-knowledge on the part of humankind.

The second aspect of particularity which can be identified in the will is given by a specification of its *content*. As the will of a subject, as elaborated above (and not as the will of a dog or jellyfish – Knox's example!), this content is understood as the ends or purposes of the willing agent. In the chapter on 'Morality' Hegel will discuss the concept of purpose at greater length. For the moment it is enough to notice the two manifestations of the agent's ends which Hegel describes: purpose may be evinced in the activity of the will which formulates and acts out a plan – which may or may not be successful – or it may be recognized in the achievements of the successful agent.

§10. Will Free in-itself, for-itself, for-us and for-others[9]

In §10 Hegel introduces us to some distinctive terminology, which has further implications for our understanding of his method and direction of argument, both in this chapter and in the book as a whole. What is required, Hegel believes, is a developing phenomenology of the experiences of the willing subject. He will begin with a description of will which is free in-itself and elaborate this description to the point at which will which is free in-itself has itself as its object. Will becomes 'for itself what it is in itself' (§10). This terminology needs further explanation. In the lecture notes Hegel uses two examples to illustrate it – speaking of the child as man in-itself and the seed as plant in-itself. I find neither example particularly helpful. The plant, lacking consciousness, cannot develop a for-itself and the child is in the unhappy, if familiar, position of getting it wrong whatever it believes. It cannot *truly* be a child for-itself since it isn't a child in-itself. But neither can it be a man for-itself since then it would be man in-and-for-itself and not a child. 'I'm only a child', says the child. 'That's no excuse', replies the parent. Hans Christian Andersen gives us the best example. For-itself and for-others, notably for its fellow-nestlings, the Ugly Duckling is a duck. (But not for us, who know the story well.) They all get it wrong. In-itself it is a swan and as the cygnet grows it becomes more and more apparent that it is no duckling. Finally, when it is clear to all that it is a swan, we understand it to be a swan in-itself (*an-sich*), for-itself (*für sich*), and for us (*für uns*), that is, the ducklings and ourselves. The real moral of this story is not Andersen's politically ambiguous conclusion – 'It does not matter if one was born in a duckyard, if only one has lain in a swan's egg' – but the more pleasing thought that any child can grasp the sense of the Hegelian terminology!

An entity, we may conclude, is truly for-itself when it *recognizes* itself as being the kind of thing it essentially is, in virtue of its having, fully developed, the properties essential to its being a thing of that kind. Only humans can be in-and-for-themselves on this account, since the for-itself is a reflexive perspective which only consciousness admits of.

Let me summarize the qualities of man in-and-for itself. First, mankind has a nature or essence which may be expressed in terms of the associated notions of reason and freedom. (This nature has not been fixed in history – only at the end point of the historical process, i.e. at the moment of Hegel's delineation of his system, can we reflexively describe it.) Second, these qualities of reason and freedom have to be worked for within the individual who is to realize his potential. This, Hegel explains later, is the function of education which aims to procure liberation, 'the hard work of opposing mere subjectivity of conduct, of opposing the immediacy of desire as well as the subjective vanity of feeling and the arbitrariness of caprice' (§187).[10] Third, the struggle for self-development requires an ever more cultivated self-consciousness. The agent does not mechanically act out his potential as the sportsman might train in the pursuit of fitness. It is not a rigma-role; it is accompanied throughout by self-examination in the pursuit of self-understanding. Freedom is the prize of transparent self-awareness. Beginning with the simplest elements of free action, Hegel concludes the *Philosophy of Right* with the description of actuality (*Wirklichkeit*) which is nothing less than a portrait of the modern soul as a display of will in the full dress of freedom. No philosopher has been so ambitious since Plato aligned his conceptions of justice in the soul and justice in the city, in the *Republic*.

Thus far, we have gathered together evidence of how Hegel anticipates the argument of the Introduction – and, indeed, the whole book. He begins by giving an account of the simplest, most straight-forward, first-shot characterization of the will – 'will in-itself' is the formal description he employs. Criticism of this account takes him in the direction of greater complexity and sophistication as structure is imposed on the activities of the willing subject. At the conclusion of the analysis, we shall understand will to be free in-and-for-itself: will somehow understands and commands its own operations. The integration of the universal and abstract capacities of the willing subject (§5) with the particular and concrete activities of the subject of desire (§§6, 8–9) are complete. The oracular pronouncements of

§7 are elucidated by a full account of what a self-determined life involves. So let us get down to the detail and investigate the theory for which his early analysis and subsequent methodological interventions have been preparing us.

§§11–14. The Indeterminacy of the Natural Will and the Necessity of Resolution

Hegel now takes up the analysis of the particular desiring subject which he broached in §§8–9, describing it as 'the *immediate* or *natural* will'. Such a will is composed of 'the *drives, desires and inclinations* by which the will finds itself naturally determined'. I identify with these desires as mine, yet don't recognize myself as their source, although they may be the products of my rationality. They *may* be, but they may not. They may simply be caused in me, as when I slaver before the ice-cream stall on a hot day, or they may be irrational. Taken together, their description is the province of the 'empirical psychologist'.

Why does Hegel describe a will so conceived as 'free in-itself'? The answer must be that there is a conception of free action associated with it. And we can recognize it as that of Hobbes, or perhaps Hume's liberty of spontaneity (Hume 1888: 407–8) – we act freely when we aren't stopped from getting what we want. Hegel will proceed to criticize this account; it is importantly incomplete. He does not deny that the will thus construed is free in one important dimension, free in-itself. It turns out that there will be more to freedom than this account suggests, but there is never, so to say, less. That my actions are the product of drives, desires and inclinations may never give the full measure of my freedom, but, in an important sense, they could never be the product of anything else. At this point in the analysis, though the implication is not signalled, Hegel is distancing himself from Kant, who insists that these active powers of the mind, being themselves caused in us, cannot be the sources of free action. When I act to satisfy a desire or pursue an inclination, my action is unfree ('heteronomous' is Kant's word, contrasting with free, or autonomous, action). We enter here one of the great debates of philosophy: Must desire, or some other conative attitude, enter into the explanation of action (the Humean position) or can reason, typically in the form of duty, suffice to motivate us (as Kant insists)? Both stances find distinguished modern protagonists. I take Hegel to side with Hume, admitting that this affiliation may oversimplify a complex story. Perhaps better, and certainly more dialectically, Hegel wishes to combine central elements of both Hume's and Kant's positions in a more inclusive, coherent and satisfying unity.

So let us, for the purposes of exposition, take the immediate or natural will to be the will of a Hobbesian subject, one who is merely the locus of a constellation of desires, impulses and inclinations; a subject driven, pushed and pulled by sequences of appetites and aversions, more complex than the iron filing drawn by the magnet but equally locked within the causal powers of its physical constitution and the external world with which it interacts.

The detail of Hobbes's account, whereby will is the *last* appetite in a sequence, is absurd. But we could think of desires in the way of vectors which, alone or summed, tip the agent into action when a given level of potency is reached. The will is now the strongest (not the last) appetite in deliberation. Hegel shows us that the picture must be more complex than this. The subject of empirical psychology is a 'multitude of varied drives, each of which is mine *in general* along with others, and at the same time something universal and indeterminate which has all kinds of objects and can be satisfied in all kinds of ways' (§12). The condition of the desiring will requires that determination be effected at two points. The subject has first to determine which desire, of several desires, is to be satisfied (supposing that they conflict or that they cannot all be satisfied together – this is the normal predicament: Do I go to bed early or do I go to the cinema tonight?); and second, he must decide how the desire is to be satisfied (which of the available drinks do I choose to have, when thirsty – a cup of tea in the cafe or a beer in the pub?). No amount of detail concerning the variety of a subject's desires, or the ways in which a selected desire can be satisfied can determine how one may act. Along both dimensions – which desire to satisfy; which way to satisfy it – options remain open. The agent must decide what to do. The decision cannot be taken for him. So Hegel is able to conclude that 'it is a resolving will, and only in so far as it makes any resolutions at all is it an actual will' (§12).

Let us review briefly the importance of this conclusion. When Hegel introduced the determinate and differentiated element of the will in §6 it might have appeared that he was begging important philosophical questions against such as Hobbes and Hume in insisting that this was a mere one-sided moment of the operative will. Why not, as Hobbes had done, simply identify the will as the action-directed consciousness present in desire? Why suppose that there is another prior element of universality with which the determinate will has to be unified for it to be a will at all?

This question is especially pertinent if we conceive of desire along the lines described in the *Phenomenology of Spirit* and the later *Phenomenology* incorporated into Part 3 of the *Encyclopaedia* (ES §§413–39). Recall that here the first glimmerings of a self-consciousness are realized as the self encounters a specific external object which prompts desire.[11] The individual object which motivates consumption furnishes the content of the desire and, as an individual external other, shapes the experience in which the self first encounters itself as the subject of a specific task. Desire which does not have a specific object (which being internally generated might be defined as the *lack* of any available object as with the thirsty desert traveller) could not generate the required self-consciousness. Later in the *Encyclopaedia* when Hegel is discussing the will, he distinguishes desires of this object-directed sort from the desire which is constitutive of the activities of the will.

> Impulse [Drive] must be distinguished from mere appetite [*Der Trieb muss von der blossen Begierde unterschieden werden*]. The latter belongs to *self-consciousness* . . . it is something *single* and seeks only what is single for a single, momentary satisfaction. Impulse, on the other hand, since it is a form of volitional intelligence . . . embraces a series of satisfactions, hence is a whole, a universal.

> (ES §473A; SW 10: 374)

Hegel's objection is best put as the thought that not all desires are of the objected-directed sort, and much fun is to be had discussing the question of whether all desires are to some degree general or indeterminate. 'I do want that doggy in the window', ran the dreadful song and I guess I'd be distressed if I was told that it was there for display purposes only, that another identical pup with an equally waggly tail could be brought, pre-packaged, from the back of the shop.

It is reported of a distinguished philosopher, Professor Donald Mackinnon, that he walked into a post office and asked to see a whole sheet of 3d postage stamps. 'How beautiful', he exclaimed to the bemused postmistress who had carefully unfolded the sheet across the counter, 'I'll have *that* one!', pointing somewhere in the middle of the sheet. Roger Scruton explains well the phenomenology of desire, suggesting that one question (a key one in this context) is whether or not the desire is transferable 'from object to object; or, if you prefer, objects can be substituted for one another, without precipitating a change of mental attitudes' (Scruton 1986: 103). He believes that sexual desire is non-transferable in this way, contrasting it comically with 'sexual hunger' or 'randiness, the state of a sailor who storms ashore, with the one thought "woman" in his body' (1986: 90).

The important point is that many desires do not have a specific object. Choice or resolution needs to be effected if I am to act. It is the need for resolution which is the first chink in the Hobbesian armour and the point from which the Hegelian account will develop, for we can identify the will that resolves as self-determining in the simplest way. It is not acting in the grip of desire. The twofold indeterminacy which Hegel points to is cancelled by an act of thought which operates independently of the force of any given desire. Since the standpoint of decision must enable the agent to inspect all of her desires and the possible ways of satisfying them, it can only be reached by the employment of those powers of abstraction characteristic of the first one-sided element of will (§5). 'As such, it stands above its content' (§14). Resolution is, then, activity of the will which requires both of the one-sided elements isolated at the beginning of the analysis. In the resolution of the will we have the first experience of freedom, but will is free *in-itself* only.

§§15–18. The Arbitary Will (*Willkür*)

The advance has been made beyond simple-minded Hobbesian compatibilism to what Hegel believes is the common conception of freedom – a midpoint 'between the will as determined solely by natural drives and will which is free in and for itself '(§15R). This midpoint characterizes freedom of action as this is understood by most philosophers. He mentions Wolff, Kant and Fries as adopting this perspective. The will which resolves is the arbitrary will, the *Willkür*, following Kant's usage. The following points are distinctive of the *Willkür*.[12] First, there is a difference to be noted between the form of the will and the content of it. When I resolve, it is I who choose between the range of alternatives; each possibility of action is reviewed as potentially satisfying a desire of *mine*. Hence, 'by resolving the will posits itself as the will of a specific individual and as a will which distinguishes itself from everything else' (§13). (These latter may be either other desiring consciousnesses or, following the *Phenomenology*, other objects of desire.) The form of the will is given by the perspective of the chooser as he stands between his desires and their fulfilment in action. He claims actions as *his*, since in resolving he has converted the determinations of nature into *his* purpose. The content of the will, however, is not the product of the will. It is still given by nature. The fact of choice does not render me independent of nature since the entire range of possible actions is geared to the satisfaction of desires which assail me, desires which I do not choose to suffer. The arbitrary will is thus free in form, but restricted in content. It experiences itself as free and in choosing is conscious that it *is* determining itself. Nonetheless, its whole content is determined.

Second, we can recognize in this description of the *Willkür* a familiar understanding of free action in terms of the counterfactual possibility of the agent's acting otherwise than he does. To say one is free is to say one could have acted otherwise, if one had wanted to.[13] Hegel insists that 'whatever the will has decided to choose it can likewise relinquish' (§16). It demonstrates an ability to go 'beyond any other content which it may substitute' (§16). Hegel's contribution is to insist that the ground of my possibly acting otherwise lies in the fact that for humans drives and desires of themselves do not usually necessitate action, since they are multiple and general.

Third, the conclusion that the *Willkür* is free in a sense, but not free enough – free in-itself but not for-itself – points towards a fuller account of freedom, wherein the content of the will is not to be represented as elements of a predetermined package of options, however wide. In the operation of the *Willkür* 'every such content is different from the form [of the will]' (§16); it is the '*choosing* between these determinations which the "I" must in this respect regard as external' (§14). The fuller account of freedom will explain how the form of the will can itself be integrated into the will's content.

In §17, Hegel takes one step backward and two steps forward. He reminds us that drives and inclinations get in each other's way – 'the satisfaction of one demands that the satisfaction of the other be subordinated or sacrificed, and so on' (§17), and insists further that the conflict cannot be resolved naturally. Rejecting the Hobbesian model of appetites and aversions having some intrinsic motivational push, he argues that 'a drive is merely the simple direction of its own determinacy and therefore has no yard-stick within itself' (§17). A similar point is made by David Wiggins who distinguishes two different ways in which we might understand the notion of the strongest desire – distinguishing a definitional claim that the strongest desire is just that desire in respect of which one acts – 'the desire that wins'– from the phenomenological claim that a desire is strong if it feels strong or pressing. In this latter, empirical, sense a desire may be strongest amongst a set of competitors, yet not cause one to act. The severest, most forcefully felt, temptations may be resisted (Wiggins 1987b: 244–6).

Hegel is correct to insist, in the absence of a plausible psychology, that desires do not come on the scene already weighted so that that which weighs strongest gets satisfied first. Hitherto, Hegel has taken this point as showing the necessity for resolution and resolution is not described further. Clearly choice and decision are required, but the doctrine of the *Willkür* does not explain the mechanism of choice or the kind of decision-making involved. It could be, and this would be the extreme of arbitrariness, just *plumping,* or it could be choice with a clear criterion in mind. He does alert us, though, to a further dimension of arbitrariness in the operation of the *Willkür* – for the sense that what the will has chosen it could equally well have renounced applies not merely to the selection of desires from a range of competitors and to the selection of objects or states of affairs which may satisfy the desires; there is scope for further, deeper, arbitrariness in the selection of principles which one might apply in resolution.

He notices several candidates in the field. Initially, one has to decide whether the choice is to be criterionless plumping or whether to apply criteria. In the second case, one may be 'guided by calculations of the understanding as to which drive will afford the greater satisfaction, or by any other consideration one cares to name' (§17). And, if the reader thinks that criterionless choice makes no sense (unless one is, say, tossing a coin) and that the pursuit of maximal satisfaction is dictated by rationality, Hegel reminds us that there are two candidates in the field here, too. One can take the Hobbesian, simple utilitarian, view that the objects of desire are good and their achievement produces happiness (or Rousseau's view of natural man) and conclude 'thus man is said to be *by nature good*' (§18) or one can take the contrary view, associated with Protestantism, Rousseau's conception of civilized man, and Kant's moral psychology, that the determinations of desire are, in general, 'opposed to freedom . . . they must be eradicated; thus man is said to be *by nature evil*'. At this point, he concludes, 'a decision in favour of one assertion or the other likewise depends on subjective arbitrariness' (§18).

§§19–21. The Purification of Desires

At §19 Hegel affords us a glimpse of the direction of his argument. What is called for is the purification of our impulses or drives. This is a vague demand which calls attention to the possibility that desires may be worked on in different ways. Since we can acknowledge our desires without being driven by them, we can stand between our desires and their satisfaction; the whole gamut of desires and impulses lose their immediacy and determinative power as they are open to classification, ordering and scheduling. Daniel Dennett has drawn attention to the importance of 'the value of this meta-level activity' in Locke's account of free will.

> For . . . the mind having in most cases, as is evident in experience, a power to *suspend* the execution and satisfaction of any of its desires; and so all, one after another; examine them on all sides, and weigh them with others. In this lies the liberty man has . . . this seems to me the source of all liberty . . . For during

this suspension of any desire ... we have the opportunity to examine, view and judge of the good or evil of what we are going to do; and when, upon due examination, we have judged, we have done our duty, all that we can, or ought to do, in pursuit of our happiness; and it is not a fault, but a perfection of our nature to desire, will, act according to the last result of a fair examination.

(Locke 1975:2, 21, §48, cited in Dennett 1984: 36)

The questions we want to ask of this account draw attention to the distinctive features of Hegel's theory. There are two which are of particular importance. First, how can we weigh desires and compare them with others? Desires, Hegel has insisted, have no measuring rod in themselves. Whatever strength they possess is not discovered so much as assigned to them by the *Willkür* and revealed as they issue in action. It follows therefore that any ordering that is achieved within a set of desires is going to be the product of an external assessment and evaluation of that set. The self somehow has to step outside its constitutive desires and order them as it wills. We know that the self has the formal resources to achieve this since it is a fundamental element of the will that it can abstract from any given content ('suspend the execution of desire', in Locke's idiom). What we now have to understand is how the self can go further than this, how it can inject its own content into its network of desires and so merit the judgement that it is truly self-determining.

The second question prompted by Locke's thoughts concerns the input of morality. How do we judge our desires in the light of good and evil? The two alternative principles we have already encountered, stating respectively that the satisfaction of desire is good and evil, are neither of them any help in discriminating between desires. Hegel's answer, briefly given in §19, is that when our desires 'become the rational system of the will's determinations' this can be revealed as 'the content of the science of right' (§19).

There are no short cuts in this science, sadly. We might think that we can distinguish the more important desires, those with a moral dimension say, and examine the regulatory role which they assume *vis-à-vis* the common-or-garden items in the inventory. Thus we may conclude that 'man *has* by nature a drive towards right, *and also* a drive towards property and morality, *and also* a drive towards sexual love, a drive towards sociability, etc . . .' (§19). Or we might make the same point in the language of philosophy rather than psychology, insisting that man can simply discover 'within himself as a *fact of his consciousness*, that he wills right, property, the state etc . . .' (§19R). Both of these approaches are dismissed as superficial – theft rather than the honest toil involved in the labour of the concept. This prompts two good questions, which I shan't tackle here: first, does Hegel achieve anything more substantial than the philosophically sophisticated empirical psychology he adverts to here? He believes that he does, because he takes himself to be offering a speculative deduction of this material which displays its validity. I can't endorse this claim since I've never been able to see what this might involve beyond a standard philosophical defence of the positions Hegel canvasses. Hence, second, one may ask whether Hegel needs to do more than give an acceptable philosophical dress to what we take as a 'fact of [our] consciousness' (§19R) concerning the duties that bind us. I shall say more on these topics in Chapter 3.

Hegel expands his remarks about the purification of impulses in terms that uncannily repeat Locke. He writes:

> When reflection applies itself to the drives, representing them, estimating them, and comparing them with one another and then with the means they employ, their consequences etc., and with a sum total of satisfaction – i.e. with *happiness* – it confers formal universality upon this material and purifies it . . . of its crudity and barbarity.
>
> (§20)

Exactly how is reflection brought to bear on this material? Hegel tells us that one style of reflection on our desires is to investigate them in point of how they conduce to our happiness. We could think about the range of desires we respond to, the value of their typical objects and the costs of achieving them. In the light of this deliberation we may fashion a strategy for maximizing their satisfaction, promoting our happiness. This is a major step forward since it gives us an inkling of how we may take a role in working self-consciously on the collection of desires we acknowledge. It implies a contrast with the unreflective pursuit of immediate gratification. Having said this, Hegel does not proceed down this route. He does not believe that the systematic pursuit of happiness, however sophisticated or long term, affords an adequate perspective on the good life of the individual or the community. Like Kant, Hegel rejects happiness as the foundational value of morality.[14] Some of his suspicions surface in the Addition to §20. As a universal, happiness is a cypher; we need to spell out what happiness consists in if it is to be defended as a rational goal. But although we can make formal discriminations, distinguishing happiness as a long-term project from immediate gratification, for example, we find ourselves unable to characterize it independently of the drives in the satisfaction of which it consists. In modern terms, happiness reduces to desire or preference-satisfaction – a move which contemporary utilitarians will recognize. But if we go farther and identify happiness in substantial terms, as the satisfaction achieved through the successful living of a life of our own ordered creation, we find that the value of happiness is not intrinsic. We value it because we desire the freedom of self-determination.

Thinking about happiness is an advance because it exemplifies rational deliberation about the ends of life and the means of attaining them. We confer 'abstract universality' on the material (drives, desires, inclinations) we investigate, that is, concepts are applied to it. Hegel adds that 'this cultivation of the universality of thought is the absolute value of *education* [*Bildung*]' (§20).

If we take Hegel's advice and look ahead to §187 for clarification, we find there that education refers to two distinct processes. First there is the education which is represented by the transition from immediate and natural ethical substantiality to that ethical substance which contains subjectivity and the capacity to theorize itself. These are code words for the historical development in human culture represented by the progress from the simple cultural unity of the early Greek *polis* to the modern age which incorporates a principle of individual freedom within the common values of society. The second kind of education is that of the individual subject. It is, to repeat, 'the hard work of opposing mere subjectivity of conduct, of opposing the immediacy of desire as well as the subjective vanity of feeling and the arbitrariness of caprice' (§187). Both these kinds of *Bildung*, the cultural development of the species and the acculturation of the individual, are described as liberation (*Befreiung*) and again the process of liberation is best understood as the detachment of the individual from the imperatives of immediacy – whether these are the demands of a society with which the individual unreflectively identifies or whether these are the desires which he must master in the course of self-determination.[15]

The focus on education here alerts us to what we might call the public dimension of freedom. Thus far the emphasis of the story has been on the control and organization of desires, with the self emerging as free after a heroic struggle against forces which would determine it – forces which end up as material for the self's own determining activity. The difficulty of this picture has been that of understanding precisely how this has been achieved. We haven't solved this difficulty yet – but we are a step further towards a solution. We know *when* it is achieved, that is, we know that it is the product of an education which the individual undergoes as the free subject of institutions which have themselves developed in history to the point of explicit rationality.

Purification proper requires the application of self-knowledge. Desires are revealed to be ordered in the light of a definitive answer to the question 'What am I?'

> Here is the *point at which it becomes clear* that it is only as *thinking* intelligence that the will is truly itself and free. The slave does not know his essence, his infinity and freedom . . . for he does not *think* himself. This self-consciousness . . . constitutes the principle of right, morality, and all ethics.
>
> (§21R)

Education will bring us to self-knowledge. It will teach us, individually, lessons which mankind struggled hard to learn: that we are persons, bearers of rights and not slaves, that as moral agents we are not subject to the moral authority of kings or priests, and that we fully understand the duties placed upon us by the ethical relationships in which we stand to others, in the family, civil society and the state. At this point, 'will has universality', in the sense of some determinate conception of the self, 'as its content . . . it is free not only *in itself* but *for itself*' (§21).

§§22–8. The Full Story

One can't pretend that this is clear – and the murk gets dimmer in the paragraphs that follow. I select for your astonishment a few characterizations of the ideal of freedom:

> The will which has being in and for itself is truly infinite, because its object is itself, and therefore not something which it sees as other or as a limitation . . .
>
> (§22)

> Only in this freedom is the will completely *with itself* [*bei sich*], because it has reference to nothing but itself, so that every relationship of *dependence* on something *other* than itself is thereby eliminated.
>
> (§23)

> It [the will] is *universal*, because all limitation and particular individuality are superseded within it.
>
> (§24)

> The absolute determination or, if you prefer it, the absolute drive, of the free spirit is to make freedom into its object – to make it objective both in the sense that it becomes the rational system of the spirit itself, and in the sense that this system becomes immediate actuality.
>
> (§27)

How can we make sense of all this? It must be admitted that here Hegel seems to be pulling one rabbit after another out of a hat, each fantastical, each magical, each mystifyingly unintelligible. Only the most committed Hegelian could suppose that conditions of this sort determine a novel and crystal-clear conception of the free will. We shall have to take what may be called a dialectical short cut; that is, we shall attempt to understand this introductory material in the light of the substantial doctrines which it is meant to introduce! And to achieve this we shall need to employ resources furnished by contemporary philosophy.

But before we look in this direction, there is one strand in the passages cited above that needs to be disentangled. Hegel says that for the will to be wholly free (have being in and for itself) it must not have an object which it sees as '*other* or as a *limitation*' (§22). It must be 'completely *with itself* [*bei sich*] . . . so that . . . every relationship of *dependence* on something *other* than itself is thereby eliminated' (§23), 'all limitation and particular individuality are superseded within it' (§24). This may be expressed, in hardly popular parlance, as the thought that freedom consists in being 'at home [*zu Hause*: §4A] with the other'. Let me explain this terminology and the philosophical intuition behind it.

Hegel takes the view that, in point of knowledge or cognition – how things *are* to us, perceivers and actors – we are not caused or determined by this or that to believe things to be thus and so. To make any claim to theoretical knowledge, to have any intellectual grasp of objects in the world, one must *master* them by applying concepts to them. '[I]t is only by comprehending it that I can penetrate an object' (§4A). (I can't refrain from commenting, mischievously, that this quotation should be grist to the mill of those feminist philosophers who believe that traditional logic, epistemology and metaphysics amount to a phallocentric discipline.) This is a philosophical position that takes us far away from the *Philosophy of Right*, so I shan't discuss it further. On the other hand, this thought – that free will is a matter of 'being at home in the other' – should have resonances for those who think about the philosophical problem of free agency in traditional terms. For what condition of the will can be described as its not being thus free?

The answer, in Hegelian terms, is that the unfree will is one that is limited by the 'Other', that is, dependent on the 'Other'. This condition, of limitation or dependency, can be explained in terms that are familiar to students of the 'free will/determinism' debate. Metaphysically, the opponent of free will claims that one's will is dependent on, or necessitated by, those features of the world (the 'Other') which cause her to act in this way or that. Hegel's claim is that she is *never* thus dependent, because she (the agent) is always in the position of being able to act otherwise. In respect of ethics, the study of how folks ought to behave, the threat to freedom arises from the possibility that persons' actions are caused by the socio-psychological circumstances in which they find themselves, willy-nilly. A congeries of social circumstance dictates that, for the most part, people will abide by the rules they are taught. They do what they are told by the 'Other', now construed as the forces of social conformity. So you and I follow the rules: we do what is expected of us. But if we feel, comfortably, 'at home' (*bei sich, zu Hause*) in these social conditions (and if we are not the deluded creatures of some manipulative ideology), we do so because we *don't* experience the rules and prescriptions of the social life we inhabit as the impositions of an alien culture, an illegitimate authority, or a coercive regime.

Abstractly, this is a nice prescription. Freedom, which we prize, is the condition of being 'at home in the other': (1) when the 'other' is intelligible to us in light of concepts we deploy; (2) when the 'other', taken as the natural world which causes us to desire objects within it, is integrated into our freely devised plans and projects, when we, not the world, dictate how we shall respond to felt desires; and (3) when the actual ethical norms of the social world are not experienced as alien impositions, as the commands of some 'other', but rather are understood as the norms of an institution with which the agent knowingly identifies. Thus, for example, a loving parent will not consider the duties of family life to be an onerous burden, fashioned by the social forces which have produced a canonical model of domesticity which the laws of the state reinforce. To think of oneself as a parent just is to accept that one loves and cares for the dependent youngsters one has created. This is the perspective of Ethical Life (*Sittlichkeit*) which we shall explore in Chapters 9–13.

Notwithstanding this sketchy exegesis, the statements I have quoted are still very puzzling and I think we need to step away from Hegel's text for a moment to unearth a conceptual framework in which they might be considered plausible, if not true. In particular we need to find good arguments that force us to conceive of the will in a complex and structured fashion and then we need to ask whether the structures we recognize can illuminate Hegel's programme. There are two ways of attributing structure to the will which are helpful here and we can see how, in the full conception of the will, they pull together. The first structural dimension is displayed when we distinguish first- and second-order desires. An example of a first-order desire is the desire that currently assails me for a cigarette. A second-order desire is a desire whose object is a first-order desire; thus I presently (and which grown-up smoker nowadays does not?) desire to be rid of any first-order desire for a cigarette. Matters are a little more complex than this; taking a smoker to be one who desires cigarettes and satisfies his desires in this respect, we can conclude that my desire to be a non-smoker is a second-order desire which operates on first-order desires through the concept of a person of a specific kind, delineated in terms of characteristic constitutive desires.[16] For a smoker, wanting to be a non-smoker just is wanting not to want a cigarette.

It has been objected that this distinction of levels does no real work, since one may be a *wanton* in respect of one's second-order desires (Watson 1975: 108). One may have a range of second-order desires and yet believe that these are not organized or prioritized in the light of a desire of higher order still. Thus one may desire both to be temperate and self-controlled, valuing desires which one appraises as moderate, and yet also desire the pleasures of loss of self-control, of a passionate, uncontrolled responsiveness to powerful stimulations. Sometimes one acts reflectively – and sometimes not. There is no overarching conception of how one should react that fashions one's disposition to respond one way or the other.

We must accept this as a phenomenological possibility. We can understand how both self-control and spontaneity can appeal – and how neither may be decisive. One 'may not care which of the second-order desires win out' (Watson 1975: 108). If so, whilst having second-order desires to which one is committed and with which one identifies may be necessary for truly free agency, as Frankfurt believes, simply having second-order desires is not sufficient to accomplish this.

The second way of attributing structure to our desires carries Frankfurt's analysis further, integrating the crucial element of evaluation into the structure of the will. It is revealed as soon as we recognize that we already possess an evaluative vocabulary which enables us to describe persons in terms of their attitudes to their own desires; we speak of puritans and sybarites, the moderate or the temperate, the self-indulgent and the self-denying. These character descriptions pick up echoes throughout the tradition of Western moral philosophy, reminding us of the doctrines of Plato, Aristotle, Stoics and Epicureans and, not least, Christian moralists of various sorts. In his essay 'What is Human Agency?', Charles Taylor has argued that there is a range of contrastive predicates ('strong evaluations') which we apply to our desires in so far as they are constitutive of ideals of personality.

We might have noticed something of this in the example of the smoker adduced above. Think of the force of contemporary anti-smoking campaigns – how they direct attention to the personal qualities of the poor smoker: at best, she is weak, unhealthy, addicted; at worst anti-social, the public exponent of a nasty, dirty and dangerous habit. In speaking of strong evaluations, Taylor claims that

> if we examine my evaluative vision more closely, we shall see that I value courageous action as a part of a mode of life; I aspire to be a certain kind of person. This would be compromised by my giving in to this craven impulse. Here there is incompati-bility. But this incompatibility is no longer contingent. It is not just a matter of circumstances which makes it impossible to give in to the impulse to flee and still cleave to a courageous, upright mode of life. Such a mode of life *consists* amongst other things in withstanding such craven impulses.
>
> (C. Taylor 1985a: 19)

Other strong evaluations of desires are given when desires are described as noble or base, integrating or fragmenting, alienated or free, saintly or merely human.

We can say more about the connections between different conceptions of the self and their associated desires. There are two views of this relation which one might take and both are false. On the first view, our having a specific desire is to be *explained* in terms of the conception of the self which is employed. Thus my desire to be a non-smoker, my desire not to want a cigarette, is explained by my thought of the character of the smoker as weak and pathetic. Alternatively my view of the non-smoker as strong and athletic, brimming with health and effi-ciency, might be thought of as the cause or motivation of my desire not to be a smoker. This sort of relationship between a strong evaluation of character traits and consequent desires is suggested by Thomas Nagel's account of the desire of the prudent man for his future well-being as *motivated by* a conception of the person, as one whose life has a future which he acknowledges as *his* future (Nagel 1970: 27–46). The second view of the relation between self-conception and associated desire puts matters the other way round. It is my desire not to weaken before temptation, my desire to glow with freshness and vitality, my desire not be scoffed at by my friends and sent to the rear compartment of the train, my desire above all, not to want a cigarette which causes me to evaluate disapprovingly the character of the smoker.

Both of these views make the same mistake. The relation of self-conception to desire is not that of explanans to explanandum, cause to effect, motivation to manifestation, or vice versa. That I have an evaluatory conception of myself in terms of the alternatives smoker/ non-smoker, is just the condition of wanting to be grown-up or like Humphrey Bogart in the case where I value smoking or the condition of wanting not to be or to be thought to be an addict where I disvalue the condition. Being disposed to accept or endorse some conception of the person consists in the having of a constellation of appropriate desires. The relation I have in mind is constitutive, not causal, though no doubt interesting causal stories may be told of specific incidents of these conditions.

We are concentrating now not so much on the intermeshing, ordering and scheduling of desires as on the self of which such arrangements are an expression. Let me elaborate. So long as we are not seeking knowledge of the essence (a word Hegel is prone to use in this context) of things of our kind, of our being members of a natural kind (*Homo sapiens*, presumably) or in terms of a philosophically anchored designation (as with Descartes's claim *sum res cogitans* – I am a thinking thing), we can answer questions of the sort 'What am I?' as calling for descriptions of what I take myself to be. The fullest such description would be given by an autobiography (or its later chapters) which details all my actions ('What the subject *is, is the series of his actions*' (§124)) and provides a check on what I claim to be my characteristic dispositions. There is a third way of conceiving of the self, however, which lies midway between the blank abstraction of the Cartesian *res cogitans*, or the specification of the human genome, on the one hand, and the explicit autobiography on the other. It is a conception of the self built up in accordance with the categories of valued self-ascriptions which men and women in history have learnt to deploy of themselves and to which they attach significant moral potency.

§§28–30. Freedom, Will and Right

The remainder of the Introduction to the *Philosophy of Right* spells out, in formal terms, the connection between freedom of action and right – 'right' being construed as a range of conceptions of the self and their associated normative orders. Hegel has told us that 'The abstract concept of the Idea of the will is in general the free will that wills the free will' (§27). We are now ready to unpack this thought.

What would it be for the free will to will the *unfree* will? I take it that this would amount to a characterization of the arbitrary will, the *Willkür*, will-in-itself. Such a will is free because it resolves, fixing on an option amongst a range of alternatives; it is unfree because the options in the range are each of them determined and because the resolution is achieved in an unprincipled (or incorrectly principled) fashion. Perhaps it is the will of the wanton, as described above, or the will of one who is unable to act in the light of the True and the Good,[17] perhaps because of a defective education or degenerate social surroundings. By contrast, one wills the free will who acts, knowingly, in the light of those moral rules and those social institutions which express and promote a valued conception of human agency. Hence, Hegel tells us, '*Right* is any existence in general which is the existence of the *free will*' (§29). In the Remark to §29, Hegel amplifies this claim by taking an unfair swipe at Kant and Rousseau (whose arguments Hegel regularly distorts: often their views were too like his for Hegel to relish the coincidence or the debt). The unfairness of the charge that these distinguished predecessors conceived of right as a limitation on freedom cannot be pursued here; the important implication is the assertion that the principles of right embody universal principles which are objectively manifest in social rules and institutions ('*true* spirit') which have proved themselves necessary for freedom.

This point is made explicit in §30. The rules of right are 'utterly sacred' since they embody the human (sometimes, unblushingly, Divine) aspiration to 'self-conscious freedom'. What are these rules? They include, but go beyond, the formal demands of agents who see themselves as discrete, atomistic, persons and express these demands as claims of right which establish their moral boundaries. They are rules which autonomous moral subjects can recognize as binding on themselves independently of any external authority. They are the rules which make it possible for persons to act in a united fashion as members of families, to act independently and interdependently as economic agents, subject to law, and lastly, enable individuals to act as citizens within a state whose political institutions fashion all these rules into a harmonious system which all agree has the authority to settle such collisions of rules and conflicts of rights as may emerge. At this final point, we shall have described the highest sphere of right since 'it is the *more concrete* sphere, richer within itself and more truly universal' (§30) than any of its components, taken singly.

How can we model this series of nested self-descriptions?[18] The analogy that first strikes me is that of the children's guides to elementary human anatomy that were sold years ago. My memory of their construction is dim, but I trust you will get the picture. Basically they consisted of a number of transparent sheets on each of which was depicted a distinctive physiological system. Thus we could build up an increasingly complex picture of the human body. To each picture there was a common outline of a human form, curiously sexless until the final sheets were reached. We began by putting down the sheet on which the skeleton was drawn in black and white. The next sheet showed the circulation of the blood, red lines of varying thickness for the arteries, blue for the veins, together with liver and kidneys, and we superimposed that on the transparent sheet with the skeleton. Next came the sheet for the respiratory system, which superimposed neatly on the circulation. Next came the digestive system, again with distinctive colouring – horribly, greens and browns, I remember. Then the nervous system, filling in the brain and tracing thin black lines into all corners of the body. Then, finally, a couple of optional sheets adding the bits and pieces of the reproductive systems of men and women. It would be nice to report that all was clear in an almost three-dimensional fashion by the time the sheets had been correctly assembled. But I suspect we were left with a messy composite and eyes fixed on the genitalia.

We can see the *Philosophy of Right* as constructed in this fashion. Each normative system (both 'shape of the Concept' and 'shape of existence') has a distinctive account of the individual and a characteristic understanding of the moral principles appropriate to that conception. In Part 1, 'Abstract Right', we are 'persons', and employ a distinctive moral vocabulary, of rights, to person and property, and a distinctive understanding of crime as the violation of rights and punishment as the necessary response. In Part 2, 'Morality', we investigate our subjectivity to locate our moral agency. We identify our will in the intentions which inform the actions for which we are responsible, understand how we take satisfaction in actions that are conducive to our welfare, explain how we seek the good through the pursuit of our duty, and diagnose our failure to construct principles of the good from this limited perspective. Part 3, 'Ethical Life', is a systematic investigation of the good, finding it in activities constitutive of three domains of human relationship which are superimposed one on the other. In the first section, 'Family', Hegel investigates the realm of domesticity, explicating the principles recognized by those who see themselves as family members. In the second section, 'Civil Society', the family (i.e. the husband, the breadwinner) is integrated into the world of work, regulated by the administration of justice and socialized by intermediate associations (the Police and the Corporations) formed to smooth the wheels and ameliorate the ill-effects of economic activity. The final section, the 'State', describes the political constitution whereby those who recognize themselves as citizens make laws which permit them to live together as persons, moral agents, family members, workers and citizens. In the Rational State, harmony (organic unity) is achieved in two dimensions: on the one hand, individuals will find their complex identities can be expressed in a fashion that does not impose conflicting duties upon them. They can accommodate and reconcile their personal aspirations and their (many and varied) social roles. On the other hand, the possibility of interpersonal conflict is obviated by careful regulation which marks off the limits of personal domains and makes possible concerted activity. Each person is an ethical virtuoso, managing a complex emotional life in the light of recognized moral responsibilities. But this triumph of self-realization is only possible within a social framework which has developed as necessary for its accomplishment. Magnificent instrumentalists though we may be, we can only achieve the consummation of our skills alongside others in the social orchestra. *Then* we are truly free.

To understand how this concomitance of personal and social freedom is possible we take apart its constituent elements and see how they structure the social whole which they comprise, much as the child (or ignorant adult) may take apart the representations of the different physiological systems before tracking down the patterns of their inter-connectedness.

The second model for understanding the structure of the *Philosophy of Right* is much simpler – to the point that I shall draw it! The concentric circles below represent the successive ethical domains. The point at the middle is the 'person' – a technical term we shall explore later. Paradigmatically a rights-bearer, the person inhabits Abstract Right. The next line demarcates the domain of the moral

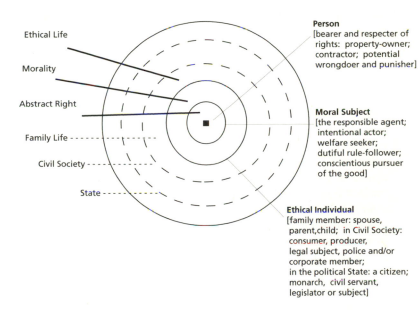

Normative Domains

Self-ascriptions

Ethical Life

Morality

Abstract Right

Family Life

Civil Society

State

Person
[bearer and respecter of
rights: property-owner;
contractor; potential
wrongdoer and punisher]

Moral Subject
[the responsible agent;
intentional actor;
welfare seeker;
dutiful rule-follower;
conscientious pursuer
of the good]

Ethical Individual
[family member: spouse,
parent,child; in Civil Society:
consumer, producer,
legal subject, police and/or
corporate member;
in the political State: a citizen;
monarch, civil servant,
legislator or subject]

Figure 1   The modern self in the rational state

subject, Morality. The next line introduces Ethical Life, with the dotted lines demarcating the Family, Civil Society and State. Moving outwards from the centre enables us to give our moral address. In my case, I, Dudley Knowles, claim rights as a person and recognize the rights of others. I engage in legitimate contractual relations with others and recognize the legitimacy of punishment imposed on rights violators, myself included, should I turn out to be a criminal. As a moral subject I claim responsibility for actions I perform intentionally and understand how they promote my welfare; I seek moral rules which determine my pursuit of the good, but recognize that the resources of the moral subject – formal reasoning, conscience and other styles of moral subjectivism, are insufficient to establish rules with a specific content. To fix the content of such rules, I need the resources of Ethical Life; marking my identity as a family member, son of Margaret and Arthur, husband of Anne and father of Katy and Helen, I endorse the duties ascribed to me in these roles. I place myself in the economy as a teacher (a member of the Police under Hegel's description, see §239), and accept the legal system which determines my duties as person, family member, worker, etc . . . Finally, In the outer ring, I see myself as a citizen – of Glasgow, Scotland and the UK, recognizing its place in the concert of nations at a specific epoch in the history of humanity.

Again, these self-ascriptions are integrated. I can be all these things at once (without the sort of inner personal conflict Hegel attributes to Antigone) only because I live in a society organized so as to permit myself and all other members to function harmoniously (unlike the ethical world of Thebes, which drew Antigone and Creon into tragic conflict) (PS ¶¶446–75; SW 2: 339–67). Thus far, I have explained the structure of the *Philosophy of Right* in terms of two models which reveal the systematicity of self-identification in the moral world. Such a system amounts to the purification of desire which constitutes freedom. Such a system expresses my freedom as well as that of all other citizens of the Rational State. But such systematicity as I have been able to invoke is entirely informal – the sort of cheap systematicity Hegel derides at §19R, where he provides a pair of informal characterizations of the content of the science of right. Can a proper science of the moral world be engaged? How does Hegel claim he has accomplished this? Asking the same question in terms of the first (organic) model: How are the different systems of right related to each other? What is the logic of superimposition and hierarchy? Putting the question in terms of the second model: Is there a logic of concentricity which explains how the rings constitute one circle, a logic which carries us from the centre to the all-enclosing circumference of the Rational State?

§§31–2. Coda: The Method of the *Philosophy of Right*

The method of argument which Hegel advertises is that of *dialectic*, which we discussed briefly in the last chapter. We can add more detail now that we have a picture of Hegel's enterprise in the *Philosophy of Right*. Dialectic charts 'the movement of the concept' and is not to be confused with dialectic of the style 'which frequently appears even in Plato' (§30R). This latter is a teasing style of argumentation designed solely to display the falsity of appearances or common preconceptions. The dialectician asks: What is justice or courage or knowledge? and immediately goes on to disparage and reject candidate answers. One thing we can say for sure about Hegel's dialectic – it is not like that. It is characterized by determinate negation, a process of achieving a positive result from a critical examination, 'a *development* and imma-nent progression' of thought. It is an open question whether there is any such thing.[19]

Readers familiar with Hegel's writing may judge that I have already gone off the rails in describing the dialectic as a method of argument. This suggests that dialectic has a common purpose with better-known canons of reasoning – deductive or inductive inference – in taking the reasoner from premises to conclusions in a process of valid inference. On this conception, dialectic is a method employed by anyone engaged in an argument. It is a tool or technique of reasoning which is quite neutral with respect to its subject matter, displaying a form of thought which may be applied to any content, 'an *external* activity of subjective thought' (30R).

Hegelian dialectic is not like this, either. (In fact, it turns out to be a good deal easier to say what dialectic is not than to describe what it is. But we shall have more to say on this topic in the next chapter, too. For the moment, let us assume that we have a grasp on the underlying metaphysics and try to describe matters in Hegel's terms.) When Hegel says that dialectic is not a process of subjective thought – as a specific argument in use may be taken to be: for example, *your* diagnosis of a fallacy in a purported syllogism – he is thinking of thought (or mind, or Spirit, or *Geist*) *doing its own work.*

This happens in two different but related ways. First, and this is the way of the concept (*Begriff*), we take the totality of modern philosophical thought about how we ought to behave (which is my informal characterization of the concept of right) and see how it discloses itself to be a rational structure. I emphasize 'discloses itself to be' because Hegel is emphatic that he is not dictating the logic of how we ought to think; rather, he is articulating the way the mind has learned to think. He is a reporter of the processes of thought about what is right, rather than a prognosticator of how we shall think once we have been persuaded that he is the authority on how we ought to think about these things.

The implication of this is that thought has its own dynamic, which we should follow as we conduct our enquiries in any of its disciplines.[20] In the *Philosophy of Right* we take our repertory of moral and political beliefs and rewrite them in the systematic form that dialectic dictates – the concept of right.

The second way that thought does its own work refers to the historical process that has bequeathed us the concept of right that we employ. History as we shall see in the next chapter is the test bench not only of ideas, but of the institutions that embody these ideas. Dialectic is the process of reason at work in history which has promoted specific beliefs and created the institutions that give them expression, filtering out the ideas and concrete ways of living that show themselves to be defective. We are left with the actual principles of right, which we find ourselves acknowledging, and the social institutions which embody them. Dialectic has formed our moral consciousness and the shapes of social life in which we give it characteristic expression. It dictates the terms in which we recognize ourselves and others, and the social reality that embodies these insights. That said, the historical formation of the modern ethical mindset, the concept of right as it has become actualized, is not studied in the *Philosophy of Right*. Hegel undertakes this task in the *Lectures on the History of Philosophy* and the *Lectures on the Philosophy of World History*.

The Idea of right, which is the topic of investigation in the *Philosophy of Right*, is the concept of right, the totality of our ethical beliefs systematized in accordance with its dialectical character, together with its actualization, the fact of its constituting personal and social moral reality. Thus 'the subject-matter of the philosophical science of right is the Idea of right – the concept of right and its actualization' (§1).

Dialectic structures our thought about right and has determined the processes of its formation. Since the text of the *Philosophy of Right* articulates the concept of right, it follows that it will have a dialectical structure and that this will explain the sequence in which topics are broached and enable us to see how the whole is gathered together by the end of the book.

There are two ways of characterizing the dialectical structure of will as delineated in the *Philosophy of Right*. They are related in a complex fashion which I shall not explore. The first identifies this structure with the 'stages in the development of the Idea of the will which is free in and for itself' which are described in §33. This adopts 'the stages of the Speculative Method' which are detailed in §§238–42 of the *Encyclopaedia*. Thus the first stage, Abstract Right, is the stage of Immediacy. The second stage, the sphere of Morality, advances beyond Immediacy to Reflection, focussing on the self-examination of the moral subject, the form of its subjectivity. The third stage, Ethical Life, represents the unity and truth of Immediacy and Reflection, the Realized Concept.

I have capitalized the formal designations of these 'moments' of the development of the Idea in order to emphasize their strangeness. No doubt you will be asking: What does all of this mean? For answer, you could go to the *Encyclopedia* and try to work it out. You may well return mystified – in which case, do not despair. Careful attention to the substantive ideas, as these are introduced and subsequently developed in the body of the text may well put some flesh on the bare bones.

The second way of understanding the dialectical structure of the sequence of parts (Abstract Right, Morality and Ethical Life) characterizes these in terms of the 'moments' of the concept, elaborated in the *Encyclopaedia* at §§163–5, as Universality, Particularity and Individuality. Again I capitalize the terms – and for the same reason.

By all means study Hegel's discussion in the *Encyclopaedia*, but my advice is that the meanings of these technical terms are even more fluid in their application by Hegel than the first series mentioned above. Their meaning is best discerned through studying their application in the different contexts of their employment. We have already found these terms at work in characterizing the moments of the free will in §§5–7 (but we should note what little part the sequence played in the subsequent discussion, which proceeded at §8 to elaborate will in its particularity).

Once again, I recommend that we move on rather than get bogged down in preparatory terminological exegesis. But we shall move on now by taking a backward step and examining the Preface. Hegel's study of the will in the Introduction has given us a rough idea of the content of the *Philosophy of Right*. This will be helpful in understanding the claims of the Preface, or so I trust.

Chapter 3

Hegel's Preface

The Preface to the *Philosophy of Right* was the last portion of the book to be completed. It serves a variety of purposes, personal, political and philosophical. Hegel uses it to settle scores with some old enemies, notably Jacob Fries, and to protect his personal position at a time when philosophers (including Fries himself) were being sacked from university positions for their political activities. Politically, it enabled him to align himself with the reactionary stance of the government of the day. Philosophically, Hegel uses the Preface to position his work in the context of his previous publications, notably the *Science of Logic* and the *Encyclopaedia* and to contrast his position with those of contemporary opponents. In this chapter I shall concentrate on the philosophical content of the Preface.[1]

Hegel takes it that his students will be familiar with the 'speculative mode of cognition', the properly philosophical manner of 'conducting a scientific proof'. We have already mentioned Hegel's method. Here we

should note that he contrasts his way of presenting his subject matter with standard philosophical treatments which employ 'the forms and rules of the older logic – of definition, classification and inference' (PR: 10/12). He is contrasting his own method of reason (*Vernunft*) with the more superficial analytical rules of the understanding (*Verstand*). We should take it for granted that this represents a philosophical advance, but Hegel identifies another response to the inadequacies of the understanding which will be one of his recurring targets in the Preface. This attitude despises the apparatus of logic and analysis, and instead has immediate recourse to 'the arbitrary pronouncements of the heart, of fantasy, and of contingent intuition'. He clearly has various species of Romanticism in mind (and particularly the doctrines of Fries). This approach may end up reproducing the work of the understanding or it may be more ambitious. It may believe that the resources of the heart and its intuitions are sound enough to grant those who have genuine insight access to new truths, novel conceptions of what ought-to-be, fresh prescriptions for how we ought to behave. We know these approaches have gone off the rails when we see their protagonists scrapping with each other and having no way to resolve the disputes that their conflicting proposals interminably create.

Hegel insists that the truth of the matter is not hard to find. 'The *truth* concerning *right, ethics and the state* is at any rate *as old* as its *exposition and promulgation* in *public laws and in public morality and religion*' (PR: 11/13–14). In other words, it is not the task of the ethicist or political philosopher to tell us how to behave. Our community has its legal, moral and religious rules. These rules, rather than the spouting of radical or out-of-date moralists, tell us what do. The task of the philosopher is not to identify or rehearse them as the principles of right. It is to *comprehend* them. We can take it that they amount to a rational system ('the content is already rational in itself' (PR: 11/14)); the job that remains for the philosopher is to display that rationality in a way that advances our understanding of why we identify with the actual system of rules that bind us.

This point is recapitulated in a provocative way. Hegel asks: Why do so many contemporary philosophers appear to be puzzled and perplexed by questions which the person in the street does not see as open? Why does the philosopher court controversy, adduce a variety of opinions where in truth one finds a consensus, take pride that his or her view '*diverges from what is universally acknowledged and valid* and manages to invent something *particular* for itself'? He sees it as perverse that philosophers should identify freedom of thought with the impulse to be different, that they endorse as distinctive of the discipline of philosophy the temperament of the bloody-minded, the sceptic and nay-sayer. It is no surprise to him, particularly when the topic is that of 'right . . . the commandments of ethics and the state' (PR: 12/15) that many people ('*basically* this includes *everyone*' (PR: 14/16)) take the rules as given and in consequence regard the philosophical comedy as 'an empty game, now amusing, now more serious, now pleasing, now dangerous' (PR: 14/16–17).

Hegel has raised what philosophers should recognize as a disturbing question. Anyone who teaches or studies philosophy will have come across this critical attitude towards the discipline, not least since so many casual students of the subject, those who have taken a closer look at it than the man in the street, *do* emerge with the view that philosophy is a game. They are encouraged to question what is taken to be received opinion and common wisdom. Some like this game; some don't. But large numbers take the view that, since questions don't seem to be settled, since they are told that there is always something to be said 'on the other side', since so many modern controversies reproduce (in a contemporary idiom) the philosophical street fights of ancient Athens, philosophy really *is* a game, to be played and replayed eternally.

For Hegel, philosophy is not the game of attacking or defending inherently controversial positions. In the Preface he is staking out his ground on the nature of philosophy, on the proper contours of a philosophical question. Do persons have rights? What are they? Can persons determine *for themselves* on grounds of reason or conscience what is their duty? Should citizens obey the law or revolt? Should they see poverty as a moral problem or a fact of life? Is marriage an arrangement between families or dynasties, or a personal commitment on the part of the loving couple? It is important to understand that for Hegel these (and many other questions in like vein) are not *genuine* philosophical questions, despite what one may think of their urgency or contentiousness, because they are not *open* questions. Despite the game-playing of sceptics or fantasists, the answers to them are explicit in the rules of the communities we inhabit. There is no game to be played once the truth is known. But there is a science to be articulated. The human mind (spirit), characteristically reflexive in its scrutiny of its own activities, demands that its own products, its characteristic concepts and doctrines, be displayed intelligibly to those who apply them.

Thus the task of the philosopher on Hegel's construal is one of stating the truth concerning the deepest problems thrown up by human enquiry, showing how the truth of any subject of enquiry is ('scientifically', 'dialectically', systematically) demonstrable, how it is connected up with other truths that we avow, explaining in a philosophy of history and a history of philosophy how and when the truth dawned, and, along the way, criticizing a multitude of false and one-sided views. So the philosopher does not discover, articulate and disseminate fresh truths and novel concepts. His subject matter lies before him as the truth of the world. His problem is primarily intellectual, not political or rhetorical, definitely not evangelical. Again, the task of the philosopher is that of *comprehension*, of demonstrating the rational credentials of the knowledge claimed by modern man, of articulating to true believers *why* the truth *is* the truth. And when comprehension is achieved and the light clearly dawns, the philosopher has done all that is necessary to *justify* the domains (of world and thought together) that he has been examining. Hegel is quite right: if this is the task of the philosopher, it is not a game, however serious. It is an enquiry, a real research project, as they say nowadays.

This explains why Hegel emphasizes what readers should see as an extraordinary contrast. He asks (surely disingenuously in light of the lengthy Addition recorded in the 1822–3 lectures (PR: 13–14/15–17)): Why should scientists, students of the natural world, be able to take nature 'as it is', assume that nature is 'rational within itself', and take their task to be the investigation and conceptual elaboration of that rationality, whereas students of the ethical world are taught to regard their subject matter as inherently problematic? (PR: 12–13/15).

Actuality, Reality and Reason

This is the time to stop and examine what is going on. The topic of the *Philosophy of Right* is, broadly, ethics. Its subject matter is the personally avowed and interpersonally valid structures of will analysed in the Introduction and detailed in the rest of the book. Readers should be well aware of standard distinctions: between anthropology and sociology, which tell us how people do in fact behave, and ethics, which considers how people should behave; between political science, which tells us how folk in fact organize their political lives, and political philosophy (or theory) which deliberates how best they might live together, what values their political activity should serve. Thinking about morality and politics, we distinguish positive or scientific studies on the one hand from critical or normative investigations on the other, and we worry (and examine) whether these professional territories can be kept apart. What is central to this cluster of distinctions is not so much a simple philosophical contrast of fact and value; rather, it is an insistence that once we have a clear view of the facts of the matter concerning how persons judge that they ought to behave and how these judgements are expressed ('objectified') in their behaviour and the institutions that govern it, the field is open for an examination of whether people ought to believe what they do, ought to act as they do, and ought to support the institutions that make it possible for them to act in the light of their ethical beliefs.

The distinctive feature of Hegelian ethics is his insistence that there is no rational space for this latter type of free-wheeling enquiry. Having established that physical objects obey the laws of motion, it would be very strange to consider whether they might be better doing something different, whether there might be alternative laws that they ought rather to obey. 'Since philosophy is *exploration of the rational*, it is for that very reason the *comprehension of the present and the actual*, not the setting up of a *world beyond* . . .' (PR: 20/24). More succinctly and more famously:

> What is rational is actual;
> and what is actual is rational.

This conviction is shared by every ingenuous consciousness as well as by philosophy, and the latter takes it as its point of departure in considering both the *spiritual* and the *natural* universe.

(PR: 20/24–5)[2]

This looks clear enough: if a state of affairs is rational, then it exists; if a state of affairs exists, then it is rational. But paraphrasing Hegel's saying this way, giving the terms 'is rational' and 'is actual' (in the latter case, as near as we can get to) their common meanings, makes it alarmingly conservative and obviously false, as many critics claimed as soon as the book was published. Off-hand, using prosaic and uncontroversial criteria for determining whether or not a state of affairs is rational, we can think of rational social structures that do not exist (are not actual) and social structures that do exist (are actual) which are not rational. An integrated transport policy for the UK would be an example of the first. As against the second element of the formula, since there is evidently *some* transport policy, or policy mix, in place, in existence, that is, *actual*, why on earth should we suppose that it is the best or even one of the best? It is awful: the poor wait too long for dirty but expensive buses; the rich are stuck in traffic jams. As read, we have no reason to believe either that the rational is actual or that the actual is rational. If the social world is a mess and a muddle, not to say riven with conflicts deeper than those between users of public and private transport in inner cities, we should reject Hegel's saying on a first reading.

The Actual is Rational

We must interpret it more carefully. It is most important that we distinguish 'actual' (*wirklich*) from 'real' (*real*), actuality (*Wirklichkeit*) from reality (*Realität*) and existence (*Existenz, Dasein*). Actuality is a technical term. In the *Science of Logic* (and recapitulated in the *Encyclopaedia)* Hegel tells us that 'Actuality is the unity of essence with Existence' (SL: 528; SW 4: 662 / EL §142). Since I want to avoid an excursus explaining Hegel's concept of essence, readers should take it that this implies one of two things: *either* that actuality is that portion of the existent world which accords with, or has achieved the potential of, its nature as disclosed by reason, *or* that actuality is that condition which will exist when the reason which modern social life prefigures is fully, as against imperfectly, realized. Both of these conceptions of actuality are at work in an example Hegel gives us in the *Encyclopaedia*:

> The education and instruction of a child aim at making him actually and for himself what he is at first potentially and therefore for others, viz. for his grown-up friends. The reason, which at first exists in the child only as an inner possibility, is actualized through education: and conversely, the child by these means becomes conscious that the goodness, religion, and science which he had at first looked upon as an outward authority, are his own and inward nature.

> (EL §140R)

Referring back to the example used in the last chapter, the Ugly Duckling exists in the real world as an appearance (*Erscheinung*) only, undeveloped, ignorant of its own nature, and misunderstood by others. The fully grown swan, by contrast, is *actual*: respecting Hans Christian Andersen's conceit, it is fully developed, understands what it truly is (a swan), and is recognized as such by others. Since the world contains both Ugly Ducklings and swans, 'existence is in part mere appearance, and only in part actuality' (*Encyclopaedia* §6). And so, if we look around us, we shall find that the social world, the normative structures of will, with which we identify and by which we guide our behaviour, 'is in part mere appearance, and only in part actuality'.

It follows from this analysis of Hegel's terminology that the second half of his famous saying is an analytic truth: what is actual is rational, since if it were not a feature of some existent element of the social world that it is rational in the sense of being an intelligible institution or mode of behaviour for persons who truly understand their nature, it would not be actual. The institution or mode of behaviour would exist in the modern world, but it would be an anachronism, or it would be based on superstition; it would betoken an error or a misunderstanding of how persons should conduct themselves (which is not to say, as in the case of crime, that such mistakes might not be wilful and liable to punishment – see Chapter 6). Which is to say: it would not be rational. This reading of the second element of the famous saying threatens to deprive it of its cutting edge. Who would deny that the actual is rational, if the true judgement that an existent state of affairs is irrational entails that it is not actual? Thus one might for the moment accept that Hegel can defend himself against those opponents who say he is a conservative but argue that this defence succeeds at the price of denying that he is saying anything interesting or controversial.

We should not make too much of this charge that the second element of the saying is a tautology, therefore uninformative and uninteresting. Since the actual does not coincide with the real, there is still work to be done in specifying the elements of the real social world that are rational. To do this we need an operational concept of the rational, and we shall move on to discuss this shortly. But for the moment we should notice that there are two distinctive ways in which reality can fall short of actuality. We can see this first of all in the way Hegel clearly limits the ambitions of his philosophical science. The existent social world reveals 'an infinite wealth of forms, appearances and shapes [which surround its rational core] with a brightly covered colouring . . . this infinite material and its organization, are not the subject-matter of philosophy' (PR: 21/25). Philosophy should not pretend to be able to explain every detail and facet of the social world as a demand of reason. (Hegel joshes Plato's instructions to nurses and Fichte's prescriptions for passport regulations.) The world is multifaceted, as he implies, multicoloured; philosophy articulates its monochromatic core, painting a grisaille picture which captures the essential elements.[3]

If this is a distinctive feature of the actuality/reality contrast, Hegel faces a difficulty with which he never really comes to terms – that of distinguishing core and superstructure, appearances and essentials, in a principled fashion. Sometimes the reader needs more colour; Hegel can be careless and slipshod in his portrayal of the details of institutions – what *exactly* are the constituencies, 'the associations, communities, and corporations' (§308) from which representatives in the second Estate are selected to serve in the legislature? At other times, by contrast, he goes into the sort of detail that would raise even Fichte's eyebrows, noticeably where he has a personal interest in a practical problem. Readers of §§43 and 68–9 will recognize that Hegel has a proprietorial stake in the minutiae of rules ascribing intellectual property rights. There seems to be no rule to dictate what aspect of a social institution renders it amenable to rational (scientific) redescription, and what level of nitty-gritty suggests that its study can be safely entrusted to empirical studies. Thus, to take another example, it is not easy to see why *reason* should dictate that crimes and punishments should be equal in respect of their value as injuries to the victim and culprit respectively, yet disdain the task of fixing the terms of the equation. This latter issue is a matter for the *understanding* of professional judges (§§101, 227).

In a case like this, Hegel may be right to draw the boundaries of the philosophically defensible and the practically expedient at the place he selects, but often one suspects that the guiding principle is his lack of interest or his undefended belief that philosophy has little to offer in settling a particular issue. You will notice as you read the text how often he throws pearls to the swine, as topics suitable for the employment of the 'understanding' that non-philosophers characteristically employ. And sometimes you may take the view that the problem which is swept aside is apt for careful and genuinely philosophical study and debate.

The second respect in which the actual world may not amount to the real world can be seen in circumstances where the real world falls short of the actual world. This condition has to be specified with some care, since it cannot be described as a state of affairs in which the real world is judged critically in the light of some rational ideal. That is the perspective of the *sollen*, of the ought-to-be which Hegel derides. We can understand the contrast best by way of example. Let us agree that freedom of speech is an ideal which is recognized in our community. No politician would openly deny the principle, no citizen would fail to claim it as a right. The principle is objectified in institutional form: it is explicit in laws which incorporate charters of rights; it is embedded in practices such as uncensored newspaper publishing and the availability of a pulpit at Hyde Park Corner for any citizen with a cause to press in public. Nonetheless, a critic of the present regime may say that the principle of free speech is not fully actualized. Freedom of speech is impotent if there are significant restrictions on access to information. And it is compromised if the economics of newspaper publishing make it inevitable that most of the press is in the ownership of a few wealthy proprietors who use their power to press a personal agenda and make it difficult for new voices to enter the market place of opinion. Where a principle is honoured in the breach as much as in the observance, so long as that principle is rationally grounded we have identified logical space for the claim that the real is not actual, or fully actual. We haven't spun a novel principle out of the realm of ethical fantasy; rather, we have taken up a principle to which lip-service is universal and demonstrated how it is imperfectly respected (or cynically ignored). We have identified an opportunity for *immanent criticism*.

Criticism of this style is dubbed 'immanent' because it is criticism of an institution (in this case, the press) on the basis of principles which it conspicuously endorses. Immanent criticism is the best sort of criticism of social practices, since it begins from premises which all parties accept. It says to the professed democrat: If you subscribe to democratic principles, why don't you have a referendum on matters which in Parliament are decided by free vote, as a matter of conscience? It says to the professed egalitarian: If you believe in equality of opportunity, why do you send your child to a public (i.e. in the UK, private) school? It is a social version of *ad hominem* argument, requiring a society to take seriously the principles which it explicitly endorses and, in consequence, to amend its practices. Hegel's distinction of reality and actuality opens up the space for this sort of criticism. It does not conjure critical principles out of fresh air; it identifies those with clear and acknowledged roots within the beliefs and institutions of the community, and it demands transparent compliance with them.

To my knowledge, every fair-minded commentator on Hegel's *Philosophy of Right* emphasizes the space between actuality and reality which Hegel opens up for immanent criticism. In the Rational State, but *not* in Prussia c. 1820, there is trial by jury, constitutional monarchy, a representative legislature, to give a few examples of institutions which rationality requires (and philosophical science describes) but which reality does not attest. But it is one thing to say that Hegel is not a slavish apologist for the reactionary Prussian state which confronted him in all its grim detail; it is quite another to claim that he is a strong critic. To my knowledge, despite his description of institutions which would fulfil the potential of his underdeveloped present, which would fully objectify reason, he is never once *directly* critical of the institutions of the Prussian state of which he was such a prominent citizen. He never once draws attention to the criticism which his philosophical practice implies. Maybe he expects his students to read between the lines. Whether this is timidity or humility or deviousness on his part (and it may be a mixture of all three) it is noticeable that he is much more restrained in his criticism of the political institutions of contemporary Prussia than he is of political conditions in Britain.

The Rational is Actual

Now that we have a clear(er) view of the claim that the actual is rational, let us examine in further detail the thought that the rational is actual. We should begin by considering what this element of the saying excludes. Most obviously, the point is epistemological; it excludes the possibility of reason being accessible to enquirers in structures of will which are neither manifest in personal ethical beliefs and institutional forms nor immanent in beliefs and institutions which are imperfect realizations of reason. In the context of Hegel's grand metaphysical scheme, this is entailed by the conception of reason as spirit's (mind's) knowledge of itself. If reason isn't there to be known (i.e. actualized) how can spirit have that knowledge of it which amounts to self-knowledge? If reason isn't actual, in respect of being either existent in the social world or being an identifiable development of the social world as we experience it, how could it be an object of knowledge? How indeed? is the proper, albeit partly sarcastic, response.

To understand this position fully, we would need to master the fundamental elements of Hegel's absolute idealism, and we cannot pursue that task here. The central claim is that thought, mind or spirit is necessarily embodied in some medium: 'this principle of necessary embodiment, as we may call it, is central to Hegel's conception of Geist, or cosmic spirit' (C. Taylor 1975: 83).[4] In the context of the *Philosophy of Right* this amounts to an insistence that reason, the governing principle of spirit, is actualized in the structures of will which compose the social world.

Having abandoned the task of summarizing Hegel's meta-physics, I don't want to leave the matter there, since there are useful things to be said about the location of reason in the actual social world. First, pointing us forward to Chapter 8, we should see Hegel's claim that the rational is actual as a rejection of the Kantian thought that practical reason is a distinctive faculty of moral subjects which permits them freely to legislate rules of morality in a quasi-algorithmic fashion, quite independently of their natural embodiment and their given social context. This conception of reason, as an autonomous instrument of moral prescription, will be demonstrated to be inadequate. Hegel's claim is that the Kantian conception of normative ethics, paradigmatic of the ethics of the ought-to-be, cannot deliver on its promise to serve as a test of putative moral maxims. Moral rules are actual in the domain of Ethical Life.

Second, we know from the Introduction what the form is that reason will take in the social world as comprehended by the *Philosophy of Right*. It will characterize the structures of will manifest in the social world as structures of freedom. As we have seen, Hegel tells us in §4 that this much is obvious, but as we have also seen, he is careful to spell out analytically what freedom involves and, as the argument proceeds, he will put flesh on the analytic bones. In the Preface he anticipates the result of his enquiry: philosophy will enable the student 'to recognize reason as the rose in the cross of the present and thereby to delight in the present'. That philosophy which enables its practioners to comprehend the social world, to achieve 'rational insight', grants them a '*reconciliation* with actuality', which is to say, it enables them 'to preserve their subjective freedom in the realm of the substantial' (PR: 22/26–7). To understand the social world as rational is to endorse the ethical demands which the social world places on the individual. Subjective freedom is attained when the individual recognizes the validity of substantial ethical norms, identifying with those institutions and their constitutive ethical principles which compose a realm of objective freedom. Of course, all these terms (subjective freedom, objective freedom) will have to be cashed out in the argument that follows, but we should have a clear idea of the agenda. Hegel will disclose how the social world which he describes in the chapter on Ethical Life is a harmonious and coherent structure of will, a realm of freedom. It follows, if freedom is the key to the manifestation of the rational in the actual social world, that we should take particular care to investigate Hegel's argument from this perspective. We shall find ourselves asking, over and over again, whether or not, in what way, the social world of the *Philosophy of Right* truly is a world in which freedom is realized.

This task would be a lot easier if we had a simple concept of freedom to work with, but as we have seen from our preliminary study of the Introduction, we don't. The account of freedom which Hegel sketches there and elaborates in the rest of the book is irremediably complex (and none the worse for that). It embraces freedom of action and social freedom, negative freedom and positive freedom, freedom as self-knowledge and freedom as self-control. Most difficult of all to grasp, it embraces as the *subjects* of freedom individual persons, social groupings such as families, the rational state as a whole, as well as the quasi-divine, human spirit which is the subject of history. All of these strands of Hegel's thought will have to be teased out before we come to a final judgement on whether the social world as he describes it is a realm of freedom. But we should note now one source of conspicuous tension.

Subjective freedom as understood in the Preface is the achievement of the *philosopher*. It is attained when one comprehends the existent social world as rational and thereby 'delight[s] in the present'. The freedom which is attained objectively within the substantial norms of ethical life is objective. It must be recognizable as freedom quite independently of the formal condition that it is comprehended as rational by the philosophical enquirer. Objective freedom must connect with familiar, though not necessarily uncontroversial, thoughts that we have concerning which social arrangements are free and which are not. Reason which is actual must be recognizable in institutions which are substantively free.

The tension between subjective freedom understood as a cognitive state and objective freedom, the freedom that social institutions permit and promote, is revealed whenever Hegel comes across a conflict between the assertion of individual freedom and the claims of the state. We *know* that some individuals are likely to cite freedom of conscience in the face of the demands the state makes upon them.

Conspicuously, these claims of conscience are asserted against (let us assume) the state's legitimate imposition of conscription to fight a just war. Such claims are familiarly made on religious grounds, as with Quakers, but sometimes they are not. A. J. P. Taylor's uncle Harry

> was amongst the first conscientious objectors [to conscription, in 1916], and an 'absolutist' at that. His particular conviction was unusual. Previously, though a Radical, he had not been particularly interested in politics. Unlike most conscientious objectors he had no religious beliefs, still less was he a Marxist. His objection was based simply on a belief in individual liberty. The State had no right to conscript him, and that was that.
>
> (A. J. P. Taylor 1983: 28)

I surmise that every state there has ever been has, that all states presently do, and that all states in the future will, meet such challenges. I believe that these conflicts are to be approached delicately, employing (on the part of the state) the most sophisticated moral resources. I would argue that this heightened moral sensitivity is one of the few beneficial consequences of the First World War, though such sentiments have their origin in pre-Hegelian conclusions about permissible toleration. I think Hegel sometimes approaches such issues with a blunderbuss.[5] Having worked out what reason requires, what freedom demands, he feels able to insist that

> the right of insight [§§120, 132] applies to insight into *legality* or *illegality*, i.e. into what is *recognized* as right, and is confined to its primary meaning, namely *cognizance* [*Kenntnis*] in the sense of *familiarity* with what is legal and to that extent obligatory. Through the public nature of the laws and the universality of customs, the state takes away from the right of insight its formal aspect and that contingency which this right still has for the subject within the prevailing viewpoint [of morality].
>
> (§132R)

When discussing moral conscience, in §137, he insists that 'the state cannot recognize the conscience in its distinctive form, i.e. as *subjective knowledge*, any more than science can grant any validity to subjective *opinion, assertion*, and the *appeal* to subjective opinion'.

Why should he feel such confidence in the face of conspicuous opponents? What is crystal clear is that the voice of authority which Hegel familiarly bespeaks is grounded in knowledge claims. And if knowledge equals self-knowledge (of Spirit), and if self-knowledge equals freedom, freedom as self-knowledge trumps freedom as the self-determination of the conscientious objector, the true but contrary believer, or the bloody-minded sceptic. We can all see the genuinely philosophical difficulties raised by practical confrontations such as these. My thought is that these are steamrollered, flattened out beyond the possibility of careful philosophical appraisal, by Hegel's cognitive conception of freedom.

This criticism may seem harsh, and I accept that a more nuanced view of Hegel's position is possible, particularly one that makes use of Hegel's treatment of the religious, as against the moral, conscience. (See the careful discussions in §270R and EL §552.) I accept, too, that my reading is based on the difficult business of identifying the tone, as much as the letter, of Hegel's writings. So readers of Hegel will have to come to their own view of the matter. But they should be aware that the crucial question of how far Hegel respects his own doctrines concerning the centrality of subjective freedom in the modern world is wide open.

Reason and History

We should read the *Philosophy of Right* as an ahistorical text delineating the structure of the social world as rational in virtue of its multidimensional, multilayered manifestation of freedom. It is not essentially a historical study,[6] although as I have mentioned, Hegel's description of our ethical life, which locates us in the framework of social norms, concludes its account of our moral address by placing us at the concluding point of world history. Nonetheless, each of the structures of right that he investigates – Abstract Right, Morality and the domains of Ethical Life – has a historical provenance. And there is a historical story to be told about the establishment of these norms and about their integration in the consciousness of modern man. This is the third aspect of Hegel's doctrine that the rational is actual that I wish to discuss – the role of reason in history.[7]

This is the subject matter of probably the most famous passage Hegel wrote – the penultimate paragraph of the Preface. I shall rehearse it here in full. It bears repetition.

> One word more about giving instructions as to what the world ought to be. Philosophy in any case always comes on the scene too late to give it. As the thought of the world, it appears only when actuality is already there cut and dried after its process of formation has been completed. The teaching of the concept, which is also history's inescapable lesson, is that it is only when actuality is mature that the ideal first appears over against the real and that the ideal apprehends this same real world in its substance and builds it up for itself into the shape of an intellectual realm. When philosophy paints its grey in grey, then has a shape of life grown old. By philosophy's grey in grey it cannot be rejuvenated but only understood. The owl of Minerva spreads its wings only with the falling of the dusk.
>
> (Knox: 12–13; *Werke* 7: 27–8)[8]

Hegel, in the *Philosophy of Right*, reconstructs the social world as 'an intellectual realm'. But this philosophical enterprise is only possible because reason has been at work in history fashioning actuality in its own image. How has it done this? It has ensured that those elements of our social life which are necessary for freedom have been preserved, that those elements which have denied, frustrated or compromised humanity's drive for freedom have gone under, or, maybe, can be studied as anachronistic relics, still inhibiting freedom in societies which have not progressed or have never started. (The time–space worm of spirit developing and articulating its rationale of freedom follows a spatial as well as a historical track, moving westwards from its oriental origins in China, India and the Middle East into Greek and Roman territories before moving north to the Germanic realm.[9] Africa and South America do not feature in the narrative of world history except by way of their colonization. Is there a great dead philosopher who has offered more hostages to political correctness than Hegel? Aristotle perhaps.[10])

How much of this speculative philosophy of history do we need to know to make sense of the arguments of the *Philosophy of Right*, to understand the opportunity offered to philosophy to comprehend (to disclose the rational core of the social world, to paint its grisaille, its grey in grey)? The more the better, one should insist. But the essentials are these, for the reader who can excuse my brutal condensations: once upon a time (in the ancient world), folks unreflectively identified with their communities. They lived in harmony with each other, with nature and with their gods – in harmony because these relationships were unexamined. Incredibly they had no sense of themselves as individuals; they identified themselves as members of the clan or instruments of the state. Persons had to learn how to identify themselves in the first-person singular, as an 'I' as well as a 'We', and this dimension of self-understanding began to dawn with Socrates' questioning of traditional beliefs in fourth-century BCE Athens. In the Roman world this embryonic sense of individuality was enhanced with the introduction of the concept of the person as a legal subject, but this concept was not fully explicit until Protestantism taught Christians that they are discrete souls, each with immediate access to their God, which is to say, access without the mediation of priests or saints. This sense of individual atomicity is amplified by political doctrines which assert natural rights, emphasizing the boundedness of particular human beings who make claims of right against their fellows.

Thus far, history has disclosed to humanity that it is *universal*, in the sense that persons inhabit communities of belief, identifying themselves as members of organically unified societies, and that persons are *particular*, which is to say that they have also learned to think of themselves as unique, as essentially different from their fellows. As Hegel writes, the apotheosis (better, nadir) of particularity has been witnessed in the atrocities of the Terror in revolutionary France. Reason requires that we identify the present as a social world in which the claims of universality (of social membership) and particularity (as personal discreteness or atomicity) are integrated and given due recognition. In the modern world this is possible for the first time. The rational has become actual through a historical process that we can chart.

To understand the *Philosophy of Right*, we don't need to know the history, but we do need to know that we are historically situated beings, inhabiting social structures that mankind has formed and that have formed mankind in turn. We also need to know that Hegel locates us at the end of history. There are different ways of understanding this thesis. The first is innocuous: we are always at the end of history, conscious beings moving forward at the point of time's arrow, depositing human history behind us, looking back at the layers of spiritual sediment. The second is controversial, and I confess that I cannot even begin to sort out the controversy here. Stated crudely, the thesis that the rational is actual and the actual is rational implies that the end of its history which mind has reached is that stage of maturity and completion where it can survey clearly the skeins of rationality (the grey in grey painted by philosophy) in the social world of the present time. That aspect of freedom which consists in mind's self-knowledge and which has hitherto been limited by the fact of mankind's ignorance (as revealed in poor science, misguided religion and false philosophy as well as institutions which inhibit freedom) is now manifest in the world. Genuine philosophy, 'the thought of the world', is only possible 'when actuality is already there cut and dried after its process of formation has been completed'. This looks clear enough, for all that it is fabulously ambitious or optimistic. But we should notice the possibility of two different readings.

The first is the sharp thesis, expressed in the claim that we do have complete knowledge, absolute freedom; and this is expressed in Hegel's philosophy, most compendiously in the *Encyclopaedia*, but with respect to the social world, in more detailed fashion in the *Philosophy of Right*. The distinction of actuality and reality suggests that there are t's to be crossed and i's to be dotted, but that the practical application of immanent criticism is all that remains to be done. There is no more ethical knowledge to be sought, no fresh ethical truths to be discovered, no novel institutions to be designed. Thus put, Hegel's claim is clearly false, as can be seen if we contrast Hegel's moral vision with our own. Hegel was just wrong about the role of women in the family and in the worlds of work and politics, wrong about the value of colonialism and warfare, wrong about mankind's relationship to the natural world, to name a few (and maybe there are only a few) radical shifts in moral perspective that have occurred in the last two centuries. We can, so I believe, chart moral advances between his time and ours which should lead us to dismiss his thesis if it is construed in this severe, absolute fashion.

But there is another, third way of understanding the end-of-history thesis which cannot be dismissed so easily, although it is obviously controversial. This last account agrees with the absolute reading in that it sees history not only as a process, but as a progress. At any time of study of the social world, we can identify institutions and concomitant moral beliefs as rational if they promote freedom. Our perspective is necessarily conservative since the only elements of the social world that are open to understanding and endorsement are either those that are in place, or those that immanent criticism will lead us towards. One need not insist that the social world has reached a completed state, but one can claim that bankable moral assets have been deposited in mankind's moral history and that these are available for inspection. This is the more plausible Hegel, if not on my reading Hegel as he aspired to be read (though I stress again that this is controversial).

What programme for ethics does this last (Hegelian, if not quite Hegel's) way of construing the end-of-history thesis leave us with? On this account, the task of the philosopher is that of (social) self-examination, of elaborating as rational the normative resources of the social world we inhabit. How do we identify these resources? We severally ask the questions 'What am I?' and 'What does my being thus demand of me?' We interrogate the 'I' to disclose the 'We'.[11] Hard questions, these, but we have cheated. We already have a grasp of schematic answers from our study of the Introduction. And, to anticipate the rest of the *Philosophy of Right*, Hegel delineates those ways of identifying ourselves which have moral potency, which carry with them subscription to a set of moral norms. The first task is to describe these. Thus he explains how we recognize ourselves as discrete persons, claiming rights on our own behalf, respecting the rights of others and legitimately punishing the violators of rights; how we see ourselves as moral subjects, accepting responsibility for actions we fully intend, achieving satisfaction through their successful accomplishment, and demanding that we should be able to recognize as valid any duties imputed to us. He shows how we must pursue the good, but concludes that we are unable to legislate for ourselves what it might be, and we are unable to test the voice of conscience as it speaks directly to us. Rather, in order to act well, we need to identify with the forms of social life which enhance our freedom by enabling us to express our spiritual, human nature as this has been formed through history. We seek to understand the opportunities and demands of family life, civil society and the state. We articulate how, severally and most importantly, together, these ethical domains serve the end of freedom.

Allen Wood characterizes Hegel's ethics as a 'self-actualization theory'. As I read this, normative ethics, the study of how we ought to behave, proceeds by persons interrogating what reason tells them that they are, what their nature demands of them. Meta-ethically, this perspective is described as historical naturalism since it explains the conception of the good (and the good life as it is lived) as a historical achievement on the part of humanity (or mind, or spirit), as what historically conditioned humanity is nowadays naturally disposed to seek. So we have Hegel espousing a historically naturalist self-actualization theory (Wood 1990: 30–5). This is a mouthful, to be sure. But it tells us exactly what sort of philosophical theory we can anticipate. As we shall see, it is a strange and exotic creature, but that should make the study of it an exciting prospect.

Coda: Introduction §§1–3

Happily, we are now in a position to understand the difficult first three sections of the Introduction. First, Hegel announces that the 'subject-matter of *the philosophical science of right* is the *Idea of right* – the concept of right and its actualization' (§1). This tells us that we are going to study two things at once: the concept of right, the structures of reason manifested in the domain of right (roughly: our ethical thought) together with the actualization of the concept in the social world, which is to say those patterns of ethical norms and the institutions which they constitute which make the social world a structure of freedom. We shall be studying together rationality and actuality.

The method of study that we shall employ will not be that of analytical ethics or jurisprudence. We shan't be searching for definitions or engaging in conceptual analysis as that is presently understood. Hegel believes this approach is dangerous as well as superficial, since our definitions may well encode philosophical errors and anachronisms. Moreover, however competently this task is done, it will never get down to the heart of the matter. It will never reveal the *necessity* of the subject of study, the manner in which reason is actualized. Nor should we substitute for this misplaced rigour the conception of right which he attacked in the Preface, the immediate assertion of '*facts of consciousness*, and our natural and intensified feelings, our *own heart* and *enthusiasm*' (§2R). It remains to be seen whether there is a method for ethics which goes beyond the careful analysis of our modes of self-understanding. I confess, I can't see it. Beneath the technical vocabulary, Hegelian argument looks to me like most other species of reputable philosophical argument, so I shall present it and examine it in that vein.

The one final topic for introductory comment concerns the notion of right itself. Phrases such as 'the concept of right' and 'the science of right', and indeed the title of the book *The Philosophy of Right*, read oddly in English, though one can lose sight of the fact if one uses them often enough. *Recht* in German, like *droit* in French, has a range of meanings for which there is no English equivalent. It can mean a common-or-garden 'right', it can mean 'justice' or it can mean 'the law'. (See Inwood 1992: 259–61, '*Recht*', for a lovely discussion of these issues.) Hegel's use of the term in the book title is philosophically knowing, since he uses the concept of *Recht* in a broader sense than some of his philosophical opponents, for example Kant, for whom *Recht* has a primarily legal or jurisprudential significance. That said, Hegel never reaches philosophical conclusions about *Recht* on the basis of his semantic or stylistic decisions. As we shall see, his disputes are always posed in philosophical terms and arguments are always brought forth or (less admirably) intimated.

In translation, 'right' as used broadly is probably best understood as 'ethics' or perhaps even 'morality', so long as we are aware that Hegel himself uses the term 'morality' for a distinctive and limited conception of ethics. Ethical rules or prescriptions as these are studied in Part 3, 'Ethical Life', include both rules of morality and laws. 'Right' also has the narrower meaning, in 'Abstract Right', of a specific claim, as when we speak of natural rights or human rights and designate a limited segment of ethics.

We are familiar with contrasts between natural law and positive law, between positive morality and critical morality, and the way these distinctions are drawn may lead us to take these contrasts as signalling, on the one hand, statements of what the law or morality is, and on the other hand, judgements of what the law or morality ought to be. And of course it is an implication of this distinction that systems of positive law and morality may be incompatible with natural law or critical morality. Lawyers, moralists and sociologists describe the content of positive law and morality. Philosophers work out principles of natural law and critical morality, and prepare the way for legal and moral reform. It is important that we understand that these distinctions and contrasts are *not* Hegel's. Given his views on the rational and the actual and his regular disparagement of the morality of the ought-to-be, it is clear that this familiar cluster of distinctions is not available to him. The distinction he is prepared to draw between, say, natural law and positive law is that between the general principles of ethics and the rational structure of will as disclosed in the (grey) philosophical science of right, on the one hand, and ethics, including law in its full (multicoloured) positivity, on the other hand.

Positive right can be identified in terms of both its form and its content. It has the '*form* of having validity' in accordance with the authoritative legal norms of the state (§3, 211–18). Read strictly, this has the implication that the entire ethics of, for example, family life will be codified in positive law. This cannot be right, though it is hard to think of a society in which the kernel of domestic duties is not enacted in family law. On the other hand, it is hard to think what the validity test of positive morality might be as it governs domestic and other civil relationships.[12] In terms of *content*, right is declared to be positive first as a specific structure of ethical norms such as a sociologist or anthropologist might describe as fitting to the contingent circumstances of time and place; second, in virtue of the applicability of the general act-descriptions which comprise the content of the law to the societies which these laws govern. Thus, if there is a law proscribing bigamy, this will require an actual practice of monogamy, otherwise the law has no sense or point. Third, right is positive in the specific judgements made in particular cases. Thus the wrongness of theft is explicit in the moment of conviction of the thief. (We shall see later, in Chapter 6, that this point is important in explaining why punishment is justified.) We must understand that particular moral judgements too ('It was wrong of you to deceive your mother like that') attest the phenomena of positive right.

Hegel makes it quite clear that the judge or sociologist and the philosopher have different tasks, though they cover the same ground and deal with the same subject matter. But to repeat a point I made earlier, it is not clear in principle where the lines of demarcation between these different activities are to be drawn. We shall have to see, as we go on to study the book in detail, how fine-grained the disclosure of the rational in the actual turns out to be. Mercifully, we can now proceed to engage that detailed study.

Chapter 4

Abstract Right 1. Persons and their Rights: §§34–43

Persons

'What am I?' we have now moved on to ask in our characterization of the free will. The first-shot (*immediate*) answer that we give when we put this question to ourselves is that 'I am me'. This answer is both wholly abstract – it says nothing about me or my world except that I confront myself as 'pure personality' (§35A) – and yet wholly determinate – I am, after all, all the things that are true of me, of such a height, weight, age, and so on . . . I am a Cartesian ego, 'totally pure self-reference' (§35), yet also a finite and spatio-temporally fixed locus of beliefs and desires.

From this exercise in self-examination, a number of conclusions are drawn by Hegel. First, although the exercise is conducted by a particular finite self, say me, the self that is immediately disclosed is '*infinite, universal* and *free*' (§35). The self is universal in the same sense as the element of will which is encountered in §5. In answering the question 'What am I?', I detach myself from any content of consciousness, becoming

conscious of myself as 'a completely abstract "I" in which all concrete limitation and validity are negated and invalidated' (§35R). In so doing, I abstract from any distinctive feature of myself that might distinguish me from other selves; I discover my universality. Second, this capacity for detachment, as we have seen, is an element of the free will. Third, I disclose the infinite, in the sense that the self thus revealed is not limited by the desires and inclinations of the natural self from which it has abstracted. This conception of the self is entirely empty in point of content. It is the self as a person.

'Person' is evidently functioning here as a term of art. To say that someone is a person says nothing about her beliefs or desires, but it does impute a formal character which is important but easily over-looked. The person thus disclosed is an 'exclusive individuality [*ausschliessende Einzelheit*]' (§34). Later Hegel will speak of the person 'as atomic individuality [*als atome Einzelheit*]' (§167). This is to say that the self as we first encounter it is a distinct individual, discrete and bounded from other selves and from the external world which they inhabit. (It is nonetheless universal in that this atomicity is a property which self-enquiring selves share with all other selves.)

So, if I ask, 'What am I?' my first-shot answer will express the formal difference of myself from other things – 'I am me, not you nor it', which is to say I shall apply to myself the formal concept of a person: 'I am a person'. Why is this of any interest, still less impor-tant? Hegel believes, and to modern ears this should be a striking claim, that there are other, different, ways in which we might imme-diately identify ourselves. I might, for example, not think of myself as distinct from others. The first way that I think of myself may be as the appendage or instrument of another, as a slave, ascribing to myself no independent status. Or I might identify myself with some social group, a family or a clan or a nation: I am one of the Knowles family, or a MacKnowles or English. It is Hegel's interesting thesis that folk have not always thought of themselves as persons. He thinks the light began to dawn in the Roman world, but of course the concept was not applied universally since there were slaves. The concept of a person developed with Christianity and particularly with Protestantism which empha-sized each person's unique relationship with their God. To us, having done some philosophy, it is perhaps most familiar from the natural rights doctrines of the seventeenth century – but more on rights later. Humanity has had to *learn* to apply to itself this conception of the self as a discrete, bounded individual. That it has succeeded so well is indicated by the very strangeness of thinking of ourselves in other terms. That I am, in the first place, different from you may seem so obvious that it is not worth saying. But it is a truth that the well-treated, acquiescent slave, for example, may miss (§57).

Nor should we think of the concept of a person as ethically inert. Personhood amounts to a distinctive moral status as indicated by the commandment of right: 'be a person and respect others as persons' (§36). To be a person, on this account, is not to have specific sorts of interests or a concern for one's own welfare; persons don't have particular motives *qua* persons (§37). But there is a distinctive moral vocabulary that they employ when they act as persons and accord others the respect that their personhood is due. They use the language of rights.

Rights

There are two formal features of this language. One who claims rights demands the recognition of others for a domain in which they can act as expressive of their freedom. Thus if I claim a right to walk up and down Sauchiehall Street, I assert that walking up and down Sauchiehall Street should be a possibility for me. I don't say that I want to or even that I intend to do so some time. Who knows? But I do say that it should be possible. This takes us to the second aspect of the language of rights as used by persons. To have the possibility available that my right requires is to place a requirement on other persons. In the case of my right to walk up and down Sauchiehall Street it will be a requirement that they don't interfere with me. Hence the logical form ('the necessity') of claims of right 'is limited to the negative – *not to violate* personality and what ensues from personality. Hence there are only *prohibitions of right*, and the positive form of commandments of right is, in its ultimate content, based on prohibition' (§38). The commandments of right, therefore, have this form: 'Don't . . .'

This account of persons, and the logical grammar of the rights claims they assert, should be familiar to readers of modern political philosophy from the work of John Rawls and, most conspicuously, Robert Nozick. First, it asserts the priority of the right over the good. The ethical status that individuals demand when they conceive of themselves as persons is established independently of any account of characteristic human interests or the sources of human happiness or well-being. Second, presaging both Rawls and Nozick, it asserts (indeed, claims little else than) the distinction or separateness of persons (Rawls 1972: §§5, 6, 30; Nozick 1974: 28–35). Third, the normative vocabulary appropriate to an ethical ontology of circumscribed, discrete social atoms is that of rights construed as 'side constraints', to use Nozick's term. 'Side constraints express the inviolability of other persons' (Nozick 1974: 32). They do so by prescribing 'Whatever your goals, don't . . . in pursuit of them', where the blank is filled in by action descriptions which entail the violation of the rights of others. Being a person involves the assertion of side constraints against others. Respecting a person involves accepting such side constraints as inhibiting one's conduct *vis-à-vis* others.[1] The rights which are claimed are, all of them, negative rights, rights that others should not do such and such. They correlate with and, indeed, are expressed as, duties on the part of others, duties formulated as injunctions not to x, y and z. (We shall investigate the content of these duties in the next chapter.)

Notoriously, Nozick has little to say in justification of his conception of rights as side constraints and nothing to say in respect of the derivation of the particular right to private property which is the foundation of his entitlement theory of justice. The first omission is fair enough; it is an omission of detail only, since he gestures towards Kantian doctrines of autonomy, of the importance of treating persons as ends in themselves and not as means merely, of the wrongness inherent in using other persons as instruments of one's own purposes. The detail, one supposes, may be filled in by a sympathetic application of Kant's insights and there are plenty of modern Kantians for us to follow. This prompts the question 'How does Hegel vindicate his claim that we are persons with "the capacity for right"?' (§36).

It is tempting to say that Hegel takes this route as well. There are undoubtedly Kantian elements in his articulation of the groundwork of Abstract Right. In the first place, the universal element of the will of the person, stressing the detachment of the self from its desires, echoes Kant's contrast of desire and duty (GMM: 52–6 / Ak 4: 397–400). Associatedly, the insistence that personhood is a formal concept, detached from any account of human interests or desires, which, in modern terms, is one dimension to the priority of the right over the good, is a recognizable Kantian theme. Also, Hegel's announcement of the commandment of right (*das Rechtsgebot*, §36) surely mimics a categorical imperative, as does the form of rights claims as prohibitions or side constraints. Such a reading though would be anachronistic, notwithstanding Hegel's proclivity to tease his readers in the matter of inexplicit or unacknowledged references. There is an argument behind his claim that we see ourselves, first of all, as persons, and we find its origins in Rousseau and Fichte as much as in Kant. It is a doctrine of recognition.

Recognition

As described in Rousseau's second discourse, *The Discourse on the Origins of Inequality*, natural man is pre-eminently independent, but independence has been lost as mankind was first of all compelled to associate, then formed a taste for association and the goods it brought.

> Free and independent as men were before, they were now, in consequence of a multiplicity of new wants, brought into subjection, as it were, to all nature, and particularly to one another; and each became in some degree a slave even in becoming the master of other men: if rich, they stood in need of the services of others; if poor, of their assistance . . .
>
> (Rousseau 1973: 86)

Rousseau finds the growing condition of inequality a dismal state of affairs which bred, according to the different characters of men, 'dominion and slavery, or violence and rapine' (Rousseau 1973: 87). These are evils enough, one may think, since they lead to the horrors of war. As with Hobbes's state of nature, this is a war of every man against every man, and is settled only by means of a fraudulent contract engineered by the rich which transforms inequalities of wealth into inequalities of social status and political power. Rousseau was adamant, though, that inequality spawned a deeper evil. It corrupted the minds of all parties, entrammeling the rich as well as the poor in the chains of social dependency. As summarized in the first sentences of Chapter 1 of *The Social Contract*, 'Man is born free; but everywhere he is in chains. One thinks himself the master of others, and still remains a greater slave than they' (Rousseau 1973: 165). Inequality has a terrible psychological cost which no-one can escape. It undermines everyone's sense of their equal worth.

Rousseau's depiction of the psychological horrors attendant on inequality and dependency was emblematic. It may well have inspired Kant's formulation of the categorical imperative as the principle of humanity: '*so act that you use humanity, whether in your own person or in the person of any other, always at the same time as an end, never merely as a means*' (GMM: 80 / Ak. 4: 429), since this is targeted at the use of other persons for one's own ends, a use which violates their moral status as autonomous creatures. Kant's argument for this conclusion is formal in a way that Rousseau's is not. Though he knew Rousseau's work well enough, he does not derive the postulate of equal moral worth from an anthropological understanding of human nature, nor does he dwell on the psychological effects of its denial.

Fichte is the first to develop this account of equal moral worth into a principle of recognition.[2] There are two strands to Fichte's argument. The first is transcendental. He claims to deduce the necessity of a principle that persons must reciprocally respect the demands they make of each other for a sphere of free agency from the very possibility of self-consciousness. An agent cannot identify itself unless it can distinguish itself from others. But that very act of distinguishing the self from others presupposes that others are recognized as other self-consciousnesses, capable in turn of distinguishing themselves from other selves. Put crudely, I cannot apply the concept 'I' to myself without understanding how it is applied by others to themselves. I understand this, in turn, by respecting the agency of the other, by acknowledging in their case what I demand in my own – an external domain in which free agency is possible. Self-knowledge and self-respect require the acknowledgement of the independence of others and respect for their rights.

It is hard not to think of such transcendental arguments as pulling rabbits from hats. The slide from conceptual or epistemological constraints on the application of the concept 'I' to the ethical standing of an agent who demands recognition is too quick to be convincing. Wood identifies more promising ground in a second strand of argument, reading

> Fichte's theory of recognition as an account of an ideal social-ization process for individuals in a culture in which values such as individual freedom and autonomy hold an important place. In teaching people to think of themselves as rational beings, we teach them to think of themselves as having the right to an external sphere for free action, and we teach them to employ the same conception in thinking of other rational beings.
>
> (Wood 1990: 83)

But such a theory does not explain *why* values such as individual freedom and autonomy are values, *why* they should have an important place in a process of socialization. One way of reading Hegel's doctrine of recognition is to see him as attempting to remedy this defect in Fichte's argument – and doing so by returning to its roots in Rousseau's characteristically undeveloped insights.

Masters and Slaves

The centrepiece of Hegel's argument is the 'Self-Consciousness' section of the *Phenomenology of Spirit*. This develops themes first worked up in the Jena lectures and anticipates the examination of self-consciousness in the *Encyclopaedia* (EL §§424–37). Hegel refers to this cluster of arguments twice in the discussion of Abstract Right, at §§35R and 57R. In the first section of the *Phenomenology*, 'Consciousness', Hegel has demonstrated the failure of conscious-ness to articulate itself as knowledge which has the form of a subject's knowledge of an object which is distinct from the subject. The lesson is that consciousness had better turn in upon itself, seeking knowledge of itself (self-certainty) through an examination of self-consciousness.

According to Hegel, the first glimmerings of self-knowledge occur when a living creature identifies an object as 'other' in the course of desiring it. At this stage, 'self-consciousness is Desire' (PS ¶174 / SW 2: 146). The thought is that I first encounter myself as an object of self-knowledge when I distinguish myself from an object of desire. The sort of object of desire that Hegel has in mind are objects that I intend to consume, for an aspect of the self-knowledge that is gained invokes a contrast between the object which I see as a 'nothing' – the apple vanishes as I consume it – and myself as permanent and objective.

The sense of self that is achieved by the consuming subject is radically incomplete. It is achieved by a reflection back upon itself in the process of its consuming an other which it desires. I am not the apple. It is a nothing. But then it is not an other, either, so it cannot afford me a sense of myself as distinct from it since it has vanished as it has been eaten. It follows that the self which has been identified in the act of consumption is as transitory as the object consumed, itself consumed in the consummation of its desire. It re-emerges as desire re-engages with the world it seeks to consume but is as transient as the objects which feed its sense of self. Just as the object cannot be both objective other and an ingredient of the consuming self, so the self cannot be both enduring and sustained by its reflection of a transient other. We shall think harder about this argument later, but for the moment let us accept Hegel's conclusion: the element of self-consciousness that is attained through action in pursuit of desire is as flimsy and insecure as the objects that periodically sustain it. My sense of self had better be more permanent than the objects I eat. Severally, they are reduced to nothing. Serially, they are a sequence of nonentities. That cannot be *me* – surely?

Indeed it can't. To achieve a truer conception of myself I need to be confronted with an other which is not consumed just as soon as its reality affords me a glimpse of who I am. I need to actively confront, not yet another object of my consuming activities, but another self-consciousness. I need to to recognize myself in an other which is independent but enduring, despite my intentions – which apples are not. I need to experience others like me, others whose crucial likeness to me enables me to recognize myself (as one of a type of thing – my essence) through the particular quality of my interactions with things of that type. I need to see myself as *one of* a community of independent spirits, so that I can recognize them and they can recognize me in terms of a concept that we each apply to each other, seeing ourselves as ' "I" that is "We" and "We" that is "I" ' (PS ¶177 / SW 2: 147). In such a community individuals '*recognize* themselves as *mutually recognizing* one another' (PS ¶184 / SW 2: 150). This condition of mutual recognition proves hard to achieve.

The first attempt to achieve recognition is almost comically self-frustrating. On encountering another self-consciousness, the self presents itself 'as the pure negation of its objective mode . . . showing that it is not attached to any specific *existence* . . . not attached to life' (PS ¶187 / SW 2: 151). Each self seeks to display what Hegel believes to be a uniquely human characteristic – that it is not attached to life, to the natural processes that sustain it. A person can detach itself from its natural desires and inclinations to the point that it is able to put its own life at risk, and this complete detachment from natural existence is a display of freedom. He continues,

> It is only through staking one's life that freedom is won . . . the individual who has not risked his life may well be recognized as a *person*, but he has not attained to the truth of this recognition as an independent self-consciousness.

So each separate consciousness parades its independence, from nature as from the self that confronts it, by engaging in a life-and-death struggle. Each seeks the death of the other, not because the other is perceived as a threat – this is not the war of all against all that Hobbes and Rousseau envisage wherein security demands the launching of pre-emptive strikes – but because the presence of the other is required for that display of insouciance in the face of death which marks the beginning of freedom. It is worth noticing that the aspect of freedom which is foregrounded here is that same capacity of detachment from one's desires which Hegel introduces in §5 of the *Philosophy of Right*. It is another form of the pursuit of freedom through self-oblivion that the Brahmin pathologically seeks.

As a strategy for the achievement of self-knowledge it is doomed to frustration. Since the struggle must be one in which the protagonists put their lives at stake, self-knowledge is not achieved by the loser. He is dead – stuffed. (I confess: I can't read these passages without thoughts of Monty Python – the figure of the life-and-death struggle has an inescapable quality of comic grotesquerie.) But then self-knowledge is not achieved by the winner either, since he has killed the figure who was the occasion of his insouciant postures. Since there is no audience for the terrible display of freedom, no other against whom the reality of freedom can be enacted and proven, there is no true freedom either. Again, as with the objects of desire, only a glimpse of freedom is obtained in the process of deadly combat. Then, inexorably, one way or another, the vision is lost.

Somehow, with the lesson learned that life is as essential to the self as is pure self-consciousness, a cunning plan is hatched. Instead of one protagonist being dead and the other facing an emptiness with no other self to reflect his gaze, the dual imperatives of freedom and continued life are distributed between the two parties. The winner retains his sense of independence and the glory of his experience of freedom. The vanquished is 'the dependent consciousness whose essential nature is simply to live or to be for another. The former is the master, the other is the slave' (PS ¶189 / SW 2: 153).[3]

But this strategy too turns out to be self-defeating. The master seeks recognition of his standing as a free agent from another consciousness, but finds that the recognition he is afforded by the slave is as unsatisfactory as the recognition he gets from the corpse of a vanquished opponent. In holding fast to his life, believing that 'his essential nature is to live', the slave has slipped below the threshold of respectability, he has become less than a person. In which case, the quality of recognition he is able to grant the master is diminished. The master fails, too, in respect of another element of his strategy. With a slave to do his work for him, he no longer needs to be active in pursuit of the objects of his desires. These are served up to him on a plate by the hard-working slave. He still *has* desires and still seeks satisfaction, but these no longer compel him to engage with the objective world which occasions them. He leaves the productive, physical work to the slave, himself concentrating on pure enjoyment. But this simply shifts the object of dependence. Whereas formerly it was the external world which sustained him, demanding the expenditure of his efforts, now his dependence is on the slave. Contrary to his aspirations, the master finds that he is neither recognized in a fashion sufficient for him to achieve true self-consciousness, nor has he achieved independence. The achievement of self-knowledge is compromised because recognition is expressed in false coinage. It is 'one-sided and unequal' (PS ¶191 / SW 2: 155).

We have rehearsed enough of the tale to have unearthed the moral that we have been seeking: that true recognition is mutual, requiring that both of the parties be of equal standing. (What does this tell us of those who seek recognition through the public display of their domination of a savage dog?) But still: never tell half a story. The master–slave dialectic concludes in seductive ironies and it would be a pity not to rehearse them. The failure of the master's project is now clear; the slave now emerges on to centre stage.

The bravery of the master in the struggle gave him a glimpse of transcendence as he cast off the burden of earthly desires and experienced 'our power (not one of nature) to regard as small those things of which we are wont to be solicitous (worldly goods, health and life)' (Kant 1952: III / AK5: 262).[4] But if the master's experience of the possibility of death was real but transient, the experience of the slave was harder and truer and left a deeper mark. He

> experienced this his own essential nature. For this consciousness has been fearful, not of this or that particular thing or just at odd moments, but its whole being has been seized with dread; for it has experienced the fear of death, the absolute master [*des absoluten Herrn*]. In that experience it has been quite unmanned, has trembled in every fibre of its being, and everything solid and stable has been shaken to its foundations.
>
> (PS ¶194 / SW 2: 156)

Hegel's thought is that fear for one's life is as authentic an experience of self-consciousness as is raw, physical courage. The hero experiences his continued life as a nothing, compared with the experience of transcendence in the face of death. This is Yeats on how 'An Irish Airman Foresees his Death':

> I balanced all, brought all to mind,
> The years to come seemed waste of breath,
> A waste of breath the years behind
> In balance with this life, this death.

Hegel's imaginative reconstruction of the experience of the coward (the slave) is equally moving in its evocation of humanity. And it is plausible in its suggestion that the ignominious fear of death is as authentic an experience of what freedom truly is as is the joyous putting at gratuitous risk of one's life, one's whole (physical) being. Further, we should not think of the slave in this dialectic as a happy sort of fellow, well fed and acquiescent. The superior power of the master exists for him as objectively as the sword hanging over his head. He is dragooned into service, but his service is the saving of him in more ways than one. 'Through his service he rids himself of his attachment to natural existence in every single detail; and he gets rid of it by working on it' (PS ¶194 / SW 2: 156).

How does this happen? Hegel tells us that the slave becomes absorbed in his labour for the master. He doesn't consume the natural world. He works on it. Think of him as the master chef who keeps his appetite in control as he directs his attention to the preparation of exquisite dishes for others to consume, who sees his care and skill in the product of his labour served up on a plate. The slave learns what he is because he sees what he does: 'Work . . . is desire held in check, fleetingness staved off; in other words, work forms and shapes the thing' (PS ¶195 / SW 2: 156). In other words, the slave experiences his freedom as he identifies the products of his labour as his own fashioning, notwithstanding the fact that the master has ordered their preparation. The slave 'acquires a mind of his own' (PS ¶196 / SW 2: 157).

Don't think this is a happy ending. The slave, after all, is still a slave in respect of the legal determination of his status. There are plenty of respects in which he isn't free, although he is not rotting in the fleshpots of desire and the chains of dependency in the manner of his master. Things will improve for both of them – but slowly, as they traverse the shapes of stoicism, scepticism, the unhappy consciousness and explore the realm of spirit. Read the *Phenomenology* (skipping bits) and the *Lectures on the Philosophy of History* for the denouement. Read the *Philosophy of Right* for an account of how Hegel believes mutual recognition is possible in social life.

Mutual Recognition

We should return to the beginnings of this story since we have told it uncritically. The theme, or the moral, is that true, un-self-deceived self-consciousness is only possible for agents who accord each other the respect due to equals. Self-knowledge and the freedom that issues from it is a social achievement, in a community of equals. One-sided recognition is a failure. There must be some terms, some concept, in respect of which we recognize each other, some language of mutual recognition. The minimal concept, the simplest of terms, is that of the person, the atomic individual, the claimer and respecter of rights.

How does the story we have told support or illuminate these insights? What kind of story is it? I don't want to delve into the interpretation of the *Phenomenology* with the seriousness that enterprise deserves. So let me assert a series of judgements about the different stages of the argument, the different shapes of experience it charts, and then let us come to some assessment of how well it vindicates the preliminary statements of Abstract Right in the *Philosophy of Right*.

The first, obvious question concerns Hegel's intentions in the 'Self-Consciousness' chapter. It is obvious that he is not engaged in the kind of conceptual anaysis with which most of us are familiar. And yet this should be surprising. After all, our philosophical reflections on the nature of self-consciousness have probably begun with the study of Descartes, and a swift study of Descartes should convince us that analytic philosophy, the close, careful study of how we apply concepts such as 'I', is not the unique province of academic philosophers in the twentieth century. A reading of Kant should alert us to the radical nature of Hegel's intervention, since Kant's study of the self outdoes Descartes in the closeness of its attention to the way we acquire and employ the concept of the self. And Fichte and Schelling advance the project of the investigation of the implications of the self-evident success of the ascription to the 'I' of the first-person mode of identification – 'I' = 'I'.

Hegel does not pursue this route in the chapter on 'Self-Consciousness' in the *Phenomenology* because he believes that he has already rejected it as a mode of achieving 'self-certainty'. The chapter on 'Sense-Certainty' has established that the self is neither available to immediate self-identification nor identical with any description that may be advanced to capture its essential nature. If we take the first route, we find that we cannot distinguish the self as we experience it from the self as it is experienced by others as they engage in the same task. If we take the second route, we identify the self in terms of properties which we believe the self possesses (if, in fact, it does possess them – which it may not) but their attribution is in any event entirely contingent, in which case *I* could be *me* without having any of those properties at all. Hegel's conclusion, massively debatable, is that the investigation of the nature of the self as a theoretical exercise, in advance of our understanding of how the self *interacts* with 'the other' (the world of objects and other consciousnesses), is doomed to failure.

Suppose he is right. It is now plausible to see the first step in the acquisition of self-consciousness as attained when the self distinguishes itself from the objects of desire. Perhaps it is attained at the mother's breast or when the baby is confronted with or denied the feeding bottle. We can leave the task of description to developmental psychologists. But it is evident that what is being described is not the nature of self-consciousness but the process of its dawning. These facts, if true, probably yield a necessary condition on the acquisition of self-consciousness: that the self-conscious individual be able to distinguish itself from others – other things and other people.

Hegel is right to conclude that self-consciousness cannot be as transitory and episodic as it would be were its whole content to be given by its experience of activity in the pursuit of desire. So we should expect him to move on to supplement this primitive phenomenology. He does so in a way that is both natural and peculiar. It is natural in that he proposes to expand his account of self-consciousness by tracing the impact of the encounters of the self with other selves. It is through one's interactions with other self-consciousnesses that full or complete self-consciousness is achieved. It is peculiar in that the mode of interaction he describes in the *Phenomenology* is both limited and antique. It is the experience of the life-and-death struggle. It is limited in that very few properly self-conscious agents can have experienced such a struggle.

Hegel may well be right about the unique sense of freedom attained by one who voluntarily puts his life at risk; this is the experience of the finest mountaineers, the cave diver and the bull-fighter, as well as the daring airman, and the experience may be narcotic for some. And, since the risk is real, it may be fatal too. But Hegel cannot pretend that such an experience operates as a necessary condition for the development of self-consciousness – and indeed, he doesn't. This emblematic figure is presented as typical of a mythical prehistory, recalling the struggle of Hector and Achilles outside the walls of Troy. It is not even echoed in the practice of duelling, which Hegel describes as a pathetic relic of feudalism (EL §432). The duellist seeks a kind of honour, or its restoration, just as Hobbes's fighter seeks self-preservation. Hegel's protagonist, in contrast to both of these figures, seeks freedom and an enhanced self-consciousness.[5] At this point, Hegel's emphasis has shifted from an exploration of the experiential and social conditions necessary for a person's acquisition of self-consciousness to a speculative aetiology of mankind's acquisition of the concept of the self. And the story continues with the master–slave dialectic, which tracks the mindset of the Greek and Roman worlds, and proceeds through the examination of stoicism and scepticism to the 'unhappy consciousness', the self-experience of medieval Christianity.

The trail is evidently historical, although the content of the argument as well as the resonances it has evoked establish that there is more going on than a simple conjectural history of mankind's developing self-consciousness. Some have argued, plausibly, that the structures of self and other which are rehearsed in the story have a universal applicability to the logic of our understanding of the phenomena of self-consciousness (Kelly 1966: 189–217). Others have identified the pathology of the underlying structures of the dialectic in phenomena as diverse as the ownership of pets, patriarchal domestic structures, sado-masochistic (as well as standard varieties of) sexual behaviour, class structures in the capitalist economy, and colonialism, with more or less plausibility and without, of course, attributing these insights to Hegel. This is one of the greatest and most fertile passages of Western philosophy, which is to say (and in part, it is because) its lessons are not entirely clear.

What does the argument (or story, or allegory, or diagnosis) tell us about personhood? This is a hard, hard question, but it must be attempted. First, it tells us that the concept of a person is a social concept in this sense: the sense of oneself as a free and independent individual can be attained only by persons who live in communities which permit mutual recognition between equals. Societies which permit individuals to wantonly aggress against or dominate other individuals, or which exhibit social structures characterized by behaviour of these sorts, are likely to be psychologically crippled and practically unstable. (This last thought may be wishful thinking. As Dent points out, social structures may effectively stabilize pathological personal traits. Nature's masters, i.e. bullies, may succeed in gaining each other's respect – and the respect of their dreadful peers may be all the respect they seek (Dent 1992: 161).)

Second, personhood, a status concept, if not in Hegel's sense a moral one, is constituted by the fact of reciprocal recognition. The aspect of personality which is recognized is persons' jural standing or capacity for right (*Rechtsfähigkeit*, §36), their status as makers of rights claims, and, reciprocally, their duty to respect the claims of right which others legitimately make against them.

Does the account so far given, of personhood, recognition and rights, amount to a justification or vindication of the judgement that we are all of us persons, bearing rights and respectful of the rights of others? It tells us that we cannot be persons if we do not recognize others as persons, since *person* is not a concept that folk can apply to themselves if they do not respect the claims of others. To be a person requires that one be recognized as such, and recognition must be mutual; it cannot be one-sided, it cannot be afforded to persons by non-persons, as it cannot be afforded to masters by slaves. But these are conditions imposed on those who claim to be persons. They establish who cannot be regarded as persons, namely, those who do not respect the claims of others; but they do not tell us that we *are* persons, and that we ought to make such claims.

But nothing could serve as a foundation for such claims. The fact of our being persons is wholly constituted by the fact of our claiming to be persons, and our concomitant recognition of the claims of others. Hegel's 'argument' here amounts to nothing more than a judgement that people do in fact make such claims nowadays, having learned in the course of history that they *can* make them, and *can* get them recognized, because all people make similar claims, having learned that recognizing the claims of others is a necessary condition of their being recognized in turn.

This is the basis of what I dub the 'No-Theory Theory of Rights', and as theories go, it is not a bad one. Historically, and the philosophical battles are still being fought, those who disavow utilitarian theories of rights have felt compelled to search for some alternative grounding to the ascription of rights, and Kantian theses concerning the value of autonomy have looked the likeliest source for deriving them.[6] But these arguments are notoriously difficult to handle as soon as they purport to derive the content of specific rights. By contrast, the No-Theory Theory has no such ambition.

Arthur Danto tells the story of how he found himself a member of a committee charged with drawing up disciplinary procedures which his university could employ in the aftermath of student rebellion in 1968, when one member of the committee asked the others if they were certain that they had the right to do what was asked of them. As they were just starting to worry about this question,

> a man from the law-school said, with the tried patience of someone required to explain what should be as plain as day, and in a tone of voice I can still hear: 'This is the way it is with rights. You want' em, so you say you got 'em, and if nobody says you don't then you do.' In the end he was right . . . there are no rights save in the framework of declaration and recognition.
>
> (Danto 1984: 30)

Basically, this is Hegel's position. We have all learned to think of ourselves as discrete persons, free and independent as Rousseau believed we once were: which is to say, we have all learned to claim rights and to recognize others as they in turn make claims of right against us. This is just a fact about the modern ethical world. Things were not always so, as the struggles of heroes and the institution of slavery attest. But nowadays self-conscious agents express one element of their freedom by insisting that they are persons and finding that this claim meets the recognition of their fellows.

Concluding remarks

The next question is 'What rights do modern persons claim?' and this will be the topic of the next chapter. But before we attend to it, I want to make two points, one concerning the substance of the argument, and the other concerning the interpretation of the *Philosophy of Right*.

First, I want to defend Hegel's concept of the person as the minimal element of one's moral status in a way he does not attempt, although to be generous (or patronizing) one might argue that his account implies the thoughts that follow. I want to insist, on the basis of phenomenological truisms (aka anecdotal evidence of a mainly first-person sort) that a metaphysical difference between persons and non-persons is crucial to our ethical perceptions and moral experience.

I remember working in a pub years ago, when a customer shouted at the boss, 'You there. Geeza pint. You. C'mon. Geeza pint.' (Cognoscenti will recognize the vernacular: *Parliamo Glasgow*.) The boss was miffed. 'You. What do you think I am? A f****** vending machine? Learn some manners if you want a drink in this bar', and moved on to serve another customer. (He could afford to teach his customer a lesson. The nearest alternative bar was three miles away.)

Courtesy, I suggest, is the recognition of personhood. It marks the distinction we want to draw. It embodies the recognition of another as having a distinctive moral standing. You are due it (as my father used to say – another piece of anecdotal evidence) even in a pawn-shop. Courtesy doesn't denote friendliness or solidarity or even respect in the customary sense in which respect has to be earned. It denotes respect in the philosophical sense as a proper recognition of moral boundaries, because it stops us short as we execute our projects in the vicinity of other persons. Courtesy demands that we formally recognize the presence of the other as the presence of a person – so you say 'Good afternoon' when you meet a stranger in the mountains. You needn't, of course, acknowledge the sheep.

This exercise in popular phenomenological ethics can be extended. 'Give me some space' demands the oppressed teenager, and we should be able to cash out the metaphor with literal examples of the wilful boundary crosser. I had a colleague who shall be nameless (but I hope some readers can pin a name on him) who thought the best way to clinch an argument (philosophical, political, religious, departmental . . . any variety) was to place his nose about two inches in front of other folks' faces and claim victory when they didn't sock him. This is discourtesy (and it may amount to aggression, depending on the vulnerability of the target) because it doesn't respect the personhood of the sufferer of these overclose attentions. It crosses boundaries which are not spatial and are barely moral, boundaries that delineate the person, hence boundaries which ought to command respect.

No doubt there are other ways of filling out the concept of a person, its implications as the most minimal of status concepts and its constitution in practices of recognition, but having amplified Hegel's insight, we should now note its application in the *Philosophy of Right*. Most commentators remark on the way Hegel's thoughts concerning the necessity of mutuality or reciprocity for recognition to be genuine are worked out in Abstract Right as he explores the concept of the person. In this context, mutual recognition is particularly apt since the concept of the person has minimal substantial content and is entirely constituted by practices of recognition. To be a person just is to be recognized as an ethically significant other, bounded and discrete. It would be a mistake, though, to conclude that the dialectic of recognition does no work elsewhere in the argument of the *Philosophy of Right*.[7]

We shall explore the details later, but it is worth putting down a marker that we should expect to encounter the constraints on patterns of social life that the requirement that proper recognition be mutual imposes throughout Hegel's discussion of social norms. Mutual recognition of each other as free and independent beings demanded, for Rousseau, a homogeneous society, a republic of citizens of severely equal standing, and a consequent exclusion of partial associations and delegated hierarchies that may blinker this clear moral vision or corrupt the ethos of republican citizenship. Hegel, by contrast, wishes to embrace the glorious variety of modern society, to celebrate the fact of difference as we encounter it in domestic life, in the workings of the economy, and as recognized in the operation of a complex political constitution. This gives him a problem.

Mutual recognition is easier to achieve the thinner the ethical-cum-ontological basis for its ascription. It demands little of any of us when we insist, and costs little for any of us to concede, that we are all persons. In a direct Rousseauian democracy, we are all citizens and all subjects. But in Hegel's model of family life, husband and wife, parents and children, have different roles and different statuses. How is mutual recognition possible between the different parties? Arguably, in Civil Society, Hegel's vertical division of classes (agricultural, business and civil service) ignores horizontal differences (between, say, landowner and farm labourer, or businessman and worker) that might prevent mutual recognition. In the state, the differences of political standing, as measured by the opportunities for effective political participation, are radical. How can such differences fail to compromise the ideal of mutual recognition?

These are lovely critical questions. They open up a line of interpretation that permits Hegel to give answers, and they reveal the inadequacies of those answers. To anticipate both the interpretation and the criticism to follow: Hegel espouses a doctrine of separate but equal roles. Difference need not compromise ethical standing. I use the terminology of 'separate but equal' deliberately because we have heard it before, notoriously in defence of unjust and discriminatory practices in the United States prior to the Civil Rights legislation and the reforming Supreme Court decisions of the late 1950s and 1960s. I use the terms pejoratively because, at the end of the day, I judge that Hegel was not true to the demands for mutual recognition which were made so strikingly and so eloquently in his earlier work. But this is to prejudge the issues. We still have to see what mutual recognition entails in Abstract Right.

Chapter 5

Abstract Right 2. Property and Contract: §§44–81

Property and Political Philosophy

Hegel makes a distinctive and valuable contribution to philosophical thinking about private property. For good reasons, given the history of competing property claims as sources of conflict, strife and bloodshed, and given the philosophical impulse to articulate our sense of justice into a specification of the conditions under which holdings of property are just or fair, philosophers have concentrated on the task of justifying systems of property distribution. They have distinguished practices of common or public property holding from institutions of private property and presented arguments for and against the alternatives. The focus here has been on the justification (or otherwise) of property systems.

A different, but obviously related, clutch of philosophical problems concerns our understanding of the property relation in the particular case of private property. What exactly is the relation between persons and the property they claim to own? In part, the easy part perhaps, this is a matter of analysis. For the

purposes of our discussion we can suppose the core concept is that of a person's transferable right to the exclusive use of an object.[1] I advance this as the core concept, knowing full well that every term in this statement is subject to clarification, qualification and modification in the course of articulating any recognizable application of the concept in terms of the provisions of a legal system. For some, the analysis of the concept in terms of a set of rules governing acquisition, use and exchange constitutes the whole exercise of explaining the property relation. But for others the concept of private property has a metaphysical dimension which requires philosophical exploration.

A tree is a tree is a tree one might think, whatever that is. But what is the difference between a tree that is owned as private property and a tree that is not? How is the tree that is owned related to the owner, so that one may judge that the owner, but not the tree, is harmed if someone else cuts it down or harvests its fruit? What do we recognize in the tree when we respect it as the property of another, leaving alone the apple that dangles temptingly from the branch that reaches over our path? It may be that these questions are illusory once the issue of analysis of the concept is settled. They may turn out to be pseudo-questions, as they used to say. But it may also turn out that the concept of property invokes a distinctive view of persons and the property to which they lay claim which itself constrains the process of analysis and has severe implications for the first philosophical enterprise – that of justification.

Thus, to anticipate a detail of the argument to follow, Hegel argues that property is a relation of will between the owner and the possession. Since, as we have seen, the person is a bounded, discrete individual, the will which is embodied in property is exclusive. It thus follows that all property must be in some sense private, that the concept of common property is unintelligible or incoherent. Hence it follows that systems of common property, as advocated for example by Plato in the *Republic* for the Guardian class, and as recommended by socialists, are unjustified. It is fair to say that, although Kant recognized the perplexing metaphysical quality of the property relation, it was Hegel who brought these questions to the fore.[2]

Before we go on to discuss the detail of Hegel's theory, it is worth canvassing briefly the major modern theories of property which formed the background to his discussion, if only so that we can begin to measure the debts and differences in Hegel's contribution. One thread can be traced through Hobbes, Rousseau and Kant, and holds that prior to, or independently of, the institution of political authority there is no private property. In Hobbes's state of nature, 'there is no Propriety, no Dominion, no *Mine* and *Thine* distinct' (Hobbes 1985: ch. 13, 188). Persons contract with each other to establish (or are to be understood, being rational, as disposed to accept) a sovereign power which is assigned 'the whole power of prescribing the Rules, whereby every man may know what Goods he may enjoy . . . Rules of Propriety (or *Meum* and *Tuum*)' (Hobbes 1985: ch. 18, 234). On this account, the rules of private property are justified as the imposition of a sovereign power which citizens (hypothetically, on my eccentric reading of Hobbes) have agreed to authorize. This contractualist justification of private property (supposing, as Hobbes does, that it is a system of *private* property (of *Meum* and *Tuum*) that the sovereign will prescribe) may be supplemented by a proto-utilitarian argument to the effect that citizens would only accept the sovereign's judgement on who owns what as decisive if they were convinced that his decisions were to the advantage of everyone.[3]

Rousseau's views on private property are complex and hard to disentangle since in the *Discourse on the Origins of Inequality* he is clear that it was the direst of human inventions.

> The first man who, having enclosed a piece of ground, bethought himself of saying 'This is mine', and found people simple enough to believe him, was the real founder of civil society. From how many crimes, wars, and murders, from how many horrors and misfortunes might not any one have saved mankind, by pulling up the stakes, or filling up the ditch, and crying to his fellows: 'Beware of . . . this impostor . . . the fruits of the earth belong to us all and the earth to nobody.'

> (Rousseau 1973: 76)

In *The Social Contract*, by contrast, he employs exactly the same argument as Hobbes. We must suppose that persons who believe their lives and possessions to be at risk would contract with each other to establish a sovereign who will procure security and stability of life and property. The rules of secure and stable possession are then devised and enacted by the sovereign as laws expressing the general will (in a direct democracy which respects freedom and equality). Again the system of private property is dictated in its particulars by the sovereign and justified in terms of a hypothetical contract between persons who agree on fundamental values.

In the social contract tradition (Hobbes, Locke, Rousseau) there is an endemic ambiguity in the contract argument between actual and hypothetical contract arguments. Or so one would judge from the commentaries.[4] Kant, by contrast, distinguishes sharply between the actual and hypothetical contract arguments and applies the hypothetical contract mode of argument – 'rational agents would agree . . .' – to vindicate private property. Kant's use of hypothetical contract arguments is both *direct* in that it applies the categorical imperative to yield the wrongness of violating another's possession (MM: §2, 52–3 / Ak. 6: 246–7) and *indirect* in that it establishes the legitimacy of the sovereign power which fixes the rules concerning legitimate possession, the rules of private property (MM: §47, 80–1 / Ak. 6: 315–16).

To summarize: we have before us examples of actual and hypothetical contract arguments. These (Locke excepting) generally legitimize private property indirectly as the prescription of a legitimate sovereign which legislates to give effect to the values of its citizens. The hypothetical contract argument, as in Hobbes, may be reducible to arguments resting on an account of the interests of all citizens, or of each citizen severally, which have a distinct utilitarian ring.

In the writings of Hobbes and Rousseau, property is a minor theme. They think of the importance of life before they consider what 'commodious living' involves. And Rousseau elevates the values of liberty and equality above that of private property. Gross inequalities of property holdings threaten democratic equality (as we newspaper readers know well – do you have the political clout of a proprietor?) and should therefore be restrained (Rousseau 1973: 178–81).

There are other arguments in the field, notably those of John Locke.[5] Locke has other arguments up his sleeve. I shall mention them successively. In the first place, persons own their bodies. And so persons own the powers of their bodies, which is to say their labour power. So, when they mix their labour power with the unowned portion of the world they work upon, tilling a field or carving a block of marble, they mix their labour with the world. And mixing it, own it. This is a hard argument to sustain. Is the mixing literal or metaphorical? If literal, it faces the challenge of Nozick's impertinent question 'why isn't mixing what I own with what I don't own a way of losing what I own rather than a way of gaining what I don't?' (Nozick 1974: 174–5).

If, by contrast, the mixing is metaphorical, then the argument reads as a typical argument from desert. The acquisition of private property is fair reward for my investment of effort as I labour. A final strand of Locke's argument is broadly utilitarian. Had a system of private property not been established, mankind would have starved. Private property, we would say nowadays, is both a more productive and more sustainable method of using nature and garnering her fruits than a condition of no-ownership or of common ownership.

What is striking about Hegel's contribution is that he does not seek to use any of these familiar arguments (broadly contractarian, utilitarian or desert-based) in his discussion of private property. His major concern is to illuminate the ways in which a system of private property promotes freedom.

Private Property and Freedom

Hegel's discussion in Abstract Right has the following structure: first, in §§41–53 he outlines his basic theory of private property. Since 'I, as a free will, am an object [*gegenständlich*] to myself in what I possess and only become an actual will by this means [this] constitutes the genuine and rightful element in possession, the determination of *property*' (§45). Free will becomes objective in private property. This is a highly abstract characterization of the property relation, so we shall elaborate it carefully. Hegel helps us to do so in the three subsections to follow. He believes that this basic insight can be supported (i.e. more fully articulated) if we examine three fundamental modalities of the property relation. So, second, he explores our intuitions concerning the practices of taking possession of objects which are unowned. In fact, this subsection, 'A. Taking Possession [*Besitznahme*]', §§54–8, could be just as well entitled 'Displaying Possession', as we shall see when we investigate its content. Third, subsection B, §§59–64, examines our ideas and practices concerning the 'Use of the Thing', and fourth, subsection C, 'The Alienation of Property', §§65–70, examines the possibility of withdrawing the will from the objects in which it is embodied as property. We shall follow the sequence of Hegel's discussion, but the underlying strategy will be to explain how the basic theory is substantiated by an interpretation of the practices which constitute private property. In other words, the *argument* of Hegel's treatment of private property involves the statement of an insight concerning the relation of persons, their wills and the world to which they lay claim, and the defence of that insight through an explanation of the institution of private property as we encounter it. Hegel will explain to us *why* we accept the institution of private property. It never occurs to him, as it occurred to others (e.g. Proudhon and Marx, to name a couple of sceptical successors) that this institution may be judged unacceptable.

In Chapter 3 we examined the distinctive self-consciousness of a person – the sense that individuals have acquired that they are discrete entities, bounded atoms, separate and different from each other. Hegel argues that this capacity for identifying the self in its difference is radically incomplete. It is a 'wholly abstract determination' (§41); the person can say of himself, 'I am me and not you', but nothing more. The distinctiveness of the personal self is thus far a condition of 'mere subjectivity' (§41A) which must be superseded. It needs 'an external *sphere of freedom* in order to have being as Idea' (§41).

Here we encounter one of Hegel's distinctive theses: Spirit (or *Geist*) must be embodied.[6] In the context of Abstract Right, this amounts to a requirement that the sense that I have of myself as a distinct person must be publicly recognizable by others – self-consciousness, quite generally we have seen, requires social structures that permit mutual recognition. This requirement is satisfied if my personality is embodied in some portion of the external world. The fact of my difference as a person is established when personhood is displayed in a 'sphere distinct from the will' (§41), a sphere which attests my distinctiveness through its own evident difference, the sphere of 'the external in general', of things which are 'unfree, impersonal, and without rights' (§42). Hence, 'a person has the right to place his will in any thing [*Sache*]. [This is] the absolute *right of appropriation* which human beings have over all things' (§44).

This looks deeply implausible, not to say equivocal. The sense that I have that I am different needs to be registered by the publicly recognizable location of my difference in the radically different, non-human, world of external objects which I appropriate as my property. I become *actually* different by appropriating what *is* different. I establish my essential exclusivity by making claim to the exclusive use of the things of this world as my private property. I demonstrate my boundedness and atomicity through the demarcated portion of the external world which I control.

These ideas prompt an obvious question: Why do I need to embody my personhood in the external world for my discreteness to become actual, to be apparent to myself as well as others? Why, in particular, is it not sufficient that I am embodied in my own physical body, which has a distinctive physical location in time and space so long as I am alive? To my knowledge, Hegel does not address these questions directly, though as we shall see, he has something to say about my taking possession of my body as an item in the world, and he does regard this as a necessary dimension of my freedom. So we shall have to answer the question for him in a way that would be a plausible reconstruction of his views. The answer must be that the fact of my physical embodiment is an insufficient or incomplete display of my *freedom* as a person. This is a good answer to be going on with, because it requires us to elaborate just how the freedom of persons is promoted by their making claims to private property, and this is the direction that Hegel's argument takes. As so often in Hegel's writings, we should take the initial, puzzling claims of §§41–4 as programmatic. They scream out for elaboration, but then elaboration is given in what follows.

The crucial claim is made in §45, which I shall now quote in full:

To have even external power over something constitutes *possession*, just as the particular circumstance that I make something my own out of natural need, drive, and arbitrary will is the particular interest of possession. But the circumstance that I, as a free will, am an object [*gegenständlich*] to myself in what I possess and only become an actual will by this means constitutes the genuine and rightful element in possession, the determination of *property*.

113

Hegel accepts that for the most part persons acquire something because they want it or need to use it. This explains their possession of goods, but it cannot explain why their possession is rightful. It cannot justify a specific claim of right for a very simple reason: ownership precedes legitimate use. In this statement he explicitly disavows the attempt to justify private property – either the core elements of a system of private property or, derivatively, a particular person's claim to a specific item of property – in terms of the usefulness of bits and pieces of the world in the service of natural human purposes. He makes this point again later when he insists that it is only superficial thought (*Vorstellung*) that regards use as the '*real* aspect and actuality of property' (§59). My use of an object is legitimate only if I own it or if its owner permits me the use of it. Legitimate use presupposes legitimate ownership or a valid contract. The legitimacy of a claim to property cannot be derived from the usefulness of an object to a claimant. On the contrary, one's making good use of an object is legitimate only if one can claim a property right to it. We must suppose that a claimant has the (property) right to use an object before we can judge that use to be legitimate.

This argument is evidently directed at most of the alternative justifications of property that I canvassed at the start of this chapter. The contract accounts focus on the disutility of strife and the mutual advantage secured by the regulation of property claims. Locke mentions (and Hume emphasizes) the utility of a private property settlement. Hegel insists that all such considerations are secondary:

> the will of the owner, in accordance with which a thing is his, is the primary substantial basis of property, and the further determination of use is merely the [outward] appearance and particular mode of this universal basis to which it is subordinate.
>
> (§59)

Private property, I suggested earlier, is the transferable right of exclusive use of the things of this world. We can now see that for Hegel exclusivity comes first, usefulness comes next, and transferability (alienability and thereby contract) follows in order of importance. Why *exactly* is this so? If we can answer this question, we shall have unearthed the distinctive connection between will, property and freedom that makes systems of private property fully comprehensible elements of our moral world. And, of course, from a Hegelian perspective, this amounts to a justification of them.

To be free is to be self-determining, to make something of oneself, to be able to step back and detach the self from its desires and inspect the self as its actions in pursuit of its desires reveal it to be. Then, and only then, can the agent judge whether she is as she ought to be, whether she acts as she judges she ought to act. And, in the light of such judgements, the agent can endorse her dispositions or seek to alter them. In Abstract Right, Hegel privileges the actions of the property-owner as revelatory of her status as a person. The actions which conspicuously permit an external self-appraisal are those of taking possession, private use and alienation of property. All such actions are in pursuit of the agent's desires and inclinations. I want this piece of ground because I judge that I can cultivate it to yield a harvest that will feed my family through the winter. I wish to use it to grow vegetables that I can't be sure of finding in the market. I plan to sell or barter some of my surplus in order to acquire other goods that I cannot produce for myself. Hegel claims that I acquire, use and alienate goods in the service of my desires, yet insists that the utility of these goods, whilst it may explain my actions, does not justify the system of private property which facilitates these activities.

So we can now see what is truly important in my dealings with those bits and pieces of the world that are my property. Since I can reflect upon the self thus exposed in its transactions with the things of this world, things external to me, so, too, can others:

> My *inner* idea [*Vorstellung*] and will that something should be *mine* is not enough to constitute property, which is the *existence* [*Dasein*: Knox, 'embodiment'] of personality; on the contrary, this requires that I should *take possession* of it. The *existence* which my willing thereby attains includes its ability to be recognized by others.
>
> (§51)[7]

The crucial connection between ownership of property and freedom is revealed as the possibility which the location of will in property affords of the agent being able to identify herself in that portion of the physical world which she has appropriated for use in the satisfaction of her desires. Private property enables us to take an external measure of our desiring selves, and because the measure is external, it affords others, too, the opportunity of identifying the workings of our will in the things that we own. Freedom requires, as we saw in Chapter 2, that the self be able to detach itself from its desires in order to appraise and order them, in order to determine itself. This detachment is explicit for the first time when the self is recognized (by itself and others) in the publicly accessible medium of private property. Now that I (and others) can see what I am, I can either endorse the pattern of desires thus revealed or alter them. I can use the property or alienate it. Whatever transactions I engage in with respect to my property will attest my freedom.

It is important that we distinguish this argument from another which is very close to it.[8] Everyone knows that Hegel believes private property to be justified because of its contribution to personal freedom. And we can easily reconstruct an argument to this effect: my property comprises the resources I have at hand to employ as means to whatever ends I select. If I had a bit more money, for example, I would be freer than I am now because there would be more opportunities available to me when I decide what to do. I could choose to visit Timbuctoo without restraint of finance if that is where I want to spend my holidays. I would no longer be restricted to the choice of Blackpool or Morecambe. Property rights make it possible to *plan* for the future in the knowledge that such resources as are necessary for the plan to be brought to fruition are likely to be available. In similar vein, we can tell a story about how those who lack private property are unfree, driven from pillar to post as they attempt to satisfy basic needs. This line of argument is strong and familiar. Hegel's later discussion of the system of needs (§§189–98) and the evils of poverty (§§241–6) trades on it. Yet it is important to see that this is not the argument Hegel relies on when he is explaining the rationale of the private property system in Abstract Right. He does not argue that we *seek* private property in order to be free, as the means to our freedom. We acquire private property because we want what we can find a use for in the satisfaction of our desires.

His claim is not (the plausible one) that property enhances freedom as it broadens our opportunities. It is the different claim that property is necessary for the self-consciousness and thereby mutual recognition that is integral to freedom. Here the crucial point concerns the achievement of objectivity in respect of the will of the private property owner. Property enables us to accomplish what Robert Burns despairs of – that we might see ourselves in the only way that can give us a true sighting, that we see ourselves as others see us. To repeat: 'I, as free will, am an object to myself in what I possess' (§45); 'my will, as personal and hence as the will of an individual, becomes objective in property' (§46); 'The existence which my willing thereby attains includes its ability to be recognized by others' (§51).

It is through our claiming rights to private property that we identify ourselves as having the status of being distinctive as persons, since our property portrays our distinctiveness and the exclusiveness of our right to it commands the respect of others. As we claim rights of exclusive use against others, we display to others, as we encounter in ourselves, a history of activity in pursuit of desire (and in prudent persons this history may include our making provision for putting into effect choices we may make in the future).

To summarize: the freedom which private property promotes is the freedom which requires us not merely to think of ourselves as different and discrete, but to identify that particularity in a public medium (goods held as property) which permits our recognizability by others as the locus of unique claims. Personhood is integral to the modern self, but to be true it needs to be objective. It becomes objective when it is embodied in claims to private property that command the recognition of others. Private property becomes a necessary element of freedom as it permits such appraisals of the self as are required for self-determination. As we acquire, use and alienate property, we work on the self in a manner that demonstrates our freedom to ourselves and to others.

Problems and Implications

This is an intricate account of private property which requires very close examination.

Anthropocentrism and environmentalism

First we should notice, parenthetically, an important presupposition of Hegel's theory. Hegel presents the natural world as a moral vacuum (*Rechtloses*). Taken as a whole, or considered in respect of its animal, vegetable, or mineral constituents, it has no moral standing, and certainly no rights that may be cited in its defence against uncontrolled human use. 'A person has the right to place his will in any thing [*Sache*] . . . – the absolute right to appropriation which human beings have over all things [*Sachen*]' (§44).

At the time Hegel was writing, this idea was a commonplace in the West. The earth is mankind's dominion, to treat as it sees fit. Nowadays such opinions have become controversial. Many ascribe a moral status to animals; some even accord them rights. Some believe a moral wrong is effected when old trees are felled gratuitously; many believe that the destruction of the rainforests is an evil quite independently of the imprudence of such operations. And here is an excerpt from a letter by Jim Crumley of the Scottish Wild Land Group to the *Scotsman* (3 May 1986) concerning the extension of skiing facilities on Cairngorm:

> Where the landscape is recognized as being of outstanding quality – as the Cairngorm massif is throughout Europe – there should be a legally enforceable 25-year moratorium between a public enquiry like the Lurcher's one and any subsequent planning application for the same area. That way the needs of the landscape can be shown due regard and the opportunity will be created to confer long-term stability on a priceless and unique piece of wild land. *Landscape, too, has rights, for its own sake.*
> (my italics)[9]

Such environmentalist views are morally respectable, if philosophically puzzling and controversial. Philosophical journals have been created in order to provide a forum for the specialized discussion of them. Nowadays Hegel would have to *defend* the supremacy of the human will in relation to all the things of this earth in a way which he does not attempt. At the very least, he would have to respond to explicit rejections of his anthropocentric assumption.

We should note, too, a further implication of the fact that views which were commonplace and practices which were unquestioned in Hegel's time have now become morally questionable, controversial if not shown to be downright mistaken. Hegel believed that the unearthing of error and folly was the story of human history, but, as we saw in Chapter 3, he believed that the history of human moral education was just about complete. Environmental ethics of the kind that do not grant an unimpugnable right to the implementation of human purposes in the natural world represent the kind of deep moral sea change that the end-of-history thesis deems impossible.

Fortunately, all of these perplexing moral questions can be bracketed since they cannot be resolved through the establishment of moral principles which rule out *altogether* mankind's destructive, exploitative use of the materials of the earth. In some measure and in some ways, the earth must be available as a resource for food, clothing and shelter. And if, as Hegel thinks, it must also be available as the material condition of freedom, the most such animal rights or environmentalist arguments could achieve is a set of principled constraints on *untrammelled* exploitation.

Property and personality

Second, we should consider just what it is that we recognize when the will of the owner takes an objective existence in her property. In the first place, and minimally, we recognize the normative status of the owner as a person bearing rights. As Hegel notes later (§96) the precise significance of crime is that it is an injury to the will of the victim. If you kick in the headlights of my car, you don't harm *it*, you injure *me*. Private property enhances my freedom since it permits persons to achieve mutual recognition of each other's status as discrete moral beings. Recognition is afforded when respect is granted to the authority of the will of other persons concerning the property at their disposal. But further, the possession of goods as property always has a '*particular* aspect' (§49). My holdings tell a particular story concerning 'subjective ends, needs, arbitrariness, talents, external circumstances etc.' (§49, see also §45). The fact that some such story can be told, and the fact that it will be a public manifestation of my particularity, do not themselves attest my freedom (or do not attest it at this stage of the argument: a philosophy of action of the kind that is explicit in §§115–27 is necessary before such conclusions can be drawn). But this story will be visible to me (and to others) as *my* story. The pattern of natural needs, drives and arbitrary choices which my property witnesses is essential raw material for the achievement of freedom. So it is an important question whether or not property is readable in this way as a disclosure of personality, and it is an equally important question whether personal freedom is possible without private property.

I don't see the first question as a philosophical question. We either do see property as a display of a person's character or we do not – and as a matter of fact, I think the former claim is true. We are not simply looking for something to read when we scrutinize another's bookshelves. We are finding out what interests them. We may be conducting a detached aesthetic appraisal when we enter someone's living room and look around, as a connoisseur might examine a picture in a gallery, but more likely we are investigating their taste. Possessions reveal preferences, though the revelation may be partial or misleading given the element of sheer contingency in the accumulation of property. But advertisers are not wrong when first they sell us an image of the type of character we wish to be, then go on to tell us what items of property will promote that image. I shall take it as a fact that self-understanding is enhanced by a clear-sighted view of our possessions. And self-understanding is integral to personal freedom.

But what of the person who has no private property? Can the naked guru wandering the countryside and fortunately in receipt of gifts regard himself as a person if there is no objective testament to his freedom? Isn't this way of life chosen, after all? And might it not be chosen by one who regards private property not as necessary for freedom, but as a burden? Since the answer to both of these questions must surely be 'Yes', it behoves us to seek the particular form of the guru's freedom elsewhere. We can perhaps find it when we understand the philosophical nature of human action, and Hegel gives such an account in the first two subsections of the next chapter, 'Morality'. An alternative would be to regard such an aberrant display of personhood as pathological, perhaps because it is parasitical upon an economy of private property and the generosity, or piety, of proprietors. I leave the reader to construct such a diagnosis if they judge this line of argument to be promising.[10]

Persons and self-ownership

A third line of questioning concerns the relationship between the person and her body. Locke, as we saw, begins one of his arguments for private property ownership with the thought that we own our bodies and their powers and we extend these rights over the world that we work on. Shouldn't Hegel have argued in the same fashion, first linking personality with the thought that our bodies are our own as a condition of any free agency, next explaining how such agency is further promoted by the acquisition of goods? This looks a tidy and plausible argument and something like it has found favour with modern writers, not all of them supporters of capitalist free-market systems.[11]

Fortunately, we do not have to speculate over whether Hegel thought we own our own bodies. He discusses the issue in a way that makes it plain that we cannot be said to *fully* own ourselves, though something akin to this relation may be judged to hold. Hegel says that 'as a person, I at the same time possess *my life and body*, like other things [*Sachen*], only *insofar as I so will it*' (§47).

In order to understand this we have to identify the default position: what is it for one *not* to be in possession of one's life or body? Following the discussion of §57, it is clear that this is for one to be in the possession of someone else, to be a slave. But even this is not enough. If the slave rejects the master's dominion, claiming to be a person with rights that slavery violates, this insight, this claim to rudimentary moral status, undermines the fact of the master's possession, because it refutes the validity of his claim. A free entity cannot belong to anyone. The only circumstance in which one might truly be described as being in the possession of another is that of the slave who takes himself to be a slave, who is immersed in his condition, who has not yet worked out that he is a *person* (though to us moderns, who understand that personality is universal, he ought to be – he ought to assert himself as a person).

We are all of us natural creatures, but there are no natural slaves, *pace* Aristotle. Nowadays, we take possession of our bodies and spirit by absorbing the lesson that mankind learned as it developed in the course of history: the understanding that we are persons – by 'self-consciousness comprehending itself as free' (§57). It was once possible for slaves to think of themselves as slaves ('in the transitional phase between natural human existence and the truly ethical condition' (§57A) in the Greek and Roman worlds, and doubtless in other benighted states), but no longer.

The major difference between the possession that I take of myself when I claim to be a person and the possession that I take of objects when I make them my property is that in taking possession of my person, willing is enough to make it so[12] (though physical training may render more complete my possession of my body) (§52R). For other people, it is enough that they recognize my bodily difference, and a right to physical integrity must be presumed. 'Violence done to my body by others is violence done to me' (§48R). By contrast, in the case of taking possession of objects, social conventions are necessary, dictating which activities count as establishing possession. The detail of the specific rules cannot be elicited by philosophical reflection. In the modern state it will be a matter for legislation (§55R).

This talk of taking possession of oneself, of one's life and body, strongly suggests that Hegel is adducing a relation of self-ownership. But this is to ignore an important difference between self-possession and the ownership of goods. Although we take possession of ourselves as we realize that we are persons, we cannot alienate ourselves from another, nor can this status be taken away from us.[13] In contrast to virginity, which can be lost but not acquired, personhood can (and in the modern world *must*) be acquired, and once acquired cannot be lost.[14] Hegel's discussion of personality and the relation of the person to his life and body (and conscience and religious beliefs) would have been a lot clearer had he never used the language of property and possession. Everything he has to say could be expressed in terms of self-consciousness and recognition. The metaphors surrounding the concept of self-ownership obfuscate the important claim that slavery is indefensible as the importation of property rights into a domain where it is singularly inappropriate – the domain of persons wherein it should be evident that they mutually recognize each other's status as the bearers of rights which disqualify any such institution.

Private property

A fourth matter for discussion concerns Hegel's insistence that property must be private. For Hegel, this is a matter of necessity. Property is justified as necessary for the objective identification of the person as a discrete existence. It permits the self-identification necessary for freedom and displays this moral atomicity to the world at large: 'Since my will, as personal and hence as the will of an individual [*des Einzelnen*], becomes objective in property, the latter takes on the character of *private property*' (§46). It is easy to see why Hegel emphasizes this. His argument for the rationality of property requires us to triangulate our distinctive position as rights bearers back from the objects we own, and this would be impossible were all property to be owned collectively (as with the property of a family or the state) or communally (as in the common land of a crofting township, wherein all crofters have an individual inclusive right to graze).[15] Grant him his argument concerning the role of private property in establishing the freedom of persons and we can endorse his conclusion that the property which serves this purpose must necessarily be private property.

So far, so good – but Hegel goes further and suggests that there is something odd and anachronistic about systems of common or collective property. There is absolutely no reason why he should claim this. His target is Plato, who suggested that the Guardians (but the Guardians alone) should be forbidden to hold private property, as well as the sort of regime of common ownership exemplified by monasteries. It is perfectly reasonable that regimes of private and common or public property should exist together and for societies to work out for themselves the parameters of the different systems of ownership. In fact Hegel will acknowledge this later. Family property, as we shall see, is a species of collective property – and the patriarch is not at liberty to dispose of it by capricious bequests (§§170–2, 178–9). We must suppose, too, that the Corporation has property resources sufficient to carry out its proper functions – so, too, the State.[16] Other legitimate limitations on private property rights include the requirement that the property of the families who comprise the estate of landowners be entailed and 'burdened by primogeniture' (§306). Only if the state sees a point in preserving these fundamentally irrational forms of property holding may they be validated. But then, of course, contrary to the necessity adduced at §46, they will not be irrational. Marxists at this point will hoist Hegel on to the petard of spurious logic which drives the argument and marvel as the edifice of idealism vanishes in a puff of smoke.[17] The critic who wishes to retain some of Hegel's insight into the importance of private property for freedom will settle for the more important task of demarcating an appropriate domain for private property without according to it a paramount rationality.

This task can be engaged in a constructive manner, for Hegel's insight concerning the role played by property in the identification of persons can be deployed in the identification of the collective, corporate or artificial persons which have rights quite as exclusive as those of ordinary persons. It is a mark of a distinctive form of social unity, of a family, a business, a university, a city or a state that it claims exclusive rights against persons and other social groups to an exclusive property domain. Recognition of such social unities will involve respect for the property rights they assert. This will be true, too, of common property. The crofters each have an inclusive right to graze, say, up to five cattle, but the common right to the common land of the township will exclude non-members from use of the land.

Justice and the distribution of property

A fifth question which we should raise concerns the distribution of property. Hegel's remarks on this topic are very confusing. To the modern mind this question will be crucial, since who should get how much of which goods is the central problem of distributive justice. Hegel's approach to these problems looks unfashionable but promising. It is unfashionable because he does not direct his attention in the first instance towards *theories* of just allocation. But it is promising because, as many critics of standard theories have emphasized, a theory of justice which does not follow from, or respect the constraints of, a proper understanding of the property relation is bound to fail or be radically incomplete. The failure of Nozick's entitlement theory of justice in this respect is conspicuous (see Knowles 1979: 263–5). The charge that Rawls's theory of justice is inconsistent with deep intuitions concerning desert may have a provenance in a desert-based account of private property. So one might think that Hegel starts off on the right track in the construction of principles of justice in distribution.

If so, Hegel's contribution must be judged to be a disappointment. In §49 he announces that '*What* and *how much* I possess is therefore purely contingent as far as right is concerned', and by this he means that who owns what is contingent on a whole host of facts of the matter concerning 'subjective ends, needs, arbitrariness, talents, external circumstances etc.'. The theory of abstract right has nothing to say on the question of distributive justice. Those who believe that it has, proclaiming a principle of '*equality* in the distribution of land or even of other available resources', for example, betray a 'mediocrity of spirit', an understanding which is 'vacuous and superficial' (§49R).

There is an obvious objection to Hegel's position – and it is exactly the same objection that can be put to Nozick's rejection of any patterned theory of justice. If private property is *so* important, valuable to the point that one cannot be a person and hence free in the modern world without the possession of it,[18] hadn't everyone better have some of it at least? Thus we open up, *within* the sphere of Abstract Right, questions of what property and how much of it persons need to be free, questions which Hegel explicitly puts to one side.

I think this objection is decisive against Hegel's refusal to take up the question of distributive justice in Abstract Right. But there is a defence of that position, which I shall state, then leave the matter to the reader to adjudicate.

The first strand of this defensive case notices that in the Addition to §49 Hegel argues that human beings are equal in respect of their status as persons, and in respect of this status 'everyone ought to have property [*müsste jeder Mensch Eigentum haben*]'. There are two ways of reading this: on the first, it amounts merely to the claim that it should be possible for everyone to own some property in the sense that institutions which disallow private property or restrict the class of property holders are unjust. This plausible reading is consistent with Hegel's indifference to the questions of what and how much, but it does not disarm the objection. The second possible reading is clearer and its implications are more subtle. On this account, Hegel accepts the minimal distributive requirement that everyone should have *some* property – presumably enough for them to recognize themselves and be recognized by others as persons – but in Abstract Right he brackets the issue of *what* or *how much* property this should be, taking up these matters later.

We can specify several contexts in which these issues come up for further discussion. In §49R he tells us that it is 'a moral *wish* . . . that all human beings should have their livelihood [*Auskommen*] to meet their needs', and the moral wish is cashed out at §127 as the assertion, against the rules of Abstract Right, that it may be justifiable to enforce a right of necessity against a property owner if this is necessary for one's survival. Thus although the starving person who steals the loaf of bread violates the property rights of the baker, her action is not straightforward theft. To be free, a person must be able to live. So one may judge that Morality, if not Abstract Right, vindicates the allocation to all of sufficient private property for them to survive.

But is this all that justice in distribution demands, that the conflicting rules of right and considerations of welfare be adjudicated within a statement of the rules of morality (the good) which allows that persons who steal in order to survive should go unpunished? No – for Hegel later insists that the institutions of Civil Society must make provision for the alleviation of poverty. Hegel's discussion of poverty, of which we shall have more to say later, is remarkable in that he insists that poverty is not merely the consequence of personal inadequacies, of idleness or extravagance. Poverty may be the consequence of structural economic factors, and subsequent overproduction and market collapse deepen the crisis (§§240–5). In these circumstances Civil Society cannot rely on charity; institutional mechanisms must be in place to alleviate the inevitable poverty and this is a particular responsibility of the corporations (§253).

For Hegel, then, a just distribution of property does not require equality (this point is reinforced in §200). But it does require that no-one fall below a poverty line which is set at a level relative to the sense persons have of what is a respectable amount of wealth within their particular society. Persons must have sufficient resources to maintain a sense of themselves as rights-bearers, persons of integrity and honour. However unequal a distribution may be, if all have the opportunity to work, if no-one's rights are violated, integrity compromised or honour demeaned, redistribution is unnecessary.

In modern terms, this amounts to an endorsement of market capitalism supplemented by a welfare system, supposing, that is, that the welfare system itself does not demean or compromise the dignity of recipients – evidently a delicate issue. In philosophical terms, it is a defence of entitlement principles of acquisition and exchange, qualified by principles of need. It is not fully worked out, either in its institutional specifications or in respect of the philosophical articulation of principles of need. But plenty of modern philosophers have covered this ground,[19] so that we can see how a modern version of the Hegelian position could be elaborated. Whether or not this amounts to a satisfactory account of justice in the distribution of goods, I leave to the reader to decide.

Taking Possession, Use and Alienation

Thus far we have stated and examined the philosophical core of Hegel's discussion of property. The three subsections of 'Abstract Right' following on from the initial presentation amplify the philosophical insights by describing practices governing the acquisition, use and alienation of property which make sense only if we construe property as the embodiment of a person's will. Or, to put the same point a different way, these practices, when correctly understood, reveal to us how we are to identify a person's will in the property he owns.

What kind of practice is Hegel describing? He does not seem to be summarizing the property law of contemporary Prussia, since he gives us no references. To judge from the detail and references he does give, one might think that he is giving us an idiosyncratic digest of Roman law, but this, too, would be an error. Perhaps he is glossing the natural law of property relations, construing natural law as a set of rational principles governing acquisition, use and alienation and taking the glosses as pointing up the abstract theory of property canvassed earlier. The positive law governing property relations will be altogether more detailed and specific than the treatment Hegel affords the practices of property. Hegel is quite clear that the philosophical deduction of the central features of the natural law concerning property cannot be used to vindicate or refute every particular provision of positive law (§55A). We need positive law because natural law cannot dictate how all disputes about property rights ought to be settled in the circumstances in which they arise.

This might lead us to think that Hegel is operating with a traditional distinction of natural law and positive law – natural law comprising the rationally defensible principles which should guide the conduct of individuals and which operate as a constraint on the content of positive law, and positive law consisting of the specific prescriptions of a municipal legal system.[20] If this is so, Hegel would be in a position where he could use the principles of rational, natural law to criticize the positive law of his day if it fell short of the critical standards he has deduced. In which case, Hegel is not describing practices that he observes at *any* level of generality. He is prescribing the form that rational, defensible, practices must take.

We are on familiar terrain here. We discussed in Chapter 2 the distinctive form of Hegel's ethical theory. Now we see that form exemplified. In the terms of this dichotomy – of natural and positive law – of course it is possible that natural law and positive law may conflict. This is the fate of Roman law. As Hegel insists, Roman law was dead wrong in its treatment of domestic relations. 'Roman family law [*Familienrecht*], slavery etc. do not satisfy even the most modest demands of reason' (§3R). But Roman law isn't Hegel's law or indeed our law, and it is the central thesis of Hegel's ethical thought that conflicts as sharp as this are not possible in the modern world. 'Natural law or philosophical right is different from positive right, but it would be a grave misunderstanding to distort this difference into an opposition or antagonism' (§3R). That superficially critical posture is what Hegel derides in the Preface as the 'vain reflection', 'the vainglorious eloquence', the 'arbitrary sophistry' of those who think they have the philosopher's stone in their grasp (PR 14, 17/16–17, 20–1).

What we find in the subsections on taking possession, use and alienation is a philosophical articulation of the governing principles of a private property regime. We can think of it as a statement of the natural law concerning private property (and other personal rights), but we should not understand it to be God-given and universal since it is evidently a historical product. We should see it as a digest of 'best practice' in the modern world, or, since there may be no one model of best practice, as a construction from a range of sources amounting to an 'ideal-type of existing practice'.[21]

Such principles as constitute the practice are appropriate to human nature as it is *now* encountered, having developed through history to the point, in particular, where all see themselves as persons and require this moral status to be recognizable (and recognized) through the display of their free will which property effects. The science of this natural law, or, as one might put it, the thread of argument, consists in the elaboration of the key aspects of private property in terms of the thought that private property is necessary to personal freedom in so far as it makes possible the display and recognition of will.

Taking possession

Some of the property we own has been given to us, but most has been purchased. We vindicate the claims that we make to it through showing receipts. But Hegel reserves discussion of these modes of acquisition to the section on Contract (§§72–81). At this stage of the argument he is discussing the taking into possession of things that are unowned, *res nullius*. He is discussing *original* acquisition. It may be thought that he fails to make a fist of it since he ignores what for many is the obvious philosophical problem: in taking an unowned good into ownership, I not merely claim a liberty right to it in the minimal sense that I have no duty not to acquire it; I assert a claim right against others who may wish to acquire or use what I have taken into possession. Through some act, I impose, unilaterally, a duty on others. Others thereby acquire a duty where hitherto they equally had a liberty right – to use or acquire the good in question. Put in this way, it becomes a very hard task to justify original possession. Whether the stock of acquirable goods is taken to be the common property of everyone (as Locke believed) or whether, as Hegel believes, it has no moral entailments, it is difficult to see how anything *I* might do can impose duties on *all other* people where they recognized no such duties before.

There are good reasons for believing that this problem is both unsolvable and unreal, for a theory of private property can be developed which ignores it (Wenar 1998: 799–819). If we accept these reasons, and suppose further that Hegel is attempting to justify a set of natural law prescriptions concerning legitimate original acquisition, we must conclude that his arguments fail. I leave the detail of the case to those who would pursue further the question of principles governing original acquisition. In any case, even at the time Hegel was writing, original acquisition was not a major problem concerning the property regimes of the societies he held under review. Hegel knew this well enough. In the modern world 'property is . . . based on contract and on those formalities which make it capable of proof and valid before the law'. 'The original, i.e. immediate, modes of acquisition and titles (see §§54ff) are in fact abandoned in civil society' (§§217, 217R). Original acquisition must have taken place hundreds of years back and the details of whether this conformed to any putative principles would be unrecoverable.[22]

In which case we must recast his arguments concerning original acquisition. His arguments concerning 'taking possession' are best read as a speculative survey of our intuitions concerning what would generally be taken as the marks of someone taking something into possession, were any opportunity available to do so. Such a survey would reveal how rules of the form he describes are comprehensible given the role of property in contributing to free agency. The argument thus works almost as a thought experiment which purports to vindicate Hegel's theses concerning the relation between will, property and freedom. We might judge, if his speculations are plausible, that since these are the sorts of acquisitive behaviour we would naturally endorse, this must be because we recognize the distinctive contribution that private property makes to the freedom of persons. We must understand the various modes of taking possession as articulating how private property is a public expression of the will of the owner.

Hence the first mode of taking possession, *physical seizure*, as when I pick up a pebble from a beach or a mushroom from a field, makes sense since 'I am immediately present in this possession and my will is thus also discernible in it' (§55). I and others see my will in the object which I grasp. 'What I hold I have' seems to be the operative principle and it may be extended as my grasp is extended in artificial ways.

The second mode of taking possession is that of *giving form* to something. I give form to an object when I make something of it. We are well used to identifying the will of the maker in the product of his work, the will of the ploughman in the furrows of the field just as much as the will of the artist in the painting. Hegel trades on the familiarity of this association, this combination of the subjective and the objective (§56) in supposing that this would be recognized as a mode of taking possession. It would certainly be a way of elaborating Locke's mysterious claim that we own the unowned goods with which we mix our labour (Locke 1960: ch. 5, §27, 328–9). The principle would state that we own those unowned things that we have formed in line with our intentions, the will of the agent thus being recognizable to himself and to others. In this specific context, Hegel's claim is that recognition of the will is not simply the identification of the maker – as we might spot a painter's familiar style from 20 yards away – rather recognition amounts to endorsing the property-claim of whoever imposed form on the natural materials.

This is an intuition I find hard to test. Of course I do wrong when I kick over the sandcastle you have laboriously constructed, but is that because your work has given you rights of ownership? Does the falconer own the bird he has taken from the nest and trained? I suspect our intuitions in this area are only confident where we are sure that the maker already owns the raw material she fashions. To echo Rousseau's criticism of his social contract predecessors (Rousseau 1973: 45), Hegel would have us transfer to the state of nature intuitions educated in society.

The third mode of taking possession involves the marking of things with signs. Again the process is familiar: we mark out our lawn with wee ornamental fences, we put up notices saying 'No trespassers' or the like, not as a means of keeping other folks out, but as proclaiming to ourselves and others that this is our territory, much as a fox will mark a tussock by dropping a turd. In Britain there used to be an engaging practice of lovers sticking their names on car windscreens above their respective seats (but never, to my keen eye, was there a woman driver or a homosexual pairing; we, the vulgar, are non-PC too). The sign as interpreted indicates that 'I have placed my will' (§57) in the object I have marked. Indeed, in the addition,

Hegel proclaims this 'the most complete mode of all, for the effect of the sign is more or less implicit [*an sich*] in the other ways of taking possession' (§58A).

Again, I find the intuitions canvassed opaque. Indeed, they invite Nozickian contempt: imagine some clownish frontiersman, breathlessly racing round as large an amount of ground as he can encircle, desperately dragging a ball of string or splashing paint on rocks before anyone else arrives. This is Monty Python philosophy – the intelligible practice of the evidently absurd. But of course these activities do make sense in the context of established rules governing private property. If, foolishly, you decide to rent a water meadow prone to regular flooding from a wily farmer who has no other use for it, as a place to park the caravan you use for odd weekends, I guess you are entitled to advertise your rights and thereby yourself to the world at large by putting up notices galore.[23]

Again, the intuitions enlisted by Hegel do not find a response in our experience of state-of-nature scenarios; rather, they trade on the peculiar, but I suppose universal, implications of private property regimes. As regards the acceptable practices of taking into possession things which are *res nullius*, we know next to nothing beyond the realities of force and fraud. As regards the display of the will embodied in objects of private property, we are connoisseurs of the variety of strategems of personal display and public recognition. As a series of statements of natural law governing the taking into possession of unowned objects, Hegel's analysis is worthless, for all that its categories are deduced from the concept. As an interpretation of all too human practices concerning the display and interpretation of the will we take to be embodied in private property, it is perfectly intelligible.

Use of the thing

Use is integral to ownership because all ownership is in the service of the possessor's needs, desires and preferences. Recall: desires and the like explain ownership, freedom is the source of its moral standing, the fact of ownership being a relation of right. That a good serves the owner's need is the fact of its use (§60).

Hegel has interesting things to say about the value of property. Since the aspect of the will which is displayed in ownership is evident in the use made of goods which satisfy desires, it is impossible for one person to have the whole use of property and another to be the owner in a deeper sense. 'Ownership is therefore essentially *free* and *complete* ownership' (§62) and this thought is held to show that some distinctions of Roman law are empty and some practices of feudal tenure are illogical. He tells us that it is only in modern times that the full implications of freedom of personality have been worked out, one and a half millennia after the moral potency of the concept of the person was first discovered (§62R).

Those who have an interest in the history of economic thought will be intrigued by Hegel's account of value. To summarize brutally, the value of a good is purely a function of its usefulness as compared both with other goods that serve the same need and as compared with other goods that service more or less stringent needs (§62). If one insists on a distinction between the use value and exchange value of commodities, Hegel can be charged with conflating the distinction. If one holds that exchange value is explained in terms of the socially necessary expenditure of labour power upon the production of commodities – a thesis famously maintained by Marx developing errors of Hegel's contemporary, Ricardo, themselves derived from earlier sources – Hegel should be acknowledged as an opponent. Most modern economists (and philosophers of economics) would acknowledge that Hegel was on the right track, but I leave these matters for students of these questions to judge.

All readers should note, as Hegel follows the trails of ancient and modern disputes concerning the relations of valid ownership to proper use that the regulative principle of his discussion is the insistence that property exhibits the will of the person who is the owner of it. Should we respect ancient burial sites when we plan our motorways, supposing that no-one living has titles to the lairs? Not if there are none of our contemporaries who can demonstrate how conservation might serve their active projects. Should the copyright on novels, plays and poetry be transmitted *for ever* to the author's descendants? Such works become ownerless when they cease to register the actual will of the defunct author (§64R).

Alienation

One might think that whatever I take into possession as an embodiment of my will I can give up or alienate. Whatever I can put my will into I can take it out of. This sounds sensible. Private property invokes rights against others that they shall not ... steal, damage, trespass against, otherwise use without permission, objects in which the will of the owner is embodied. But if the owner relinquishes such rights, disembodies her will, either the thing reverts to the status of ownerless *res nullius* or is transferred to the ownership of another. Immediately the duties of others are altered; either they have no duties in respect of the item alienated (and so may acquire it) or they have duties which follow the route of transfer. Most things are like this. I can't complain if some alert DIY exponent takes the oak panelling I have stripped from the rubbish skip in which it has been deposited. I can't reclaim the Fabergé knife sharpener which I have given to a friend, mistaking the provenance of the ugly miniature obelisk.

Hegel spends most of his time in discussion of this thesis dealing with exceptions to it. If the thing is 'external in nature' (§65) no problems arise. But we should recall that he gets himself into trouble by speaking of other goods which the agent takes into possession. I take myself into a kind of possession when I recognize that I am a person, but the appropriation of this status is irrevocable. It debars me, for example, from selling myself as a slave. How can I sell myself as what I am not? How can I alienate what I understand to be, and have declared as, inalienable?

Hegel believes that what is true of personality in general is true of 'my universal freedom of will, ethical life and religion' (§66). We can see the logic of this. If a person who recognizes herself as a person cannot surrender the rights in which her personhood consists, how can a free agent, one who thinks of herself as free, renounce that freedom upon pain of self-contradiction or, more vividly, personal fragmentation? If I recognize as distinctive of my ethical life (on which much more later) specific duties to my family, colleagues, or state, how can I give these up? If, in matters of religion, my conscience dictates that I should worship my God in this ritual fashion, how can I reject its demands? All of these prescriptions have to be 'owned' in the nice terminology of modern management-speak, but this talk isn't literal, because the things Hegel lists cannot be properly owned. And that is why they can't be alienated either. And that is why he should not have spoken of inalienable ownership in this connection. They are prescriptions of such a kind as disallows their alienation.

Sure: we can give some of them up in their specifics: once persons, always persons; once free always free; but I can repudiate a demand of ethical life and I can see the light of another religion. But then it isn't *truly* my ethical life that I repudiate, and the religion I forswear worships a false god. As folks began to recognize in the seventeenth century, allegiance can't be *commanded* in the heart of the citizen nor faith to the congregation. These obvious points can be made without our claiming that these personal duties are explained as encumbrances of property or that they need metaphorical elaboration in terms of property rights. Hegel muddies the waters when he suggests that our understanding of these matters amounts to an *appropriation*, a taking into ownership, of moral status, and when he claims that the language of appropriation adduces a property relation. He inadvertently tells us that we should drop the Lockean language of 'self-ownership' because it cannot be consistently or profitably employed to illuminate the relationship of the person to the self it holds as integral to its deepest beliefs.

The remaining elements of Hegel's discussion of alienation put in turn the questions of 'wage slavery': How much of one's time and effort is alienable short of the impossible outcome (in the modern world) of self-imposed slavery (a good question, but not one that the brief exposition in §67 can possibly answer); of intellectual property and copyright (topics which were close to Hegel's heart – as the author of text books stating the truth); and finally, as any reader of classical texts of ethical or political theory might expect, an a priori one-paragraph rejection of the moral permissibility of suicide (§70)? Students of philosophy should regard this paragraph as a challenge: first, to formulate Hegel's argument in terms which permit its careful appraisal; second, to consider the assumption upon which the argument rests – that the ethical permissibility of suicide is settled by considering whether or not it is a personal right.

Even if Hegel is correct in this assumption (and the defence of it would require a more sophisticated analysis of rights than he provides, assessing whether it is best thought of as a moral power or a Hobbesian liberty-right rather than a standard claim-right), his argument looks straightforwardly fallacious. If a property-owner can eliminate her status as property-owner by giving away all her goods to the poor, why can't a person eliminate her status as a person by making herself a corpse? I mention what I regard as a paragraph of historical philosophical trivia because many people, quite cogently, have considered whether or not the world might be a better place without their presence and have decided in favour of suicide. I suspect some of these latter have taken the right decision. If Hegel is right, then all these poor folks have done wrong. But those who agree with him had better find an argument which is more cogent than the one he presents.

Contract

Hegel's discussion of contract contains three elements of note which I shall consider briefly. First, we should think about the argument which prompts the transition. There are many reasons why a full philosophical treatment of private property rights should consider valid principles of contract: if the right to private property is essentially the transferable right to exclusive use, one had better be able to articulate valid principles of transfer governing interpersonal transactions. One would expect these to outlaw forceable seizure and to legitimate gift, sale and the like. Certainly, if the institution of private property is grounded in its usefulness, principles of legitimate exchange will readily be incorporated, not least since the calculation of utility will be constructed upon or corroborate the reasons ('need in general – benevolence, utility etc.' (§71R)) which Hegel acknowledges as the motivation of contractors. But Hegel's philosophical explanation of private property identifies utility as a secondary feature of a private property regime. The crucial aspect is the mode in which it expresses the freedom of persons. We should remember, too, that the freedom which is promoted is primarily a matter of property enabling persons to recognize themselves in a public medium which entails their recognizability by others. It is not simply a matter of their being able to exercise more choices the more possessions they have at their disposal. Rights of exclusive use serve this purpose as citizens claim the respect of others and respect others as they recognize their rights in turn.

Recognition in respect of the processes of taking possession, use and alienation, is a matter of mutuality and reciprocity, of the owners' thinking through the logical implications of the claim rights they assert. In respect of acquisitions which are the consequence of interpersonal transactions (i.e. *most* acquisitions in the modern world) a further dimension is added to the core element of recognizability since holdings will now display a genuinely common will. After we barter goods, it is *our* will that the pattern of ownership displays, yet it is each person's unique will that is objective in his own subsequent holdings. Each contractor will identify his will in the new dispensation which therefore expresses a truly common will.

So far as the necessity of the transition is concerned, we might ask whether it is possible to have a private property regime that consists of rules governing the acquisition, use and alienation of property but without rules of contract. It would be a very odd institution and it would not be Hegel's, since arguably he (inadvertently? illegitimately?) introduces the element of contract into his account of alienation: see his discussion of the alienation of labour power in §67. But this is an odd question. If there is a logic to this transition it is revealed in the incompleteness of an account of entitlement which does not incorporate principles of legitimate transfer, and an explanation of that incompleteness in terms of the enhanced opportunity for, and modality of, interpersonal recognition which contract permits. The advance which the discussion of contract marks is thus an advance in freedom.

The second feature of Hegel's discussion is a swift dismissal of Kant's account of marriage which he announces as 'disgraceful' (§75). In brief, Kant considers that marriage is a contract between heterosexual adults for the reciprocal use of each other's genitalia – and this sounds disgusting! This is a celebrated *contretemps* in the history of philosophy but I shall reserve full discussion of it until Chapter 11 when we consider Hegel's account of the family. For the moment (and to be academically po-faced), we should notice that it is not clear from Hegel's charge against Kant which of the three necessary conditions of proper contracts is violated in such a contract. It cannot be the first condition, 'that (a) the contract is the product of the *arbitrary will*' (§75), since marriage *does* have this origin in common with contract (§§75A, 162). It may be condition (c) which stipulates that 'the object of the contract is an *individual external* thing [*Sache*]', but in §80 Hegel implies that we should not take the language of 'things' too literally, arguing that a person's output or services can be the object of a wage contract. So why not think of marriage as the mutual, reciprocal prostitution of equal partners? In principle, then, it cannot be the 'unthingliness' of the content of marriage vows (love, comfort, honour, keeping, obedience, service and fidelity: to collect together the objects listed in the Anglican Book of Common Prayer) which disqualifies marriage as a contract. It is perhaps a violation of the second condition (b) that Hegel has in mind, that the '*will posited by the contracting parties* [is] only a *common* will, not a will which is universal in and for itself' (§75), but the argument must be stated very carefully, since marriage certainly seems to be an expression of a common will between the marriage partners alone.

The third interesting aspect of Hegel's discussion of contract is similarly announced as an implication of the necessary conditions of a contractual relation that I have articulated above, namely the rejection of social contract accounts of the state. Again, it is not wholly clear which conditions are violated by social contract accounts of the state (probably all three), nor indeed which versions of social contract theory are the targets of Hegel's criticism. Assessment of the argument as condensed in §75 will again be reserved, in this case for Chapter 13, where I discuss Hegel's account of the state. At §258 he discusses the contract theories of Rousseau and Fichte, in particular, at more length. The emphasis of the discussion here, as §75 heralds, is that the political relationship which holds between the state and the citizen is not to be understood as a relationship which holds between 'persons' in the technical sense outlined in Abstract Right, nor between persons and the state.

Rational persons will endorse the rules of right concerning personality, property and contracts, but it is a contingent matter whether individual persons with their particular wills act in conformity with these principles. They may assault or try to enslave other persons; they may damage or steal the property of others; or they may violate properly binding contracts. When they do so, they do *wrong* (§81). What does the fact of wrongdoing and the range of legitimate responses to it tell us about rights? This is the topic of the next chapter.

Chapter 6

Abstract Right 3. Wrongdoing and Punishment: §§82–104

Introduction

Hegel makes a celebrated and distinctive contribution to philosophical thinking about one of the great, enduring, philosophical problems – the problem of punishment. Punishment standardly involves hard treatment. Those who are judged guilty of offences are punished by being killed or made to suffer physical hurt, are imprisoned or otherwise lose some measure of their liberty, are fined or have property confiscated. All measures of punishment involve actions which would in any other context be judged morally wrong through the violation of rights or the infliction of suffering. And so the practice of punishment screams out for a philosophical justification. It is natural, therefore, that the student approaches Hegel's discussion of punishment in Section 3 of Abstract Right (§§84–104) in light of this perennial philosophical enquiry, and unless one thought that Hegel's treatment of the subject made a valuable contribution to the specific problems thrown up by penal practices, the study of his discussion would have only historical value.

This natural focus may lead us to misplace Hegel's prime concern in Abstract Right, which is to fully elaborate the nature and structure of personal rights. Even if we recognize this point, we might take him to be focussing on a slightly different problem concerning punishment and rights. Punitive activities of the sort that I listed above all involve actions which violate the rights Hegel has been explaining in Abstract Right. Again, it would be natural to think of his discussion as trying to square the legitimacy of punishment with a doctrine of rights. This is an obvious and serious problem for any strong theory of rights: how can one both endorse rights and accept the standard practices of punishment? But this does not seem to be Hegel's main concern, either.

Hegel tells us that thus far, particularly in respect of contract, we have been studying the *appearance* (*Erscheinung*) of right (§82). What this term tells us is not that we have been studying a mere surface phenomenon, the appearance as against the reality of rights. Essence (of rights or anything else) is not something that is concealed by appearance; it is rather the necessary, structured, totality of all appearances.[1] Without expanding on the metaphysical claims that Hegel's use of this terminology invokes, we can see that his crucial claim here is that the doctrine of rights so far developed is incomplete, a part only of the whole truth about rights. What is missing? To find the missing ingredient, we have to consider the phenomenon of wrongdoing. When folks do wrong, in particular when they violate rights, the appearance of right becomes a *semblance* (*Schein*) (§82–3), which is to say a truth about rights is denied. Wrongdoing thus presents a problem, since we have a world in which rights are claimed and recognized as necessary for freedom, yet in fact these rights are rejected in the event of their violation.

In dealing with what Hegel has thus diagnosed as a contradiction, we come to recognize something that heretofore was missing from the analysis of rights, namely, that rights which are actual and valid, that is, not merely an appearance, must be effective – which is to say, enforceable (§82R). The prime purpose of Hegel's discussion of Wrong (*Das Unrecht*) is to establish this last claim, that genuine rights must be enforceable in principle and in practice. This conclusion is reached through an argument which covers the familiar ground of crime and punishment and which offers a solution to the problems which these practices create. But we should remember throughout this chapter that Hegel's chief interest has not changed. He is concerned primarily to understand the modern theory and practice of rights and judges (surely correctly) that this requires an account of punishment.

The Varieties of Wrongdoing

We do best to consider the semblance of right as a false claim about personal right made by a particular agent whose action is in conflict with the rules of right which are universally valid. Wrongdoers get wrong the rights of the matter and the false claims which they make or which their actions imply come in three varieties. First, they may commit an unintentional or civil wrong. Suppose Tom plants a hedge of *Leylandii* which grows to enormous proportions, obliterating the sunlight from Dick's garden, killing off some of his plants and preventing him from sunbathing – as they say, a severe loss of amenity for Dick. But does Tom have the right to do this? He thinks he does, but Dick disputes his claim. Or to stick with Hegel's example of conflicting property rights to the same object, think of a squabble over the terms of a will. Neither party disputes the rules governing the dispensation of the property. Both parties insists that they are in the right. Such '*collisions of rights*' (§84) can be resolved by an authoritative adjudication, and when this judgement is delivered one or other party will be shown to have right on their side. The will which is *particular*, expressing the (probably self-interested) judgement of the party which is in the wrong, will be negated as the rules governing the case are applied against the wrongdoer. The wrongdoer is obliged to renounce her claim, notwithstanding the genuine claim to self-interest which she avows in the matter in question. What is essential to this variety of wrongdoing – non-malicious wrong – is that the wrongdoer does not deliberately reject the rules which determine which actions are right.

The second variety of wrongdoing occurs when a contractor deceives the second party. I sell you mutton but dress it as lamb or I sell you as my mutton a beast I have rustled. Both of us abide by some of the rules. I send you a bill of sale and you pay up; the wrongdoing consists in my following a rigmarole, mimicking the procedures of legitimate commerce but deceiving you as to the nature or provenance, and hence the true value of the commodity I exchanged. My intention is fraudulent, but I execute it by trading on the valid rules governing legitimate contracts. In exploiting the rules, I recognize them in the moment I violate them. One might think that Hegel's specification of this category of wrongdoing has more to do with his love of trichotomies than it illuminates the variety of wrongdoing. I wouldn't argue with such a claim, except that it foregrounds a distinctive feature of the final species of wrongdoing – that of crime.

Criminal activity is conceived of as *coercion*, as the exercise of force upon the will of another person as this will is embodied in their property. Thus you coerce me when you damage or steal my property, or when you threaten to do these things as a means of enforcing your will (§90). Other examples of crime include breach of contract and the failure to fulfil duties to one's family or the state (§93R). Hegel also mentions perjury, treason, counterfeiting, forgery (§95), murder, slavery and religious coercion (§96). No doubt we could add to the list physical assault and rape and many more violations of right. With some of these examples, the dividing line between fraud and crime looks pretty arbitrary, but so be it. The central feature of Hegel's understanding of crime is an interpretation of the coercive behaviour of the criminal as an all-embracing rejection of right.

Hegel describes this rejection as 'a negatively infinite judgement' (§95).[2] Suppose you steal my car. We should take this as your denial that the car is rightfully mine (just as you might in a disputed claim of possession) but in addition we should take you to be denying my status as a person, 'my *capacity for rights*' (§95), and, by implication, the whole regime of rights, 'right as right' as stated in the *Science of Logic*, to which Hegel refers his readers. The point of punishment is to reject in turn the criminal's rejection of rights in each of these modalities. Hence crime is described as a nullity manifested in the subsequent nullification of the infringement of right; punishment is the negation of the negation, 'the actuality of right, as its necessity which mediates itself with itself through the cancellation [annulment, sublation, negation, *aufhebung*] of its infringment' (§97).

This is the sort of language which has given Hegel a bad name with impatient critics and which has generated some crude critical responses. Benn and Peters argue, for example, that crime, unlike marriage, cannot be annulled. The annulment states that the marriage never properly took place, whereas the criminal act certainly did. To say that the criminal pays a debt is one thing; to say that punishment asserts that the crime never really took place is something very different (Benn and Peters 1959: 177). This argument trades on ordinary language associations which are remote from the German text. It has no critical purchase on Hegel's discussion, since the term *Aufhebung* which Hegel uses in this context is much richer than 'annulment' as found in common usage. In particular, *Aufhebung* frequently in Hegel's writings, and in this context specifically, has positive connotations; the *Aufhebung* of crime will preserve the right in a manner to be described.

These murky phrases serve one specific point, then, most importantly: they function as trailers for the closer arguments which follow. The specific point is a denial of Kant's view that 'right and authorization to use coercion therefore mean one and the same thing' (MM: 389 / Ak. 6: 232). Hegel's thought is that we cannot appeal directly to the meaning or concept of right to establish that rights are enforceable in the sense of carrying an authorization for coercion to be used against their violators. 'Abstract right is a *coercive right*' he tells us at §94, but this is not a matter of definition nor an analytic truth. To reach this conclusion, further argumentation is necessary – and fortunately, this is what he provides. The argumentation to follow will enable us to flesh out the hard language which Hegel employs to advertise his programme.

The Restoration of Right

In the case of a dispute about rights, or in respect of damage to or destruction of property (which is a tort, a civil wrong, and not a case of criminal damage), the person who is in the wrong has not rejected either the moral status of the injured party as a person, nor have they challenged the normative order of rights. Adjudication is necessary, and in the case of personal injury or damage to property compensation is due in the measure of the value of the damage (§98). The case is different in respect of crime proper. Hegel has insisted that the criminal has rejected the capacity for rights, that is, the personality of the victim together with the regime of rights which expresses the personal standing of all. Nonetheless, we cannot inspect the victim's capacity for rights and find it impaired. (If it is impaired, we must suppose that the victim has willed his own coercion (§91) – an old Stoic doctrine which is at odds with Hegel's views on the inalienability of freedom.) Nor can we identify the injury done to the regime of rights. 'Right or law in itself is rather something which has no external existence and is to that extent invulnerable' (§99). So how do we identify the particular form that rejection or denial (semblance) of the right takes in the case of criminal behaviour?

'The *positive existence of the injury* consists solely in the *particular will of the criminal*' (§99). Which is to say, we can recognize the criminal's will to deny the personality of the victim and the regime of right in her behaviour, although we cannot see the marks of this denial. We know the attitude of the criminal to the victim – which is not one of respect for his personhood – and we know that the criminal has no respect for such freedom as the rules of right embody, though we cannot inspect freedom and see evidence of the disrespect the criminal has shown. On the other hand, in the character of the criminal's action, in her rejection of the principles of right, both generally and in the person of the victim, we can identify a challenge to the regime of right. Unless this challenge is met by way of an injury to the will of the criminal, we must suppose that her challenge is successful, that she is not dealing with a person and that the rules of right are not universally applicable, if at all. Punishment, coercion against the will of the criminal, is necessary for the restoration (better: reaffirmation) of the rules of right (§99).

This is an obscure argument and it is a good question as to whether a clear and persuasive case can be drawn out of the shadows. The crucial claim is evidently the concluding sentence of §99: 'Thus an injury to the latter [the criminal] as an existent will is the cancellation [*aufheben*] of the crime, *which would otherwise be regarded as valid*, and the restoration of right.' This sentence, if not the full argument which precedes it, has produced a dense and useful literature in recent years (Cooper 1971; Steinberger 1983; Wood 1990, 1992; Houlgate 1992). Discussion has focussed on Cooper's claim that

Hegel's talk of punishment restoring the right expresses a logical or conceptual thesis: 'Unless people are generally apprehended and punished for preventing others doing x, there is reason to suppose that the latter do not have the right to do x' (Cooper 1971: 162–3). Although Cooper stresses the conceptual connection between the assertion of rights and the application of just punishment, Steinberger argues that the conceptual connection has not been drawn tightly enough. Since Cooper's formulation of it relies on empirical judgements to the effect that only the *punishment* of offenders (i.e. hard treatment, and not, e.g., public denunciation) can vindicate the rights which the criminal challenges, it misrepresents the logical or conceptual groundings of Hegel's defence of punishment (Steinberger 1983). Allen Wood notices Hegel's talk of restoring the right but claims that Cooper's explication fails on all grounds: it is not explicitly stated in the texts, and, if it were, it would be a poor argument (Wood 1990: 111–13). Houlgate has challenged Wood's rejection of a conceptual thesis, claiming that 'a [criminal] violation cannot therefore be allowed to stand but must be negated so that the necessary validity of right is restored' (Houlgate 1992: 12). In the same volume, Wood replies forcefully, challenging the 'conceptual' interpretation of the restoration of right theme and rejecting the argument, once more, as 'just no good' (Wood 1992: 44).

We can begin to adjudicate these disputes by paraphrasing Hegel's statement of the position at §99. If an ostensible right is violated and the violator is not punished (supposing him to be known and available for punishment etc.) we must regard his deed as innocent; if he has taken some property, we must regard that property as his. This, we must take it, is the implication of Hegel's claim that the criminal act 'would otherwise be regarded as valid' (§99).[3] *Contrariwise*, if the criminal is punished, the *status quo ante* crime is publicly restored; both the victim's moral status and her specific rights are vindicated. The deed cannot both be a crime and right. This reading is also suggested by a later note (if we read 'impossible' as 'logically impossible', as I think we should): 'it would be impossible for society to leave a crime unpunished – since the crime would then be posited as right' (§218A). It is either not a crime or not right – and the response, by way of condonation or punishment, demonstrates one's judgement of it.

Examples suggest that this view is plausible. Mark Tunick illustrates this point with a good story from the Upper Congo. An old woman confronts and publicly denounces a young warrior who has unrepentantly broken a minor taboo. The warrior runs off in shame. Tunick concludes that 'without the old woman's response [of denunciation] there would have been no crime: not because if nobody discovers it happened it didn't happen, but because if nobody declares it's wrong, it's not' (Tunick 1992a: 78–80). Likewise, if technical violations of the law go openly unpunished, as was the case in Scotland before the law on consensual homosexual acts was brought into line with the reforms effected in English law, we may judge that no wrong is committed. Where prosecution is capricious and arbitrary – this is the early history of boxing in Britain; sometimes the magistrates stopped the fights, sometimes they sat in the front row – the law is an ass because the right is indeterminate.

Does this argument advance a conceptual claim? As they used to say, it all depends on what you mean by 'conceptual', and the commentators above differ in this respect. As we have noticed, Hegel is quite clear that the justification of punishment for violations of right is not a matter of definition. Argument is needed, but then an argument has been given which amounts to an analysis or articulation of conceptual linkages revealed by a discussion of examples. I don't think we need to confront the methodology of Hegelian argumentation, the possibility of a distinctive speculative science, to reach a conclusion.

If what we are faced with is conceptual analysis of a familiar sort, as Wood points out (Wood 1992: 43–5), the conclusion will be parochial and conservative – but then perhaps 'we' can find agreement about how 'we' think in 'our' parish, and maybe this enterprise can afford *comprehension* of that 'truth concerning *right, ethics, and the state* [which] is *as old* as its *exposition and promulgation in public laws and in public morality and religion* (PR 11/13–14). If, by contrast, we are tracking the path of a speculative logic, we still have to unpack the metaphors which fill the conceptual space of 'right re-establish[ing] itself by negating this negation of itself' (§82) and what better way of doing this can there be than to find a valid argument? One point should be agreed by all: that Hegel's argument at §99, even as paraphrased lengthily above, is elliptical. As such, we should expect any plausible reconstruction of it to read the texts at their most capacious and go beyond them if the argument requires supplementation.

It is on these grounds that I am content to endorse the drift of Cooper's original reading. Following my earlier remarks about Hegel's focus on our understanding of rights and his interest in what a philosophical examination of our practice of punishment contributes to that enterprise, I shall state the conceptual truth at the heart of the restoration of rights argument as: 'Rights are not properly recognized (actualized) as valid claims, binding on others, unless their violation is met with punishment wherever possible'. As conceptual truths go, this is parochial. It applies to *our* world, supposing that alternative responses would not serve the purpose of public recognition. For all I know, there are other worlds wherein a public judgement of wrongdoing may suffice to restore the right. But then, I suspect (and this is suggested by Tunick's example) public judgement would amount to denunciation, and this in turn would be regarded as hard treatment (being explicitly a cause of public shame) and hence as a measure of punishment. I speculate, on the basis of the sort of common sense that is acknowledgedly fallible, that in our world rights cannot be protected, right cannot be restored, by non-punitive communications. Punishment is necessary, and as necessary, is justified to persons who claim and respect rights as expressive of their freedom.

This argument can be supported by looking ahead to Hegel's discussion of the administration of justice in Civil Society. Punishment can only restore the right if the institutions whereby punishment is effected constitute the means of public recognition of rights. Public recognition requires public institutions. And so it proves. In the institutions of Civil Society which administrate justice, Abstract Right is posited objectively as law, universally promulgated and intelligibly codified, publicly dispensed in open court following trial by jury (§§209–29). The practice of punishment, following court proceedings which have established the fact of criminal behaviour, makes it clear to all parties (victim, criminal and the general public) that the rights of the matter are as the law states them to be. The victim's rights are vindicated, her moral (now legal) status as a person with the capacity for rights is affirmed, the public's interest in countering a danger to society is satisfied (§218). But what of the poor criminal?

If the criminal is left out of the picture, a telling objection emerges.[4] Even if, instead of the usual suspects (happiness, pleasure net pain, preference satisfaction, objective list), the value to be maximized is respect for rights, or freedom, it is hard to see Hegel's account as distinctively retributivist. This is because the restoration of rights thesis seems to articulate the social functionality of punishment and seems to ignore that aspect of punishment which is directed towards the particularity of the specific violation. The dealings which the punitive agency has with the criminal seem to be secondary to the efficacy of punishment as the instrument of a social purpose – the restoration of right. If we reconstruct Hegel's argument in the fashion that I have reconstructed it, we must conclude either that the theory does not accomplish its retributive intent or that it is incomplete. This latter is my claim. The restoration of right *is* a public function. It is the objective face of what Hegel later calls 'the genuine reconciliation of right with itself' (§220), which the fact of crime necessitates and punishment effects. The argument, so far, is incomplete because it does not consider the perspective of the criminal. This is the subjective aspect of the reconciliation of right with itself which is revealed in the response of the criminal.

> reconciliation applies . . . subjectively . . . to the criminal in that *his law, which is known by him* and is *valid* for him and *for his protection*, is enforced on him in such a way that he himself finds in it the satisfaction of justice and merely the enactment of *what is proper to him*.
>
> (PR §220)

We need to understand these ambitious claims. And we need to show how they amplify, rather than contradict, Hegel's concern for the restoration of right.

The Criminal's Right to Punishment

Reviewing the position we have reached thus far we can fairly conclude that we have one good argument in the bag which links the legitimacy of punishment with the necessary enforceability of rights. But we have not reached the heart of the Hegelian doctrine, which, loosely put, claims that punishment is the right of the criminal.

This is a very hard doctrine to understand. The important text states that

> The injury [*Verletzung*] which is inflicted on the criminal is not only just *in itself* (and since it is just, it is at the same time his will as it is *in itself*, an existence [*Dasein*] of his freedom, *his* right); it is also a right for the criminal himself [*ein Recht an der Verbrecher selbst*], that is a right *posited* in his *existent* will, in his action. For it is implicit in his action, as that of a *rational* being, that it is universal in character, and that, by performing it, he has set up a law which he has recognized for himself in his action, and under which he may therefore be subsumed as under *his* right.
>
> (§100)

The argument needs to be unravelled carefully. Look at the first extended clause: in what respect is the punishment which is inflicted on the criminal just in itself? I take it that Hegel is reminding us that the punishment is enforcing the rules of right. Since the criminal is a person and persons claim and respect rights (§36), it is the criminal's will that rights-claims be effective, it is the criminal's freedom that effective rights claims express and protect. It is therefore a right of the criminal, as of every other person, that criminals suffer punishment. (I shall expand on this argument later, since I believe it to be substantially correct.)

I take the argument that follows to be a real mistake. This is how I read it: the key statement is that by performing his criminal action, the criminal has 'set up a law'. What is the law that is implicit in the action of the criminal? As we have seen, the crime bespeaks the criminal's rejection of the victim's rights, personhood, and the regime of rights in general. It bespeaks these rejections in accordance with what Hegel later calls, teasingly, the 'right of the *objectivity* of the action ... to assert itself as known and willed by the subject as a *thinking* agent' (§120), as distinct from the subject's right of intention. The rational agent knows that his actions disclose his intentions (and speak louder than any words of disavowal), since he employs the same rational schema as others do to understand the actions of his fellows. And he knows how they will interpret his actions when he commits a crime, just as he knows how to interpret their actions when they do so. This is one cost of rationality.

So what is the law that he recognizes in his action and under which he may 'be subsumed as under his right'? We must take it to be a universalized rejection of the specific rights his action infringes. Thus when Tom steals Dick's car, he is saying the car isn't Dick's by right, Dick is not a rights-bearer in respect of his possessions, and it is permissible to take property that others claim of right. (Dick's rights are not infringed in their entirety – that would be to kill or enslave him (§96).) If this is what Tom's action bespeaks, then the principle, the universalizable rejection of the normative force of rights claims, can consistently be applied to him.[5]

I say this is a bad argument. It says little more than, since the criminal knows or ought to know that he will be taken as implying that it's fine to violate the rights of a person, this 'principle' can fairly be applied to him. The subsequent punishment is justifiable *ad hominem*, in accordance with a principle which as a rational agent he cannot disavow. This does little more than dress up the thought that the criminal cannot complain if he is treated in exactly the same fashion as he treats his victims. This thought has much to be said for it, but it is hard to see how it can be acceptable to the punishing agency. The criminal's act, we recall, has the dimension of a 'negatively infinite judgement', denying the victim's capacity for rights – and in Civil Society, the law, the whole regime of rights as it applies to its members. The punishing agency cannot be thought to assert *this* as the principle of *its own* action, and explicitly it does not. As we shall see, punishment recognizes the standing of the criminal as a person, as a rights-bearer; through his punishment he 'is *honoured* as a rational being' (§100R). This response to Hegel glosses an old saw: Two wrongs don't make a right; but it is none the worse for that. Indeed, it is a rather well-judged application of it. The last thing the punishing agency should be doing is adopting the moral perspective of the criminal. Cack-handedly, that would be to endorse the semblance of right rather to establish its actuality.

To find a sound argument hereabouts, or the suggestion of one (but explicitly, not one that Hegel endorses), we need to return to the earlier part of §100. In Abstract Right, all agents assert the status of being persons. Each person is distinguished by a capacity for rights, by their standing as rights-bearers, and each person recognizes the commandment of right requiring them to be persons and to recognize others as persons. The content of the rights-claims which persons characteristically address to each other is sketched in the sections on property and contract. All of this should be clear to the criminal who one can expect to have as full an understanding of the regime of rights as any other person. If it is not clear to the criminal, then in an important sense he is not a rational agent; he has not absorbed the rational demands of the order of Abstract Right as this is essential for his freedom.

From these initial postulates, we ought to be able to develop a full justification of punishment on the model of a hypothetical social contract argument. Thus:

1. Individuals claim rights against each other and recognize that others claim equivalent rights against themselves.
2. They see no prospect of others respecting their rights whilst they themselves are immune to the rights claims of others.
3. They suspect that others may attempt to become free-riders on the convention of respect for rights, since they understand that the attraction of wrongdoing with impunity on their own part is enhanced by the predictability of others' behaviour – which they may be able to exploit.
4. Hence, they demand a guarantee of good faith in the principles of rights from those others who avow them, and they are willing to give such a guarantee themselves.
5. The guarantee which is universally offered and taken up is a recognition of the legitimacy of punishment exacted against criminals; a guarantee taken up against criminals on the part of all contractors, against themselves, of course, should they turn out to be criminals.
6. They accept that punishment may take the form of actions which, in other contexts, would amount to a violation of their rights.
7. Hence, those who wish their rights to be promoted and protected are willing to alienate their rights should they, themselves, violate the rights of others.[6]

How much of this argument can we recognize in Hegel's texts? At first sight, admittedly, not much; 1 certainly is a Hegelian thesis, and so is the conclusion at 7. This explicates the thought that, both in itself and explicitly, punishment is the right of the criminal. In some sense, the criminal consents to his punishment. What of the steps in between? I would be prepared to defend 2 as a Hegelian position. Besides being one of the sources of the universality explicit in the imperative of right, it is a clear implication of the demand that law be universally valid and universally known through its promulgation in a public legal code and its prosecution in transparent legal processes (§§209–11, 215–17). We can take it, too, that the rational agent will endorse the principles of Abstract Right on which the administration of justice is, in part, founded. Similarly, I think 6 can be defended as an implication of the Hegelian texts, which stress that the appropriate measure of punishment will be equal to the crime in point of its value (§§101, 214). But that is as far as the texts will take us.

Hegel knew this form of argument well enough. He was well aware of the work of Rousseau, who puts it with characteristic succinctness. Speaking of the death-penalty, but using an argument which can be applied in full generality across the variety of punishments, Rousseau asserts that 'the death-penalty inflicted upon criminals may be looked on in much the same light: it is in order that we may not fall victims to an assassin that we consent to die if we ourselves turn assassins' (Rousseau 1973, Bk.2, ch. 6: 190). The canonical source for a contract argument in favour of punishment (and *pace* Rousseau, a rejection of the legitimacy of capital punishment) is Beccaria, whom Hegel cites in §100R. This suggests to me that Hegel knew quite well that a contract argument is in the background to his own discussion, but he makes strenuous efforts to dissociate himself from it.

His reasons for doing so appear confused. First he insists that 'the state is by no means a contract' (§100R – see also §§75, 258). Whether this means that the state is not to be understood as having its origins in a contract or whether this means that the citizens' allegiance or political obligation to the state is not founded on a contractual relationship matters little in this context, for Hegel is not discussing the state; he is discussing punishment as an element of Abstract Right. Of course, as the argument develops we shall see how the practice of punishment is located in Ethical Life, in Civil Society in the Administration of Justice, and this element of Civil Society evidently needs the State in order to legislate the rules employed within the Administration of Justice. But this relocation of the practice of punishment should not compromise any arguments in favour of punishment which can be advanced from the premises of Abstract Right any more than the State and Civil Society can ignore altogether the insights of Abstract Right concerning citizens' rights.

In fact, the defence of punishment which Hegel elaborates in his discussion of the Administration of Justice (§220) merely recapitulates the philosophical points made in the discussion of crime and punishment of Abstract Right, although it adds much more detail concerning its institutional articulation and practical application, and of course, in this context, crime is taken to be a rejection of the positive rules of civil society which protect citizens' rights. Hegel could perfectly well have developed a contract argument for punishment while denying that contract arguments have any part to play either in explaining the origins of states or in vindicating our obligation to obey the law of the state. That he never did so, is in part a product of a further confusion I detect in his discussion. He insists that right embodies rational principles, 'rationality *in and for itself*' which the state must enforce *with* or *without* the consent of individuals', and says that this is implied through 'the formal rationality of the *individual's volition*' (§100R). This latter I take to be the formal universalizability of the principle of the criminal's action, which universalizability holds whether or not the criminal recognizes this implication.

Hegel's mistake is therefore that of confusing a hypothetical contract argument with an argument from actual consent: he concludes, on the basis that the criminal may not in fact recognize the principles of right or the legitimacy of his punishment for violations, that he cannot be supposed to have actually contracted to accept punishment. This conclusion is quite fair. What he does not realize is that this objection, devastating against arguments which rely on actual consent or actual contract, has no purchase on arguments from hypothetical consent. I have suggested that such an argument is available to him on the basis of premises advanced within Abstract Right, and further that such an argument would serve his purposes better than the argument he does employ. Concerning punishment, if not our obligation to obey the state, Hegel should have accepted the hypothetical contract argument.

There is a further aspect to Hegel's claim that punishment is the right of the criminal which we should take up at this point. Hegel insists that although the criminal rejects the personhood of the victim, he himself remains a person and must be treated as such, 'honoured as a rational being. – He is denied this honour if the concept and criterion of his punishment are not derived from his own act' (§100R). Which accounts of punishment do not derive the concept and the criterion of punishment from the criminal's own act? In respect of the concept of punishment, Hegel has in mind theories which are non-retributive, which do not focus on wrongdoing and the requirement of justice as retribution (which he glosses in §101R as 'the universal feeling of peoples and individuals towards crime [which] is, and always has been, that it *deserves* to be punished'). It would take us too far away from our present remit to enquire deeply into this terminology,[7] but retribution is best understood in two distinct ways, though they may be related in the work of particular philosophers. The first conception of retributivism is of a theory which establishes as the 'general justifying aim'[8] of punishment its intrinsic justice as a response to crime. The second conception of retributivism is a doctrine concerning the appropriate measures of punishment – an eye for an eye and so forth – on which subject we shall have more to say shortly.

Retributivism of the first stripe is of course Hegel's position and he contrasts it with a number of non-retributive, generally consequentialist approaches. Such 'theories of punishment as prevention, as a deterrent, a threat, a corrective etc.' all make the same mistake: they conceive of punishment as an (otherwise) evil which is to be inflicted in order to promote some consequent good, generally the prevention of crime by the deterrence of the criminal or others, or else through the reform or treatment of the criminal. If this is true, then the criminal is conceived as the means to produce that good. If the good of crime prevention is achieved by threatening punishment, as Hegel judges Feuerbach's theory of punishment to imply, then this 'means treating a human being like a dog instead of respecting his honour and freedom' (§99A). If we use criminals as the instrument of social purposes, seeking to deter or reform them, we treat them as we would treat 'a harmful animal which must be rendered harmless' (§100R). In other words consequentialist accounts of the justification of punishment which defend the practice in accordance with the social good it promotes, fail to respect the criminal as a bearer of rights, fail to honour him as a rational creature.

This is evidently so where, for example, the judge in sentencing says 'There is far too much of this sort of behaviour going on. I intend to impose an exemplary sentence so that those inclined to act in this way will think again.' Here the convicted criminal is being used as the instrument of a social purpose. The objection would be even clearer were the courts or a rogue sheriff to punish an innocent person in order to advance the public good. Hegel's thought that punishment is a right of the criminal looks very plausible if it is read in this fashion as insisting that the rights of the criminal should constrain the criminal process, disallowing excessive punishment of the guilty or punishment of the innocent. The underlying conception of the criminal as an autonomous agent whose rights must be respected within the criminal process has found favour amongst many modern philosophers writing on punishment.[9]

We have identified two strands of argument in Hegel's case for the justification of punishment. The first calls for the restoration of right in the face of the criminal's challenge, but is vulnerable to the charge that it is essentially non-retributive in so far as it holds up the restoration of right as a consequential good. The second argues that punishment is the right of the criminal, in accordance with a law to be deduced from his own action. This argument, too, has a weakness which critics have noticed. For we may conclude from it, not that the state ought to punish the criminal, but that it does no injustice if it does so. The argument shows that punishment is permissible but not mandatory. Hence the argument is incomplete.

In §220 Hegel gives the argument for punishment in its final version. Here in Civil Society punishment is explicitly the function of the legal authorities involved in the administration of justice. It is not a matter of persons, whether victims or those who have their interests at heart pursuing punishment as a private project. This is the full statement of his position:

> When the right against crime takes the form of *revenge* (see §102), it is merely right *in itself*, not in a form that is lawful [*Rechtens*], i.e. it is not just [*gerecht*] in its existence [*Existenz*]. Instead of the injured party, the injured *universal* now makes its appearance, and it has its distinctive actuality in the court of law. It takes over the prosecution and penalization of crime, and these thereby cease to be the merely *subjective* and contingent retribution of revenge and are transformed into the genuine reconciliation of right with itself, i.e. into *punishment*. Objectively, this reconciliation applies to the *law*, which restores and thereby *actualizes itself as valid* through the cancellation [*Aufheben*] of the crime; and subjectively, it applies to the criminal in that *his law, which is known by him* and is *valid* for him and *for his protection*, is enforced upon him in such a way that he himself finds in it the satisfaction of justice and merely the enactment of what is *proper to him* [*des Seinigen*].

I think we can now see how the defects critics have identified in each of Hegel's arguments can be remedied, since it is clear from the text cited that they are intended to pull together as the objective and subjective aspects of the reconciliation of right which punishment effects. In the first place, we should adopt the contract version as the superior statement of the subjective strand of argument. Then we should add to it a lemma to the effect that the criminal must recognize that his punishment is legitimate *in so far as it procures the restoration of right* – a goal which he himself endorses as appropriate for the law. Thus all citizens accept the validity of the goal of the restoration of rights, not because this is a valuable social function of punishment, but because it is necessary for the protection of the rights which they themselves claim. So the state *must* punish criminals if it is to serve the purpose of protecting rights. This now amounts to a positive reason for the state to punish, and not merely a licence.

Second, viewing the matter from the perspective of the concern to restore the right, this becomes a properly retributive function just as soon as it is realized that the specific institutions which effect the restoration do so in a manner which enlists the rational endorsement of citizens. The transparency which is at the heart of the administration of justice serves to embed the reasoning of the contractor in the institutions which identify, prosecute and punish criminality. The restoration of right is accomplished by social mechanisms which demonstrate to all, honest and criminal citizens alike, the nature of their rights, their concomitant duties and the penalties to be imposed for non-compliance. The institutions make explicit, through their laws, processes and punitive regime, the rights for which persons demand protection.

This knowledge, explicit in the alignment of subjectivity and objectivity, is not available to the criminal in Abstract Right where punishment takes the form of revenge and revenge breeds vendetta (§102). But it *is* available in Civil Society. The restoration of right is achievable wherever the administration of justice is so structured as to make transparent to citizens the rights they may justly claim, the duties they must fulfil, and the penalties they will incur for non-compliance. In Civil Society, the reconciliation of right with right, which is necessitated by the fact of crime, is achieved by the rule of law, serving ends which all citizens endorse as promoting their rights, and dispensed in courts of law which make that endorsement evident to reflective, rational agents.

The hypothetical contract device explicates the structure of practical reason by which all rational agents, criminals included, can be presumed to accept the legitimacy of punishment. By embedding the necessity of the restoration of right within the practical reason of all rational persons, by treating the criminal as a person and by describing how the administration of justice articulates the self-understanding acquired by these practical reasoners, we deflect the outstanding objections. Against all his instincts, but following through on his most convincing arguments, Hegel should have employed a hypothetical contract argument to defend the institution of punishment.

The Measure of Punishment

I mentioned above that retributivism may be a doctrine concerned with the general justifiability of punishment, or a doctrine which fixes the appropriate level or measure of punishment, or both. For Hegel it is both. It is easy to grasp the intuitions which show how retribution works as a measure of appropriate punishment, but hard to state the argument with sufficient precision. Let us attempt this task using Hegel's suggestions as a guide.

The *lex talionis* (Exodus 21: 23–5) is the simplest version: 'life for life, eye for eye, tooth for tooth, hand for hand, foot for foot, burning for burning, wound for wound, stripe for stripe', but there are obvious objections to this which the Old Testament writers knew well, as commentators, if not some fundamentalists, reassure us. The list of strict equivalences soon runs out. It transpires that if a master puts out the eye of a servant or knocks out a tooth, he does not lose his own eye or tooth, but should let the servant (a chattel-slave presumably) go free. Other punishments by contrast look more severe than the crimes. The penalty for bestiality is death, though sheep are a placid breed and do not hold grudges. As Hegel says, 'it is very easy to portray the retributive aspect of punishment [thus construed] as an absurdity . . . one can even imagine the miscreant as one-eyed or toothless' (§101R). What then?

We should abandon the idea of 'specific equality' or exact reciprocity of crime and punishment. Instead we should seek an equality of value between crime and punishment. Equality of value (§101) looks right, but it is easier said than specified. Hegel has already told us that not all crimes are equally serious. The law of Draco (Hang 'em all) and the gangster honour codes which insist that lack of respect is reason for immediate execution fail to acknowledge the difference in seriousness amongst crimes which derive from 'the quantitative extension and qualitative determinations' (§96R) of the infringements of right. Both the crime and the punishment are injuries, and 'as injuries [*Verletzungen*], they are comparable' (§101R).

Hegel has little to say about how judgements of equality are made, how sentences can equate to the criminal's just deserts. This for him is a matter of detail, to be settled at the level of a community's custom and practice, but we can take the matter a little further. One implication of the doctrine of equality of value of respective injury to the victim of crime and the criminal set for punishment is an ordinal principle: the more serious the crime, the more serious the punishment ought to be. If we judge crime A to be a greater evil than crime B, it would be inconsistent for us to punish crime B more seriously. This principle looks trivial, but it is not. If we accept it as a philosophical conclusion, it opens a way to the rejection of consequentialist, specifically utilitarian, accounts of the proper measure of punishment.

The success of policies of deterrence depend upon the strength, frequency and ubiquity of the impulses towards wrongdoing, the likelihood of detection, and the propensity of citizens to take these facts into account in the regulation of their behaviour. Suppose driving at speed is very exciting to many people, is hard to detect, and even harder to deter since offenders (irrationally, let us suppose), discount too heavily the prospect of conviction in their decision-making. We may then need to impose the most severe penalties in order to deter drivers from speeding. We can imagine that a few sentences of ten years in jail or worse might concentrate the minds of otherwise obtuse speeders, and the very great harm to the unfortunate bad examples who are convicted would not outweigh the benefits of increased road safety. On the other hand, the murder of spouses does not attest a widespread proclivity, the chances of detection are very high, and since these crimes tend to occur in the heat of the moment, the chance of any tariff of punishment preventing them is very low. This suggests that strong punishment is unnecessary. The prospect of a couple of years in jail will deter the (few) calculators and why punish heavily those beyond the use of reason? The upshot, assuming that the facts of the matter are as described, is that speeding should be punished more heavily than the murder of a husband or wife.

This example trades on assumed facts, but these scenarios are not implausible. Utilitarians are not entitled to assume that the facts of the matter concerning deterrence will always be consistent with the ordinal version of the principle of equality of injury in respect of crime and punishment. If so, they may endorse a response to the lesser crime with the greater punishment or the greater crime with the lesser punishment as the facts of the matter concerning the utility of outcomes dictate. This possibility does not settle the question as to which party is right – the utilitarian or the retributivist – but it does serve to sharpen our perception of the differences between these approaches to ethical sentencing policy. It is not hard to determine what Hegel's position would be in this grand debate.

At this point the utilitarian will object that the ordinal principle is incomplete, and in principle incompletable. We can agree that murder is more serious than burglary and that burglary is more serious than being drunk and disorderly, but many different tariffs of punishment can meet this ordinal constraint. To many, life imprisonment, a jail sentence and a fine look appropriate, but a tariff of fines of ten sweeties, five sweeties and one sweety, respectively, is equally respectful of the ordering of the offences. How do we fix the right level? How do we equate incomparables? Hegel points out that we do so in other contexts. Contracts generally realize an equality of value between the disparate goods that the contractors bring forward for exchange and in the case of civil suits we do not feel that awards of compensation for injury are irrational on the grounds that cash cannot be equated with, say, the loss of limb caused by a botched operation (§101R). Punishment is not compensation, but compensation teaches us that rational persons can apply canons for assessing equality of value.

How do we find acceptable canons? Hegel is clear that philosophy cannot help. This is the task of the community, specifically that of the legislators and judges who take account of such factors as the incidence of the crime and the danger criminal conduct poses to a society. The more stable and secure a civil society, the less grave the threat or the challenge posed by crime. 'A penal code is therefore primarily a product of its time and of the current condition of civil society' (§218); 'a criminal code cannot be valid for every age' (§218A). We must suppose that the administration of justice will be sensitive to changing conceptions of the gravity of offences in the circumstances in which they are committed. If the processes of law are transparent and publicly reported, and if the reactions of the public are carefully gauged, sentencing policy can be the product of continual fine-tuning. A community may even take into account considerations of deterrence or reform when it decides on 'the *modality* of punishment' (§99R), supposing the value of alternative measures is roughly equal. These proposals look eminently sensible to me.

Revenge and the Limitations of Abstract Right

Abstract Right is abstract in a number of different senses. It should now be clear that one obvious dimension of abstraction concerns the fact that we have been elaborating a conception of normative status (that of the person), an account of the rights that personhood demands (rights to physical integrity, property and contractual exchange), together with an argument to the conclusion that these rights are properly enforceable (by civil judgements and the punishment of criminal violations). Although I have corroborated my interpretation of these arguments (and augmented the detail) by incorporating material from Hegel's account of civil society, the core arguments all abstract from the economic and legal context in which the claiming, exchanging and enforcing rights takes place. It is as though we have been describing a state of nature and outlining the law which is natural to that province.

Hegel believes that such a device can induce clarity in our reflections concerning persons and their rights, but he is equally sure that it is a limitation. The limitation becomes especially clear when we reflect on the possibility of finding agreement on the problems we have just been considering concerning the appropriate measures of punishment. Just punishment requires the sort of social mechanisms which are available in Civil Society, itself an element of the State, but not in the regime of Abstract Right, which is susceptible to a kind of tragedy of innocence. Borrowing an argument from John Locke (1960, §§7–13: 312–17) Hegel suggests that retribution will take the form of revenge, that punishment will inevitably be judged as the exercise of a particular will (§102). The criminal may be punished too harshly, but even if he is not, the contingency which is concomitant to the victim's punitive response will probably lead the criminal to the view that he in turn has become a victim, that his rights demand restoration and vindication, and that this can be accomplished only if he in turn may coerce the coercer. 'Thus revenge . . . becomes part of an infinite progression and is inherited indefinitely from generation to generation' (§102). The persons of Abstract Right correctly see themselves as persons, they claim rights and find that these are generally acknowledged as they recognize the rights of others in turn, they correctly judge that these rights are enforceable by punishment, yet they find themselves unable to agree on a correct measure. They become enmeshed in vendetta.

Their attempts at justice express a subjective interest and take a subjective shape, since in Abstract Right we have abstracted from the actual institutions which alone can confer objectivity on the processes of justice. Subjectivity, conceived in terms of the particularity of the wills of both the punisher and the punished, poisons the pursuit of justice, and the defect cannot be remedied within the sphere of Abstract Right, using only the normative resources of persons, abstractly conceived. But if subjectivity is the problem, this suggests that we investigate subjectivity itself to see whether it, when properly understood, can furnish the resources persons *qua* persons lack. Perhaps we can specify how a will which is particular and subjective can yet will the universal (§103), which is to say can generate principles which command the intersubjective agreement lacking at the final stage of Abstract Right.

In sum, we have an argument which concludes that social norms cannot be a matter solely of individuals' claiming rights. Such rights need to be enforced, but the only measures of enforcement which are available under such a limited normative regime themselves conduce to further violations of right. We need a more capacious understanding of the human subject and its moral agency than is provided in the abstract domain of persons. Following Hegel we have a criticism of Abstract Right and we have an agenda for moving forward: to supplement our understanding of the freely willing self as a person with an understanding of how that self is also a subjective moral agent. This is the transition from Abstract Right to Morality.

Abstract Right: a Brief Review

We have now concluded our discussion of Abstract Right. It represents for Hegel the most primitive and rudimentary normative conception modern humans have of themselves – that of the atomic and discrete person. In the history of human self-understanding, the history of spirit, the knowledge that we are each of us persons has been hard won. So, too, has been our understanding of the implications of this mode of self-conception – that we claim recognition for ourselves and accord recognition to others as the bearers of rights which, further, we recognize must be enforceable by the infliction of just punishment if they are to be actual, if they are truly to enhance our freedom.

Two questions arise, and from the perspective of the liberal who accords prime importance to rights, they are related. The first question concerns the adequacy of Hegel's account of rights. As we noticed above, the rights Hegel delineates, rights to life and bodily integrity, private property and exchange, are a limited set. Hegel mentions other rights of personality, rights to freedom of will, ethical life and religion (§66), which may be denominated rights of conscience, but still the set may be circumscribed as negative claim rights, rights that Nozick has dubbed side constraints. Many modern rights theorists would judge this list insufficient. Positive or welfare rights, rights to the provision of goods and services such as education and health are not mentioned. This is not an oversight. Arguably doctrines of rights had not been elaborated in Hegel's day which extended their remit in this positive direction. More important than this, though, is the thought that such rights typically make demands not on persons severally, but on institutions such as the family, the state or even international agencies. On standard accounts of the right to education, duties are placed on parents and/or municipal authorities to make provision for educational services. As such, they would have no place in Abstract Right, which is the study of interpersonal norms.

A second species of right which Hegel does not consider in Abstract Right is that of political rights. Typically these include freedom of information, speech and discussion, freedom of association, and, most importantly, the right to participate in the making of government policy, a right that Cobbett, writing in 1829, designated 'the right of rights . . . the right of having a share in the making of the laws'.[10] Again, these are not rights which have a place in Abstract Right, since Abstract Right is not a political regime. It has rules and principles but not laws. It is akin to Locke's moralized state of nature. In respect of both positive or welfare rights and political rights, Abstract Right reveals itself to be necessarily incomplete – so long, of course, as one admits such rights into the domain of universal human rights. (In respect of welfare rights, in particular, the issue has been found controversial.)

This incompleteness opens up the second question concerning Abstract Right: How far is the domain of rights which is articulated therein respected and, concerning the missing species of rights, extended in the argument that follows? We can certainly agree with Hegel that Abstract Right is an impoverished conception of social norms, of morality in a general sense, if not for his specific reason that in practice it would be unenforceable. But the insights and principles of Abstract Right are taken up (*aufgehoben*) in the structures of Ethical Life, and they are quickened and given a specific context in Hegel's account of the Family, Civil Society and the State. It is therefore an important issue, from the perspective of the liberal critic, how far Hegel not only accords a secure place to those rights he has defended as integral to personhood, but also makes provision in these ethical domains for those species of rights that are necessarily absent in Abstract Right. We shall see that these are truly vexed questions concerning both the interpretation of Hegel's writings and the evaluation of them.

Chapter 7

Morality 1. Hegel's Philosophy of Action and Moral Psychology: §§105–28

Introduction

If we follow the logic of Hegel's official transition from Abstract Right to Morality, our prime concern will be to examine whether or not we can find, in our study of the phenomena of subjectivity, philosophical resources to determine the proper tariff of punishment to be employed against criminals, supposing that the 'proper tariff' will be agreed by all: criminals, victims, all of their friends, relations, gang members and fellow-travellers, as well as impartial observers. Hegel believes that we are now forced to confront the question of persons' motivation, since it is vengeance that corrodes justice in Abstract Right. The limitation of Abstract Right is revealed in the motivation of those who engage in vendetta, who seek to get their own back or restore the honour of their family, who pursue a private agenda when they should be serving justice. '[T]his constitutes a requirement for a will which, as a particular and *subjective* will, also wills the universal' (§103). So we need to explain how a subjective will

can 'will the universal' in the sense of understanding, adopting and guiding its behaviour in accordance with moral principles which are universally applicable.

Thus the particular problem of the just punishment of criminals disappears from view, to be replaced by a general investigation of the subjective freedom of the moral agent. The investigation is profound and wide-ranging, but we get a clearer view of Hegel's agenda if we identify, as a central feature of it, his scrutiny of the central claims of the ethics of his near-contemporary Kant[1] and those who adopt his ambitions. If Kant (as read by Hegel) is correct, each moral agent expresses her freedom through the employment of her rational will in deliberation about how to behave. As moral subjects, agents have the power to determine (to test or to generate) the principles which ought to govern the conduct of all those persons of good will who are motivated to do their duty.

In ethics Kant's ambition was quite Cartesian. Just as Descartes rejected the claims to knowledge of those who appealed to authority and sought to derive first principles which alone could vindicate the results of modern science, so Kant believed that in matters of morality, too, established authority was defunct.

> Our age is the genuine age of *criticism*, to which everything must submit. *Religion* through its *holiness* and *legislation* through its *majesty* commonly seek to exempt themselves from it. But in this way they excite a just suspicion against themselves, and cannot lay claim to that unfeigned respect that reason grants only to that which has been able to withstand its free and public examination.
>
> (Kant 1998: 100–1 / Axiii)

As written, Hegel may well agree with this passage, but then Hegel's conception of reason was not Kant's. Kant's striking claim may be paraphrased thus: 'If you want to know how to behave, if you are unsure what is the right thing to do, don't ask a priest or a judge or a political superior. Work out for yourself what to do, using those resources of reason which you possess and which are sufficient to the task.' Do we possess such resources? Are they sufficient to the task of dictating where our duty lies? Hegel's final answer to these questions is 'No': at least, not as Kant describes the resources or their application. But a lot of ground has to be covered before we reach this conclusion.

The introductory paragraphs of the Morality chapter are as hard as any that Hegel wrote. How do we distinguish the order of Morality from Abstract Right? One important point of contrast seems to be that in Abstract Right Hegel insists that personal freedom does not concern the *motivation* of the agent who pursues personal security and claims property rights. 'With right in the strict sense [i.e. Abstract Right] it made no difference what my principle or intention was' (§106A).[2] There will always be some story as to why *this* agent took *that* object into their possession, but the details of it, the specification of their desires and inclinations, is irrelevant in point of the justification of the property relation. What is crucial to their ownership of the house, say, is not that they purchased it in order to have comfort and shelter, or to provide a rental income for their retirement, or whatever, but that the objectivity which their will thereby attains attests their freedom. Freedom is afforded through the external perspective that the person has attained who can recognize herself, and see herself recognized, as a bearer of rights. But then the inadequacy of a practice of punishment that degenerates into vendetta reveals that this conception of freedom is impoverished through its inability to comprehend the subjectivity of the agent as a modality of freedom.

In Morality, by contrast, the prime focus is on the motivation of the subject. This makes perfect sense. Grant the central claim of Abstract Right that, in order to be free, persons need to recognize themselves, and to be recognized in turn by others, as possessing the distinctive moral status of rights-bearers: this is clearly an incomplete account of freedom of action. It is hard to think of a philosophical discussion of free agency which does not focus directly on the motivation of the agent. To use the hackneyed example, whether I act freely in walking down the aisle and saying 'Yes, I do' in the marriage ceremony depends in part on such factors as whether the bride's father is behind me holding a shotgun or whether I have been drugged senseless. If I do these things in the belief that otherwise I shall die or if I parrot the words uncomprehendingly, we would judge that I haven't acted freely. The issues are massively complicated and controversial, but it seems clear that my freedom of action is, in some part at least, a function of *why* I act as I do.

In moving towards an investigation of subjectivity as integral to persons' freedom, Hegel is not simply addressing the conclusions of Kant, he is developing his account of freedom in a direction that ensures that he covers the ground of traditional debate concerning freedom of action. I repeat, it is useful to see Kant as the stalking-horse of this chapter, but it is important to see that Hegel's investigation of subjectivity brings him back to the mainstream of philosophical thinking about freedom.

Hegel's introductory remarks on Morality (§§105–14) are bedevilled by jargon. It is fair to say that no philosophical concepts are as confusing as those of subjectivity and objectivity. Great philosophers deploy these concepts with cavalier insouciance, trusting (correctly) that those who follow will work out the detail of their argumentation with the great effort their great contributions deserve. The finest of contemporary philosophers, under-labourers all, will use these terms but be utterly scrupulous in their analysis and employment of them.[3] Hegel, unfortunately, writes as a great philosopher and has turned out to be one, so it behoves his expositors to work out the implications of his use of this terminology at every turn, understanding the variety of meanings that it may encompass. It can't be said that he doesn't attempt to help us. As early as the Introduction to *The Philosophy of Right* he disambiguates these terms (§§25–6) and in §§107–13 we find further analysis. My advice is that we move quickly over this material since the important philosophical ideas will all come out in the wash as we discuss his detailed argumentation.

For the moment, it is sufficient that we understand the focus on subjectivity to encompass matters which concern the mindset of the conscious agent and the features of it which attest his freedom. One must assume straightaway that readers will grasp the philosophical agenda this topic opens up. Do we know our own minds, having transparent and incorrigible access to their contents? What can we know of the minds of others, supposing, correctly, that we do not have the access to them that they, themselves, employ? In *The Philosophy of Right* Hegel finesses philosophical problems of this profundity – the philosophy of objective mind is, after all, the outer reaches of his metaphysics – and concentrates instead on the implications of his general view that mind, though subjective to the conscious subject, must be objective, too.

It must be objective, in the sense that it is a phenomenon available for scrutiny and of which one's investigation must yield truths that others can recognize if it is to be a subject of knowledge at all. So we must be able to distinguish statements which are true and false in respect of subjects' minds. It must be objective in the further sense that subjective mind, if we are to have the knowledge of it that our investigation assumes is possible, must be embodied or actualized in the world that we encounter. As Charles Taylor has emphasized, this is a ground-level proposition of Hegelian metaphysics.[4] Arguably, the requirement that subjective mind have objective standing in both of these respects is a presupposition of any human intercourse.

Hegel proposes that we investigate the subjectivity of the will – how our willing seems to us – and the objectivity of the will – how our will is actualized in the world of public experience – independently. Then we shall see that subjectivity and objectivity are related as two sides of a coin, posited as identical (§109). Subjectivity and objectivity are disclosed as the will is engaged in action, the self-conscious implementation of an end in the public world. Since the public world upon which my actions impact is the world of other agents, likewise pursuing their own goals, agents must seek to understand the agency of others just as they accept that others will take a view on what it is that they themselves are doing. 'The implementation of my end therefore has this identity of my will and the will of others within it – it has a positive refence to the will of others' (§112).

Thus Hegel announces that the domain of subjective will that he seeks to comprehend is that of action. 'The expression of the will as *subjective* or *moral* is *action*' (§113). These are the things we shall need to understand about action if we are understand it as the expression of a free subjective will:

1. How I can identify external happenings in the world as mine, how I determine those events for which I am responsible.
2. How normative judgements are possible, how it is that I determine what I *ought* to do, in the widest sense of 'ought'.

3. How my actions, and the normative judgements which motivate them, bear on the will of other free agents; how far my judgement that I ought to act in such and such a way entails that others ought to act in a similar fashion.

As we shall see, Hegel has good and interesting things to say on all of these questions, but we should not expect to find an exposition which fully matches the ambition of this prospectus.

Purpose and Responsibility

When I act, it is against the background of an external world, a complex state of affairs with its own laws which limit and affect what I can accomplish. This background establishes 'the finitude of the subjective will' (§115). A little knowledge of this background will convince me that although I would like to fly like an eagle, this is not something that I can properly *will* because I know that I can't put it into effect. My intervention [deed; *Tat*] creates an altered state of affairs. If I can truly describe (some aspect of) the altered state of affairs as '*mine*', then I am *responsible* for effecting it (§115). There may be cases of dispute, responsibility may be more or less. If my tup charges the sparkling radiator of the stationary Rolls-Royce causing thousands of pounds' worth of damage, I do well to consult my lawyer and inspect my insurance policy (§114). Most grown-ups have a rough idea of the impact their interventions will have, but the world has its own laws and the consequences of my deeds may surprise me. The farrier in the familiar rhyme would have been surprised to learn that a kingdom was lost as a result of his shoeing the horse with a poor quality nail. '[T]he objective phenomenon [was] *contingent* for [him]' (§117). So, of all the things that happen when I intervene in the world, which of them can be imputed to me (or can I claim) as mine, for which of them can I be judged responsible (or claim responsibility for)?

> It is, however, the right of the will to recognize as its *action* [*Handlung*], and to accept *responsibility* for, only those aspects of its *deed* [*Tat*] which it knew to be presupposed in its end, and which were present in its *purpose*. – I can be made *accountable* for a deed only if *my will was responsible* for it – *the right of knowledge*.
> (§117)[5]

Thus Oedipus was not guilty of parricide because he did not know that the old man he killed was his father (§117A). So far, so conventional. This is the source, well known in law and ethics at least since Aristotle discussed the matter in the *Nicomachean Ethics*, of the doctrine of *mens rea*. A guilty act requires a guilty mind, and Oedipus couldn't have had a guilty mind if he was completely unaware that that (parricide) was what he was committing.

On the other hand, this is only the beginning of wisdom on this topic, since the right of knowledge is not a clown's licence to disown all and any unpleasant consequences on the grounds of ignorance, as we shall see. One question which is opened up by the right of knowledge concerns the range of my responsibility. Of all the things that happen consequent to my intervention in the world, for which am I responsible? Hegel well understands the philosophical problems which this question raises, and briskly discusses a few of them.

He briefly discards two philosophical nostrums which many have taken to have significant moral import. The first of these 'enjoins us to disregard the consequences of our actions' (§118R), presumably requiring agents to focus solely on the nature of the action as disclosed by their subjective will, their motivation. This is a crude and simplified version of a central feature of Kant's ethics, his thought that the only unqualified good is the good will, the only action of moral worth that which is motivated by duty. The second nostrum which Hegel pins down is a bowdlerized version of a central insight of utilitarianism which 'enjoins us to judge actions by their consequences and make the latter the yardstick of what is right and good' (§111R). Both of these views are products of the 'abstract understanding'. (Whenever you come across these terms in Hegel, you should note that they signal contemptuous dismissal.)

Both positions make the same mistake of operating with a simple-minded distinction of action and consequences. Since, as we shall see, there is no sharp distinction to be drawn between action and consequences, since in some measure the consequences give shape to the action and frame its proper description, neither of these familiar positions is tenable in the terms in which they are formulated. Hegel's own position is not crystal clear, but he seems to have this model in mind. First we should think of the agent's intervention as comprising all those things that happen in consequence of the impact of his (physical) bodily movements on the track of events in the world; next, we should narrow down our conception of the agent's action in terms of those consequences of his intervention which he intended should happen. 'These consequences, as the [outward] shape whose soul is the end to which the action is directed, belong to the action as an integral part of it' (§118). This is a familiar thought. We often describe actions in terms of consequences, as when we judge it to be murder when a victim dies of his injuries months after the initial assault. If the victim's death is what the agent sought, his purpose gives a shape to the action which is properly described as murder. The victim's death is an integral part of the action as thus described. Finally, we take stock: we deem all those events which are left over from our subtraction of the action from the whole course of events which follow the impact of our bodily movements upon the world as irrelevant to the judgement of action.

Hegel distinguishes this sort of consequence – which need not be immediate – from another sort which we cannot suppose the agent to have intended, as in the loss of the kingdom for want of the horseshoe nail. Here is a consequence which is so remote as a causal consequence and so alien to the farrier's intention that he can fairly repudiate any responsibility for it other than his featuring as a distant and partial cause. Hegel concludes that 'The will has the right *to accept responsibility* only for the first set of consequences [those that give shape to the action], since they alone were part of its *purpose*' (§118).

Hegel is quite aware that this distinction between two kinds of consequences – those which are integral to the action and those which are utterly contingent – is a forensic minefield. Legal reports yield a multitude of cases where the distinction is difficult to apply with confidence, not least because there is a whole category of cases wherein we judge not that the agent intended the action as described in terms of some evident consequence but that the agent ought to have known that such a consequence was likely and hold him responsible for the action in point of his negligence. Suppose the killer throws a stone at his victim and hits him on the side of his head. The victim dies because unfortunately he has a fragile skull. We are reluctant to call this murder unless we are prepared to judge that this is the kind of consequence that those who assault others should bear in mind, in which case it becomes a sort of murder-by-negligence. '[O]nce the crime has developed more fully, the crime itself is made responsible for them [its further adverse consequences]' (§118R). Hegel later endorses, as a sort of subsidiary principle that should guide our intuitions in such complex cases, the old proverb that 'The stone belongs to the devil when it leaves the hand that threw it' (§119R). This is a hard saying. Mercifully, the judgements of the criminal courts are generally more nuanced.

These sorts of distinction are meat and drink to the philosophy of the criminal law, but they cause difficulties in moral theory, too, under the contemporary heading of 'moral luck'. As Bernard Williams and Thomas Nagle point out, 'moral luck' is a blight on moral theories as different in structure as Kantianism and utilitarianism, since how things (contingently) turn out makes a difference to our judgements about what actions agents are responsible for, and, derivately, how their actions should be appraised (B. Williams 1981; Nagel 1979). Hegel recognizes the problems: 'the criminal stands to benefit if his action has less adverse consequences, just as the good action must accept that it may have no consequences or relatively few' (§118R). The would-be murderer is lucky if there is a nurse on hand to give life-saving first aid to his victim. The philanthropist with infinite good-will may see all her projects fail.

What has emerged from Hegel's preliminary foray into the philosophy of action is the conclusion that the concept of action presupposes the attribution of the subjective will of the agent, since the identification of an action amongst all those changes that are consequent upon an agent's intervention requires that we have knowledge of the agent's purpose. Only then can we demarcate the consequences which give shape to the actions from those consequences which are contingent and extraneous to it. On the side of the agent, he will claim responsibility (or accept its imputation) only in respect of those aspects of his intervention which were encompassed in his purpose in acting. These conclusions open up exactly the right question: how do we attribute purposes to agents, whether the agents in question be ourselves or others? This question Hegel will take up directly in the next section.

Intention

Of all those things that happen when I engage with the world, which am I responsible for? As Hegel puts the matter, it looks as though lots of things happen. As a famous modern example has it: 'I flip the switch, turn on the light, and illuminate the room. Unbeknownst to me I also alert a prowler to the fact that I am home' (Davidson 1980: 4). From Davidson's perspective, it looks as though Hegel is taking the wrong route when he says that 'The external existence [*Dasein*] of an action is a varied set of connections which may be regarded as infinitely divided into *individual units*' (§119), since this suggests that every action construed as a complex physical occurrence is in truth an ensemble of lots of little actions. This has the further implication that the real action, the action for which the agent is responsible, is one or a subset of these – 'the action can be thought of as having *touched only one of these units in the first instance*' (§119). But Hegel turns away from this conception of action, adopting a position which is recognizably akin to that of Davidson himself in modern times. There are not lots of things going on when I flip the switch, turn on the light, and so on; there is only one action which is described truly in a variety of ways.

Which is the appropriate description for purposes of assigning responsibility? Hegel would put this question by asking which universal content is most aptly ascribed. This is not a matter of singling out a component unit amongst the many events that comprise the action. '[T]he determinate character of the action for itself is not an isolated content confined to one external unit, but a *universal* content containing within itself all its various connections' (§119). The action description that is most appropriate for capturing responsibility is that which specifies the subject's purpose in terms of his intention. To amplify and re-employ Davidson's example, if I return home and go through my normal rigmarole, probably the most apt description is that I turn on the light. If on the other hand I am colluding with a burglar who is at work in the apartment facing mine and switch on the light as a pre-arranged signal, 'alerting the burglar' best captures my intention. In both of these cases, differently because the stories are different, I highlight the 'universal aspect' of the deed in terms of my intention.

When I describe an action as one of murder, 'it is not the piece of flesh as an individual entity which is injured, but the life within it' (§119R) that is central (otherwise I might be describing a botched surgical operation). Oddly, Hegel says that one can apply a universal predicate like 'murder' or 'arson' without first having determined whether the action is right or wrong (§119R); this is surely a slip. Prior to having come to such a judgement, all that one could say is that one person killed another or set light to such and such. Whichever form, moralized or not, the action description takes, it succeeds if it captures the agent's intention. This leads Hegel to announce as 'the *right of intention* . . . that the *universal* quality of the action shall have being not only *in itself* [viz.: be true], but shall be *known* by the agent and thus present all along in his subjective will' (§120). Thus when we ascribe responsibility to an agent by describing his action in terms of the intention that captures his purpose, we presume that the agent will agree with this description on the basis of his knowledge of what he was doing.

It follows, of course, that where agents are unaware that their action can be described in the terms we employ for the judgement of it, they are not responsible. 'The right to such insight implies that the *responsibility* of children, imbeciles, lunatics,[6] etc. for their actions is either totally *absent* or diminished' (§120R). I think we should accept this implication as humane and correct, but there is a danger to which Hegel is fully alert. We might put it this way: in insisting that agents are responsible only for what they know themselves to be doing, are we not granting them a privilege which they might employ to exculpate themselves from any blame and consequent punishment? If agents have privileged access to their own intentions,[7] can't they tell us just any story about what it was that they were doing? Imagine the nonsense we might hear: 'I didn't intend to murder her; I was just testing the strength of the hammer.' The strict requirement of agents' knowledge looks as though it may paralyse judgement. Of course, the agent may not be telling the truth, but how can we tell, if the agent's right of intention presupposes a kind of knowledge that is not available to observers?

Hegel is emphatic that this is not so, for a crucial reason that resonates through the argument of the *Philosophy of Right.* Alongside the right of intention, Hegel postulates the curiously named 'right of the *objectivity* of the action'; 'the right of the action to assert itself as known and willed by the agent as a *thinking agent*' (§120). It is important to see how and why this constrains the right of intention. When observers attribute actions to agents, they generally grant the agent a status or 'dignity [*Ehre*] of being a thinking individual and a will' (§120R) – that is a free will rather than a will which is incapable of reflecting on what it is doing. The will which is subjectively free is not free to describe itself in any way it chooses, it cannot ascribe to its agency a universal content that others in the circumstances would not accept. The saying tells us that actions speak louder than words; the rational agent knows that his actions bespeak his intentions to others in accordance with a schema of interpretation (rationality) that is common to all. Thus the agent knows which actions will be imputed to him by others, which action-descriptions they will employ as they impute responsibility to him. He knows these things at the time of action, as he forms his intention and puts it into action. The price of a severe dislocation between the agent's conception of what he is doing, as articulated when he claims his right of intention and publicly discloses his reason for action, and the judgement of others as to what he is really doing, is a charge of unreason, of insanity or the like in the case of adults. So the murderer may tell a crazy story in order to escape blame, but we are unlikely to believe him unless we think he is genuinely crazy – and then he is in a different kind of trouble.

It is the supposition of rationality – the claim of agents to be thinking agents, the imputation of that dignity to them by observers – that establishes the common ground necessary for the right of intention and the right of the objectivity of the action to coincide in attributions of agency. Subjectivity, in the form of the agent's distinctive knowledge of his own intentions, and objectivity, the requirement that this knowledge be available to others, coalesce in the nature of intelligible action. The thinking agent will act in accordance with those intentions which he knows that his actions bespeak to others. Action we might think of as the public language of intention, and as a language, it permits its own special kind of deliberate deception. I might pretend that I love you dearly. I never tell you so, but I act in a way that inclines you to express your gratitude by leaving me a large bequest. I even help you draw up the will. This devious kind of agent deception presupposes that actions generally speak the truth concerning their motivation. It is the abnormal case; like lying, it operates against a background of reliable mutual interpretation.

How do we acquire the knowledge, the rationality, that enables us to project our intentions to others and acquire knowledge, in turn, of what it is that they are doing? What is this schema that self-interpreters and the interpreters of others systematically employ? In a sense we need to read the rest of the *Philosophy of Right* to find out, particularly the detail of Ethical Life. This will disclose, in the philosophical trappings that are necessary for full intelligibility, our characteristic motivations as we interact with each other in the domains of family life, economic activity, legal regulation, co-operative ventures and political activity. It will reveal the norms that govern our behaviour in these different spheres: norms that explicate expedient as well as properly moral agency, that permit judgement as well as understanding of the success and dutifulness of our conduct. But this is the material of later chapters. Is there anything we can say at the moment about the categories of rationality that permit self-understanding and public judgement?

Hegel believes that there is. In the first place, the appropriate description of the action must bear on 'the particular content' which the agent seeks as his end. '[T]his is the soul and determinant of the action' (§121). We must read this as a requirement on free action that the end which the agent pursues is one which he has given himself. Achievement of that end, whatever it may be, will give the agent satisfaction since he has brought about the end which he determined for himself. This amounts to '*subjective freedom* in its more concrete determination, i.e. the *right* of the *subject* to find its *satisfaction* in the action' (§121). Hegel, here, seems to be distinguishing two levels of description as appropriate for capturing the intention of the agent. The first level of description, the universal, applies a predicate to the complex event which fixes the nature of the action: what it was that the agent did. In different cases, the answer might be murder or arson. But such answers do not 'constitute my positive content as a subject. If someone has perpetrated crimes of this kind we ask why he committed them' (§121A). So as well as asking what he did (murder, charitable donation), we can also ask why he did it (revenge, generosity). This gives us the second, particular, level of description of the action. This level will describe the action in terms of the desires that it satisfies and the passions that it gratifies. These levels of description may be related systematically, as means to ends. Thus murder is the way I satisfy my desire for revenge, a charitable donation is the way I satisfy my desire to do good to another. It is always possible that these ends may be further construed as means to still more precise ends, which may be elicited by repeating the why-questions: Why do I have a desire for revenge? Why do I wish to do good to another person? Hegel suggests, improbably but in a way that may be recognizable to the exasperated parents of young children, that there may be 'an infinite progression' of such means–end relations (§122).

Can we say anything systematic about the ends which persons select as the particular content of their actions? Two things: the first is an entirely formal point. Nothing can count as an agent's end unless he is active in its pursuit. '[T]he subject actively commits itself to whatever it is to regard and promote as its end' (§123).[8] This formal point does not amount to a trivial truth; it counts *against* someone's affirmation of an end if they have made no effort at all to accomplish it. The second point is more philosophically potent (as well as controversial). Hegel insists that the determinate content of an action can always be specified in terms of the 'natural subjective existence [*Dasein*]' of the agent, which is to say 'its needs, inclinations, passions, opinions, fancies etc. The satisfaction of this content is *welfare* or *happiness*' (§123).

We shall discuss the credentials of this view shortly. For the moment, let us follow Hegel's discussion of its implications, for Hegel is certain that his analysis of the concept of action is already sufficiently powerful to have refuted one of Kant's most distinctive doctrines. Section 124 commences with a ringing declaration:

> Since the *subjective* satisfaction of the individual himself (including his recognition in the shape of honour and fame) is also to be found in the implementation of ends *which are valid in and for themselves* [Knox: 'ends of absolute worth'], it is an empty assertion of the abstract understanding to require that only

an end of this [latter][9] kind shall appear willed and attained, and likewise to take the view that, in volition, objective and subjective ends are mutually exclusive.

We need to understand the target of Hegel's attack, recalling the dismissive connotations of the phrase 'empty assertion [Knox: "dogmatism"] of the abstract understanding'.

In the *Groundwork of the Metaphysics of Morals*, Kant discusses the example of the shopkeeper who deals honestly with his customers (GMM: 53 / Ak. 4: 397–8) A proper judgement of the moral worth of the shopkeeper's actions – not even children are short-changed or overcharged – requires that we know not only the nature of his actions (fair dealing) but also the wherefore of it. He may give his customers good measure because he judges that, if he does not, sooner or later he will be found out as a cheat and his business will vanish. The prudent shopkeeper deals fairly with his customers but his action is of no moral worth because its motivation is good business – enlightened self-interest. Perhaps the honest shopkeeper loves his neighbours; born and brought up amongst them, blessed with the sentiments of *caritas*, fellow-feeling and neighbourly concern, he finds that these quite disable him from fiddling to his own advantage. Bless this innocent soul, but if his motivation were the expression of sentiments bred in him, if his honesty and decency were his natural or nurtured response to his neighbours, again his actions would be of no moral worth. (Basically, because, as expressions of his unreflective, kindly nature, they are not free.) By contrast, the shopkeeper who has worked out that he can successfully diddle his neighbours but doesn't, who has worked out what duty requires of him when the opportunity of self-interest (or favour) tempts him, and who follows these stern grounds – that is your honest man. That is the shopkeeper whose actions are of true moral worth.

Kant's harsh doctrine, much mollified by sympathetic readers (and much weakened as a contribution to philosophy in the process) is intuitively correct when it contrasts the motives of morality and self-interest – and intuitively incorrect when it derogates those actions of common decency which are the habitual response of good moral citizens who cannot bring themselves to deal dishonestly with their neighbours. Be that as it may, Hegel chooses to tackle it on the strong ground. Suppose I decide to risk my life to save another, knowing that if I succeed and live to tell the tale I shall be honoured for it, famous maybe if my action is conspicuous and, in the silly season, well reported. Suppose I know I shall feel pleased with myself, as well as receiving the benefits(?) of celebrity for doing well. Does this mean that my action is the less praiseworthy? Hegel (as opposed to Kant, on this reading) says 'No'.

Hegel's view has the merits of honest complexity over theoretical simplicity. A careful reading of the text of Kant's *Groundwork* reveals that Kant is uncomfortable with cases where agents have mixed motives. The fact that the shopkeeper stands to benefit from honest dealing precludes us from giving credit to him and assigning moral worth to his action.[10] Kant's distinction of types of motive (self-interest, inclination and duty) best serves his view that true moral worth attaches only to actions done from duty when self-interest and/or inclination pull in one direction whilst duty pulls in the other. It is in my interests to promote my daughter to a better-paid position. My love for her would prompt me to promote her even if it were not. Nonetheless, as a public servant, my duty is to appoint the best candidate for the job. When I appoint the best candidate instead of my daughter, it is evident that my action has moral worth since it so conspicuously goes against both my own interests and my inclinations. This conception of duty 'produces a view of morality as a perennial and hostile struggle against one's own satisfaction, as in the injunction: "do with repugnance what duty commands"' (§124R).[11] In modern times, this dour perspective on morality is best captured in Ogden Nash's 'Kind of an Ode to Duty':

> O Duty,
> Why hast thou not the visage of a sweetie or a cutie?
> . . .
> O Duty, Duty!
> How noble a man should I be hadst thou the visage of a
>   sweetie or a cutie!
> Wert thou but houri instead of hag
> Then would my halo be in the bag!

(Nash 1985: 141)

I think it is fair to say that Kant's discussion invites this reading since he believes that there is always something suspect about actions which are in conformity with duty, yet promote the agent's interests or serve his inclinations. '[T]hough much may be done *in conformity with* what *duty* commands, still it is always doubtful whether it is really done *from duty* and therefore has moral worth' (GMM: 61 / Ak. 4: 406). Kant's problem arises because so many actions which are *in conformity with* duty are suspect in these ways: either in the agent's interests or in service of his inclinations. For Hegel, this dilemma is old-fashioned. It rests on the analytic psychology of the Enlightenment that would attribute a distinctive faculty of the mind to each distinct kind of motivation. It presupposes a model of the mind wherein kinds of motivation struggle for supremacy. Where Kant seeks to recognize supremacy amongst competitors with moral worth as the prize when duty wins out, Hegel looks for accord and harmony. What could be better than that our self-interest, our inclinations, and our knowledge of our duty all pull in the same direction? The familiar condition of mixed motives that generates (often insoluble) puzzles for Kant – What was the agent's real motive? Given the strength of self-deception, how can I know that I am doing the right thing? How can I judge the actions of others? – is meat and drink for Hegel – 'What the subject *is, is the series of its actions*' (§124).

Kant's classification of motives is suspect because it opens up a range of questions that cannot be answered since it divorces the subjective and objective aspects of action. It opens up the possibility of a radical distinction between agents' real (but concealed) motives and their ostensive (but self-deceiving) reasons. The *reductio ad absurdum* statement of Kant's position is his view that 'it is absolutely impossible by means of experience to make out with complete certainty a single case in which the maxim of an action otherwise in accordance with duty rested simply on moral grounds and on the representation of one's duty' (GMM: 61 / Ak. 4: 407). If we grant, as Kant concedes, that there is always *some* reason for aligning the dutiful action with the self-interest of the agent, this altogether debars us from moral judgement in cases where action is in conformity with duty.

Why should Kant worry so much that otherwise dutiful acts might be in the interests of the agent or might be the response of a loving or generous person? Why does he think that we should be suspicious or withold our judgement as to the moral worth of such an action? Why does the coincidence of self-interest or inclination taint the moral worth of the action upon which these motives converge? The answer must lie in his conviction that such actions are (or, to read him sympathetically, may be) heteronymous – which is to say, essentially unfree. Hegel has no such grounds for worry. As we saw in the Introduction and as I shall explain in what follows, there must always be some conative element in human activity.

Free agency, for Hegel, is not a matter of rejecting desires, acting against them and actively frustrating them, nor a matter of their being phenomenologically eclipsed, or ignored, or abstracted from that aspect of human nature which is subject to natural, causal laws. They do not represent the other, base side of human nature or even the gracious side of human nature which has been bestowed, in step-motherly fashion, to some persons but not others. They represent the raw material of freedom, the natural will which is freedom-in-itself. Freedom in-and-for-itself requires that such natural tendencies be, not absent, but in the control of the moral agent. If we run down the lower slopes of a mountain, desperate for a pint of beer and determined to get to the pub before it closes, we don't need to worry that our actions are unfree because we are caused to have a beer, or necessitated to celebrate our good day out with our friends. This isn't the animal or addicted side of our nature getting the better of us and forcing us into the bar. Isn't everyone agreed that this is the best thing to do?

We should conclude that Kant's theory of moral motivation gives him severe problems concerning the appraisal of actions. Hegel goes further. He believes that it also encourages an iniquitous propensity to attribute self-serving motives to the best of actions. Take a common or garden example: I see an old lady needing assistance to cross the street. It is one of the great truisms of the moral life that if I help her across I shall be pleased with myself for helping her. In fact, it is a foolproof way of enhancing my self-esteem and I know this well. (We all know this – but if you doubt it, try it out: do someone a good turn.) I find, as I could have predicted, that when I have safely delivered her across the road, I feel all the better for being able to pat myself on the back. My having done a good deed gives me great pleasure, and the more unusual my good deed, the greater the pleasure I will derive from the remembrance of it. None of this should suggest that I help the old lady *in order to* gain the satisfaction I know I will derive from doing a good deed. That imputation is characteristic of a snide 'valet psychology' which debunks even the finest efforts of great men as the pursuit of power, honour and fame: 'since this particular aspect is a consequence [of the individual's action], it is also supposed *for this reason* to have been the end, and indeed even the sole end in view' (§124R). Hegel is surely right here. Suppose I find that I have found great satisfaction in helping others and decide I want more of it, seeking out folks in desperate straits who will benefit from my assistance. 'Oh good!' I exclaim when I find another old lady having trouble crossing a street, 'This is another opportunity for me to experience that unique pleasure which I gain from doing good works.' If this is how I think, I am a very odd bird indeed. I hesitate to diagnose a contradiction in such a thought, but I cannot see how my sense that I am engaged in good works can survive my explicit engagement in them as a source of pleasure. Of course people often rationalize their work in soup kitchens and the like by saying that the work gives them a great deal of satisfaction, but for most of them this is undue modesty. Kant is suspicious of ostensibly good deeds:

> [M]ost of our actions are in conformity with duty, but if we look more closely at the intentions and aspirations in them we everywhere come across the dear self, which is always turning up; and it is on this that their purpose is based, not on the strict command of duty, which would often require self-denial.
>
> (GMM: 62 / Ak. 4: 408)

Hegel believes that such a view is the product of philosophical error, rather than the reasonable conclusion of the elderly, cool observer who is shrewd in judgement and acute in observation.

But if we concede, as we should, that Hegel is right, what remains of his thought that the '*subjective* satisfaction of the individual himself' is always to be found in the implementation of even the noblest ends? I read this, controversially I suspect, as a Humean point, reminding us that in the explanation of action something of the nature of desire, need, inclination or passion — in modern terms a pro-attitude

– must always be present if the action is to be intelligible. To insist on this is not to subscribe to egoism, since such a view says nothing about the content of the pro-attitude. I may be motivated by love (or hate); I may desire the well-being of my beloved (or the downfall of my enemy). If my action is successful, I shall be satisfied however its content is specified. The mistake is to infer that, since all my actions are motivated by desire, say, and since the achievement of my desired ends brings me satisfaction, all my actions are motivated by the desire for my own satisfaction. This, I propose, is the tidiest reading of the texts, and it brings out the specific character of Hegel's dispute with Kant over the question of moral motivation. Further, if my desires are well formed, ordered and controlled in light of my reflections on how I ought to behave, the fact that desire is present in the aetiology of action should not incline us to judge that the action is unfree – heteronymous in Kant's terms. I act freely when the desires and passions that drive me to action are within my autonomous control.

There is one final implication of Hegel's account of action that we should review before we move on. In modern times, dispute has raged over the proper way to characterize the relation between actions and the reasons for them. We explain actions in terms of reasons, but are reasons causes? Is the explanation of actions in terms of reasons causal explanation, or is it a distinctive kind of explanation, rational explanation, say? Charles Taylor distinguishes two different conceptions of action. The first, causal, theory of action sees actions as physical events, most often bodily movements, brought about by psychological causes, primarily intentions – these latter conceived as a combination of desires, broadly construed, and beliefs. The second conception of action, the qualitative conception of action, 'involves a clear negation of the first: we cannot understand action in terms of the notion of undiscriminated event and a particular kind of cause' (C. Taylor 1985b: 78). On the first conception, reasons are causes. On the second conception they are not; action and intention are not discriminable as separately identifiable events, they are, in Taylor's words, 'ontologically inseparable'. 'Actions are in a sense inhabited by the purposes which direct them' (1985b: 78). On Taylor's reading, 'Hegel is clearly a proponent of the second qualitative conception of action' (1985b: 80).

I think it would be anachronistic to investigate Hegel's philosophy of mind and action on the assumption that he was making a contribution to the actions–reasons–causes debate, not least because this debate is in turn entangled in other philosophical disputes concerning physicalism and determinism. On the other hand, the questions framed by this debate do enable us to gain a sharper picture of Hegel's position. At first glance it might look as though Taylor is mistaken. Hegel describes the particular end of the agent, an end to be characterized in terms of the agent's 'natural subjective existence' (§123), his desires, needs, inclinations and so on, as 'the soul and determinant of the action' (§121). Desires are no less potent for having been selected in a process of resolution (§§12–13), and if a given desire motivates an action, that action is determined by the desire. Some will object to this reading as a cavalier misappropriation of the notion of determination (das Bestimmen and its cognates), which has so many varied and contextually relative meanings. I accept the difficulties, but in The System of Logic Hegel is quite clear that the language of causality is perfectly appropriate in its application to action: 'The cause [die Ursache] of an action is the inner disposition in an active subject, and this is the same content and worth as the outer existence which it acquires through the deed' (SL: 561 / SW 4: 706).

On the other hand, Taylor cleverly implies that the crucial issue is the 'ontological separability' of the intention and the action. As I read Hegel, these elements seem at first sight to be independent. The agent has a subjective mindset composed of dispositions, desires, inclinations, passions, opinions, fancies and so on – 'a multitude of varied drives, each of which is mine in general along with others' (§12). This necessitates resolution, but resolution between desires which cannot be satisfied simultaneously does not eliminate the drives which go unexpressed. It is easy to see how a particular passion, against which the agent struggles for all of his life, might never issue in action. Such a passion might always be inhibited in its expression, yet the story of that agent's (mental) life would be incomplete if it recorded just those dispositions which turned out to motivate his actions. Some paedophile schoolteachers do no harm. Their sexual desires, though potent, are forever inhibited by their sense of duty, and so they come into no closer contact with the children in their charge than the supervision of under-14 cricket matches.

But desires which are never selected are not intentions, which is not to say that all intentional action succeeds. The crucial connection is that between intention and action. When Hegel describes intentions as 'the soul' of the action, he does imply that the action cannot be identified independently of our knowledge of the intention which the action expresses. A complex event has taken place and this event will have numberless consequences as the world takes a different track to that which it would have taken without the intervention. But unless we know the intention of the agent, whether the agent be oneself or another, we have no means of characterizing the action. This is not merely the logical point that events can be described in terms of their causes or effects, as I might describe my alerting the prowler as my switching on the light or describe switching on the light as my alerting the prowler. Hegel's point is stronger. The nature of an action consists in part in its being the putting into effect of an intention. In Taylor's terms, the intention and the action are ontologically inseparable.

At least since Hume, many have insisted that cause and effect must be distinct existences. If this condition holds, then Hegel cannot believe that reasons for action, as capturing intentions, are the causes of actions. The matter is made more complicated still because Hegel does not accept this condition on causal relations – and this is the major reason why it is anachronistic to see Hegel as contributing to the modern debate. He does *not* believe that causal relations hold between 'two several independent existences' (EL §153). That is 'the common acceptation of the causal relation' and the common acceptation is mistaken. He believes, for a variety of reasons, some good, some bad, that there is an identity of cause and effect.[12] This, basically, is why he has free licence to use the language of cause and effect when discussing the relation of intention to action and yet also maintain that the intention is an integral, non-separable element of the action.

Welfare

I feel satisfaction when my actions succeed in meeting my needs, fulfilling my desires, expressing my inclinations. Such pleasing conditions amount to '*welfare* or *happiness*' (§123). We already know that it is a mark of maturity when individuals can reflect on their competing desires and order them from a perspective of maximizing satisfaction overall (§20). This is the pursuit of happiness and it is only made possible by a proper education that cultivates the capacity to distance oneself from one's drives and evaluate them as it were externally. Happiness is not an intrinsic value for Hegel; it becomes a value, and is important to us, because only a free agent can achieve it. It is a by-product of what is truly valuable, that is, freedom.

Hegel next tells us that

> Subjectivity, with its *particular* content of *welfare*, is reflected into itself and infinite, and consequently also has reference to the universal, to the will which has being in itself. This [universal] moment, initially posited within this particularity itself, includes *the welfare of others* – or in its complete, but wholly empty determination, the welfare of *all*.
>
> (§125)

What is the argument here? I take it that the conclusion is something like this: subjects who have a concern for their own welfare also have a concern for the welfare of others, indeed, the welfare of all. An argument of this form is the Holy Grail of utilitarians since it takes us from premises that are weak, attesting agents' concern for their own well-being, to a conclusion that is strong, that they thereby have a concern for the well-being of all. There are two ways of filling the gaps in Hegel's argument. The first I shall call the strategic reading and this points forward to Hegel's discussion of Civil Society. In the economic world of Civil Society we begin with persons who are pursuing their own particular ends. (More precisely, we begin with persons – male heads of families, most likely – who are seeking to promote the well-being of themselves and their dependants.) The mechanisms of Civil Society, which Hegel describes in great detail, entail that those who engage in such selfish pursuits find their interests enmeshed with those of others as patterns of co-operation develop. 'Thus the subsistence and welfare of the individual and his rightful existence are interwoven with, and grounded on, the subsistence, welfare, and rights of all' (§183). Strategically, the worker can attain his particular ends most effectively within a system that equally procures the ends of others. In pursuing his own ends, he is contributing to the well-being of others. Further, as the individual becomes enmeshed in projects which advance his particular ends, he loses that sharp sense of particularity which motivated his initial activities. He associates with others and takes on the social perspective of the association; his self-interest becomes absorbed in the interest of the collective.

Hegel could have been anticipating the results of his later analysis of the mechanisms of Civil Society, but I don't think he was (cf. Siep 1983: 140–1, 147–9). Otherwise he would have no reason to describe the welfare of all as a 'wholly empty' end. In any event, Civil Society does not procure the welfare of all. It secures the welfare of its members only. The argument still needs filling out. I think we should take a conceptual route, made familiar in the nineteenth century by Mill (on some charitable readings of his 'proof' of the principle of utility (Mill 1910: ch. 4), and Sidgwick (Sidgwick 1907: 380–2), and more recently by Thomas Nagel (Nagel 1970: 90–124)) . The argument runs as follows: suppose that the egoist tells us that his own happiness is a value and that value is promoted by his pursuing it. If this is a value that we are expected to recognize, that can only be because his happiness is an objective value. But then his happiness has value not because it is his, but because happiness *per se* has value. If this is true, then the happiness of others, indeed the happiness of all, is a value, too. The upshot is that one cannot take one's own happiness to be an objective value, without according value to the happiness of all others.

Is this the argument that Hegel employs? It would certainly serve his need, but that is not good enough evidence to attribute it to him. Against such an attribution is his statement at §122 that the 'particular aspect gives the action its subjective *value* and *interest* for me'. But this should not settle the matter since it does not rule out the possibility that what has subjective value has objective value as well. This latter thought is prompted by Hegel's further claim (§123) that happiness has both a particular determination, in its source for the individual, and a 'universal aspect – the ends of finitude in general'. When Hegel tells us in §125 that subjectivity which reflects upon its nature 'also has refence to the universal', I think he is telling us that we can't value the satisfaction of our own interests without accepting that it is the satisfaction of interests quite generally that has value. This is how the universal (objective) value of happiness is 'posited within this particularity itself'. What we don't know is what the value of happiness consists in for all other people, since we don't know which states of affairs would count as satisfying their desires. That is why the determination 'welfare of all' is empty. This is a speculative reading, but it has the virtue of some (albeit sketchy) textual support and considerable plausibility.

We feel satisfaction, gain welfare or happiness, whatever the particular content of our ends. I have discussed this already in the case of noble ends, the sorts of ends we recognize as our duty. But the same is true of base ends. The ends of particularity may or may not conform with moral principles which have universal validity (§125). It is likely that a spiteful action will not conform with duty, but it is always possible that a good-hearted intention likewise goes wrong. I should not lend a crowbar to a burglar nor sympathize with a noble-hearted terrorist.[13]

The 'right of *subjective freedom*' requires that the particularity of subjects be respected as they work out for themselves a lifelong itinerary that will give them satisfaction. They may get things wrong, but their particularity cannot be discounted. For Hegel, this 'is the pivotal and focal point in the difference between *antiquity* and the *modern* age' (§124R). The right of subjective freedom establishes the value, to the agent who undertakes them, of the projects to which he commits himself. The totality of the particular interests that comprise the natural will of the subject is that subject's life. If the subject's life is threatened, he may claim a right of necessity against the rightful property of someone else (§127). In like manner, creditors should accept the benefit of competence, recognizing that debtors cannot be expected to surrender their tools or their clothes, whatever is the wherewithal of minimum support in their accustomed station in society. Life (and a decently commodious living) creates its own rights which may come into conflict with the norms of Abstract Right, with rights to private property and rights established by contracts. If I am starving and can survive only by stealing the loaf of bread from the market stall, that should not be treated as common theft. If I would be destitute were my creditors to take from me the necessities of personal support, I would be right to keep hold of them.

Such hard cases demonstrate the importance of both right and welfare and show how these may give rise to competing claims which need to be systematically resolved. They ground the necessity of a theory of the good and an exploration of the possibility of our knowledge of it, that is, conscience. We shall follow Hegel's discussion of this project in the next chapter.

Chapter 8

Morality 2. The Good: §§129–41

Thus far Hegel has assembled a variety of elements as
integral to our practices of moral judgement. Thinking
of ourselves as persons, we claim and recognize rights.
Taking ourselves to be moral subjects, we insist that
our actions be attributable to us in the light of our intentions and we pursue the well-being that accrues to us
as our projects are accomplished to our satisfaction.
Personal freedom is achieved in the domain of abstract
right. Morality as so far specified is a domain of subjective freedom. Freedom in either domain is an individual
achievement, the province of a particular will, though
that will is constrained by the recognition of other
persons as bearers of rights and other moral subjects as
entitled to welfare. If the good were entirely a matter
of respect for the claims of oneself and others to rights
and welfare, the concept of the will (the articulation of
the demands of freedom) would be exhausted by the
content of the moral imperatives established within
these individualistic domains. The good would be
entirely a matter of individuals working out what was

191

demanded of them in respect of claims of right and (interpersonal) welfare. The *good*, 'as the unity of the *concept* of the will and the *particular* will' (§129), would simply(?) be a matter of working out what rights and welfare dictate.

But we have seen that the imperatives of these different ethical domains may conflict. The imperative of right (assert rights and respect rights claims) may, in specific circumstances, conflict with the demands of welfare (preserve life, serve dire need). We can work out what is required if we are to abide by the moral rules which respect for rights enjoins, but this is incompatible, in circumstances where the right of distress is invoked, with the demands of welfare. We can, and must, insist that the good is '*realized freedom, the absolute and ulti-mate end of the world*' (§129) but we cannot say what the good is, we cannot determine with the resources at our disposal what freedom requires when norms conflict.

At this point, Hegel reminds us of a crux of contemporary normative ethics: 'welfare is not a good without *right*' (§130). To employ hackneyed examples, much used in discussions of utilitari-anism: if welfare demands that the rights of the innocent be sacrificed, welfare may require too much. We should not hang a plausible but innocent culprit in order to prevent a rampaging mob wreaking havoc. We should not take the body parts of a healthy person to ensure that five needy patients survive. But if these intuitions look secure, we should also consider that 'right is not the good without welfare (*fiat justitia* should not have *pereat mundus* as its consequence)' (§130). There may turn out to be circumstances wherein it is necessary that the rights of an individual be violated in order that some massively catastrophic evil be averted. The practice of constraining rights is familiar in wartime as politicians spout the demands of the national interest, but even the strongest advocate of rights must be stumped by the (thankfully – so far, so good – hypothetical) example of the inno-cent who must be killed in order to prevent terrorists detonating a nuclear weapon in the middle of a city.[1] Hegel is right. Claims of right may conflict with the demands of welfare. Examples show that neither is decisive. To work out what is good we need a moral theory which advances beyond the claims of either to moral hegemony. In his terms, we need a theory of the good.

The Right of the Subjective Will

What can we say of such a theory? We have some formal apparatus available. We can say, as a matter of abstract principle, that if something is good the subjective will ought to pursue it as an end. The good is normative and motivating, determining how agents *ought* to conduct themselves. Next, we should recognize that the good does not characterize a state of affairs that may come about quite independently of the activity of agents. 'It is only in the subjective will that the good for its part has the means of entering actuality' (§131). These formal conditions look trivial, but from them, together with the rights of intention and objectivity introduced in §120, Hegel derives a principle of the highest importance:

> The *right of the subjective will* is that whatever it is to recognize as valid should be *perceived* by it as *good*, and that it should be held responsible for an action – as its aim translated into external objectivity – as right or wrong, good or evil, legal or illegal, according to its cognizance [*Kenntnis*] of the value which that action has in this objectivity.
>
> (§132)

Assessment of the implications of this right for the argument of the *Philosophy of Right* will be crucial to our judgement of the success or failure of Hegel's project, so we should subject it to the closest scrutiny. The first clause must be understood as the ground rule of modern ethical liberalism. Its importance can be explained in terms of what it denies: no rule of conduct can be valid if subjects cannot perceive it as conducive to or constituent of the good. Read in this fashion, the principle denies any claim to moral authority made, for example, by church or state. Neither priests nor princes have established authority independently of the powers of subjects to investigate and endorse such claims to authority, and, in consequence, such rules as these would-be authorities might promulgate. For Hegel, as for Kant, this assertion of subjective right is the decisive shift that ethics has taken in the modern age.

The principle might be glossed as 'no-one can just *tell* me what to do' and immediately we see its danger. Does it offer a licence to the bloody-minded moral renegade to fix for himself the rules by which he is to abide? Does the right of the moral will entail an extreme moral subjectivism wherein what is right is whatever the subject chooses as right? Hegel insists that it does not (and we shall encounter his criticisms of these positions later). Just as the right of intention is qualified by the right of objectivity, so the right of the subjective will is qualified by what Hegel calls 'the right of the rational' (§132R). The good, however its content is spelled out, will be articulated as a set of substantive moral principles which determine how the subject must act. Such principles, again following Kant, will be universal in form. It must be possible for everyone to act in accordance with them; if they bind one person, they bind all. Hence we have to employ our rationality and *work out* what the good requires of us. '[T]he good therefore exists without exception only *in thought* and *through thought*' (§132R), which is to say that the good is a rational demand on moral subjects.

Once again, this enables Hegel to take a swipe at the targets of the Preface, those who insist that doing the right thing is a matter of following the heart, of expressing natural, uncorrupted feelings. '[T]he assertion . . . that thought is harmful to the good will, and other similar notions [*Vorstellungen*: "nostrums" probably catches Hegel's tone in this passage], deprive[s] the spirit both of intellectual and of all ethical worth and dignity. – The right to recognize nothing that I do not perceive as rational is the highest right of the subject' (§132R). But of course I can't *choose* which moral demands are rational. Rationality is a constraint which my reflections on the good must respect. As I think through what is demanded of me in the name of the good, as I must, I may get things right, but I also have the capacity to get things wrong. '[I]nsight is equally capable of being *true* and of being mere *opinion* and *error*'. And this remains the case however scrupulous I am in insisting that 'an obligation should be based on good reasons'. Whatever set of constraints I may impose on my deliberations in order to secure that my judgement of what is good is properly rational 'in no way detracts from the right of objectivity' (§132R).

This is a hard conclusion to accept. On the one hand, Hegel tells us that nothing is good unless it can be disclosed as rationally compelling. In principle, there must be some story available which will convince us that a moral demand is grounded in reason. On the other hand, the possibility that we might get it wrong, despite a decent upbringing and our best efforts at finding a rationale for what we judge the right thing to do, means that we must defer to what is generally regarded as the best thing to do, independently of our reflections on the topic. In respect of action generally, we must 'conform to what is *recognized as valid*' (§132) in our social world. In respect of the demands of the state, we must conform to the letter of the law. So long as the laws are clear and publicly stated, we cannot err in our judgement of what we ought to do.

In which case, we should ask exactly what the right of the subjective will amounts to. What exercise of thought does it require? What is needed for the agent to perceive a course of action as good other than the observation that others will judge it to be good, or that it is required or not forbidden by the law of the land? Suppose a child is well educated in the laws and customs of her community and mindlessly, habitually, conforms with its rules. Does this count as sufficient insight for us to judge that her actions are the product of her exercise of the right of the subjective will? If it does, it is hard to see how Hegel can effectively contrast the uninhibited response of the feeling heart with the unexamined life of the habitual conformist. Both act unreflectively.

At this point, and to anticipate a question we shall ponder in later chapters, Hegel might respond that rationality is guaranteed by the institutions of ethical life. If the structures of domesticity, economic, legal and civic order, and the political constitution of the state, are rational, then the demands made by these institutions are also rational. Hence conformity, however mindless, amounts to rational behaviour. But this response is too quick. Rationality surely demands that the subjective will understands and endorses the claim that the objective ethical life of the community is a valid set of social norms. Ethical life must pass inspection by the rational enquirer before its demands can be recognized as valid. Hegel is surely right to stress our fallibility of judgement in specific cases, but rationality also demands that the enquirer accept that, in principle, before an enquiry is complete, the demands of a specific form of ethical life may be wrong. We shall have more to say on this topic later, but at the moment it looks as though Hegel has debarred this possibility in the modern world.

Suppose, what is false, that Hegel has described the complete set of rational norms in his description of ethical life. One question is still on the table. The description he gives us of ethical life is the product of a philosophical exploration of rationality in the social life of the present. Hegel, the philosopher, and those who follow his writings and accept his conclusions, are the guardians of rationality. Suppose the citizen is not mindless, suppose she judges that the institutions of ethical life are probably for the best – the nuclear family is the best way to bring up children, the regulated free market is the best way to run an economy, the best constitution is monarchical, and so on – how deep should this understanding run if her endorsement of it is to be judged appropriately reflective? I suggested that mindless conformity to the demands of the rational state does not amount to rational behaviour, but it would be equally absurd to require that rationality demands a full understanding of the argument of the *Philosophy of Right*, that the right of the subjective will can be exercised only by those who have a full philosophical comprehension of how freedom is realized in the rational state. Between the two implausible extremes, there is a lot of controversial ground.

The second element of the right of the subjective will concerns the imputation of responsibility. Again, as Hegel insisted in §120, our responsibility for an action requires that we know what we shall be taken to be doing. The right of intention was the right not to be assigned responsibility for an action under a description of which the agent is ignorant. The right of the subjective will correspondingly excuses 'children, imbeciles and lunatics' (§132R) from responsibility for their deeds. Hegel is chary of being more specific than this; he is reluctant to credit lesser conditions as grounds of excuse, since valid excuses derogate severely from human dignity. In insisting that we should bring to questions of culpability the assumption that criminals have full knowledge of the rights and wrongs, legality or illegality, of the types of action available to them, he once again lowers the reflective threshold for attribution of an exercise of the right of the subjective will. It is enough, he suggests, that we suppose the agent to have the nature of an intelligent being for him to be deemed responsible, although on the occasion of his acting he may have no clear idea of the wrongfulness of what he is doing.

It is natural to judge, from Hegel's discussion of the right of the subjective will, that he takes away with the left hand the moral stature he concedes with the right. It is one of the hardest tasks in the reading of the *Philosophy of Right* to establish the precise content of the right of the subjective will. Following from a judgement on this, one is also forced to enquire about its standing in the argument that follows. Does it represent a severe constraint on ethical principles – that agents must be shown to have a clear perception of the validity of the moral demands made of them – or does Hegel take this to be the default position? If it is a significant constraint on the rules of ethical life, does Hegel himself respect it when he describes the operative rules? We shall try to keep these questions in focus when we discuss the detail of ethical life.

Formal Aspects of the Good

Hegel's assertion of the right of the subjective will, however interpreted, establishes a further formal condition on the good – that it be perceivable before a norm is judged to be valid. Suppose a norm is perceivably constituent or productive of the good. As we saw earlier this is not merely a matter of the subject having knowledge of what is good; the good in this case is 'the *essential* character of the subject's will, which thus has an unqualified *obligation* in this connection' (§133). By this Hegel means to remind us of the connectedness of theoretical and practical reason. We recognize the fact of the good not merely as motivating but as furnishing us with an unqualified obligation, an obligation which we must take to be binding regardless of other considerations which might motivate us to act otherwise. Competing moral considerations, as in the case of conflicts of right and welfare, we must take to be settled in our judgement of the good. Other competing considerations, for example prudential reasons, we must suppose are either integrated into the judgement of the good or have no standing against that judgement. 'Unqualified' means much the same as 'unconditional', as Kant uses that term to describe the obligations yielded by the categorical imperative. Once established, such obligations hold independently of any other consideration which might motivate the subject, any reason the subject might have for acting otherwise.

We should read Hegel here as stalking Kant, perhaps as taunting Kantians, by establishing points of agreement in order to highlight strong differences. Thus §133 continues by identifying the formal (universal) condition of abstract essentiality in the will of the subject who recognizes the good as an obligation with that person's duty. It is therefore tautological that '*duty* should be done *for the sake of duty*' (§133). In Hegel's formulation, this reads as tautological in the same fashion as 'obligations should be fulfilled because they are obligatory' or 'self-interest motivates because it promotes one's own interests'. In Kant's writings, 'duty for duty's sake' has a different implication. Actions which *conform* with duty (objectively specified by application of the categorical imperative) have no moral worth unless they are *motivated by* duty, done *for the sake of* duty. And as we saw in the last chapter, actions which conform with duty will have no moral worth if they are in fact motivated by self-interest or an inclination such as natural sweetness of character or generosity. Hegel, having rejected the faculty psychology which underpins Kant's substantive position, can accept his conclusion as a tautology.

In other words, who would deny the imperative 'Do your duty'? If a particular action is accepted as one's duty, one should do it because it has been accepted as such. This is a formal condition on the good, that it furnishes duties to the agent who recognizes it. Hegel stresses that this is a formal condition by insisting that it opens up (rather than settles) the question 'What is duty?' (§134). We can give a partial answer. 'All that is available so far is this: to do *right*, and to promote *welfare*, one's own welfare and welfare in its universal determination, the welfare of others' (§134), but the answer is obviously incomplete because, as we have seen, right and welfare may issue contradictory imperatives, notably in circumstances where the right of distress is invoked.

Hegel's Criticism of Moral Formalism

I said earlier that Hegel is stalking Kant in these passages because they are preparatory to the dismissive criticisms of Kant which Hegel directs in §135. They are preparatory to Hegel's specific criticisms of Kant because they enunciate formal constraints on the good, and the distinctive charge that Hegel brings against Kantian ethics is that it is formalistic. In Hegelian terms, Kant erroneously believes that one can derive specific moral principles from reflecting on the formal properties that a moral principle must exhibit. Hegel, by contrast, believes that when all the formal characteristics of moral principles have been specified, the question still remains open: What is duty? What *exactly* does duty require?

This brings us to one of the great *contretemps* of modern philosophy – Hegel's charge that Kantian ethics amounts to an empty formalism. It has been treated exhaustively by commentators, but exhaustion does not demonstrate that a definitive judgement is available for us to explain and endorse. The issue is wickedly elusive because there are questions of both interpretation and substantial moral philosophy at stake. One can agree or disagree with readings of the two philosophers on which the various interconnected disputes are predicated. When one has defended one's reading of each of Kant's and Hegel's positions, including Hegel's reading of Kantian ethics, one has to defend a philosophical judgement of the issues as these have been presented. It is fair to say that the controversy would not be so intractable, such an elephant's graveyard of ancient disputes, had Hegel taken the care necessary and proper to articulate his own critical position.

In the *Philosophy of Right* the discussion merits one paragraph – a couple of pages. Fair enough, one might think, if the argument summarizes material available elsewhere, and, to some degree, it does. In the Remark to §135 Hegel refers us to the *Phenomenology* and the *Encyclopaedia*. Of course, he would discuss Kant's ethics later in the *Lectures on the History of Philosophy*, but in fact his lengthiest treatment occurs in the early (1802–3) *Natural Law* essay. The good news is that neither the substance of Hegel's reading of Kant's ethical writings, nor the chief lines of criticism, change very much over this lengthy period. The bad news is that the interpretation and discussion is sketchy and condensed throughout, and nowhere does Hegel do justice to his subject matter. To be fair to Hegel, perhaps one reason for the cursory, almost off-hand nature of his critical discussions of Kant is the thought that the main lines of criticism are not original to him, that he is summarizing the results of earlier reviewers of Kant's work,[2] and that he can presume his readers have covered the familiar ground. This is entirely speculation on my part, but it is a pity that he did not treat Kant as expansively as he would treat, for example, contemporary varieties of subjectivism in the long note to §140 which follows.

The conclusion of Hegel's criticism of Kant is 'From this point of view, no immanent theory of duties is possible' (§135R), which is to say that Kant can give no determinate, unequivocal, non-arbitrary answer to the question 'what is duty?' (§134) as the question arises in specific circumstances. We know that a conception of the good tells us how we ought to act and is thus normative for us; we know that if we do not perceive an outcome as good we shall not recognize the prescription which enjoins it as valid for us; we know that if we do recognize an action or state of affairs as good, we have a duty to fulfil it; we know that if we recognize an action as our duty that we ought to do it, for duty's sake. But all these considerations are entirely formal. They do not disclose the content of the moral principles that bind us. They do not tell us in what it is that our duty consists in the specific circumstances of action. That formal considerations alone cannot dictate the content of our duties is the nub of Hegel's 'emptiness' charge. Duty, on the Kantian conception, amounts to 'abstract universality, whose determination is *identity without content* or the abstractly *positive*, i.e. the indeterminate' (§135).

To work out what is going on in this dialectic, we need first of all to understand the nature of Kant's formalism, at least so far as Hegel understood this to be Kant's ambition. Kant was quite clear that ethics, which consists of the laws free agents give to themselves to regulate their behaviour, cannot have its source in the empirical facts which determine human nature. Such facts are contingent, yet moral laws should be deemed necessary truths and should constrain all rational creatures who have the faculty to discern them, not merely human beings as nature has constituted them. Moral laws are not a posteriori, dependent on the facts of human behaviour as we discover them, but a priori, binding us quite independently of our psychological ancestry and personal history, the product of reason working out how we ought to behave, rather than an anthropology which tells us how we tend to behave. This is because moral laws are the voice of human freedom whereby reason detaches itself from nature, investigating the question of how humans ought to behave quite independently of facts which suggest how they are disposed to behave, given their nature.

It follows from this grand picture of the domain of ethics that as rational creatures we have the capacity to deploy our faculty of reason to determine the rules which should govern our conduct. Just in case this prospectus for the study of ethics looks uncontroversial, advocating that humans should use their reason to determine how they should behave – who would deny this? – we should notice that in modern terms there are herds of sociobiologists who tell us that the beginning of wisdom in ethics is to understand that humans are a species of animal which cannot escape those imperatives of nutrition, reproduction, and so on, which most successfully reproduce the species.

The upshot of this rationalistic orientation is that Kant believes careful philosophical thought concerning the *form* of a law which inscribes one's duty should determine the *content* of how rational creatures should behave. In the first place we must recognize that any law which has its foundations in reason must be a law that any rational agent must adopt as a matter of necessity. Such a law must be both universal (governing all those who ponder the matter) and overriding (since the demands of reason cannot be subordinated by a free, rational creature to the demands of nature). If there are such laws, universally applicable and overriding any natural desires or inclinations, they should determine our duties.

How can we tell what such laws might be? We can say what such laws must be and then check whether there are any such. We can say that a law of conduct which satisfies these formal requirements has this double modality: it is necessary that it be possible that all rational agents be subject to such a law. This (summarizing swiftly) gives us the *form* of the categorical imperative, the imperative that is binding upon all rational agents in virtue of their rationality, regardless of their natural inclinations, namely, '*act only in accordance with that maxim through which you can at the same time will that it become a universal law*'. It is Kant's claim that all moral principles, 'all imperatives of duty can be derived from this single imperative as from their principle' (GMM: 73 / Ak. 4: 421).

How do we use the categorical imperative to derive our actual duties? The ground here is littered with alternative interpretations, but there seem to be two clear ways of understanding the process of derivation.[3] In both cases we are to suppose that one who employs the categorical imperative brings forward for testing a maxim, 'a subjective principle of acting' (GMM: 73 fn. / Ak. 4: 421) which the subject, perhaps erroneously, believes should govern his conduct. Thus a man contemplating suicide might proffer for his maxim 'from self-love, I make it my principle to shorten my life when its longer duration threatens more troubles than it promises agreeableness' (GMM: 74 / Ak. 4: 422). A woman wondering whether to steal an apple from a grocer's might advance the maxim 'When I am hungry and have no money to feed myself, I shall steal the necessary food.'

We must suppose that the circumstances of action prompt, through recall of the rules of some moral code or through the press of desire, a maxim as a candidate moral principle. This maxim must now be tested and the first way to do this is to hypothesize a possible world in which everyone acts in accordance with this maxim. The categorical imperative enjoins us to conduct the thought-experiment of describing such a world. We may find we cannot construct such a world without describing inconsistent conditions. Suppose I am deciding whether I should enslave myself if I judge that I would be happier selling myself into slavery than remaining free.[4] My maxim would then be something like 'I may sell myself into slavery if it promises to be advantageous to me.' To test this we imagine a possible world in which everyone behaves in the same way. Everyone sells themselves into slavery. The thought is that such a world would be logically impossible, since there would be slaves without slave-owners. Another way of judging the permissibility of slavery would be to test the maxim 'I may justifiably take others as slaves if it is to my advantage', and we would then, illogically, try to envisage a world of slave-owners, but no slaves. Both hypothesized worlds would be contradictory – worlds with slaves but no slave-owners, with slave-owners but no slaves. This test is dubbed the 'contradiction in conception test' (O'Neill 1989: 96–8) since it tests for contradiction or incoherency when a maxim is universalized. We could not will such a maxim as a universal law because, as rational agents, we could not will a contradictory state of affairs.

The second way of deriving principles from the categorical imperative employs the alternative formulation of the categorical imperative that follows shortly after the first statement: 'act as if the maxim of your action were to become by your will a *universal law of nature*'. To motivate the use of this version of the categorical imperative, we must suppose that there are cases where we find that we can consistently hypothesize a possible world wherein all follow the maxim, yet we are unable to consistently will such a world. Such a case is given by Kant as the third example discussed in the *Groundwork*. The maxim that he is testing prescribes that it is permissible to neglect one's natural gifts, and Kant sees that the world one hypothesizes might be something like the world reported in the travellers' tales of the South Sea Islanders which so fascinated eighteenth-century Europe. In such a world, everyone would be basking in the sun, playing games and having sex, waiting for the coconuts to drop. (I confess that it is impossible to discuss this example with a straight face in Glasgow in the middle of winter.) Kant sternly remarks that one who hypothesizes such a world

> cannot possibly will that this [neglect of talents] become a universal law or be put in us as such by means of a natural instinct. For as a rational being he necessarily wills that all the capacities in him be developed, since they serve him and are given to him for all sorts of possible purposes.
>
> (GMM: 74 / Ak. 4: 423)

Kant's thought here is that willing is not mere wishing; it requires a practical attempt to realize one's intentions. But how could one generally will to realize one's intentions in action if no-one (oneself included) made any effort to cultivate the skills and capacities necessary for successful accomplishment?

I trust I have given a fair account of the application of the categorical imperative test as outlined in the *Groundwork*. I recommend that readers study these pages carefully and think hard about Kant's discussion of examples. It is fair to say that Kant's efforts to derive moral principles from the categorical imperative have generally been judged a failure, but curiously, since around the 1970s, there have been defenders of Kant aplenty. Many of these require that we switch our attention from the two formulations of the categorical imperative that I have discussed and use the further two formulations, the formula of humanity and the formula of autonomy, as central to Kantian ethics. Another interpretative strategy which is used to defend Kant is to downplay the *Groundwork* and stress the arguments of the *Critique of Practical Reason* and the *Doctrine of Virtue*, Part 2 of the *Metaphysics of Morals*. Of course these defensive strategies may be used in tandem. Since it is not part of my project to give a comprehensive account of Kant's ethics, I shall not judge the accuracy or otherwise of Hegel's presentation of Kant's *oeuvre* taken as a whole. Sufficient to say that, so far as such a comprehensive reading diminishes the formalism of Kant's ethics, so far it disarms Hegel's criticism (and so far, in my view, it diminishes Kant's stature as a moral philosopher). To understand and evaluate Hegel's criticisms, we have to read Kant as developing formal principles to derive moral rules, specifically by applying a universalization test to check the validity of candidate rules and the permissibility of actions that fall under them.

Before we look at Hegel's criticisms in more detail, we should make one concession to Kant. It may well be possible to take a maxim as germane to specific circumstances of choice and derive a contradiction through use of the first formulation of the categorical imperative. In fact, the example of slavery mentioned earlier seems to work perfectly well, and there may be plenty of other cases. I think Kant's test works with examples which have propositional content, which concern lying or false promises. So long as one formulates the maxim carefully, licensing the supposition that lying or promise-breaking takes place most of the time in the world described by the thought-experiment, we find ourselves hypothesizing a world in which folks say, for example, 'I promise', yet never in fact promise because the promisee will not take their words to express an intention to comply with their undertaking. Speech acts of promising take place but do not amount to promises because they are unsuccessful in inducing expectations. Oddly, and inconsistently, this is a world in which there both are and are not promises. Since there could not be such a world, the maxim permitting false promises cannot be universalized and so we should judge that the making of false promises is not permitted by the moral rules. It thus looks as though, through a careful specification of the maxim, the categorical imperative test can disqualify some candidate maxims.

Hegel's first criticism alleges that purely formal mechanisms, notably the criterion of duty as '*absence of contradiction*, as *formal correspondence with itself*' (§135R) cannot be decisive since to operate the categorical imperative one has to bring in 'material *from outside*' (§135R). It is an interesting question whether this is true of the cases discussed above. Certainly, in order to review the permissibility of slavery, one has to understand the institution of slavery. This involves understanding the meaning of the term 'slavery' and presumably some further knowledge of how a system of slavery works in the real world. One can then give an answer to questions such as: Could everyone be a slave-owner? Could everyone be a slave? Grant that it is logically impossible for both A to enslave B and B to enslave A, could there, for example, be a world in which A enslaves B, B enslaves C, C enslaves D, and D enslaves A? I think not, but in truth I don't have much confidence in this first-shot answer. It may be that one has to have a much fuller description of the social relationships in this strange world before an answer can be given. Likewise in the case of false promises, one clearly has to have fairly precise knowledge of how much promise-breaking there would actually be in a world where promise-breaking was permissible in order to decide whether, as described, the hypothesized world contains a contradiction. One can certainly imagine a world in which promise-breaking is permissible, yet there is no contradiction, since no or few promises are in fact broken, promisors recognizing, in good Hobbesian fashion, that promise-breaking would be imprudent since the institution of promising promotes mutual advantage. If this were true, making promises would induce expectations and thus be successfully effected.

All then depends on the precise specification of the maxim. Consider the maxim 'I shall break my promise if I am sure that this will be to my ultimate advantage, supposing that I can discount any damage to my reputation and any general weakening of the institution of promising.' (Some deathbed promises would be an example.) I see no reason why this maxim cannot be universalized without contradiction. In fact such a world, with plenty of promises made and not a few broken, is rather like the actual world we inhabit. This alerts us to the possibility of rigging the maxim, as soon as we are free to bring into our calculations a particular content. This is why, I take it, Hegel believes that 'it is possible to justify any wrong or immoral mode of action by this means' (§135R).

There is a further way of considering the application of the categorical imperative. Consider a world in which there is a practice of private property; individuals make and respect claims to private property. Then suppose a property-holder puts forward and universalizes this maxim: 'I shall not respect the property of others.' We now conjecture a world in which everyone adopts this maxim and discover as we work through the details of the thought-experiment that private property vanishes. Thus we have people living in a regime of private property envisaging that that institution vanishes if everyone acts in the way they propose. Is this a contradiction? Yes it is, if we take it that everyone both endorses the institution of private property and then acts to undermine it. But for this contradiction to be clear we must assume that folks believe that private property is a valuable institution – and this is the belief that is up for testing. If we do not make this assumption, if we suppose that someone is genuinely reviewing the institution, the fact that the institution would vanish is neither here nor there. A world without private property may be a better place. This is not a contradictory supposition and the thought-experiment cannot help us decide whether this outcome may not be welcome.

Hegel sees this clearly:

> The fact that *no property* is present is in itself [*für sich*] no more contradictory than is the non-existence of this or that individual people, family, etc., or the complete *absence of human life*. But if it is already established and presupposed that property and human life should exist and be respected, then it is a contradiction to commit theft or murder; a contradiction must be a contradiction with something, that is, with a content that is already fundamentally present as an established principle.
>
> (§135R)

It is worth mentioning at this point that this fairly imprecise way of operating the categorical imperative (something like: Do not act in a way that would undermine the very institution that makes your action possible were everyone to act in similar fashion) also disallows actions that are distinctively valuable (giving to Oxfam) or clearly morally neutral (paying off your credit cards each month).[5] As Hegel notes in the *Natural Law* essay,

> [T]he determinate injunction [*die Bestimmtheit*] to help the poor expresses the supersession of the determinacy which is poverty; but if the maxim whose content is this determinacy is tested by raising it to a principle of universal legislation, it will prove to be false, because it annuls itself. If it is thought that the poor should be helped universally, then either there are no poor, or there are only the poor (in which case no-one remains to help them).
>
> (PW: 127 / SW 1: 470)

This conclusion, that the categorical imperative disallows innocuous or valuable actions, is a persistent difficulty for Kant. As Wood remarks, it can disallow a maxim such as 'I will occasionally accompany others through a doorway, and on those occasions I will always go through the doorway last' (Wood 1990: 157).

Thus far, Hegel's objections have been targeted at the categorical imperative understood in its first formulation as 'a consistency in conception' test. As explained above, Kant's test, as exemplified in the *Groundwork* by the cases of duties to develop one's talents and help others in distress, can be conducted as an investigation into what states of affairs can be consistently willed (as against: consistently described). It is claimed that no-one could consistently will that her talents fail to be developed or that she be disposed not to help others in distress. There is a weakness in this mode of construing the application of the categorical imperative that Hegel may or may not have divined. The interpretative question – did he spot the problem or did he not? – is hard to settle. All depends on the scope of his assertion that Kant brings to his discussion of examples 'a content which is already present as an established principle' (§135R).

We can keep this question open whilst rehearsing the objection. Suppose in the case of the life of the South Sea Islanders, which we can envisage all too clearly without any inconsistency, we ask ourselves: But could we *will* (i.e. really want, and if possible work for, not just fancy) a world in which everyone lived in this fashion? What could possibly constrain us from answering, 'Yes. That is possible. We *could* will such a life'? The only constraints I can imagine are cultural or otherwise moral inhibitions, since the Polynesians (supposing their attitudes and habits to have been accurately reported) would experience no difficulty in conducting this thought-experiment. We happen to be East Prussian Protestants imbued with the work ethic, or British grammar school boys and girls in whom the self-cultivation, duty and service ethic has been inculcated, or victims of some other social pathology. Whatever way of thinking explains our reluctance to endorse this Arcadian-cum-Polynesian vision, we must be citing some cultural baggage in order to yield a contradiction. It is because we think our talents have been endowed in order that we make good use of them that we cannot envisage ourselves or others similarly blessed permitting them to atrophy. But of course this explanation of the impossibility of *our* willing such a state of affairs uses what has to be proved, namely, the thought that it would be wrong of us to live in this uncultivated paradise.

Kant's other example, that of helping others, invites us to consider a world in which no-one helps those in need. Again we must suppose such a world is possible. Arguably it has been described by Ayn Rand. Kant unfortunately asks us to envisage the possibility of ourselves stuck in such a moral desert and concludes that, as described, we couldn't will it – again with all the force of 'will' against 'merely wish or fancy'. The block he attests on such an exercise of will is erected by the thought that we ourselves might find ourselves in need of the assistance of others. We couldn't will both that no-one assist others and that we ourselves be assisted as and when we stand in need of help. I guess this is true. But why *must* we will that we ourselves be assisted at the point of need? A policy of not assisting others and not accepting their offered help would be misanthropic and temperamentally contrary, but the character trait is recognizable and far short of insanity. The obvious (if false) answer is Kant's: we cannot possibly escape the demands of self-interest. In cases where we stand in need of the love and sympathy of others we could not rob ourselves of the hope of assistance that we wish for ourselves (GMM: 75 / Ak. 4: 423). If this is the best answer we can give, it is the fact of our self-interest, and thereby a heterogeneous motivation, that constrains our will. Our duty will be determined by the brute causal fact of our being unable to will that others do not give us the assistance we require.

I can see no way of applying the test of a contradiction in the will, as illuminated by Kant's discussion of his examples, which does not either help itself to a moral principle which is supposed to be tested or appeal to the inescapable 'facts' of human nature, which 'facts' may well be wrong – the familiar fallacy of deriving an 'is' from an 'ought'. Hegel is surely right. If the heart of Kantian ethics lies in Kant's belief that all candidate moral principles can be tested against a formal principle distinctive of the rationality of the willing agent, Kant's ethics must be judged a failure. It will validate principles which should be rejected and invalidate principles which are commendable or innocuous. Where it looks to succeed, it will illicitly introduce 'material from outside' – moral principles or speculations about human nature which are probably false, but which, if true, would introduce heterogeneous motives into our moral regimen.

I accept at this point the charge that this review of Kantian ethics is incomplete. Notoriously, it does not even consider the other two formulae which Kant in the *Groundwork* believes (strangely) to be equivalent formulations of the categorical imperative: the principle of humanity and the principle of autonomy.[6] The argumentative terrain is complex, but Hegel clearly believes that some of this ground is covered by his criticisms of Kantian psychology which occlude Kant's distinction of autonomous and heteronymous sources of agency and hence he would reject Kant's account of freedom as self-legislation directed against the voices of self-interest and altruisitic inclinations. But even this reading of Kant has been disputed.

In politics it is a familiar charge that one party has stolen another party's clothes. This is inevitable as parties compete for the middle ground and the middle ground shifts in accordance with the electoral success of one party or another. Something similar seems to happen in the history of philosophy. We can't bring Kant and Hegel together in the face of a tribunal which will quiz them exhaustively to the point that the diffences in their positions are crystal clear. The best that we can do is to read their writings, take notice that the criticisms which the later writer directs towards the first hinges on a specific construal of the latter's position, evaluate that construal fairly and adjudicate the resultant conflict. It should surprise no-one that the jury on the Kant–Hegel controversy is still out. Since we can't bring them to the tribunal, the interpretation of their views is controversial. Since we may disagree on the substance of the philosophical issues at stake, our adjudication is unreliable. My firmly believed, but tenuously grounded, view on the Kant–Hegel dispute about the power of individual rationality to determine substantive questions of ethics is that Hegel is right: as individual persons, blessed as we are with the powers of rationality, we do not have the capacity to work out for ourselves, unaided, the principles by which we should guide our conduct, and, derivatively, the rightness or wrongness of what we do.

Conscience

Kant's focus, sharpened by a distinctive conception of human freedom, is on the individual's ability to work out what is the right thing to do. This ability is characterized in terms of rationality, and rationality of the Kantian variety turns out to be a meagre and inadequate resource. But the history of philosophy demonstrates that there may be other ways for individuals to work out for themselves the content of a defensible morality, other ways to come to a judgement of what is right and wrong, just or unjust, generally good or bad. Abstract right delivers principles which are universal in point of their recognition by and applicability to all persons. If universality characterizes abstract right, particularity is the mark of the moral subject who insists on her ability to recognize the good as her moral purpose. From the perspective of the moral subject, that ability to recognize the validity of the demands of the good is designated '*the conscience*', subjectivity's 'absolute inward certainty of itself' (§136).

Hegel doesn't tell us who he has in mind as the (philosophical) exemplar of the ethics of conscience. He discusses conscience at length in the *Phenomenology* at BB, vi.C.c, 'Conscience. The "beautiful soul", evil and its forgiveness', and there is good reason to think that one of its targets is Rousseau. Conscience in *Émile* is the voice of nature calling through the 'noise' of civilization in the 'Profession of faith of the Savoyard vicar'. The 'beautiful souls' of Clarens are so entitled (*les belles âmes*) in the seventh of the lovely illustrations to *Julie ou la nouvelle Héloïse*.[7] The term had been appropriated by Goethe and Schiller. An anglophone reader would suspect that Hegel had read Bishop Butler or one of his followers, though I see no evidence for such an attribution. There can be no doubt that conscience was a potent *philosophical* term in the eighteenth century and that it designated a specific faculty of moral knowledge. More than this, conscience was an indispensable category of moral phenomenology, speaking to everyone in a recognizable voice.

The voice is that of the innermost self, 'the deepest inner solitude' encountered through 'a total withdrawal into the self'. This voice is a modern discovery. Conscience was mute when moral norms were issued only in the external, peremptory voice of the priest or the political superior who claims the authority of natural law. Such ethics of obedience do not recognize conscience. Kant's 'age of criticism' may with equal justification be dubbed the 'age of conscience', since conscience, paradigmatically, can challenge established authority, whether this bespeaks the rules of 'religion or right' (§136A).

Nowadays conscience is often explained as a reducible or eliminable category of folk morality. We all talk about it, acknowledge it, examine, cite or avow it, grant it a measure of certainty or authority. We cannot reject out of hand what we hear as its peremptory voice, but we should doubt its claims to authenticity, truth or provenance. It is an epistemological category. It delivers moral beliefs. As such, it is common ground amongst epistemologists that whatever the phenomenological power (force, strength) of a belief, that power cannot guarantee its truth. We say 'x believes that p', but there is no way of building up the *strength* of x's belief that p ('x is convinced of p', 'x cannot be persuaded that p is false', 'x is *certain* that p') that can ensure that p is true. Of course, we can insist that, if x truly believes that p, then p. In this case, we speak of true belief as knowledge, for if x knows that p, then p is true. We can claim that we know that p, but if p turns out to be false, then we don't *know* that p, we merely believe it, falsely as it turns out. Conscience is like this. Let us say that x conscientiously asserts that p in respect of any moral judgement that p. Does it follow that p is true? It does not. The demands of conscience are mere *claims* to knowledge. The claims may properly be denied. Conscience, like belief but unlike knowledge, may get things wrong.

Good examples tell us that conscience can go wrong in two ways. Conscience can dictate that an action is right which turns out to be wrong and conscientious agents may do evil as they strive to do the right thing. An example, familiar to all in Hegel's day, was Robespierre, the 'sea-green incorruptible', the revolutionary orchestrator of the Terror whose (single) room contained a bed, a desk and a chair, whose wardrobe contained two suits. The purest of the pure-in-heart, he was responsible for the deaths of thousands, and these deaths of no more significance to him than the lopping off of the head of a cabbage. Conscience is idiosyncratic in principle – which is why those who frequently cite their own can be maximally evil, minimally such a pain in the arse.

But conscience can go wrong in the other direction, too. Conscience, urgent in voice and authoritative in tone, can still be resisted, and when we guiltily do what our conscience dictates is the *wrong* thing to do, when we favour friends or family against its severe constraints, we may well have done right after all. Witness Huck Finn's conscientious certainty that in helping Jim the slave to escape, he had, in effect, been stealing from Miss Watson. Worse, in colluding with the theft of her property, he had been ungrateful (Bennett 1974)!

Hegel was well aware of all of this. For him, conscience was an epistemological category familiar to and distinctive of modern man. Appeals to conscience are quite novel in the history of mankind: 'earlier and more sensuous ages have before them something external and given, whether this be religion or right; but [my] conscience knows itself as thought, and that this thought of mine is the sole source of obligation' (§136A). Which is to say: nowadays, we all respect claims of conscience. But, at the same time, we do not take these claims to be infallible. 'True conscience is the disposition to will what is good *in and for itself*' (§137), but how can I tell that when conscience speaks to me, it speaks truly? 'Within the formal point of view of morality, conscience lacks this objective content' (§137); its sense of certainty cannot guarantee its truth.

Hegel believes that it is the content of any belief concerning what is good that determines the truth of that belief. It is certainly not its form, the quality of the 'feeling or any other individual – i.e. sensuous – kind of knowledge' (§137R). However certain we may feel that such-and-such an action is required or is wrong, we may be mistaken. The Robespierre and Huck Finn examples, I take it, show that he is right. If so, if we both acknowledge the force of the demands of conscience and accept its fallibility, what are we to do in any particular case where the voice of conscience is insistent? We certainly cannot consult conscience at a deeper level in order to determine whether its claims are authoritative. Appeals to conscience are either circular or subject to a regress once the fallibilty of the claims of conscience is recognized:

> The conscience is therefore subject to judgement as to its *truth* or falsity, and its appeal solely *to itself* is directly opposed to what it seeks to be – that is, the rule for a rational and universal mode of action which is valid in and for itself. Consequently, the state cannot recognize the conscience in its distinctive form, i.e. as *subjective knowledge*, any more than science can grant any validity to subjective *opinion*, *assertion* and the *appeal* to subjective opinion.

> (§137A)

Hegel's point about the fallibility of conscience seems to me exactly right. His further point, that the state cannot therefore recognize conscience as a subjectively authorized claim to knowledge, looks grudging and dangerous. Once again, as with the right of the subjective will, Hegel seems to take away with the left hand what he concedes with the right. Of course he is correct to insist that the state cannot as a matter of course recognize the claims of conscience. If my conscience dictates that I would do wrong to permit my child to receive a life-saving blood transfusion, the state will rightly step in and command the treatment notwithstanding my conscientious objection. Some conscientious behaviour – the murder of an adulterous sister – had just better be stopped or punished. On the other hand, it has been common ground since the Wars of Religion in Europe that conscientious belief cannot be coerced and poses a special problem for the state over and above the fact of evident wrongdoing. There is a world of difference between one who does wrong for evil motives and one who does wrong because conscience errs and this is a distinction that the state should mark.

Conscience speaks truly when it motivates actions in accordance with 'fixed principles' and 'duties which are objective' (§137). Many such principles will be prescribed as constitutive of the practices of ethical life and as law by the state. Again, we insist that Hegel must find some genuine space for subjectivity and conscientious affirmation in his account of the provenance of the laws of the state. It is not good enough, as in the British Parliament, to distinguish decisions on matters of public policy and decisions on matters of conscience, as though conscience is disengaged when public policy is effected, as though conscience can be properly acknowledged only when its concerns are shifted into a peripheral domain. Conscience cannot be relegated to the choice of a vocation (§262), to the realm of state indifference and toleration of anomaly in matters of religious belief (§270R), to the state's benign neglect of the trivial machinations within corporations (§289R) and to a grudging toleration of public opinion and its expression in the safety valve of a free press (§§316–19). Subjectivity, and hence, in some sense, conscience, must recognize the validity of social norms. We should regard Hegel's respect for true conscience, as we should regard his endorsement of the right of the subjective will, as a promissory note. It requires him, on pain of inconsistency, but more important, lack of moral seriousness in respect to principles he voices, to explain how conscience (and not simply habitual obedience and unquestioning acquiescence) can play a role in the motivation of members of the state.

Subjectivity and Evil

We know that conscience can err. Once we accept the failure of the Kantian project of deriving or validating moral principles from the rational capacities of the subjective will, we must see subjectivity as Janus-faced. Considered as 'abstract self-determination and pure certainty', it has the power to 'evaporate into itself (abolish entirely) all determinate aspects of right, duty and existence' (§138). 'Everything that we recognize as right or duty can be shown by thought to be null and void, limited, and in no way absolute' (§138A) – which is to say that no action is so awful that a manipulator of Kant's categorical imperative or some other subjectivist strategem could not justify it. Thus Hare in modern times accepts that we cannot convict the fanatical Nazi, who is prepared to prescribe that he too should be sent to the camps if he turns out to be Jewish, of subscribing to an immoral rule (Hare 1963: 157–85). At the same time, we must acknowledge that the bloody-minded subjectivist, as represented by Socrates and the Stoics, has been responsible for challenging iniquitous moral regimes 'in epochs when what is recognized as right and good in actuality and custom is unable to satisfy the better will . . . when the actual world is a hollow, spiritless and unsettled existence' (§§138R, 138A). In such circumstances retreat to inner conviction is the only resort of the truly ethical spirit.

But this capacity to absent oneself from the moral world is a source of evil when the abstract will finds its content not in the objectively valid moral rules, but in the arbitrary will which finds its motivation in the desires, drives and inclinations which naturally assail us. 'In this case, the inwardness of the will is evil' (§§139, 139R). Subjectivity is necessary as a personal orientation towards the good, but it is dangerous, since it is also the source of the most conspicuous evil. Kant was right to see subjectivity as a creative power, but he wholly ignored its capacity for evil. Taking up the criticisms of his contemporaries which he voiced in the Preface, Hegel denounces his fellow-philosophers as responsible for the perversion 'of evil into good and good into evil' (§140R).

The long Remark to §140 is a sustained (and eloquent) diatribe against the forms that subjectivism in ethics has taken in (his) modern world. As so often with Hegel, it is something of a *roman-à-clef* since he rarely picks out the culprits explicitly or cites chapter and verse. But many of these doctrines, as one should expect, are with us still, so it can be fun to relabel Hegel's targets. Since in the contemporary vocabulary, Hegel is committed to *moral realism* (since the reality of the good is manifested in actions which accord with the rules and practices of our ethical life), *moral objectivism* (moral judgements are either true or false) and *moral cognitivism* (objective moral principles are knowable), this is the place where archaeologists of ideas might unearth criticism *avant la lettre* of such modern notions as ethical anti-realism or non-cognitivism, as well as other subjectivist doctrines such as emotivism, perspectivism or prescriptivism. I shall leave this task to the reader for the most part, and travel briskly through Hegel's arguments.

His initial target is a range of casuistical arguments which seek to excuse or mitigate wrongdoing. We know what it is to do wrong with a bad conscience. It is to know what is right ('the true universal' (§140R)), to have a particular end which contravenes the right, and to pursue this end whilst acknowledging the evil. This species of evil requires that the agent knows what is right and, further, knows that what he is doing is wrong. What judgement should we make if the agent does not know what is right, or knows what is right but does wrong, falsely believing that he is doing the right thing in the circumstances? It surely makes a difference if wrongdoing is the product of error and false belief, especially when the agent cannot be held responsible for the error. Think of the poor child brought up in a criminal family to think that the rich are fair game – and then caught thieving. The basic philosophical problems which these possibilities prompt are not the specific province of theological dispute. As Hegel seems to recognize in his citation of 'the subjective right of self-consciousness' (a conflation of the right of intention (§120) and the right of the subjective will (§132)) and his insistence that this 'must not be thought of as colliding with the absolute right of the objectivity of this determination [of the action as good or evil]' (§140R), the evaluation of moral mistakes takes us into difficult judgemental terrain. It is a serious judgement when we say that someone is not responsible for their action. Exculpation should not be granted too easily given its implications for the honour and dignity of the moral agent thus excused. Hegel implies, I think, that we should err on the side of harshness of judgement. But this implication is not unsympathetic if it implies in turn that we should grant wrongdoers the benefit of the doubt concerning their status as properly moral agents.

Hegel's portrayal of hypocrisy is confusing if one thinks that a hypocrite is any person who says one thing and does another in matters of morality. I distinguish the hypocrite from Hegel's wrongdoer with a bad conscience in that the hypocrite must conspicuously proclaim or manifest to other people his subscription to the universal which he disobeys, displaying himself falsely as a true believer or fellow-traveller. Hegel mentions the element of untruthfulness but has it that the hypocrite falsely represents the evil to others as good. I don't think of hypocrites as devious proselytizers of evil doctrines. I think the hypocrite is one who parades his subscription to moral rules which his actions then belie. Hypocrisy is an odd phenomenon because the great examples of literature (Volpone, Holy Willie, Casaubon)[8] all manifest a measure of self- as well as other-deception. I think Hegel knows these things (read his account of what the hypocrite says to himself) but he stresses the appearance of the element of self-certainty in the hypocrite's public performance, emphasizing the hypocrite as devious rather than self-deceiving.[9] His philosophical point is that the propensity to hypocrisy is encouraged by the necessity of subjectivity: 'this possibility exists within subjectivity, for as abstract negativity, it knows all determinations are subordinate to it and emanate from it' (§140R).

What are the typical strategies of the hypocrite? This is a nice question which should elicit that species of keen social observation which cannot be employed absent a detached interest in the human condition which in turn is facilitated by a sharp sense of humour. (Again, read Burns's 'Holy Willlie's Prayer'.) Instead, Hegel would have us read serious theological treatises, of the sort that advocate 'probabilism'. This is a most improbable doctrine, attributed to the Jesuits but manifesting a wholly human trait – that of reaching for any barely reputable reason in order to justify otherwise disreputable actions. As Hegel points out, the possibility which this doctrine presupposes of choosing one's authorities or exemplars ensures that '[personal] preferences and the arbitrary will are made the arbiters of good and evil' (§140R).

A further stratagem of subjectivity invokes the subject's right of intention. Since it is possible that even the worst actions may be truly described in terms of a witless attempt to pursue the good, those who characterize right actions in terms of the purity of the motives which inspire them find themselves justifying actions which are objectively wrong. Hegel might have named names at this point, since he judged that the subjectivist doctrines of Fries were responsible for the crackdown on universities in the Karlsbad Decrees, following Sand's assassination of Kotzebue. No-one is as pure in heart as a radical student with a dagger or a bomb in his hand, and the blinkered pursuit of the good is sure to attract sympathy when the criminal upshot is punished. (Sand was executed for his crime.) Again, Hegel believes that subjectivist doctrines, in emphasizing 'the feeling, imagination and caprice of the individual' (§140R), are responsible for this species of wrongdoing.

Hegel's opponents should be familiar to the modern reader. They believe that

> *Subjective opinion* . . . [is] the criterion of right and duty . . . that the ethical nature of an action is determined by the *conviction which holds something to be right* . . . Under these circumstances, any semblance of ethical objectivity has completely disappeared. Such doctrines are intimately associated with that self-styled philosophy . . . which denies that truth [in ethics] can be recognized . . . [and] maintains that knowledge is an empty vanity.
>
> (§140R)

Of course, if Hegel is right, if our moral beliefs do admit of truth and falsity, and if we do have the capacity to know the truth when we see it or work it out, then Hegel's opponents are wrong. Hegel would accept this burden of proof, though he finds it staggering that persons have the effrontery to cite the authority of their own convictions in the face of massive consensus – 'authorities which encompass countless individual convictions' (§140R). This is just as well, since the internal arguments which he addresses to the subjectivist are not likely to gain assent. He maintains that

> [I]f a good heart, good intentions, and subjective conviction are said to be the factors which give actions their value, there is no longer any hypocrisy or evil at all; for a person is able to transform whatever he does into something good by the reflection of good intentions and motives and the element of his *conviction* renders it good.

But of course this is false. Since some wrongdoers do wrong wilfully, there will still be hypocritical and evil actions. And to profess an innocent or worthy motive is one thing, to have the story accepted is quite another, as Hegel himself acknowledges when he insists on the right of the objectivity of the action in §120. The real weakness of this position is epistemological, as Kant perhaps realized: whatever the nature of the action, whether it conforms with duty or no, if its rightness consists in the specific quality of its motivation, we should be sceptical about the possibility of accurate moral judgement. Absent the possibility of self-deception of course, when we judge *ourselves* we are not free to transform our evil deeds into good ones by telling ourselves a false but plausible story.

The final form of subjectivism which Hegel discusses is labelled 'irony'. The ironic stance is that of one who for the most part accepts the conventional moral rules, but insists that these are not true in respect of their objectivity. Whatever force such rules have derives from the will of the person who adopts them. Such a one carefully detaches herself from the source of their objectivity, insisting that it is up to her whether she wills them or not. '[I]t distances itself from [objectivity] and knows *itself* as that which *wills* and *resolves in a particular way* but may *equally well* will and resolve otherwise' (§140R). Hegel sees this collection of attitudes as a kind of frivolous playing at morality. He clearly thought the charge of a basic lack of seriousness concerning the moral law was fairly drawn with respect to the targets he had in mind.[10] But in our own day, without repeating this latter charge, we can find ourselves very puzzled by the earnest stance of subjectivist moral philosophers of different stripes who deny the objectivity of moral judgements, then go on to advocate (as philosophical missionaries?) that as people of goodwill we should adopt a utilitarian stance or seek to co-operate with others to reduce the measure of human misery.[11] Strangely, there are plenty of noncognitivists and anti-realists about, but very few moral nihilists of the kind who will tell us directly that since morality is dead, anything goes.[12]

Conclusion

As moral subjects we will the good, we recognize that we have a duty to pursue it, but we find ourselves without the intellectual resources to determine what the good requires. Moral subjectivity is located in the phenomenology of the true conscience, but we find ourselves unable to distinguish the deliverances of the true conscience from the imposter, notwithstanding the feelings of certainty which both true and false conscience bespeak. Subjectivity descends into a hole of its own making – moral subjectivism – when it mistakes its inability to construct or recognize an immanent doctrine of duties as the opportunity to display moral authenticity or creativity.

Morality needs to be transcended. Its insights should be preserved, but its inadequacies need to be corrected by the study of Ethical Life. As we broach that study, it is vital that we keep in mind the lessons of this chapter, since the most grievous question of Hegel interpretation concerns how far the transcendence (*Aufhebung*) of Morality (and Abstract Right) in Ethical Life succeeds in preserving its central insights into human freedom – notably 'the right of the subjective will . . . that whatever it is to recognize as valid should be perceived by it as good . . . the right to recognize [as good] nothing that I do not perceive as rational'. Since this is the 'highest right of the subject' (§§132, 132R), one crucial measure of Hegel's success in the enterprise of the *Philosophy of Right* is whether or not the institutions that he commends as rational do succeed in giving it recognition. We shall see.

Chapter 9

The Concept of
Ethical Life: §§142–57

Introduction

The notion of Ethical Life (*Sittlichkeit*) is Hegel's distinctive contribution to moral philosophy. To my knowledge, it has no obvious precursors – perhaps Aristotle's *Ethics* and *Politics* are closest in spirit, but the resemblances can be hard to discern. And it has had few followers apart from the British, American and Italian idealists; perhaps modern communitarian writers, in half-baked fashion, have rediscovered some of Hegel's leading insights. Ethics, since Kant, has taken on the form of normative ethics, what Hegel took to be the philosophy of the *Sollen* or ought-to-be. It has aspired to a decision procedure whereby norms can be tested or generated in accordance with formal principles, considerations of utility or contractarian devices, to name three influential contenders. By contrast, Hegel's account of Ethical Life (Part 3 of the *Philosophy of Right*) charts three nested domains of value (Family, Civil Society and State) which govern domestic, economic, legal, administrative and political

forms of life as these are encountered in the modern world. I say these elements of Ethical Life are *nested* because Civil Society consists of families and the Rational State as a whole comprises all its subsidiary institutions.[1] In subsequent chapters we shall examine each of these elements in turn. For the moment we shall consider the concept of Ethical Life itself.

Looking back over the previous discussions of Abstract Right and Morality, we can identify an agenda to be covered in this part of the *Philosophy of Right*. We insist that we are persons, the bearers of rights, but we do not yet know how this claim to elementary moral status is to be articulated so that it is properly recognized by others. We shall find that personhood is extended over the domain of the family unit as persons join themselves in marriage to constitute a spiritual (*geistige*) union. We shall see these 'concrete persons' (§§181–2) in the form of (male) heads of families pursuing the satisfaction of their distinctively modern needs in economic activity. This activity is governed by laws which transparently protect persons' rights through a legal system which intelligibly promulgates and effectively enforces them. Personhood is threatened as well as protected in Civil Society; the economic sphere in which the particular ends of persons are pursued needs to be regulated by public agencies (*die Polizei*) and the evil of poverty, which threatens to eliminate this most basic moral status, must be remedied. Unfortunately, the rights of the person are still mainly 'limited to the negative' (§38). Thus, in the political sphere, the rights associated (often then; uniformly nowadays) with the active political participation of each person in the role of citizen, are strongly constrained. We shall emphasize this weakness, but at this stage we can look forward to a specification of what was missing in Abstract Right: an account of the interests which persons' rights typically protect and a description of the regime of law, trial and punishment that is required to make that protection effective.

In similar fashion, we look back to Morality as a statement of the demands of subjective freedom and look forward to Ethical Life as a description of the normative order which completes it. In particular, we noted the absence of concrete detail concerning the duties of the moral agent. Since no immanent doctrine of duties was to be found within Morality, since the intellectual resources of the moral subject did not extend to the specification of *exactly* what ought and ought not to be done, these are things which we should learn as the details of Ethical Life are spelled out. But we shall be asking, too, whether the regimes of duty which constitute the elements of Ethical Life require or even permit a genuine recognition by each subject of their validity.

It is easy to see why Hegel believes the insights of Abstract Right and Morality are incomplete. As these normative orders are transcended within Ethical Life, we shall have to keep a close eye on what is discarded as well as taking note of what is retained and supplemented – the *Aufhebung* of Abstract Right and Morality within Ethical Life. Hegel's basic idea, as we mentioned when discussing the Preface, is that we identify the good in an account of 'our station and its duties' as this conception of ethics was later glossed by Bradley: not merely the station and duties which are prescribed for or allocated to us, but the stations and duties which we may select, with which we identify and which effectively govern our conduct. But before we look at the detail, we need first to read through the preliminary remarks to the description of the forms of Ethical Life.

Exposition

'Ethical Life is the *Idea of freedom*' (§142). Freedom is attained when agents pursue the good knowing it to be good. The Idea of freedom has two manifestations: first, as the concept of freedom, it can be articulated philosophically as the conceptual resources of self-conscious agents who know and will the good. The good as revealed thus far comprises the ends of welfare and of rights, but we await a fuller specification granted the possibility of conflict between these different ends. The second element of the Idea of freedom is displayed in the life of the ethical community. This is the realm of actuality wherein the good (as articulated philosophically 'by the concept') is manifested in the self-conscious actions of agents who pursue it in accordance with the rules and institutions which govern them. It follows that we can display the Idea of freedom in the modern world in two complementary fashions. We can focus on the (philosophical) self-understanding of modern individuals and show how this is expressed in the norms of the ethical domains they inhabit (Family, Civil Society and State), or we can focus on these ethical domains directly, describing them as they are encountered in the modern world and explaining how the norms that structure them are internalized in the motivation of the inhabitants. Taking the first route, we portray Ethical Life as a condition of *subjective freedom*. Taking the second route, examining the institutions which make up the moral world, we illuminate the condition of *objective freedom*. As we shall see later, these should not be represented as two independent perspectives from which the details of Ethical Life can be charted. They are interdependent or complementary aspects of it. We cannot articulate the norms of subjective freedom without showing how they are actualized in the institutional structures of social life. And we cannot describe the institutions or practices of social freedom without detailing how these institutions are constructed from the intentional activity of those moral subjects whose behaviours such institutions comprise.

In §§144–7 Hegel elaborates the application of the terms 'objectivity' and 'subjectivity' to Ethical Life. As philosophers, we know anyway that the terms 'objective' and 'subjective' are tricky and dangerous: tricky because they bear so many meanings both technical and vernacular; dangerous because these meanings may easily be conflated or confused. As we investigate Hegel's employment of them in his preliminary discussion of Ethical Life, we should bear in mind here (as in so many places in the *Philosophy of Right*) that the discussion is programmatic, with details to be spelled out later. We should also note that Hegel himself was conscious that these are slippery terms and has given us a partial glossary of their various meanings at §§25–6.

The first sense in which ethics is an objective sphere contrasts it with the *abstract* good aspired to in Morality. It is a 'substance made *concrete* by subjectivity *as infinite form*' (§144). I take this to be a statement of moral ontology. Ethical Life is the sphere of objective mind in the sense that the actual world of moral rules and institutions is constituted by, made up of, the intentional activity of moral subjects (subjectivity). Analytic philosophers, for the most part, have lost the taste for enquiring into the nature of things, having a distaste for suspiciously exotic metaphysics.[2] How are we to understand the sphere of ethics? Hegel tells us that it is constituted by 'laws and institutions which have being in and for themselves' (§144).

We won't see what is striking about Hegel's thesis in this paragraph unless we get a clear sense of the ontological puzzle in the background. Let us ask ourselves a (deceptively) simple question: What is a law? Here are two unacceptable answers:

1. A law is a piece of paper produced after proper parliamentary procedures, signed by Her Majesty and lodged wherever. There are many variations on this theme, from notices strung on trees to traffic lights. (If this were true, laws would cease to exist if the physical manifestations were lost or destroyed.)
2. A law is observed in the habits of citizens whose behaviour displays patterns of conformity which sustain the hypothesis that it is rule-governed. (This would fail to distinguish rules of law from rules of positive morality and etiquette, or indeed universally habitual behaviour quite generally – one might conclude, for example, that humans observe a rule which requires them to empty their bladders first thing in the morning.)

A correct answer, which I do not propose to elaborate here, will identify laws in a pattern of understandings which circumscribe an intentional phenomenon. It will explain how persons in roles (legislators, judges) promulgate or endorse certain kinds of rule and how those to whom the rules are addressed understand these rules to have a distinctive kind of authority. Laws, we can comfortably agree, are mental phenomena, to be explained as structures of beliefs and intentions, which is to say, as structures of will (and for Hegel, a fortiori, as structures of freedom). As such they are features of the mindset or subjectivity of persons (this is their *form*), but they are objective in so far as such phenomena can be distinguished and classified (as characteristic of well-governed family life, for example) and identified in the practices of institutions which can be accurately described. Laws are perhaps the clearest examples of the phenomena of objective mind, but all the rules and institutions of Ethical Life should be so understood. Laws, and ethical norms generally, are nowhere but in the *minds* of those who actively determine, promulgate, enforce and obey them. We should note that, as constructions of will, the structures of objective mind which comprise the practices of Ethical Life are a fortiori objectifications of freedom.

The structures of objective mind which constitute Ethical Life comprise a system which is rational. We shall take up later the issue of the rationality of Ethical Life; for the moment we should notice a potentially sinister implication of the systematic quality of the totality. It gathers together its elements (Family etc.) as '*ethical powers* which govern the lives of individuals . . . these individuals . . . are accidental to them' (§145). In the Addition Hegel continues, 'Whether the individual exists or not is a matter of indifference to objective ethical life, which alone has permanence and is the power by which the lives of individuals are governed' (§145A). A careless reading will suggest that individuals are dispensable within the system of Ethical Life, which in turn suggests that the insights of Abstract Right and Morality count for nothing. This would be to mistake Hegel's point.

This is not the place to explain Hegel's views on accident and essence. In any case, like so many other of his concepts, the point of their application needs to be fathomed for each distinctive context of use. Here he is making two different points: the first of these is quite simple and uncontroversial. The existence conditions of a system of Ethical Life do not require the existence of any particular individuals. We could discuss the nature of modern family life without supposing that it is integral to that normative order that *my* (or *your*) family exists. Family life would not take a different form had my family or your family not existed. And the same is true of Civil Society and the State. These domains have an existence independent of the identity of the specific workers and citizens who are, or have been, members of them. And although Hegel does not stress the point at this stage, the different elements of Ethical Life will continue to exist when the members of their constituent associations (families, firms, parliaments) have passed away or moved on to better things, in much the same fashion that a football team may continue to exist long after any particular group of players have retired. Nonetheless, these ethical domains could not exist without *any* members to constitute them through their subjectivity.

The second point is more troubling. The specific relation of ethical substance or essence to its accidents which is adduced here is not merely that of an ongoing social group or community to its contingent and transient membership. The ethical substance consists of *ethical powers* which *govern* the lives of individuals. We shall have to examine later what these powers amount to, and investigate what this relation of government consists in.

The next aspect of objectivity which Hegel introduces is epistemological. We have said that Ethical Life consists in structures of objective mind. It presupposes that the denizens of the different social roles which constitute it know their place, their station and concomitant duties. Things were ever thus for most folk. But some were bloody-minded in the manner of Socrates, accosting citizens in the street and impertinently querying the conventional values. And some were certain of the truth of their idiosyncratic view of what was right, but acknowledgedly ignorant of anything that might justify it. Such a one is 'unconscious of himself'. In this sense, 'Antigone proclaims that no one knows where the laws come from: they are eternal' (§144A). But this is *not* true of modern men and women. Unlike Antigone, they are in a position to understand the nature of the rules and institutions which bind them, and in the light of this reflective understanding (the sort of understanding that Socrates sought), they bend their wills to conform with its demands. They know *what* they ought to do, and more, understand *why* they ought to do it. Which is to say that objective mind in the modern world (but not in the world of Antigone, nor in the world of Hegel's youth, the world of the aspirations of revolutionary France, nor in any historical condition in between) 'knows itself and is thus an object [*Objekt*] of knowledge'. '[A]ctual self-consciousness' (§146), the way moderns characteristically think of themselves, is not ignorant or self-deluding, is not historically constrained, parochial or ideological; it is true to and of itself.

Claims to self-knowledge are not immune to error. Hegel is not putting forward a socialized version of Cartesian certainty in self-knowledge. People may misidentify themselves (as they do when they think of themselves as nature's slaves). But nowadays, Hegel believes, they don't make errors of this kind. That sort of error has been sorted out as mankind in history has discovered the falsity of such beliefs and as societies which were built on them have gone under. The genuine self-knowledge that is now available will be rehearsed in his description of the forms of Ethical Life in what follows. Since these comprise objectively the will of the agents who constitute them as members, it can plausibly be said that objective mind knows its own nature.

This is a straightforward claim to realism in ethics and objectivity in respect of our knowledge of the demands of morality. Values are explained in terms of (inter)subjective intentions to pursue the good as evinced in characteristic patterns of activity. Our knowledge of these values consists in our self-knowledge, the recognition we demand as integral elements of the institutions and practices which determine how we should (and generally do) behave. Ethical Life makes its claim as objective in two distinct but related respects: ontologically, as the world of objective mind, it is constituted by the wills of agents who recognize, endorse and act in accordance with its demands; epistemologically, its demands have the provenance of genuine claims to self-knowledge.

At this point you should ask: Do folks, in fact, recognize the rules of the elements of Ethical Life as binding on them? Do they understand them in the way that Hegel portrays them? Do they endorse them in the light of this recognition, and do their actions display this measure of understanding and acceptance? The answer to the questions I have posed on your behalf should be 'Wait and see'. And a policy of 'wait and see' prompts further questions: What are the rules? What kind of folks do these rules suppose us to be? How do the ways we generally behave presuppose the quality of self-understanding that Hegel attributes to his fellows? All of these questions demand answers in what follows. What we do not expect is the confident assertion that Hegel puts forward next: 'In relation to the subject, the ethical substance and its laws and powers are on the one hand an object [*Gegenstand*], inasmuch as *they are*, in the supreme sense of self-sufficiency. They are thus an absolute authority and power . . .' (§146).

It cannot be said that Hegel equivocates on the meaning of 'object' since he uses different terms (*Objekt* and *Gegenstand*) to denote what is translated as 'object' in the text. Hegel's claim is that the substance of objective mind (the social institutions of Ethical Life), is an object in the two senses outlined above – an object of knowledge to the sensibilities of the persons governed by these institutions, and a self-contained social reality, a reality having an even more firmly grounded existence than the objects of the natural world. It is this last claim that should give us pause. The social world, Hegel wishes to say, is self-sufficient in the sense that it is a stable and self-contained social whole which persists through time, enjoying an independent existence. In the manner of an organism, it has holistic properties which cannot be ascribed to its members taken as individual components of it.[3] Prominent amongst these qualities is the property of reproducing itself: 'What is living reproduces itself' (VPR17: §69, 130 / VNS: 83).

What is it for a social entity to reproduce itself? We can understand this by contrast with Hegel's account of the family, which, on Hegel's account, does not reproduce itself and is not a self-sufficient reality. Rather it 'disintegrates, in a natural manner and essentially through the principle of personality [as children grow into independence and form families of their own], into a *plurality* of families' (§181). The state, by contrast, persists through changes in membership, through the continued existence of its component institutions. We can see the sense in this, though some may wish to argue that families, too, have a continuing existence through successive generations. What is suspicious is the corollary: that the self-sufficient object of Ethical Life has 'absolute authority and power'. But once again, since these are introductory points, we shall have to put down a marker for further discussion. We shall have to investigate the nature of this 'absolute authority and power' (of the social world over its constituent, transitory and contingent membership) in what follows.

Hegel seems teasingly to understand the worries which his language prompts, for immediately, at §147, he goes on to reassure the subject that the ethical substance, its authority and power, 'are not something *alien* to the subject. On the contrary, the subject bears *spiritual witness* to them as to *its own essence . . .*'. It is not even that the subject has faith in the institutions of his society, or trusts them to serve him. The relationship is closer than that. The relationship in which subjects stand to the domestic, economic and political institutions which constitute their social world is 'immediate and closer to identity than even faith or trust'. What Hegel has in mind here is a relation that modern communitarians emphasize, expressed in the thought that persons are embedded within the social practices and relationships which constitute their identities.

Again, we shall see in what follows what such concrete identities amount to, what it means, for example, to be a family member in the modern world. But we should notice one striking difference between Hegel and much modern communitarian thought. Hegel insists that the forms in which the modern identity finds itself expressed be *intelligible* to the enquiring modern subject. We might take on such identities in an immediate unreflective fashion; we may express our faith and conviction that we inhabit the social roles Hegel will describe. Or we may offer reasons why these roles are attractive to us in the light of what we see as particular interests, hopes and fears, or even a sense of our historical situatedness. But '*adequate cognition* of this identity belongs to conceptual thought [*dem denkenden Begriffe*]' (§147R). So it must be possible in principle to spell out the philosophical rationale of our constitutive identities. If these are challenged, we need not remain mute. We should be able to say how a rational enquirer might endorse them.

Moreover, we should *expect* our social identities to come under challenge, because they are not some fancy dress, a kind of ethical folk-costume in which we parade our distinctiveness. Our social identities comprise '*duties* which are binding on the will of the individual' (§148). They are practically potent. At this point in the exposition Hegel contrasts the account of duties which he will offer in his description of ethical life with what then, as now, would be more recognizably 'a *theory of duties*' (§148R).

This suggests we might usefully review the methodology of Hegel's theory of Ethical Life against the backdrop of contemporary conceptions of ethical theory. By a 'theory of duties' most philosophers would nowadays understand a system of normative ethics such as utilitarianism or the categorical imperative. It is fair to say that even those who treat normative ethics as the heart of ethics are not agreed as to the status of 'theory' in their enquiry. They may see the theoretical component as the provision of a testing device for putative moral truths (in the manner of Kant), or as a procedure for generating moral principles, supposing none of these beliefs or principles has *authority* in advance of the exercise of normative ethics. On these approaches, the testing device or the generative procedure must be supposed to have a priori rational credentials, or express some grounding insight, such as the utilitarian's view that the basic data of ethics are the facts concerning human happiness and suffering. We have seen this conception of normative ethics at work in the (failed) efforts of Morality to deliver a body of moral principles, an immanent doctrine of duties. Thought of in this way, normative ethics is a search for moral truth, or if we are less ambitious or more sceptical about the possibility of moral truth, the search for plausible principles or principles which command the agreement of 'reasonable' enquirers. Call this the 'prescriptive' account, since the point of normative theory, whether it be ambitious, modest or sceptical in point of moral truth, is to *tell* us what principles to adopt, and derivatively, what to do.

Alternatively, we might give credence to the moral rules which are familiar to us, and look to normative ethics as a systematic *explanation* (hence justification) of our subscription to them. On this account, moral theory works in a similar fashion to theory in science. We give intelligible form (and thus rational defensibility) to a body of data, in this case our moral beliefs, by showing how they can be *viewed as* derivations from some overall theory. Here, our intellectual motivation is not to discover what we should believe but to satisfy our curiosity as to why we believe what we do in fact believe. We can expect a further pay-off in cases where we are unsure of, or distrust, a moral principle. At this point we can apply the theory projectively and have the comfort of knowing that our moral beliefs at least form a consistent set.

This latter, explanatory, conception of moral theory is rarely stated in this unadorned fashion, since it has serious defects. What if several theories yield the same set of principles? We might go for the simplest or most elegant theory (which seems to be the practice in natural science), but why should the elegance or parsimony of an explanatory theory carry weight if we are unsure of what is the right thing to do? Alternatively, we might find that the only theory that works is otherwise implausible: the moral principles to which we subscribe are all found to be inscribed on tablets of stone carried down from the mountain by Joe Bloggs. Why should this *coincidence* be a reason for accepting the theory that moral principles are acceptable if they are inscribed on Joe Bloggs's tablets? Generally, moral theories that are advanced as explanatory of the principles we, in fact, avow (as with Hume's 'Newtonian' theory of the principles of justice as explained by utility) have some *independent* plausibility (Hume 1975:

203ff). Thus we can understand why utility or human well-being, as against Joe Bloggs's archaeological discoveries, has some relevance to our moral deliberations.

Moral theories of the sort that fuel the enterprise of normative ethics have been represented as either prescriptive or quasi-scientific. Needless to say there is a halfway house, dubbed 'reflective equilibrium' by John Rawls,[4] wherein we seek a satisfying unifying theory to explain the moral principles we find acceptable, but are prepared to amend the principles in the light of the plausibility of the theory, as we are prepared to qualify the theory if it demands revision of principles we find ourselves unable to relinquish. In brief, I think this a fair, if sketchy, summary of the theory of 'moral theory' as that term is employed in normative ethics.

We can now ask: What is Hegel's conception of moral theory? How does it fit the rough taxonomy outlined above? It should be obvious, following our examination of Morality, that Hegel rejects the first conception of moral theory as normative ethics, working as a generative or testing device, requiring that, for the purposes of doing moral philosophy, we suspend all our moral beliefs. In fairness, his investigation was limited to an examination of Kant's views. We cannot circumscribe the future of philosophy; it may well be that a different a priori investigation of the concept of morality will license a decision procedure for acceptable moral principles. I cannot find an argument in Hegel or elsewhere that moral philosophers should forgo this ambition. But we can move on if we agree that Kant did not find it.

It should be equally evident that Hegel rejects the second, explanatory, conception of moral theory. A scientific (or quasi-scientific) theory is no better than the data that it purports to be deducible from it. So if, and this is the lesson of most of human history, the data is corrupt – a record of beliefs that includes, retrospectively, many transparent falsehoods – we need to be sure that the beliefs which the theory explains are indeed the right beliefs. But given our record of unreliability in the past, and given the fact of error in benighted corners of the globe (where folks may still believe, for example, that some humans are natural slaves), we can have no confidence in our data in advance of a demonstration that it commands our rational assent.

If we accept my earlier taxonomy of conceptions of moral theory, it looks as though we are in a bind unless we endorse a conception of reflective equilibrium. Reflective equilibrium grants a certain authority to our firmest and most stable moral judgements. It accepts that they cannot all be put to the question at the same time. And it grants a necessary role to theory in unifying beliefs and projecting decisions in problem cases. But it does not specify an optimal decision procedure when beliefs and theories come into conflict. Nonetheless there are reasons for understanding Hegel's ethics as akin to a search for reflective equilibrium, notwithstanding the anachronism implied by the application of that term.

The moral beliefs espoused by persons immersed in Ethical Life are described as the constituent rules of the actual normative orders Hegel will investigate. But this moral world is not simply *found* to be in place. It has a history (which Hegel charts elsewhere, in the *Phenomenology* and the two sets of lectures on *the Philosophy of History* and *the History of Philosophy*). A study of the history of the moral world reveals it to be the history of freedom. The institutions in place have been learned, severally, to promote human freedom in the sense that they are structures of mutual recognition which permit the expression of distinctive human capacities, capacities that would be (and often were, in the past) undeveloped or thwarted under alternative institutions. But these institutions could only serve this function severally if collectively they comprise a coherent and harmonious set, if they don't coexist in a condition of conflict or tension. Coherence and harmony are important because it is important that neither societies nor individual citizens fragment under the tensions of conflicting ethical roles and norms.

The consistent, collective, achievement of social freedom requires tinkering with the details of the institutions and the revision of members' moral beliefs. The Hegelian version of reflective equilibrium requires an analytic presentation of the system of norms in accordance with an overarching theory of freedom which explains its content and structure. The requirement that the institutions of Ethical Life promote and exhibit freedom is met through a general conception of the purpose of the component institutions (Family, Civil Society and State) and a detailed explanation of their credentials. '[A]n immanent and consistent theory of duties can be nothing other than the development of *those relations* which are necessitated by the Idea of freedom, and are therefore *actual* in their entirety, within the state' (§148R). Reflective equilibrium is achieved in the articulation of the Idea of freedom as 'the Idea of Right – the concept of right [as the theory of freedom] and its actualization [in the belief systems manifested by the norm governed behaviour of Ethical Life]' (§1).

Alert readers will note that a trick has been turned. In specifying schematically the nature and content of a theory of duties, the key theoretical notion has been identified once again as freedom. We offer as the rationale of the duties we acknowledge the value of freedom. But don't duties *circumscribe* our freedom? Doesn't our freedom consist in the *silence* of the voice of (moral and legal) duty? Isn't a binding duty a *limitation* or a *restriction* on our freedom? Hegel puts these questions in §149, and answers that we are only tempted to answer them in the affirmative if we operate with defective conceptions of both freedom and duty. If we think of freedom 'in relation to indeterminate subjectivity or abstract freedom, and to the drives of the natural will or of the moral will which arbitrarily determines its own indeterminate good' (§149) then duty, which fixes a content to the good and controls natural desires, will appear as a constraint.

'The individual, however, finds his *liberation* in duty' (§149) in these specific respects:

1. 'he is liberated from his dependence on mere natural drives';
2. he is liberated from the (egoistical?) pressures which burden 'the particular subject in his moral reflections on obligation and desire';
3. he is liberated from the interminable, because indecisive, condition of 'indeterminate subjectivity which ... remains *within itself* and has no actuality', i.e. Morality.

(§149)

It follows that we act freely when we are disposed to do the right thing, as against being pushed and pulled by our drives and desires, or deliberating to no purpose. When our characters have been so formed that we act seemingly spontaneously in an ethical fashion, we demonstrate moral *virtue*. Virtue takes the form of *rectitude* when the agent does 'what is prescribed, expressly stated and known to him within his situation' (§150R). It is important to Hegel that the members of the various communities which make up Ethical Life have a settled disposition which motivates their compliance with the institutional rules. Thus, for example, family members will love each other and pursue the interests of the family in Civil Society. Citizens will identify patriotically with their state.

So it is possible to describe Ethical Life as a doctrine of virtue and Hegel's style of thinking about morality 'virtue ethics'. But this would be misleading, since the prime virtue of persons engaged in ethical life is simple conformity with the rules which they accept should govern their conduct. A virtue ethics is more appropriately spoken of 'in uncivilized societies and communities' (§150R) where the demands of institutions or the rules of conduct are not explicit. Here the best that folk can manage is a rough Aristotelian calculation of what emotional response constitutes the mean in the circumstances of action. In the modern world, by contrast, we have rules (the ethical determination of the universal quality of actions) to guide us.

Nonetheless, we are virtuous when we act with rectitude. When rectitude is a general mode of behaviour, 'the ethical ... appears as *custom*; and the *habit* of the ethical appears as a *second nature* which takes the place of the original and purely natural will' (§151). It is the task of education to make human beings ethical (§§20, 151A, 187). Duty is not a limitation on the freedom of those who have internalized the norms of a well-governed community and who follow the customary rules of that community in a habitual fashion. Freedom does not require the strenuous exercise of putting rules to the test. Rather, individuals' '*certainty* of their own freedom has its *truth* in such objectivity, and it is in the ethical realm that they *actually* possess *their own* essence and their *inner* universality' (§153), which is to say they identify with the institutions which constitute their social nature and have internalized the institutional norms.

It follows that freedom is a social achievement, to be attained only in communities governed by transparently valid, intersubjective norms. Such a community is an ethical substance, 'the *actual spirit* of a family and a people' (§156). In the rest of the book Hegel will describe the concrete forms which spirit takes in the modern world.

Before we begin our investigation of these we should conduct a quick review of the doctrine we have articulated.

The crucial doctrine that needs defence is the challenging view that the individual finds his liberation in duty. This looks odd if we read the statement with its political implications in mind. For then we shall think of duty in terms of the requirements of the law, and view legal requirements as restrictions on freedom. This conception of freedom is 'negative' in the terms of Berlin's dichotomy of positive and negative liberty (Berlin 1969: 121–31). It is the mode of liberty which, in Hobbes's words, 'depends on the silence of the Law' (Hobbes 1985: 271 / Part 2, ch. 21). If we think of duty and freedom in this way, the thought that we may find liberation in our duty is self-contradictory or paradoxical, since legal duties paradigmatically constrain rather than express or promote our freedom.

But as we saw when studying Hegel's Introduction, we don't have to think of freedom in this way. There are two contrary conceptions of freedom of action in play here. The first, 'natural' conception, deriving from Hobbes and Hume, defines free agency roughly as the condition in which we can get what we (most) want without being hindered. The second, 'moralized' conception, deriving from Locke and Rousseau, defines free agency as self-determination, as the capacity to order or control our desires and act in the light of a conception of the good, doing what we want (or believe that we ought) to want. These conceptions of freedom as we have seen clearly conflict. The drug or tobacco addict acts freely on the 'natural' conception when he sniffs his cocaine or lights up his cigarette, but if he doesn't want to be a sniffer or a smoker, his action is unfree on the 'moralized' conception of free agency. On the first conception, I am unfree if you stop me smoking; on the second, the paradigm example of unfreedom is the poor soul who smokes a cigarette in the clear knowledge that he shouldn't be doing it.

If we see dutiful conduct as the action of one who is in control of his desires and subsequent actions, either by ordering them or, in Kantian fashion, by subserving them to a different (rational) source of motivation, we shall find duty to be a liberation in one of the senses that Hegel intends: one is 'liberated from his dependence on mere natural drives' (§149). This is a *respectable* conception of free agency. Far be it from me to defend it here against the alternative. I say 'respectable' because I insist that it is not eccentric. It has strong philosophical credentials.

If Kant had said that the 'individual finds his liberation in duty', no-one would have blinked or raised an eyebrow, because Kant conceived of duty as the product of each individual's exercise of the powers of rational reflection, each person autonomously working out for herself what duty requires. The same thought is more tricky in the voice of Hegel because the call of duty is identified in the demands of the (rational) community. So we might ask: In what circumstances might one believe that having to do her duty to family, colleagues, and fellow citizens is experienced as a limitation, hindrance or constraint, as a restriction on her freedom? A straightforward response would be to say that duties are identified as limitations where they are experienced as alien impositions or where they are judged to have an alien source. If I experience my wife as an alien 'other', no wonder I think of her as a ball-and-chain. If I regard my colleagues or employer as strangers or as the class enemy, I will experience their demands on me as alien impositions. If I regard the state as fundamentally hostile to my deepest personal projects, I will view it, basically, despite its appeals to patriotism, as an external coercive agency. The suggestion that these examples prompt is that one will judge the call of duty as a limitation on freedom just in case the duty is demanded by an agency conceived as basically 'other'. The implication of this conclusion is that if I do *not* regard my duty as an alien imposition I will *not* experience it as a threat to my freedom. Earlier, Hegel has told us that 'the concrete concept of freedom' is experienced 'in the form of feeling, for example in friendship and love. Here, we are not one-sidedly within ourselves, but willingly limit ourselves with reference to another, even while knowing ourselves in this limitation as ourselves' (§7A). Thus if I accept the norms of family life, collegiality and citizenship as constitutive of a complex social world with which I knowingly identify and in which I feel at home, my will is 'completely *with itself* [*bei sich*] . . . every relationship of *dependence* on something *other* than itself is thereby eliminated' (§23). Such a will remains '*with itself* in this objectivity' (§28) – at home in the other.

But freedom cannot consist in persons' doing *whatever* the community demands of them since in fact, as history and current affairs attest, communities may get things wrong. So Hegel's position is defensible only if the demands of the community are *rational*, which is to say, only if the demands of the community are acceptable to those who reflect on these demands and, as a result, are satisfied with their credentials. This exercise is Kantian if we can assume that any rational agent is able to do it. But it is not Kantian in another respect, since it demands that we achieve an understanding of the complexities of a historically formed human nature and the social conditions which generate its optimal expression. As we have seen, we should certainly not suppose it to require the application of reason functioning as a quasi-algorithmic device.

It follows that a philosophical verdict on the adequacy of Hegel's doctrine of Ethical Life rests on the plausibility of his account of reason, of rationality as a property of the norms of the Rational State. At this point, sympathetic readers of Hegel diverge. Some accept (one version of) Hegel's own story about the demands of rationality: that it disclose in neo-Aristotelian fashion structures of mind which exhibit universality and particularity, separately specified yet perspicuously synthesized (*aufgehoben*) in a comprehensive, individual, totality. This amounts to a *concrete universal*. Unlike Plato's forms, the concrete universal is not ideal; it is a creature of this world, a structure of objective mind (or *Geist*) which exists and can be described. It is concrete, too, in the sense that it is not a set of prescriptions or code of rules (the *Sollen*) which merely 'ought' to be authoritative. Such a set of rules would be valid quite independently of whether or not it was in place, understood and respected.

The categories which structure a rational totality (universality, particularity and individuality (or specificity)) are exemplified in Ethical Life by the Family, Civil Society and the overarching Rational State respectively (recapitulating the overall structure of the *Philosophy of Right* as a synthesis[5] of Abstract Right and Morality within Ethical Life). If the rationality of the structures of Ethical Life consists in its exemplification of these structured categories, we should be able to explain and defend their institutional embodiments, the detail of the domestic, economic, legal, administrative and political domains in terms of these formal properties. This is what I take a dialectical deduction of objective mind to amount to. I confess: I can't do it.

This task amounts to explaining, in the case of modern family life, how it can be justified (perhaps as against outmoded or fictional alternatives – the clan or Rousseau's (almost) solitary existences) in point of its universality. *Au contraire* (and this is the second route that the sympathetic reader may take): we understand how universality can be its distinguishing formal characteristic once we see the value in the typical ways in which family members are deemed to relate to one another, through love. We understand that Civil Society is the domain of particularity, not because we have an antecedent conception of what particularity in the social world demands, but because we understand the role of self- or family-centred interest in the workings of the economy and persons' rights in the administration of law. If Hegel's account of political life were more persuasive, we could give specific content to the category of individuality and understand what a concrete universal might be in the realm of objective mind.

In other words, the formal or categorial conception of rationality as disclosed by a dialectical investigation needs to be turned upside down in a fashion that Marx didn't quite envisage. Instead of deducing the optimal form of life (the Rational State) from the dialectical logic of the concept, we find that the stuctures of the concept only begin to be intelligible once we see how they serve as labels for ways of life that are independently defensible. Hegel will tell us, in succession: what is the best way for persons who love each other to conduct their relationships; what is the best way for work to be organized if it is to meet the demands of individuals; what is the best way to administrate a system of law; what purposes a bureaucracy should serve; what social ends are best promoted by interest groups; what is the constitution of the best modern state; and in each case, why this is so. Once these arguments are in place, for better or worse, we can begin to understand the dialectic and its categories.

The story that is told about the component institutions of Ethical Life will be persuasive, if and where it is persuasive, not because it obeys the canons of a dialectical logic but because it details how these institutions promote persons' aspirations to freedom. People will find their liberation in doing their duty just in case the institutions which prescribe their duties contribute, in an identifiable fashion, to the freedom of their members. When we see how this is achieved, we shall understand why these institutions found favour with humankind, why they have settled down to become mankind's ethical home. Since we value the freedom they promote, we shall have justified as well as explained their formation. We shall have demonstrated their provenance.

This mode of argumentation is not quite as novel as I have been suggesting, since it has a precursor, which Hegel did not recognize, in the work of David Hume on justice. Hume, too, tells a functional story concerning the efficacy of the institutions of justice. The rules governing property and legitimate political institutions have their origins in processes which secure utility. Utility serves to establish their provenance, both explaining their adoption and stability and justifying their demands. The major difference between Hume and Hegel is that whereas Hume claims utility does the job of explanation and justification, for Hegel freedom is the key value. It is the functional role of the institutions of Ethical Life to make it possible for persons to be free in Hegel's distinctive sense: that of being at home in social structures – the 'other' – which uniquely permit and promote the harmonious exercise of a range of personal capacities distinctive of citizens of the modern social world. We shall have to see whether he can make good his claim that the Rational State is the embodiment of freedom. Hegel's ambition is a worthy one, and his method, I claim, is philosophically defensible. But the devil, we shall find, is in the detail.

Chapter 10

The Family: §§158–81

You will enjoy reading Hegel's account of family life.
It concerns a topic with which most of us are intimately
familiar. It draws a picture of the modern nuclear
family as the ideal of domesticity, so readers will
approach it as the portrayal of a paradigm to be
supported or challenged. It offers an account of love
as the feeling distinctive of family life – and we all
have views on that. It describes the different natures
of men and women and explicitly defends a sexual
division of labour. Thus it offers feminists a clear
target. We are all experts on the topics dealt with in
his discussion, so the study of this chapter furnishes
an excellent opportunity to sharpen our dialectical
skills. We must not forget, though, that the main task
will be to use this material to gain a fuller understanding of the notion of Ethical Life. In particular, we
want to see what the duties of domesticity amount
to, and vitally, how dutiful conduct can be a liberation. The study of family life will be a good test case,
not least since it has been commonly held that its

central feature – marriage – is a ball and chain rather the locus of important freedoms.

Love

Hegel thought, and wrote, about love on many occasions. Prompted perhaps by maudlin discussions with Hölderlin, in 1797–8 he wrote and revised a well-known fragment on love (ETW: 302–8, carefully discussed in Harris 1972: 298–310) in which he analyses not only mankind's love of God, but also the physical and emotional variety of love between men and women. In both the *Science of Logic* (SL: 603 / SW 5: 39–40) and the *Encyclopaedia*, love is emblematic of that concept of freedom (i.e. the Concept generally) wherein the model is that of discrete individuals overcoming their separation by finding themselves at home in the other. 'The members, linked to one another, are not really foreign to one another, but only elements of one whole, each of them, in connection with the other, being as it were, at home [*bei sich*], and combining with itself' (EL §158A). (See Westphal 1980.) Hegel explains in detail how we are philosophically as well as literally at home with our families.

In family life, the distinctive form taken by objective mind (the *immediate substantiality* of spirit (§158)) is the feeling of love. We should note straightaway that love is a natural feeling, in the language of Kant's trichotomy, an inclination. We shall see that some of the distinctive features of Hegel's account of family life are developed in opposition to Kant's views on the topic. In fact, although Hegel does not trumpet this opposition throughout his discussion, the analysis he offers of family life as an ethical domain constitutes a recapitulation of his severe critique of Kant's moral psychology. Recall that for Kant even the sweetest inclinations amount to psychological clutter, emotional and therefore heterogeneous 'noise' that can drown out the stern but pure voice of duty. If Kant's model of dutiful conduct is the world-weary misanthrope (GMM: 53–4 / Ak. 4: 398–9), we can expect his conception of morality to offer a distorted account of family life. Loving families will be morally messy. The sharing-caring, lovey-dovey elements of family life will occlude actions of genuine moral worth.

By contrast, on Hegel's much more plausible account, all the duties, as well as the pleasures, of family life derive from the identification of love as a feeling or inclination. Marriage partners love each other; parents love their children (and children love their parents, though not to the same degree!). The model of love is that of husband and wife. We shall investigate what Hegel takes love to be and shall treat the love of spouses as exemplary. You might think this is not a good opening move. Surely the love of *lovers* is the phenomenon that needs to be studied, since spouses may or may not love each other. If the main concern were an investigation of love, this would obviously be true. But it is not. It is family life that we seek to understand, and on Hegel's account, the love of husband and wife for each other is the key concept.

Hegel tells us in the opening paragraph that love is 'the spirit's *feeling* of its own unity . . . one is present [in the unity of the family] not as an independent person [*eine Person für sich*] but as a *member*' (§158). Hegel's heroic account of love has metaphysical, ethical and psychological dimensions. Let us treat these in turn. Metaphysically, lovers are initially conceived as *persons* in the sense explored in Abstract Right. They are atomic, discrete, beings with the status of independent moral entities. But the cost of independence is isolation and an impoverished sense of self. A fuller understanding of what the individual truly is, what people can be, requires 'the renunciation of my independent existence [*meines Fürsichseins*]' (§158). This is achieved when the independent self is united with another. Metaphysically, the phenomenon of love attests the existence of a novel unity, of loving persons united through their renunciation of independence. It is as though, through love, the number of persons in the world is halved. Where once we had two persons, now we have one, and that person speaks in the language of the first-person plural. Now we have a 'We' where hitherto there were two 'I's'.

The metaphysical 'We' of loving marriage partners speaks ethically in a distinctive voice. In the moral world of discrete persons, agents act either in their own interests or in the interests of others. If they seek to advance their own interests, they act in a self-interested fashion. If they seek to promote the interests of others, they act altruistically. When persons unite, as we shall see that they do on Hegel's account of marriage, this distinction is obliterated. Those who conjugate their deliberations in the first-person plural do not seek to advance the interests either of themselves or the 'other'. They ask what is best for 'us'.[1] Precisely because this standpoint transcends the egoism/ altruism distinction, we should not characterize it in the paradoxical modern jargon as 'self-referential altruism'.

It is a good philosophical question whether the ethical perspective of the 'We', the transcendence of the egoism/altruism dichotomy, is attainable without the metaphysical construction of an 'Us'. I can think of examples of how one might take the interests of other persons into account which are strategic and thereby prudential (for example, I will be better off if I promote his interests; he is my father-in-law), but this is not an ethical perspective. I can think of examples of altruistic behaviour which require a sharp sense of the *difference* between the benefactor and the beneficiary ('Thank God I'm not reduced to begging in the street. There, but for the grace of God, go I'). This is a moral point of view but it does not attest the transcendence of the standard 'I'–'Thou'/'self'–'other' dichotomy. There are examples of persons separately identifying a common project which is more effectively pursued collectively than independently. Thus parents who wish to improve the education of their children might institute a parent–teacher association with a committee structure that secures the advantages of division of labour. These parents, acting together and speaking as a 'we', are promoting, in Rousseau's terms, their 'particular wills' if they believe the improvement of the educational prospects of all the children in the school is the best strategic route to the improvement of the education of their own children. But, in the nature of things (and this is a point Hegel will emphasize later in his study of Civil Society) a contingent strategic alliance of this sort will often be transformed into a truly general will (= 'universal', in one of Hegel's senses of the word), since the collective activity designed to secure the will of all, the universal (= across the board) achievement of particular interests, will *create* a universal (= genuinely communal) perspective hitherto absent. The ethical perspective of parents who actively care for the education of *each other's* children is explained by the metaphysical unity which has been created 'by the back door', without a forming intention.

There is no logical or natural necessity to be observed in the workings of these creative social processes. The smug, chuckling 'We' of contingent allies is often fragile, as political history attests. Indeed, to make the point in a manner which is not tendentious, we all know that there are some games (e.g. Diplomacy, Monopoly) in which self-interest is the rule; only one person can win, so all alliances are temporary and strategic, agreements are unreliable, and profitable derogations no sin. Some would have it that this is how big business works; some say that 'all's fair in love and war'. I'm sure that these wise folks are right – sometimes, but less often than they, who spout the nostrum, believe. For the most part, they should hark the lesson Hobbes addresses to the 'Foole [who] hath sayd in his heart, there is no such thing as Justice' (Hobbes 1985: Part 1, ch. 15, 203). The Foole is lucky if he gets away with it. It won't be for long. News that he is untrustworthy will travel fast, far and wide. He will find he has few allies.

The 'we' *can* signal a transient coincidence of particular wills, but in many other circumstances 'I' will find it difficult to believe that '*our*' interests are promoted unless 'I' *identify*, in some fashion, with the person I propose to help. If she is a member of my family, or a colleague at work, or a fellow citizen (and the circle can be enlarged), I will respond as one who thinks that *we* ought to look after *each other* in circumstances of distress. Such admirable thoughts require the antecedent recognition of a common identity.

It should be clear by now that the 'identity' we have been discussing is not logical identity. Lovers use the first-person plural when they speak the language of 'We'; marriage partners, the Book of Common Prayer tells us, become one person, but this does not mean that Romeo is one and the same person as Juliet in the same way that Marilyn Monroe was the same person as Norma Jean. The identity that sincere and unchallenged use of the 'We' bespeaks is a metaphysical construction. This sounds portentous, but it is not. It amounts to a denial that what is at stake ('our' interests) can be repudiated by appeal to the self-interest of one of the parties to the alliance, other things being equal.

Hegel claims that psychologically, and perhaps logically, we cannot achieve a sense of ourselves as independent self-consciousnesses unless this status is recognized by others. This is the tragedy of the protagonists in the Life and Death struggle of the *Phenomenology* (PS ¶¶186–8) who fight to the death for their standing. It is a good question why Hegel, given his earlier thoughts on love, did not at this point in the *Phenomenology* account of the development of self-consciousness emphasize how independent persons might seek recognition of their selfhood through the pursuit of love rather than war. (After all, love achieves what war only risks – the loss of the independent self.) What the agent seeks is recognition of his ethical standing. Love affords this. 'I find myself in another person . . . I gain recognition in this person who in turn gains recognition in me' (§158A).

Hegel is right to see that there is something contradictory in love, in the strategy of an independent consciousness which expresses its nature by losing its independence in its commitment to another with whom it identifies. The identification is contingent and may not endure. The union of marriage partners may be dissolved in divorce. At this point separate persons re-emerge. A modern view would take note of the implicit contradiction. It would establish *space* within the unity of the family for the partners to carve out domains of independence for the partners. Their love would not be compromised by mutual respect for spheres of independent ambitions and activities. But, as we shall see, Hegel cannot allow this.

We should recognize, in the metaphysical, ethical and psychological elements of the loving relationship, an important modality of freedom.

If we endorse one of Rousseau's key claims, we see a condition of *independence* as a paradigm of freedom. Hegel, in firm opposition, tells us that we learn something about ourselves when, as in love, we renounce our independent existences, 'finding ourselves' in the other. We learn that we are capable of attachment, of long-term commitment to a lover, and knowing this we feel 'deficient and incomplete' (§158A) if we live an independent but loveless existence. It is as though the solitary self is a prison from which we crave release. We achieve freedom from personal isolation through love. We enrich ourselves when we lose ourselves through the love of another. I think these things are true.

Marriage

We love our friends and, hopefully, our parents and children. The love of marriage partners is different because it is a sexual relationship. The association is natural, an episode in the life history of members of a sexually reproducing species. Hegel believes that it is an error to believe that mating behaviour is all there is to marriage, as he believes most systems of natural law would have it (§161A). It is a crude error, too – 'disgraceful' is Hegel's word for it at §75R – to describe marriage as a contract which licenses 'sexual union (*commercium sexuale*) . . . the reciprocal use that one human being makes of the sexual organs and capacities of another' (MM: 426 / Ak. 6: 277). This debases marriage 'to a contract entitling the parties concerned to use one another' (§162A). Hegel doesn't make the point explicitly, but the implied, *ad hominem* criticism of Kant is obvious. How can it be right for human beings to make themselves into a thing (a sexual object, as they say nowadays) for the enjoyment of another? Kant himself recognizes the problem. The only condition under which it is legitimate for persons so to violate the right of humanity in their own persons is that *both* parties do it, having signed a marriage contract. Oddly, Kant believes that this redeems rather than compounds the felony.

Hegel himself believes that marriage originates in an act of mutual consent undertaken from the standpoint of contract (*Vertragsstandpunkte*), that is, the standpoint of Abstract Right, of individuals who recognize each other as persons. Marriage is not *itself* a contract, since that would imply that the several parties treat both themselves and each other as individual, external things. It is rather the supersession of the domain of contract (§163R).[2] The subjective origins of marriage may lie in the sentiments of the two persons or in the machinations of the parents who arrange it, but even in this latter case, the parents are making a decision on partners who, they judge, are destined to be united in love (and if they are sensible they will consult their children on their proposals). They are *not* creating political alliances or advancing commercial projects (§162A). Hegel is coy as to which arrangement is best. I suspect he believes that children who are proposing to marry would do best to be guided by their parents, but he knows well enough that the battle, in the modern world, has been won for romance, if not romanticism, by playwrights and novelists. 'Nowadays', the old man concedes wearily to his otherwise sceptical student audience, 'the *state of being in love* is regarded as the only important factor' (§162A).

The objective origin of marriage is the occasion, religious or civil, when the hitherto independent persons give their free 'consent to *constitute a single person* and to give up their natural and individual personalities within this union'. This element of renunciation may suggest that the 'union is a self-limitation, but since they attain their substantial self-consciousness within it, it is in fact their liberation' (§162). We have seen that the simultaneous loss and enrichment of the self which is achieved in a loving relationship is a liberation from (the miseries of) personal isolation. We should ask if the love of committed marriage partners promises further or deeper or more specific modes of liberation.

Hegel tells us that it does (though if we are young, bold and in love, or older but embarked on an adventure, we shall have our doubts). The union of marriage partners promises 'love, trust and the sharing of the whole of individual existence'. In this state, the sexual instinct is reduced to 'the modality of a moment of nature which is extinguished in its very satisfaction' (§163). We know what Hegel means. Sexuality is urgent and pressing. Sexual desires demand satisfaction, and release, sadly, is temporary. But in marriage these desires can be disciplined; whatever the sexual regime that a particular marriage adopts (twice a night or once a week plus Christmas and birthdays) it is encompassed in the fact of union, the 'spiritual bond ... that is exalted above the contingency of the passions and of particular transient caprice' (§163). (I cannot help myself imagining the sort of detail Hegel's terminology conceals, since he does not seem able to insinuate the comic aspects of sex before an audience of students: 'above the contingency of the passions' – this suggests that married lovers can ignore the urgencies of the moment or submit, even if they have a headache; 'above particular transient caprice' – this suggests that married men and women are invulnerable to the siren call.)

What Hegel evidently favours as an important element of freedom is settled domesticity, which finds a place, but a subordinate one, for sexuality. The best, least disruptive way, to control the sexual drive is to aim for long-term intimate companionship, to commit oneself to a union which is in principle, though it cannot be so universally in practice, indissoluble (§163A). Hegel is probably right in this. Love is easy; it is sex that is hard to manage and control. Hegel believes that mankind has found, in the love of marriage partners, the optimal mode of effecting the self-discipline that the unruly imperatives of sexuality necessitate. But it is a discipline that requires an enlarged conception of the self, a conception which embraces the other as spouse. 'The sensuous moment which pertains to natural life is thereby put in its ethical context as an accidental consequence, belonging to the external existence of the ethical bond, which may even consist exclusively in mutual love and support' (§164).

One might agree with this, but still ask why marriage is necessary. Why, as Hegel insists, must lovers go through the specified rigmarole, in a church or registry office? Doesn't the formality detract from the purity of the lovers' commitment to each other? Is it not 'an alien factor [which] runs counter to the inwardness of this union' (§164R)? The view that marriage diminishes the commitment of love is familiar nowadays. Many readers may hold to it, and if they don't, they will have friends, children or parents who do. Hegel's philosophical response to this query seems to be that mere 'relationships' will be strained by the 'contingency and arbitrariness of sensuous inclination' – which is their source (§164R). They will exhibit a tension which the objective commitment demonstrated in a public ceremony will resolve. Unmarried lovers are not more free than their wedded counterparts; they are less free because all they have to sustain them are the contingencies of passion. They are vulnerable to a force which is both powerful and transient.

Is marriage a dead hand, because it *formalizes* an otherwise and hitherto authentic commitment? Does the public ritual of the religious ceremony or the civil affirmation of wedded status detract from or demean an essentially personal, because private, relationship? Or is it, by contrast, a liberation because it strengthens a discipline in matters of sexuality which is essential to personal freedom? These questions are more live than they were when Hegel drafted the *Philosophy of Right* for his students, since, if the arguments for free love are a seducer's charter (§164A), seducers nowadays can be of either sex, with no specific imputation of dishonour against loose women. If readers find these matters perplexing, I have no advice to give. They perplex me, too.

There were free, independent women in Hegel's day, and he met them throughout his life in intellectual salons.[3] He could be uncomfortable in their presence, as several were in his. He appears to be blind to this phenomenon when he writes of the different natures of men and women and the consequent sexual division of labour within the family. No doubt you can guess the story he tells even though you may not have read it. I can't believe that anyone would accept it nowadays except for embittered misogynists or self-deceiving women who seek to conceal their good fortune or excuse their lack of ambition. These are the essential features: 'Man therefore has his actual substantive life in the state, in learning, etc., and otherwise in work and struggle', that is, *outside* the family; 'Woman, however, has her substantial vocation [*Bestimmung*] in the family, and her ethical disposition consists in this [family] *piety*' (§166), that is, the domains of '*Kinder, Kirche, Küche*'.

Matters get worse in the lecture hall.

> Women may well be educated, but they are not made for the higher sciences, for philosophy ... [they] have insights, taste, and delicacy, but they do not possess the ideal. The difference between man and woman is the difference between animal and plant [I suspect this is the only joke recorded in the text of the *Philosophy of Right*, though many critics have taken the claim seriously] ... When women are in charge of government, the state is in danger [!].
>
> (§166A)

The general issue at stake here, whether men and women have different natures in some fashion which is ethically significant, is still unresolved. Even within the feminist movement there are some who accept the claim and some who dispute it. Everyone should deny Hegel's implication: that the (ideal) family should be organized around a sex-based division of labour. Hegel believed that this family structure was liberating in the precise sense that it enabled men and women severally to employ and thereby realize their distinctive capacities. His view can be rejected on the same grounds. Freedom requires: for women, that they be able to exercise their capacities for work outside the home, if they need to or so wish; for men, that they have the opportunity to express their desire for intimacy and attachment by accepting responsibility for domestic activities within the home. The precise division of labour (or its absence) within each household should be a matter for families individually to work out, rather than a prescription of domestic natural law.

Hegel draws two further conclusions from his analysis of family life as a commitment of loving partners. The first is that marriage must be monogamous and, it is assumed, between male and female persons. Hegel's argument for this position in the main text is cursory and elliptical, which would not matter if it were a statement of the obvious. But we must take it that Hegel believes a homosexual marriage would be defective because it would be irrational. Why would this be so? Homosexual marriage would be irrational if the sole end of marriage were the procreation of children, but Hegel argues in his Heidelberg lectures (VPR17: 149 / VNS: 101) that it is not. He is obviously right in this. Otherwise marriages between pensioners would be as controversial as the marriage of homosexual partners. The prime purpose of marriage is the objective establishment of the loving union of committed partners, which is justified as a liberation. If this story is acceptable, so, too, should be homosexual marriages.[4]

Hegel clearly believes that marriage can be a true union only where there is sexual difference. We can reject this and still ask whether marriage should be monogamous. Again there are alternatives – polygamy and polyandry – which Hegel rejects. He does so because he believes that a genuine sense of married unity is possible only where there is a 'mutual and *undivided* surrender of . . . personality' between the marriage partners. Such a person 'attains its right of being conscious of itself in the other only insofar as the other is present in this identity as a person, i.e. as atomic individuality' (§167). That the surrender of personality need be undivided seems a metaphysical claim to the effect that there could not be a genuine unity if married, hence sexual, love were distributed amongst three or more partners. Love certainly could not be distributed in the same fashion if the partners were exclusively heterosexual, but who knows what permutations are possible amongst bisexual persons? The mind boggles, but what is empirically possible cannot be a metaphysical impossibility. More promising is the thought, which Hegel accepts, that polygamy in the form where several women are married to one man is a mode of slavery of the women. A polygamous union would not be a union of genuine persons ('atomic individuals'), presumably since the distribution of sexual and household labours and favours must be in the control of the husband.

The second conclusion he draws is that incestuous marriages are irrational. Hegel knows the standard explanation of the incest taboo – that it produces feeble offspring – but he emphasizes instead how incest violates the concept of marriage. The argument is that close family members (I take it he has siblings in mind) are not independent of each other in the way marriage partners are described. They live within a '*naturally identical* circle of people who are acquainted and familiar with each other in every detail' (§168). In relation to one another, they do not count as distinct personalities, as atomic individuals. It is hard to adjudicate an argument presented at this level of abstraction. There are difficult philosophical issues to be addressed concerning the prohibition of incest. But before I sidestep them, it is worth pointing out that these questions must be trickier than Hegel implies since he also believes that family members become independent of each other when children reach maturity (§177). He is left with the romantic thought that marriage is a voyage of discovery undertaken by strangers who create a unity out of the novel circumstances of intimacy. Evidently this is not possible for siblings who have been brought up together.

Family Resources

Marriage creates a new person, '*universal* and *enduring*' (§170). Just as the person of Abstract Right required property in order to be free, so does the family. In fact, family life represents the transformation of the abstract individual who is standardly regarded as the bearer of rights, notably property rights. The service of particular needs (*whatever they may be* – remember they are completely unspecified, entirely abstract in Abstract Right) 'is here transformed, along with the self-ishness of desire, into care and acquisition for a *communal purpose*, i.e. into an *ethical* quality' (§170). Just as hitherto independent persons are constituted as a single unity in marriage, so their egoistic interests are left behind in the married union. 'We' now pursue 'our' best interests rather than the interests of our formerly discrete personalities. This adds an ethical dimension to prudence. We should recall that action in pursuit of immediate, natural desires is free in a meagre sense, free in-itself. A fortiori, and at best, immediate, *self-interested* or *selfish* desires are products of the arbitrary will, the *Willkür* (§§11–12, 15). We can now see how family life represents an advance over Abstract Right, because we can now describe in fuller detail the form, if not the content, of typical desires. In the family, they will be desires for a common good, and their pursuit will serve a communal purpose. When discussing the will in Chapter 2 we saw how freedom requires 'the purification of the drives' (§19). Now we can see one concrete means by which purification (i.e. freedom) is achieved. Persons are liberated from the causality of self-interest when, through marriage, they create a '*universal* and *enduring* person' and pursue the interests of the ethical being they have created. We shall describe later the ethical sphere in which the self-interest of this universal person is pusued when we examine Civil Society.

We are now able to translate the insights of Abstract Right into the first-person plural language of the 'self-sufficient concrete person' which is created in family life. Such a person will have its own exclusive property, commonly held between its members who have an inclusive right to it, though it is under the control of the father. This creates tensions as we shall see. The concept of family property also looks to create a tension within Hegel's account of property, since he has insisted at §46 that communal property is a defective institution when compared with private property. I think he can escape the charge of inconsistency since the kind of common property he is there discussing is owned jointly by separate persons or is the possession of an anachronistic, and thereby irrational, institution. But the persons joined in marriage are not separate persons. They have given up this moral status in favour of a liberating union.

Children

Family property attests the family union. So, too, but in an importantly different fashion, do children. The social metaphysics is hard to understand, but the official story runs like this: between spouses, the substance of the marriage union is their intersubjective, loving disposition. Externally, the spouses remain separate existences, although their unity may be embodied in external *things* when the family owns property. In children, this unity attains an objective existence which is self-conscious and which the parents 'love as their love' (§173). (I can't decide whether the self-conscious unity which is created within the family with children refers to the self-consciousness of the children or the self-consciousness of the enhanced family group, taken as a totality.)

Given Hegel's earlier talk of spouses giving up their individual personalities, one might have thought that children, too, were metaphysically engulfed in the sentimental unity as parts of a whole. But strikingly, he discusses the relations between parents and children in terms of each other's *rights*. 'Children have a right to be brought up and supported at the expense of the family.' Parents have a right to their children's services, so long as these services are directed towards 'the common concern of caring for the family in general' (§174). (Children are not free labour or slaves as the Romans believed (§174R).) Parents have the right to discipline their children, 'to break the child's self-will in order to eradicate the merely sensuous and natural'. Spare the rod, or insist on giving full explanations to children (as though they are adults who require to be persuaded by good reasons), and the child is spoiled, 'forward and impertinent'. It is essential to instil a 'feeling of subordination' in children – otherwise they will never wish to grow up! (§174A). Childhood is a disciplined preparation for 'the self-sufficiency and freedom of personality' (§175) which comes with adulthood. Education is not like training a dog for a lifetime of submission. It is a structure of finely meshing rights and duties on the part of parents and children.

Of course it is more than that. When family life goes well it is a cocoon of 'love, trust and obedience', but it must be structured by a clear sense of reciprocal rights and duties which permit us to judge how well things are going. Things go badly wrong if children are ill-nourished or poorly educated. Their rights are not being respected. Things go wrong, too, if children are poorly disciplined or 'educated through play' (a fashionable theory, then as now (§175R and editor's notes)). They have a right to be educated to assume the standing of bearers of rights, of personhood. Hence 'society has a right to compel parents to send their children to school, to have them vaccinated, etc.' (239A). In these passages Hegel suggests that the place of rights within the family union is akin to a backstop, a marker for when things are going badly and a resource against the dereliction of parental duty. When a family fails, the state has a licence to step in – which is a sensible position now (as it must have been a strange if prescient doctrine when Hegel wrote). Rights will not be claimed when love, trust and obedience demonstrate that the family is in good ethical condition. The contrast between Kant and Hegel can be overblown if it is suggested that for Kant persons' rights are all that matter and that for Hegel they matter not at all.[5]

The Dissolution of the Family

Strong family values are important for Hegel, but he is not so silly as to suggest that the family is immune to the winds of hostile contingency. The family is characterized by love – romantic love, sexual love and the love of committed partners, all this underpinned by civil and religious institutions and recognized as having legal status. But this does not amount to a 'positive bond which could keep partners together once their dispositions have become antagonistic and hostile', once there is 'total estrangement' (§176). Hence, since essentially, 'marriage is based only on subjective and contingent feeling, it may be dissolved'. With one eye, as ever, on backward Catholicism, he insists that 'even the religious authority must permit divorce' (§176A), at which point the estranged parties must resume their former independent personalities.

Two other modes of dissolution of the family include the coming of age of children and, especially, their marrying and founding new families, and obviously the death of the parents. The first of these is notable since it emphasizes how clearly Hegel has in view the modern nuclear family. Not only does the family exclude the wider kinship relationships of the extended family, it also excludes diachronic relationships across generations once childhood is over. No doubt there are shades of grey, which there must be since his account of the family is based in part, but basically, on the phenomenology of social relationships founded on love. How things are is constituted by how things feel to the family members. The major and obvious lesson is that things change as children grow up, perhaps move away, and form their own novel, but equally transient families.

When parents die, fresh problems are created concerning the competing rights of bequest and inheritance. Hegel's discussion is intricate. (This is one of those subjects in which he clearly indulged a personal interest, and hence *Vernunft* (reason) penetrates the fine-grained deliberations of *Verstand* (understanding).) But the gist is that, although family resources shift in status from common resources to private resources at the death of the father in particular, the disposal of these resources cannot be entirely arbitrary. The institution of the family would be weakened if the father, in whom control of family property resides, were to bequeath the family property to his old mates, or a donkey sanctuary, upon his demise. Rights of inheritance trump both rights of bequest and such laws as, for example, privilege sons at the expense of daughters or entail property in family trusts. Such regulations violate the personal freedoms of descendants (male *and* female) to acquire, use, and dispose of their own private property (§180R).

Conclusion

In discussing Ethical Life, we learned that a fully adequate form of social life must be a stable, self-sufficient, and self-reproducing organism. Neither a society founded on Abstract Right nor a society founded on Abstract Right together with Morality could achieve this. A long story could be related to expand on these deficiencies, but suffice it to recapitulate that Morality could not furnish an imma-nent doctrine of duties (§§135, 137). How could a society work if it couldn't distinguish right from wrong? A society that *can* give a deter-minate account of its members' duties will be constituted by social relationships that are themselves morally potent. Thus to be a member of a family, as we *all* of us are or were,[6] is to accept the duties and respect the rights of family membership that we have specified. But this cannot be the whole story, since the family itself is not a self-sufficient, self-reproducing social unit. It is not self-reproducing since new families are not extensions of old ones. They are not dynastic continuations which parents authorize, though they may owe their origins to parental contrivances. They are not self-sufficient (I conjecture) since newly created families must negotiate their standing and seek their particular ends amongst a social world of other independent families. We identify, but only as an appearance (*Schein*), universality in the activity of (heads of) families in the economic world. Unlike Aristotle (whose doctrines Hegel echoes with his talk of self-sufficiency), Hegel does not explain the lack of self-sufficiency (unless he equates self-sufficiency with the property of being self-reproducing) of the family unit. He takes it for granted that once we have learned that the optimum model of domesticity is furnished by the modern nuclear family, as against the extended family, the clan or the tribe, it cannot be self-sufficient because of its limited, affective nature.

Perhaps he is right, but readers are invited to take their own views on the question. Some diachronically extended families seem to do rather well in the modern world, notably those families which are moderately wealthy. (And not all families which are fabulously wealthy crumble under the pressures created by their own excess.) No feature of individual persons (not eye or hair colour, not intellect or beauty or footballing skills), is as reliably transmitted to following generations as wealth. The full story concerning the lack of self-sufficiency of the modern family becomes clear only as the detail of Civil Society is disclosed in the following chapter. This transition, from Family to Civil Society, in the developing argument of the *Philosophy of Right* is more perplexing than most, but it can be reconstructed (as ever retrospectively) in argumentative if not historical terms. (Hegel, himself, alludes to a conjectural historical story in his Remark to §181, as though, on Aristotelian lines, families *had to* evolve into states. Perhaps the story is true; unfortunately the sparse details tell us nothing of the non-self-sufficiency of families.) All will become clear when we study Civil Society.

Put to one side the proto-logical problems of the transition. What have we learned from Hegel's discussion of family life? Are there any conclusions that we can bank? There are certainly judgements that we can reject. As intimated above, we should jettison everything he has to say about the respective roles of the different sexes. Hegel may have got some things right *accidentally*; perhaps men and women do have physical or psychological characteristics so different that a sexual division of labour within the family is justified, but we should not believe that the respective tasks of man and wife should be carved up at the joints he identifies, if at all. I don't have a clue as to what is the *right* disposition of duties. I recognize no instincts as authoritative in this domain, distrusting all references to the 'natural' state of things. And I find that even Hegel's most faithful *epigonoi* (no names; no pack drill) believe that his views on questions of sex and gender are politically incorrect. So be it. When we judge the arguments of the *Philosophy of Right* we are not speaking of Hegel, the person, as a judge we should avoid on an Equal Rights Tribunal. We are in the business of attending carefully to his arguments.

So we should notice the *nuances* of his treatment of the dialectic of particular and universal. We should not let the application of these metaphysical categories dominate and distort our reading of the detail. We should not be seduced by the metaphysics of the loving relationship into supposing that the independent parties somehow disappear into the affective unity. Marriage partners are individual persons before they (*not* their parents) signify their union in a public ritual – and they resort to their individual personhood when marriage goes wrong or after death does them part. Children are sufficiently persons to have rights against their parents as well as duties towards them. The family is a unity, but it is a unity which recognizes difference. Hegel's account of the constitutive differences will not be acceptable to most readers nowadays, and women readers who brand him as a male chauvinist pig may be dead right, anachronistically. But we should not be blinded by Hegel's formal description of the regime of the family as 'immediate universality' into supposing that he believes family life is an unproblematic domain of soppy, if metaphysical, union, of 'We's' who have forgotten their origins as 'I's', and who are disabled from making claims of right against each other, if things go wrong. Hegel has his own version of how things are when things go right. This does not prevent him from recognizing that things do, in fact, go wrong, nor from seeing how the ethical status of marriage partners or children should be reassigned should the worst occur.

Hegel values family life, structured as it is by rights and duties, as a liberation. It is a method of controlling the unruly press of sexuality and it is an objective structure that enables humans to express their capacities for long-term loving commitment through their relationships to spouse and children. It is a valuable escape from the demands of self-interest, not as representing an opportunity for altruism, but as furnishing the possibility for a wider, more capacious sense of self than abstract personality permits. For Hegel, the family, as well as being a crucial domain for the exercise of a distinctively social mode of freedom, is also a model for understanding the sort of freedom that sociability generates. 'The *family*', Hegel tells us later, 'is the first *ethical* root of the state ... [it] contains the moment of subjective particularity and objective universality in *substantial* unity' (§254). But we should not take it that the moment of subjective particularity, the self-conscious identification of union between marriage partners, occludes all individual aspirations and prevents family members from so distancing themselves from their institutional affiliation that they cannot recognize that things have gone wrong. Hegel, intriguingly, does not have the starry-eyed view of family life that has been a theme of modern communitarians; he does not describe it as an attachment that forecloses the detached investigation of either its particular demands or its general rationale. To go back to the beginning, we should recall that *every* commitment of the will is detachable in thought in the service of careful reflection (§5).[7] If family life is the first ethical root of the state, we should emphasize now, in advance of the detailed examination that will follow, that Hegel's account of the state, if it is to be true to its sources in human rationality, should permit the same kind of examination of its credentials by both philosophers and engaged citizens as Hegel believes can endorse the norms of family life.

Chapter 11

Civil Society 1: The System of Needs and the Administration of Justice: §§182–229

Introduction

Section 2 of Ethical Life discusses Civil Society (*bürgerliche Gesellschaft*). In its three subsections – A. The System of Needs; B. The Administration of Justice; and C. The Police and the Corporation – there is material of extraordinary interest. We should notice straightaway that the use of the term 'Civil Society' is quite novel.[1] Its familiar use amongst political theorists was to characterize civilized society in contrast to the state of nature, an opposition made familiar by natural law and contract theorists in their discussions of the state.[2] The most distinctive feature of Hegel's treatment is that Civil Society does not include straightforwardly *political* institutions, although some of the social institutions which he does discuss evidently presuppose the existence of the political apparatus of the modern state. This is obviously true of the administration of law which presupposes but does not describe a legislature, and the Police, which comprise a variety of executive authorities. Civil Society is therefore an abstraction from, an

element of, the Rational State which is the totality described in Ethical Life. As such, it is to be distinguished from the 'strictly political state' (Knox: §267), which is discussed in the following section.

Civil Society, therefore, stands between family life and the political state. What is the principle which governs this abstraction? Hegel takes up the stance of the 'concrete person', the newly independent adult who is striking out on his own, pursuing his own ends, or, more likely, the head of a family, pursuing the welfare of his family.[3] He is seeking these private or domestic ends in a social world where others are similarly engaged. The institutions of Civil Society which Hegel goes on to describe are those which are formed in the course of this pursuit or explained as necessary for its success. The first principle of Civil Society, the governing principle of the abstraction, is that of the self-interested satisfaction of natural needs and arbitrary desires (§182). But this cannot be a solitary achievement, since concrete persons make their way in a world inhabited by other concrete persons and their dependants. For a variety of reasons, persons find themselves locked into systems of interpersonal dependency. The private ends of individuals cannot be satisfied without structures which ensure that persons are 'simultaneously satisfying the welfare of others' (§182A). Thus particularity, the first principle of Civil Society, is mediated by universality, which is the second principle of Civil Society:

> The selfish end in its actualization ... establishes a system of all-round interdependence, so that the subsistence and welfare of the individual and his rightful existence are interwoven with, and grounded on, the subsistence, welfare, and rights of all, and have actuality and security only in this context.
>
> (§183)

The key term here is 'system'. It is the systematicity described in the institutions of Civil Society, rather than explicit design or functional planning, that interweaves the projects of the particular persons in patterns of universality.

Particularity, read here as the domain of individuals pursuing private ends, is a dangerous principle. Its content is given as individuals define and seek to satisfy their needs. Since it witnesses 'contingent arbitrariness and subjective caprice' (§185), the satisfaction of the ends of particularity, though limited by the constraints of universality in ways we shall examine, is entirely a contingent affair. 'Civil Society affords a spectacle of extravagance and misery as well as of the physical and ethical corruption common to both' (§185). Given the force of these criticisms, surely as valid and as strong today as when Hegel expressed them, one might think that we would be better off without Civil Society, that it deserves to go under and be replaced by an economic and social system which does not permit these excesses. Hegel reports Plato as believing this (and Marx was later to predict that this would be the fate of the particularistic capitalist mode of production).

But Hegel cannot agree. The modern world is stuck with the principle of subjective freedom ('the *right* of the *subject* to find its *satisfaction* in the action' (§121)) which destroyed the unity of the Greek world and emerged explicitly with Protestant Christianity. Particularity must be contained, channelled, controlled, but nonetheless respected. It is a crucial element of modern freedom that persons should be able to formulate for themselves the private ends from which they will derive satisfaction. The mercy is that such ends cannot be achieved without their aligning their pursuit of satisfaction with the efforts of others. They cannot be achieved by the self-interested exertions of aggressive competitors. '[T]hey can attain their end only insofar as they themselves determine their knowledge, volition, and action in a universal way and make themselves links in the chain of this *continuum* [*Zusammenhang*]' (§187). Conflicts and tensions there will be, the opposition of luxury and misery will never be banished, but the endemic corruption will not destroy the system that creates it. This acceptance of Civil Society, warts and all, as a necessary and stable dimension of social freedom is an important difference between Hegel and Marx.

We shall have more to say later about the characteristic desires of persons in Civil Society. But we should notice, before we go on to consider the details of the economic system, that Hegel does not take persons' desires as a brute given, as a natural fact about them which Civil Society exists to service. Desires are formed in processes of education. This belief enables Hegel to contrast his position with that of Rousseau, who believed the desires of modern man are artificial and degenerate. Only a natural man, or a throwback to the state of nature such as Rousseau evidently (sometimes) believed himself to be, is innocent. For the rest, education into the ways of sociability is a curse, creating factitious needs and desires, distorting and corrupting human nature.[4] At the opposite extreme is the theorist who takes the satisfaction of actual, present desires as an unalloyed ('absolute') good, and education as merely the means to this end. (I can't think who might have been a target of Hegel's criticisms here, but a horribly bowdlerized version of Hume – 'reason [and thereby education] is the slave of the passions' – would serve as a model for those who wish to construct one.)

The truth, Hegel tells us, is that reason works on the passions by the back door. It is operative in a community's educational practices. These are chiefly the responsibility of families, but also, as we saw in the last chapter, they are effected in default by policies distinctive of Civil Society. They will be supplemented by the educational activities of the Police (§239) and the Corporations (§252). Their result, in the citizen, 'is the *hard work* of opposing mere subjectivity of conduct, of opposing the immediacy of desire as well as the subjective vanity of feeling and the arbitrariness of caprice' (§187). Important elements of universality are inculcated in educational processes which (externally) induce the (internal) controls of self-discipline. (Hegel is not worried by the paradoxical formulation of this lesson.)

In parenthesis, it is worth stating now the central importance of education in Hegel's project. Rationality in institutions requires that members think along the right tracks, that 'knowledge and volition' are aligned, and this necessitates a process of socialization which all citizens must undergo. It may be (since our discussion is anachronistic, exploring Hegel's perspective) that for most citizens a minimal system of state education is all that is necessary, the minimum being specified, then as now, by the needs of the labour market. A more ambitious system, truer to Hegel's principles, would be designed to equip all citizens for their role as reflective agents, able to command '*the right of the subjective will*', educated to be able to 'recognize as valid [what is] perceived by it as good'(§132). A *complete* system of education would do these things, but much more besides. It would, in quasi-Platonic fashion, train the state's executive officers in a system of higher education that would accord a privileged place to philosophical studies.

One of the real oddities of the *Philosophy of Right* is that Hegel did not take the opportunity granted by his programme of describing the (actual if not quite realized) contours of the rational state to articulate in much more detail a system of state education. As tutor in Berne and Frankfurt, as schoolmaster in Nuremberg, as a university teacher in Jena, Heidelberg and Berlin, and as a close friend and colleague of Altenstein, Hegel explored the theory and experimented with the practice of secondary and higher education. In one context or another, he was an educationalist all his life. Apart from one relatively short period as editor of a weekly newspaper (in Bamberg, 1807–8) his only work was in education, as family tutor, university teaching assistant, class teacher and headmaster of a reforming *Gymnasium*, university professor and senior administrator.[5] Given his view of the *philosophical* importance of sound education as a contribution to freedom at all levels, from its most basic to its most exalted, it is incredible that he did not say more about its place in Civil Society. Hegel's *Introduction to the Philosophy of Education* must be one of the greatest imaginary, unwritten books of philosophy.

The System of Needs

Hegel saw political economy as one of the triumphs of modern science. The facts concerning the production, distribution and sale of goods and services in a modern economy are beyond description. We see farmers growing crops and raising beasts, folk walking into factories and doing a day's work, goods filling the roads as they are transported between units of production and to a point of sale, streets full of consumers going in and out of shops, examining items for purchase, discovering prices, sometimes buying goods, sometimes not. The spectacle of economic activity is astonishing in its variety and vitality. The miracle of the economists (Hegel mentions Smith, Say and Ricardo in §189) was to have demonstrated *necessity*, that is, reason at work in the 'mass relations and mass movements in their qualitative and quantitative determinacy and complexity' (§189). Everyone working in an economy seems to have their own ends, a personal narrative traced through the activity of their arbitrary wills and contingent activities. Political economy brings these phenomena together; it 'does credit to thought because it finds the laws underlying a mass of contingent occurrences', 'extracts from the endless multitude of detail with which it is initially confronted the simple principles of the thing', manifests 'rationality in the sphere of finitude' (§§189A, 189R, 189).

The nature of needs and their satisfaction

Hegel's description of the modern economy begins with a subsection discussing human needs – the *demand* side of the economy, one might say. Human beings have natural needs, just as animals do, and these frame a condition of dependence. A man must eat. What is distinctive of humans is their capacity to transcend that dependency: first, by multiplying needs – inventing for themselves more and more of them; second, by '*dividing* and *differentiating*' them – the redwing alights on an elder tree and gobbles as many berries as it can manage, human beings want a three-course dinner, *à la carte* for preference. Along with these processes of abstraction which mark human beings' distance from nature, the means of satisfaction of needs (products) are similarly multiplied and divided. Needs are created as goods are invented 'by those who seek to profit from [their] emergence' (§191A). 'Refinement' is the capacity to identify a myriad ways of satisfying desires and a quality of judgement between them (§191). It is the bourgeois equivalent of 'resolution' (§12). Needs which are 'abstract', as distanced from the necessities of nature, are nonetheless concrete in respect of their social identification and provision by consumer and producer alike. The entrepreneur who spots a market opportunity and the consumer who discovers a need for the product *recognize each other* as catering for their mutually conditioned needs and means (§192). Amongst consumers, a comical but familiar dynamic ensues. They seek *equality* in the sense of parity with the Joneses, and *distinction* to mark off their difference in point of superiority from them. Of course, the Joneses follow suit, so emulation becomes a further motor of 'the multiplication and expansion of needs' (§193).

Social needs are a combination of natural needs (say, for food) and spiritual needs (say, the thought that, if *they* can drink champagne, so can *we*). In respect of the importance of this latter element of intentional determination, the pursuit of socially created needs 'contains the aspect of liberation, because the strict natural necessity of need is concealed and man's relation is to his own opinion' (§194). Consumerism, we conclude, is liberating – an element of freedom.

We should recognize this thought. It oppressed the denizens of planned economies in the 1970s and 1980s, who saw 'The Free World' as the place where citizens could buy Levis, pop records and Big Macs. If this were the whole of freedom, freedom would not be a noble aspiration, but Hegel is clear that it is only a part of the story. He is also aware that it is philosophically contentious. At least one of the many things Rousseau had in mind when he said, at the beginning of *The Social Contract*, 'Man is born free; and everywhere he is in chains' was something he had written in the *Second Discourse*: 'free and independent as men were before [in the state of nature] they were now, in consequence of a multiplicity of new wants, brought into subjection, as it were, to all nature, and particularly to one another' (Rousseau 1973: 165, 86). What can be crazier, from this Rousseauian perspective, than for men and women to create new wants which then enslave them by peremptorily demanding satisfaction? But for Hegel, the condition of the state of nature where wants are immediately, effortlessly, satisfied 'would merely be one in which spirituality was immersed in nature, and hence a condition of savagery and unfreedom' (§194R).

If increasing attention to social needs is an element of freedom, it is limited because it is '*formal*' (§195). In this context, formality amounts to the belief that the ends humans discover to be needs are formally 'spiritual' (*geistigen*: mental) as the product of man's '*own opinion*'. Their 'necessity [is] imposed by himself alone' (§194). In point of content, human needs are insatiable. The tendency towards luxury 'has no limits [and] involves an equally infinite increase in dependence and want' (§195). Dissatisfaction is inevitable in a world where the stock of goods is finite and mostly in the possession of private owners. As so often, having criticized one aspect of Rousseau's critique of the modern world, he helps himself (without acknowledgement) to another.

Before we move on, it is worth asking one question about the nature of needs as Hegel describes them. Why does he not distinguish sharply between basic needs and human wants? Why does he discriminate instead between natural needs (such as animals share) and social needs which are distinctive of human beings? The first distinction, one might think, could be put to good use in an account of justice in the distribution of goods: a state of affairs is unjust if persons' basic needs, however specified, are unmet. The answer must be that Hegel believes social needs have the urgency of natural needs in point of their phenomenology. It is a truth about the modern world that keeping up with the Joneses is thought to be a need. Relative deprivation is as keenly felt and as powerful a motive for action as the lack of natural neccessities. This may be a miserable conclusion, and it may be, as it was to the Stoics, a real error. But it describes the needs human beings *experience* in the modern world, and it must be put on the table if we are to understand the dynamics of the modern economy.

The nature of work

Work is the means by which goods are produced to satisfy the particularized needs of modern consumers. Again the contrast with life in Rousseau's state of nature is emphatic, since it is rare in the modern world that people consume anything taken directly from nature. '[I]t is human effort which [man] consumes' (§198). Hegel might have added what a lovely pleasure it is to drink fresh water from a stream, to pick and eat plants and berries, to find young, wild mushrooms that can be eaten raw. These, for some of us, are delightful *leisure* activities, indulgences far from the world of work and, paradoxically, subsistence. (I notice, incredibly, from television programmes and bookshops, that 'survival' is a modern *hobby*.)

It is the range of human interests which forms the basis of both theoretical and practical education as humans seek the *understanding* necessary for them to achieve their sophisticated objectives. Practical education once more affords a model of liberation being achieved through discipline, through developing the 'habit of being occupied', through focussing one's attention on the task at hand with an eye to its usefulness for others, and through acquiring (would you believe it?) transferable, that is, '*universally applicable skills*' (§197).

As mankind has got cleverer (has exercised its powers of 'perfectibility' in Rousseau's sarcastic idiom), production has increasingly utilized the division of labour. Hegel speaks in two voices on the division of labour. In the first place, it increases production through the honing of specialized skills directed towards highly specific elements of the productive process. It thus increases the dependency of workers on each other (a condition of dependency which we shall see later may be a distinctive cause of poverty when structural changes in the economy mean such skills become obsolescent (§§243–5)). On the other hand, the work which is done by the machine-hand in particular is 'increasingly *mechanical*' (§198). In the *Philosophy of Right*, Hegel appears sanguine about this: 'the human being is eventually able to step aside and let a machine take his place' (§198). But he was well aware from his reading of Steuart and Smith, in particular, of the drudgery, indeed alienation, of life in the modern factory and spoke eloquently of it, necessarily at second-hand, in his Jena lectures (Waszek 1988: 211–28; JR: 232–3 / Rauch 1983: 139–40; and see Wood's notes at PR: 444). So far as the text of the *Philosophy of Right* allows us to infer, this might mean that the workers who step aside can hunt in the morning and fish in the afternoon. But he knew well that the opposites of luxury and misery capture the respective lifestyles of the owners of capital and their employees, as much as it does the conditions of the bourgeois and the unemployed. Under conditions of free labour, clever (*geistig*: spiritual, mental) work cannot be exploited with the same promise of success as mindless toil.

Resources and estates

The third dimension of modern economic life which Hegel studies is entitled *das Vermögen*, meaning capital, wealth as opposed to income, or economic resources generally. Thus far, the mediating power of the universal has been exhibited

> in this dependence and reciprocity of work and the satisfaction of needs [whereby] *subjective selfishness* turns into *a contribution towards the satisfaction of the needs of everyone else* . . . each individual, in earning, producing and enjoying on his own account [*für sich*], thereby earns and produces for the enjoyment of others.

(§199)

Society creates a pool of wealth which members have the opportunity to share and augment through their investment. How much a person acquires depends on their initial capital and the subsequent employment of their skills, if any. In this area, there are massive contingencies which result in great inequalities of skill and resource-holding. It should be no news to a modern reader that these contingencies are related. The greater a family's property, the more it can invest in developing children's skills through providing good education. The greater the skills persons acquire, the more likely is it that they can accumulate capital. Thus nothing is as reliably transmitted between generations as personal wealth. This is the nature of the beast. '[A]n inequality of skills, resources, and even of intellectual and moral education' (§200R) is an inevitable consequence of the workings of the human spirit in the institutions of Civil Society.

This not a complacent conclusion on Hegel's part. He knows there are opponents in the field (Rousseau, on one reading) who advocate a system which ensures (at least rough) equality in property holdings. But he considers that 'to oppose this right [of Civil Society to sanction a contingent and dynamic pattern of inequality] with a demand for equality is characteristic of the empty understanding' (§200R) – which is to say that he is contemptuous of any demand for material equality as betraying an ignorance of how the free-market system works. The system is an organic functioning whole. As we shall see later, the state can interfere through processes of regulation designed to secure *efficiency* and to alleviate dire distress, but there is no scope for the introduction of ideals of *social justice* of the kind to which egalitarians subscribe. Hayek, writing in the second half of the twentieth century, would have agreed (Hayek 1960, 1976). A good question for readers to address to themselves, as they ponder Hegel's discussion of Civil Society in light of his views on Abstract Right and the State, is how far *any* theory of distributive justice can be drawn from these sources.

Thus far Hegel has been writing of *one* integrated system of needs which interweaves demand and supply: need and patterns of consumption, work and methods of production. This conceals the existence of specific subsystems, which may be '*differentiated* into *universal masses*' (§201), identified as distinct *cultures* of production and administration. These he distinguishes as different *estates*. Hegel's estates are not classes as Marx identified them, as functions of persons' relations to the forces of production as owners of capital or as employees of the capitalists. They are *vertical* segments of Civil Society, gathering together all those who earn their living on the land, or by way of trade, or as civil servants. The form of capital is different in each case, as is the ethos of those who earn their living by them, which is why I described them above as 'cultures'. The detail is both ingenious and fanciful, and is supposedly 'determined in accordance with the concept' (§201). There are plenty of questions to be put which reveal the oddities of the system as well as gaps of detail. The '*substantial* or immediate' (§202) estate which works the land is based on the virtues of family life, and retains a focus on subsistence (§203). (Who then feeds the towns? *Answer*: agribusiness which 'in our times . . . too, is run in a reflective manner, like a factory' (§203A)!) The substantial estate turns out to be a peculiar mixture of old nobility (and no doubt fawning peasant) and modern entrepreneur. Hegel is no fool. His farmer will keep pigs for bacon and sausages, chickens for eggs, and cattle for milking, but he looks to the market for his income.

The 'reflecting or *formal*' (§202) estate of trade and industry is divided into the estate of craftsmen, small-scale producers responding to individual needs (e.g. tailors), the estate of manufacturers engaged in mass production (e.g. pin factories) and the estate of commerce (bankers and the like) (§204). The third estate, the *universal* estate, 'has *the universal interests* of society as its business' (§206). Since this class of civil servants (including, no doubt, university teachers like Hegel himself) cannot be self-subsistent nor put its services up for sale, it must either recruit from those with private incomes or be paid a wage by the state.

The dialectical basis of the classification of the estates – substantial, formal and universal – thus seems to segment society into those who don't think at all, those who think only of themselves and their customers, and those who think of the interests of everyone. Each estate has its distinctive mentality or culture, which constitutes the rationale of the classification. How is it then determined to which a estate a member of Civil Society belongs? In the modern world this is a matter for subjective particularity, that is, individual aspirations and capabilities. Unlike the *Republic* of Plato, citizens are not selected by the rulers on the basis of abilities inculcated and disclosed by a system of education, fitted as square pegs to square holes. Unlike the caste system, too, there is no authoritative allocation of labour. These denials are persuasive, though it is a very hard question what the right to subjective particularity amounts to in a world where the quality and amount of education and training is an element of so much contingency (§200R, but cf. §239). Nonetheless, for Hegel, a free market in labour is a crucial element of social freedom:

> The recognition and right according to which all that is rationally necessary in civil society and the state should at the same time come into effect *through the mediation of the arbitrary will* is the more precise definition [*Bestimmung*] of what is primarily meant by the universal idea [*Vorstellung*] of *freedom*.

(§206)

Members of Civil Society must commit themselves to a career and thereby assimilate the ethos of an estate, identifying one measure of their self-respect in the recognition by themselves and others of the fulfilment of the duties they have taken on. Hegel, at this point in the articulation of Civil Society, is putting flesh on the bones of concepts abstractly defined in earlier portions of the book. Working out one's aspirations, developing one's skills through education, applying those skills efficiently in making a living for oneself and one's family: these are concrete elements in the process of *self-determination* (§7). Proper diligence in performing the duties of one's self-chosen station: this is what *rectitude* amounts to (§150). Central features of Morality, too, come to the fore; 'reflection on one's own actions and the ends of welfare and of particular needs are dominant' (§§120–5, 207). Good fortune enables one to fulfil duties of care to unfortunate persons in distress, as required in §127.

Consider the university student about to embark on a career. The thought of taking up a career in banking might be appalling if that is the only job on offer at the moment. Sensitive souls might ask themselves 'What shall I be like 20 years down the road?' Prescient souls may realize that they will probably have taken on board a good deal of the ethos of the financial institution to which they have committed themselves. They will have become (God forbid!) a *suit*. So they will fear work, the disciplines of a career, as an entrapment, as a limitation of their freedom, 'as a purely *external* necessity' (§207R). Hegel's advice to his students is stern and sensible, if hopelessly indirect in its technicality: such thinking is 'abstract thinking, which stops short at the universal and so does not reach actuality' (§207R) 'Get on with it', we should read him as telling them in his fashion. Freedom requires, and does not flee from, commitment. 'Determinacy and particularity (see §7)' (§207R) are attained after a process of careful reflection. A person is not 'lowering himself if he becomes a member of an estate' (§207A). Such commitment is liberating. I think Hegel is right. (Philosophy teachers: try telling that to your students.)

Looking back, we can see that 'The System of Needs' is a tendentious, but not thereby false, description of the central features of the modern economy. Hegel believed (presciently, given the economic backwardness of Germany) that embryonic capitalism, as the economists and the newspapers described it in Britain, was the model of political economy, the actualization of reason in the private sphere. The foundation of this system is private property. We have been here before, you might think. Indeed, private property is the central feature of Abstract Right. The System of Needs is Abstract Right made actual, the flesh and bones of what, from the perspective of Abstract Right, *ought to be*. The formal weakness of Abstract Right was diagnosed as a contradiction: to be properly actual, persons' rights need to be enforceable, yet the norms of Abstract Right were insufficient to generate an institution of punishment that is recognized as just. In Civil Society, by contrast, the norms of Abstract Right are recognized as law. Rights are enforced. The 'valid actuality [of right is] . . . the *protection of property* through the *administration of justice*' (§208).

The Administration of Justice

Just as the norms of the System of Needs articulate the demands of Abstract Right, so we find that the Administration of Justice articulates the requirement that persons' rights are explicitly stated and effectively enforceable. Hegel concentrates on property rights, but we should take it that the rights of the person to life and physical integrity are protected, too. In Abstract Right, being a person was explored as the minimal claim of moral status, that of being a bearer of rights. In Civil Society, the universality of personality is 'universally recognized, known, and willed'. Human beings are educated into claiming and respecting the status of 'a *universal* person in which [respect] *all* are identical. *A human being counts as such because he is a human being*, not because he is a Jew, Catholic, Protestant, German, Italian, etc.' (§209). Persons' rights become actual in the precise sense that bearers know that they have them through a legal system that recognizes their validity. In what follows, Hegel will explain how persons' rights are '*known as universally valid*' (§210) within a system of positive law.

Right as law

Law is required for hitherto abstract right to become concrete or positive (§§3, 210–11). It is obviously needed since the principles of Abstract Right, particularly those which concern the domain of contract (§§213, 217), *must* govern the economic sphere effectively. 'Justice is a major factor in Civil Society: good laws will cause the state to flourish, and free ownership is a condition of its success' (§229A), Hegel is reported as saying. A rationally constructed legal system will demonstrate 'the objective actuality of right' in a system of norms that is '*known as universally valid*' (§210). A system of norms which are universally valid is a legal system. Hegel makes a number of points about positive legal systems which are worth noting:

1. The positivity of a regime of rights does not consist merely in the fact that it has been properly legislated, that is, has satisfied some rule of recognition[6] for the legal domain and is thus established as valid universally, for all those subject to it. '[M]ore important than this is the inner and essential moment, namely *cognition of the content* in its *determinate universality*' (§211R). Positivity, we should thus understand, is a property both of institutional form and subjective content. It is a matter both of what is declared or commanded by the sovereign authority and what is understood and recognized by the people subject to it. Positivity requires something like the '*internal aspect* of rules' that Hart describes (Hart 1961: 54–60). Right would not be positive in the sense of being actually binding on citizens if the citizens did not understand it to be *their* law.

This sounds right, but we have to ask what counts as 'cognition of the content'. There are two ways of taking this phrase and they have very different implications. The first is to suppose that one has cognition of the content, knowledge of what the law requires, merely in virtue of understanding its demands. If the law says, because a statute demands, that I should stop and bow to the West every time I leave my house I have a clear idea of the content of the law in its 'determinate universality', applying a specific rule to me and all others subject to it. I *know exactly* what the law demands and I understand that this law applies to me, although it is patently silly. The second way of understanding the 'cognition' which legal subjects attain is more philosophical: cognition requires that the demands of law be 'grasped by means of *thought*' (§211R). I take this to imply that legal subjects will understand not merely the demands of the law, but also its rationality. This should not be thought of as an entirely esoteric task since the rights and duties which subjects acknowledge have been shown to be expressive of freedom in Abstract Right (discussed in Chapters 4, 5 and 6 above) and explained in the context of the property owning economy of the System of Needs. But it *is* a philosophical task, and so it is unrealistic to expect all legal subjects to have command of the disciplines of philosophy. For this reason, I think Hegel's notion of cognitive grasp shifts between the two senses I have distinguished. And such shifts are not innocuous. As we saw in Chapter 8 when discussing the crucial 'right of the subjective will' (§132), the insight into the good which is necessary for norms to be valid may simply amount to the subject's 'cognizance in the sense of familiarity' with the law. It is worth repeating Hegel's conclusion there in full.

> [I]n the *state*, as the *objectivity* of the concept of reason, *legal responsibility* [*die gerichtliche Zurechnung*] must not stop at what the individual considers to be in conformity with his reason or otherwise, or at his subjective insight into rightness and wrongness, good or evil, or at what he may require in order to satisfy his conviction. In this objective field, the right of insight applies to insight into *legality or illegality*, i.e. into what is *recognized* as right, and is confined to its primary meaning,

namely *cognizance* [*Kenntnis*] in the sense of *familiarity* with what is legal and to that extent obligatory.

(§132R)

At this point, as at so many others, the familiar critical dialectic with Hegel kicks in. I may be perfectly familiar with an evil law or a silly law, and with law at all points between the sublimely appalling and the ridiculous. (Readers are invited to contribute their own examples, parochial or foreign, contemporary or historical.) So Hegel's positivity doctrine looks sinister. The right of personal conscience never prevails against bad but valid law. On the other hand, Hegel insists that the laws which are nowadays recognized as valid within our society *cannot* be bad laws, since they are laws which actualize right in the modern world: either right is realized in the determinate commands of law or it is actual through the validity of an immanent critique of the law's prescriptions.[7]

Is Hegel signalling a conservative (and in this context, servile) acceptance of law as we find it, peremptorily commanding us however awful its demands, or is he stating the obvious – that legal systems must recognize *some* limits on declared conscientious objection, in the name of rationality: child sacrifice, suttee, female circumcision, should be stopped, whatever the sincerity with which the beliefs that vindicate such horrible practices are asserted? My judgement inclines to the first verdict, since Hegel nowhere maintains a robustly critical attitude to positive law – but the question is open. In the immediate context of Hegel's discussion of the administration of justice he evinces no inkling of the fallibility of positive law . . . but then, on Hegel's account, law is the positive expression of right, and how could such evil practices as I have mentioned be right? Hegel may well have been mistaken about the *exact detail* of the right and the good, but nothing in his philosophy should incline us to judge that he believes all positive law to be good law. And so the debate continues.

A further implication of Hegel's insistence that positivity be witnessed in the cognition of the legal subjects is that knowledge of a system of law must not be the esoteric intellectual possession of a class of legal professionals. Hence Hegel feels able to criticize the English system of common law, a central element of which is the 'unwritten law' written into the records of countless cases. The chief weakness of the English system, as Hegel describes it, is that case law is contradictory, both authoritative ('the judges constantly act as *legislators*' (§211R)) and not authoritative, susceptible to revision when judges decide whether earlier cases are compatible with the unwritten law, and thus both dependent on and independent of past cases.

Students of jurisprudence will recognize concealed here several of the great chestnuts of the philosophical study of law: Is there a stock of moral principles which serve as unwritten but effective laws which constrain the content of positive law, say principles of rights or doctrines of natural law? Do judges make law or do they seek to give correct interpretations of it? The first question is very tricky for Hegel. There are independent principles of Abstract Right (natural law?), but these are incomplete, indeterminate and ineffective until they are established as positive within a system of civil and criminal law governing an actual social order. Hegel, I take it, would be happy with neither answer to the second question. Law must be neither the creation nor the privileged intellectual domain of a professional judiciary or of legal scholars who dress up a historical story as a positive science of right (§§3, 213, 215A). As he continues to emphasize, legal subjects cannot possibly *internalize* the demands of the law if the law is unintelligible to those who do not have a degree in the subject.

2. Law makes right positive in the further sense of deriving its specific content from the concrete social life of civil society. Hegel has described the economic system in terms of 'its relationships and varieties of property and contracts in their endlessly increasing diversity and complexity' (§212) and has delineated the (limited) role of notions of rights and duties within family life. The legal system itself is a further source of rights and duties (for example, rights of due process, the legal duty of jury service) and so is the state. The legal system cannot embrace or make positive the entire content of right – morality narrowly construed 'cannot be the object of positive legislation' (§212) since the law cannot fix the quality of a person's conscience – but law cannot have any other content than that dictated by positive right or morality. Its specific content must be determined by the objective rules of the system of ethical life to which it applies.

277

3.   Finally, the law makes right positive through the specific application of punishment (and presumably legal remedies more generally), though Hegel is careful to insist that the judgement of appropriate punishment, for example, cannot be an exact science (§214).

The existence (Dasein) of the law

We have seen how the law makes positive or actual a system of rights. The law itself is positive in the minds of legal subjects. A system of law cannot have binding force upon a population unless the laws are 'made *universally known*' (§215). This might seem obvious enough, but it does create difficulties which Hegel brushes over. Dionysius the Tyrant is said to have hung the laws 'at such a height that no citizen could read them' (§215, and see editor's note). If so, he was not a tyrant in name only – he was the genuine article, since the inaccessibility of the provisions of law is a recipe for unchallenged arbitrariness. But if this is right, there is something evidently unjust in a legal system which contrives 'to bury them [the laws] in an extensive apparatus of learned books and collections of verdicts . . . so that knowledge of the laws currently in force is accessible only to those who have made them a subject of scholarly study' (§215R). Hegel is here taking another swipe at the English common law. The ideal[8] is 'a *law of the land* embodied in an orderly and specific legal code' containing '*simple* and universal determinations' (§216).

Codification is the philosopher's stone of jurisprudence. It implies not only that the content of specific laws be clear and straightforward, but that they amount to an orderly and systematic whole, 'orderly and specific', '*complete* and self-contained' (§§215, 216). What are the principles which assign order to the set of legal provisions? Consistency is an obvious and unchallengeable constraint, but there will be difficulties as soon as the codifier attempts to go beyond this. If the structure is advertised as the speculative structure articulated in Abstract Right and witnessed in the System of Needs this will be challenged by critics of the private property system. No socialist, for example, would accept that *codification* neccessitates the pattern of ownership and control that Hegel advocates. But if we put this objection to one side, and grant Hegel his premises concerning the rationality of private rights, we should consider how deep this ethical structure goes in specifying the content and structure of laws. Hegel insists that rationality cannot go all the way down, that 'it is mistaken to demand that a legal code should be comprehensive in the sense of absolutely complete and incapable of any further determinations (this demand is a predominantly *German* affliction)' (§216R). Law is a dynamic and open-textured system which needs to be pragmatically responsive to the 'finite material'. Sensibly, Hegel abandons the rigour which the demand for codification seems to require. There is space for the understanding (cf. reason) in a process of trial and error which amounts to a *'perennial approximation* to perfection' (§216R). We should not believe that the sort of immanent criticism which takes us along the path of reason from reality to actuality (see Chapter 3) is an exact science.

The court of law

Thus far, the drift of Hegel's account of the legal system has been to explain how the positivity of rights is achieved and the positivity of law expressed: positivity is witnessed in a rational structure of norms which are authoritatively declared, systematically ordered, and self-consciously attested by legal subjects. Its content is furnished chiefly, but not entirely, by the principles of right, but also by the contingencies of time and place, 'the current condition of civil society' (§218R). In whatever form and with whatever content right is manifest, *'cognition* and *actualization'* must be witnessed in the activity of the public authority acting in courts of law (§218).

The argument for this desideratum was established at the close of Hegel's discussion of coercion and crime (Chapter 6 above). The chief flaw of Abstract Right, the reason why rights abstractly conceived do not comprise a complete or adequate system of social norms, was the failure of persons to have them satisfactorily enforced. This was both a cognitive limitation on the part of individuals (they were unable to establish the fact or measure of wrongdoing) and a pragmatic weakness of the regime of private rights (persons were unable to impose or recognize just punishment). The prosecution and penalization of crime were entirely subjective, and this subjectivity tainted retribution with the stain of revenge and the consequent evil of vendetta (§§102–4).

All these flaws are eliminated through the operation of impersonal and impartial legal authority. When the courts take over from wronged individuals the task of enforcing rights, right is actualized (and made positive in respect of the judgement of particular cases) since objectively, the law which crime has challenged is reaffirmed, and subjectively, the right of the matter is made clear to the criminal who is forced to acknowledge the validity of the law which is enforced against him (§220). I don't want to take up again the discussion of Hegel's justification of punishment (see Chapter 6), but we should notice here that these conclusions are reinforced by the detail of Hegel's account of the legal system. Prosecution and punishment are not arbitrary since they are effected with due process of law: the citizen 'has the *right to stand in a court of law*' as well as 'the *duty to submit to the court's authority*' (§221). Whatever verdict is reached 'must be capable of proof', substantiated by evidence and arguments relating to the law, the charge and the verdict. Thus due process is seen as a meta-right, a right that rights be properly determined and respected, the rights of the criminal as well as the rights of the victim, and, most importantly in this sphere, positive universal right itself, as encoded in law.

Importantly, for this is not a trivial or inconsequential demand, the right of the subjective consciousness (of subjective freedom as described in §132 and discussed above) is not merely the right that citizens should be able to cognize the law as publicly known, but that they should *see it to be done*, recognize that it is actualized in particular cases (including, evidently, cases in which they themselves have standing as criminals or victims). So the entire course of criminal proceedings should be made public. Each case brought before the courts has a 'universal content (i.e. the right within it and the decision on this right) [which] is of interest to everyone' (§224). Once again, Hegel insists, justice must not be the arcane province of professionals. Readers may judge that Hegel's stylistic practice belies his principles, but incredible as it may seem, one principle which is constant throughout his system is his admirable and absolutely sincere insistence that the truth be *effable*, clear and simple to understand in its processes as well as its promulgations.[9]

It follows, in respect of legal processes, that all the germane facts concerning an offence should be established and made public, including, in criminal cases, the fact of *mens rea* (guilty intention or premeditation as insisted upon in §§119–20), and that these should be transparently subsumable under a '*law* of the restoration of right' (§225). The second of these conditions is the province of the judge; she can insist that if the facts are as found, a tort or a crime has been committed. But a judgement on the non-legal facts of the matter – was it the butler who killed the lord of the manor with a candlestick in the library? – is a matter on which all persons, given the evidence presented in the court, can come to judgement. This doesn't call for proof as required in geometry (or, as we might say, for a knowledge of rocket science). The average punter can do it. And hence, Hegel insists (significantly, but I think very quietly) on the requirement of 'so-called *trial by jury*' (§228).

This insistence, as many critics have noticed, departs from the practice of the administration of justice in Prussia c. 1820. It is thus an example of the real not coming up to the standards of the rational, of the actual still to be achieved, of immanent critique at work. This judgement is correct, but we should see that more is at stake than the exemplification of a defensive strategy by sympathetic readers of Hegel. What he wants to vindicate is the procedures of the courts. The hardest task that his justification of punishment faces is that of demonstrating to the obtuse (as against opportunistic) criminal that he has violated the principles of right which as a rational person he ought to acknowledge. Hegel thinks this task can be accomplished if criminals at the point of conviction can recognize the wrongness of their conduct following the judgement of their *peers*.

Given the variety of criminal motivation, intelligence and stupidity, this hope is perhaps optimistic, but we should not nod complacently and move on, for it conceals a more important point about trial by jury which government ministers, minded more by efficiency than justice, are liable to overlook as they criticize and seek to constrain the practice. Verdicts in criminal cases can be an opinion on the reasonableness of the law as much as upon the facts of the case. If a jury believes a law is onerous or unjust, it can take one view on the facts of the case as established in court ('Guilty') and an entirely different view of the liability to punishment of the accused. Juries ('perverse' in the words of the law) can acquit those whose crimes are morally praiseworthy or whose punishment in accordance with a legal tariff is thought likely to be excessive – an outcome described in the United States as 'jury nullification'. This was the fate of the horrendously punitive Black Acts in eighteenth-century England. The most blatant criminals were not convicted by juries who were ready to accept that they had, for example, stolen a loaf of bread but who did not judge that the crime merited the death penalty. Correctly, juries (as against Draconian legislators) did not believe that such conduct amounted to a serious injury to society or a conspicuous threat to public order, and so did not merit the most serious punishments (§218).

Hegel does not signal this possible discrepancy between a legislator's view of the value of a crime (and consequent measure of punishment) and that of the public who are called upon to license the punishment by delivering the verdict of guilty in a trial by jury. But I cannot believe he was unaware of it, and given his knowledge of the economic, legal and political condition of England at the turn of the nineteenth century, it is not surprising that his views on a just and effective legal system create the logical space for such acts of public protest.

Before we leave our discussion of Hegel and legal justice it is worth emphasizing, no doubt for the umpteenth time, the merit of his contribution which lies in his insistence that, at all points (apart from the private deliberation of members of a team of judges or jurors amongst themselves, prior to a public decision (§224)) the legal system must be transparent and intellectually accessible to all citizens. On the meanest construal, this is a radical demand on any modern society, and Hegel should be given credit for making it insistently. That said, I have registered my doubts about Hegel's implication that the crucial right of subjective consciousness or freedom (§132) should be construed as the right simply to have the prescriptions of law thus transparent and universally promulgated. The clarity and truth of the voice of conscience cannot be determined simply by evaluating the conformity or obuseness of the citizens' responses to positive law. On my reading, Hegel does not give sufficient recognition to the possibility that the law might be an ass, or, worse, a tyrant.

Chapter 12

Civil Society 2. The Police and the Corporations: §§230–56

Introduction

Hegel has described the (optimal) form of the system of needs, and the legal system which is necessary to establish the norms of that system, as positive, that is, actual, demands on citizens. What more does he need tell us? At this point we should remember his earlier critical remarks. Civil society produces misery and displays extravagance and all varieties of corruption (§185). We should not deduce that all of these evils are remediable through the operation of due processes of law. It is the task of the justice system to guarantee 'the *undisturbed security* of *persons* and *property*'. It is the task of the police and the corporations to secure 'the livelihood and welfare of individuals . . . *particular welfare* should be *treated as a right* and duly *actualized*' (§230).[1] The social apparatus necessary to ameliorate these endemic defects needs to be more carefully described. We see this apparatus at work as the police and the corporations fulfil their designated functions. On a wider note, we should recall the main theme of Hegel's discussion of Civil Society: the first principle of Civil Society is particularity; it is the domain wherein persons (chiefly as heads of families) pursue their self-interested ends. But the achievement of these particular ends is only possible through the mediation of the universal (§§182, 186).

The terminology is, as ever, forbidding. But the idea is simple enough and the logic of practices which exemplify it is utterly familiar. Suppose I believe that my child's education would be advanced by the improvement of the facilities in her school – more books in the library, the opportunity of music teaching, better sports equipment, and (inevitably) more computers. I cannot achieve these improvements by acting alone. My fundamentally self-interested purposes can be achieved only by acting in concert with others. So first I approach the teachers with a plan to institute a parent–teacher association through which parents will work with teachers to provide such equipment as will prove most useful, the association being responsible for fundraising. At this stage, the association is entirely strategic: the best way of getting a better education for my child. But as these things go, other parents follow my lead, recognizing the advantages that their subscription and co-operation will deliver. The association turns out to be a good fundraiser too, since it recognizes that appeals to personal beneficence have limited effect and straightaway begins to organize profitable social functions – Christmas fairs, garden parties, buffet dances, whist drives (I show my age). As parents begin to meet each other on a regular basis (and committee members more often than most) in the service of a common project, a genuinely social agenda develops and the original self-interested strategic perspective is absorbed (subsumed, engulfed, *aufgehoben*) in the social project. The 'I' of the concerned parent becomes the 'We' of the member of the association. The initial focus on the best interests of the (particular) child is widened into the promotion of the (universal) best interests of the school and the social interests of like-minded parents. And everyone understands that the interests of the universal are projected into the future. No-one objects if a contingency fund for extraordinary capital projects is established, though all are clear that it is unlikely that their own children will benefit. Particular interests haven't vanished. In practice, and maybe by rule, membership of the association ceases as parents no longer have children at the school.

What I have been describing is a process wherein self-interested projects are formulated, a plan is devised to achieve these ends which enlists the co-operative but similarly strategic interests of others, and the association (community) which is thereby created works through the development of a genuinely common ethos. Such an association is unlikely to succeed if all members are constantly thinking in terms of the closely defined personal interests which motivated their joining. And in any case, the point of the example is to illustrate how, in practice, self-interest may be most effectively served by institutional affiliations which derogate its centrality or widen its focus, self-interest being expanded into self-referential altruism. Formally this will be familiar as one lesson of The Prisoners' Dilemma. Hegel's belief is that this lesson has been well learnt and is explicit in the structure of many social institutions. He's probably right.

The Police[2]

We must not think of the Police (*die Polizei*) as merely the police force (namely, the 'cops' (universal) or the 'polis' (Glasgow)). We must think of it as a public authority charged with the *infrastructural* tasks necessary for the effective operation of the economy and the administration of justice. Obviously these include police activity as understood nowadays. A police force can enhance the security citizens have in their persons and property by preventing crime. And equally the administration of criminal justice needs a police force to be bring ostensible criminals forward for trial. Hegel realizes that policing, narrowly construed, is a delicate business. There are no rational limits on the scope or depth of interference by the police in the lives of citizens. It is a matter for the understanding to determine how intrusive the police may permissibly be in light of 'custom, the spirit of the rest of the constitution, prevailing conditions, current emergencies, etc.' (§234). This element of contingency and arbitrariness, together with the culture of universal suspicion that, then as now, informs police activity, means that citizens will always view the police as in some measure hostile to the public, as inherently liable to exceed their powers. All the more reason, one would have thought, for imposing *some* principled limitations on police powers, but for reasons I cannot fathom Hegel despairs of the project: 'no objective boundary line can be drawn here' (§243A).

The public authority also takes on further regulatory powers. Although 'the differing interests of producers and consumers may come into collision with one another' (§236), we cannot expect all consumers to be checking all their commercial dealings, for example by carrying measuring scales round market stalls. '[T]he business *of one* is at the same time carried out on behalf of *all*' (§235), for example, by weights and measures inspectors. Freedom of trade and commerce represents one principle of Civil Society, but this necessitates rather than precludes systematic regulation. Other infrastructural tasks are listed as provision for 'street-lighting, bridge-building, the pricing of daily necessities, and public health' (§262A). Readers may add to the list, which as specified is concerned both with the protection of the public from specific harms and the production of public goods, sometimes both at once. This makes it clear that Hegel is not a libertarian. The task of the public authority is wider than the protection of negative individual rights.

Nowhere is this clearer than in Hegel's discussion of education in this context. Civil society requires a healthy and skilled workforce. Yet if the inculcation of appropriate skills were to remain the responsibility of families, it is unlikely in the modern world that (sufficient numbers of) parents could prepare their children for an independent existence as self-sufficient members of civil society. From the point of view of civil society, children are a resource that must be cultivated, soil that must be carefully tilled. Regardless of the possibly idiosyncratic views of parents, the health of children should be protected (Hegel mentions compulsory vaccination in §239A), and a system of compulsory public education should be instituted (§§237–9). Once more, the boundary between conflicting rights claims – of family and civil society – is difficult to draw, and he was quite right in his suspicion that controversy in this area would be endemic. Still, he is quite clear that civil society is a stronger force in the modern world than the family, since for the most part family ties are broken at maturity (§177) and civil society 'alienates the members of the family from one another' (§238). By this, I take it that Hegel is reporting the breakdown of extended family affiliations and envisaging competition in the market place between siblings (brothers, we should remind ourselves!) and perhaps even parents and children (fathers and sons). Civil society demands that its members gain their livelihoods in accordance with its basically free-market structures, and so it is incumbent on civil society to establish education policies which will ensure that its adult members can swim in these difficult waters. '[T]he individual [*Individuum*] becomes a *son of civil society*, which has as many claims upon him as he has rights in relation to it' (§238).

Civil society has established the terms on which its members can earn a living, so civil society must ensure that its members acquire skills that are marketable in point of being appropriately specialized or widely transferable (§§197–8). From the perspective of civil society, families have a duty to ensure that its (future) members become competent. So public education policies may be enforced upon bloody-minded parents and, presumably, upon recalcitrant and uncontrolled children. This looks like bad news for some. 'We aren't training children to be the labour force of capitalism', say the radical teachers. But it can be represented as good news for the children. They have a *right* claimable against society that they be properly prepared for the life of independent, self-subsistent citizens.

We can paint this situation in rosy colours. Children are to be protected against the contingency of poor or misguided parenting which would disable them from independent living. Civil society is paternalistic because its successful continuance demands that it exercise 'the right and duty to act as guardian on behalf of those who destroy the security of their own and their family's livelihood by their extravagance' (§240).

Modern Poverty

Thus Hegel delicately approaches the severe problem of poverty in the modern world. He introduces the problem in the spirit of his time – poverty is a problem caused by 'extravagance' (§240), by those whose witlessness, or idleness, or simple dereliction of duty cause themselves and their families to suffer. There is a solution to this: society must protect such indigents against themselves; it 'has the right to urge them to provide for their own livelihood' (§240A) – nowadays, workfare, compulsory stakeholder pensions, and all that. Basically, the poor create the problem of poverty, so the poor (and the old, the probably poor) should be coerced into solving it. They should be made to work (and save). So far so conventional (then), so ignorant (now).

What is astonishing about Hegel's discussion of poverty in the following sections is how he breaks out of this mindset. He has portrayed civil society as a well-oiled machine, functioning effectively in accordance with the superbly rational laws disclosed by economic science. But, as ever with Hegel, his diagnosis of necessity at work in the world admits the possibility (indeed the necessity) of disruptive contingency. Individual poverty may indeed be the consequence of individual idiocy, but more likely it is the consequence of 'external conditions' (§241). Markets may collapse as the factories in Lancashire discovered when India started to produce its own textiles. So workers in the cotton mills become unemployed. Such 'contingent physical factors and circumstances based on external conditions' (§241) induce *structural unemployment*, and hence the utterly unwilling reduction of otherwise good workers to poverty. Hegel argues that poverty is not merely a problem of personal indigence, but, more importantly, is a consequence of the economic mechanism slipping out of gear. The remarkable secret of the economic world which the political economists have disclosed is *interconnectedness*. This has its downside when well-trained, hard workers, find their skills redundant in the modern economy. They are out of work, their skills aren't needed, and none of this is their fault. They were ostlers and grooms at the turn of the twentieth century, or fitters and turners in the British motor industry in the 1970s, or coal miners in the 1980s. Hard luck.

Hegel construes poverty as relative, as well as absolute, deprivation. It becomes a problem when 'a large mass of people sinks below the level of a certain standard of living – which automatically regulates itself at the level necessary for a member of the society in question' (§244). The poor, on this account, are those who are socially excluded in virtue of their absolutely or comparatively miserable social condition. Hence it is not only the unemployed who suffer from poverty. The factory system, we have noticed, turns workers into machine hands (§198) and work into drudgery (§243). Workers develop 'an inability to feel and enjoy the wider freedoms, and particularly the spiritual advantages, of civil society' (§243).

The great evil of poverty is that it creates a rabble (*Pöbel*). This is a difficult phenomenon to describe. As Hardimon notes (Hardimon 1994: 236), the rabble is not merely a collection of the worst-off in society, it is an underclass with attitude ('inward rebellion against the rich, against society, the government, etc.' (§244A)). Hegel despises it and no doubt fears it. It poses a desperately difficult problem for modern societies to solve, now as then, since the conditions which create the rabble cannot be avoided, and once a rabble has been created the mindset of the rabble is almost impossible to eliminate.

The major features of that mind-set are clear. In the first place members of the rabble have lost that 'sense of right, integrity [*Rechtlichkeit*] and honour which comes from supporting oneself by one's own activity and work' (§244). If they are working at the bottom of the pile, they are dependent and (relatively) deprived when compared with skilled workers, independent tradesmen or their own conspicuously wealthy employers. If they lack all (or sufficient) property they may not see themselves as persons and will not be recognized as such. If they experience life as folk driven from pillar to post by the necessity of satisfying their basic needs, they will not experience and hence will not achieve even the low level of freedom attained by the arbitrary will. They are unlikely to be asking, 'Shall I have a coffee or a beer? If a coffee, shall I have . . . ? etc.' Hegel does not chart the full details of the suffering and humiliation of the poor, though earlier chapters of the book allow us to reconstruct it plausibly. The basic point is that the sort of poverty that turns the hard-up into a rabble is a moral affront. It undermines the most basic elements of moral standing that humans have learnt to assert for themselves. 'We were poor but we were honest' is *not* the mentality of the rabble. Rab C. Nesbitt's anguished confession – 'We are shite' – captures the desperation of the poverty of the underclass as it is experienced.

Hegel is not sentimental about the rabble. Their life is vicious and corrupted. With no work available for those lacking minimal capital and skills, and likely to be in poor health, the rabble become lazy, malevolent and dishonest. They find it hard to get out of bed, and knowing too well that their appalling condition is a side effect of a system that guarantees luxury and great wealth to fortunate others, they feel resentment and rebellion in face of the wrong done to them.[3] They claim support as a right against civil society, a right that Hegel acknowledges (§244A).

This frames the practical problem of poverty. It is the job of the public authority (the police) to remedy this wrong,[4] but Hegel despairs of finding policies that will work or be morally acceptable. Charity should not be demeaned. It serves the sense of morality which advocates the care of others in distress. But it is haphazard in its effects. Persons will probably direct their care to those they care most about. And if some individuals do not care at all, they cannot be summoned to exhibit the necessary emotional responses (§242). It is the task of the public authority, the police, to make charity 'less necessary, by identifying the universal aspects of want and taking steps to remedy them' (§242). The obvious remedy in a society that displays the opposites of opulence and indigence is transfer payments: take money out of the pockets of the wealthy and hand it over to the poor, or do this indirectly through tax-payers' support of hospitals or alms-houses. This is no good for Hegel, since it undermines the self-sufficency of the recipients, and thus offends the principle of civil society that an honourable person works for his living.

(There is some truth in this thought, but confiscation of the assets of the idle rich is rarely advocated on the grounds that their having to work for a living will make for *their* moral improvement. If we can contemplate the playful rich continuing in their moral degredation, we should be able to tolerate some measure of dishonour as the moral cost of the destitute being fed or given medical treatment at public expense. The dependency culture is not so awful that we hear the loud protestations of those who suffer it – but then, by this way of thinking, we wouldn't, would we, since that, too, is a further sign of the moral degeneracy of the poor. I take it that all readers, whatever their political stance, will recognize the pertinence of these reflections. The terms and tenor of Hegel's discussion are *very* up to date. It is not hard to identify contemporary voices in his discussion. For those with a knowledge of British public life, I would characterize his tone as 'anguished Tory' – Michael Heseltine in Toxteth – or 'Twentieth-Century Prince of Wales': '*Something* must be done.')

The other obvious remedy, especially attractive to those who attack the dependency culture, is to make folks work. But Hegel thinks this policy, too, has obvious defects if the structural cause of the poverty that has created the rabble is overproduction and correlatively insufficient consumer demand (§245). We can leave the discussion of the worth of this argument to those with a taste for the discussion of economic policy, in particular the value of implementing Keynesian policies – which go roughly thus: pay the unemployed to dig holes in the ground; their wages will increase consumer demand which will stimulate investment to produce the goods to satisfy it, which will in turn create real jobs. We should not blame Hegel for his ignorance of modern economics, nor indeed believe the simple-minded story I have told, which, critics will insist, ignores the effects of inflation. The important thing to notice is that Hegel is identifying poverty as a structural problem which no structural policy can easily remedy.

A final solution is canvassed. One structural cause of poverty is over-production but perhaps another is over-population (§248Z). So move your poor abroad and thus both problems are solved at once: otherwise surplus productive capacity can be enlisted to export goods to those who have been encouraged to emigrate to colonies (and to the indigenous population who can no doubt be educated to demand them). Colonization I see as Hegel's final proposal of a desperate remedy to the endemic problem of poverty (but cf. Hardimon 1994: 244, n. 14[5]), a solution to which civil society 'is driven' (§248A). Colonization might not completely solve the problem of the rabble back home, but it can appear to be a no-loss policy. When truculent colonies are conceded their independence, this, too, is to the advantage of the mother country, as Spain and England had discovered (as Hegel reads current affairs). I don't think history has proved him wrong. The final, but still inadequate remedy for the problem of poverty is found in the work of the corporations, but we shall discuss this shortly.

We can now review the philosophical orientation of Hegel's conception of the role of the public authority (police). It is *infrastructural* in two respects: concerning its limited law-and-order function, effective policing is necessary for the administration of justice, and hence the effective enforcement of the rights on which the economic life of civil society is based. Construed more widely, the public authority has the job of ensuring that citizens are enabled to be competent members of civil society through its concern for their security, health and education. It has the further task of remedying inherent, endemic, defects of which the most conspicuous is that of the tendency of the modern economy to reduce masses of people to poverty, who thereby are disposed to become a rabble. (The poor don't die off quickly and quietly.) Commentators differ on how far Hegel believed this last, truly awful problem could be solved. Suppose it can't. The poor are always with us – in Possil, Moss Side, St Denis, Zurich or the South Bronx. What does that tell us about Hegel's system?

It tells us that that even the best, most highly developed, economic system cannot be guaranteed to deliver the goods – 'despite an *excess of wealth*, civil society is *not wealthy enough* . . . to prevent an excess of poverty and the formation of a rabble' (§245). And this is a moral defect in two specific respects: civil society cannot respond to the right of the poor to public support, and the poor themselves degenerate in moral stature as they recognize that their irremediable distress is not their own fault. We can have no doubt about the force of Hegel's criticism of the poverty that is endemic to civil society, but it is surely no weakness in his account of civil society that he cannot propose effective reform, if that is the way the world is. We should remember that he is not a utopian thinker, he is not offering blueprints for the good society. He is in roughly the same position as the liberal in the modern world. Although there are plenty of ways in which the modern welfare state can respond to the misery of the poor (which Hegel, for obvious reasons, did not consider), implementing policies to deliver universal education and health care, as well as public housing, income support and much else, an underclass still persists in the richest countries of the world, and disturbingly, persists through the generations with children of the poorest 'born to fail'. Some react to this appalling circumstance with insouciance, some are minded to pursue revolutionary remedies. Hegel, and any sensible person nowadays, would criticize both temperaments. His political theory and personal instincts do not block off the possibility of limited social experiment and piecemeal reform motivated by the clear immanent critique that he has delivered. Having diagnosed the social problem so carefully and having articulated his criticisms, I am not minded to criticize him in turn for not having a stack of policy options up his sleeve. He insists that this is not the task of the philosopher, and with respect to this social problem at least, he is quite right. The mistake of Marx and (to a greater extent) of his followers was to suppose that deep and plausible social criticism somehow delivers up distinctive and effective policy prescriptions. This is not a mistake to which Hegel was prone.

The Corporations

Hegel's discussion of the corporation as a vital element of civil society (and an important constituent of the political state) should be viewed as one of the real curiosities of the *Philosophy of Right*. Readers should be familiar by now with the contrast of the real and the actual, and should be willing to acknowledge that Hegel's portrait of the actual world is drawn from a prescient reading of the entrails of the modern world as much as careful observation of its workings. (Reading the entrails of the Germanic world seemingly required little more than careful reflection on the contents of English newspapers and on reports of British society: witness his views on poverty and colonization reported above.) Nonetheless, the corporations as described in Civil Society resemble little or nothing in Hegel's Prussia, nor in the Germanic world more widely construed. If this feature of Hegel's account has not been noticed or emphasized by commentators, it is probably because institutions akin to Hegel's prescription are familiar to us, given the way the social world of capitalism has developed. In the text, we find two conceptions of the corporation, one closely linked to the focus of civil society on the economic institutions which frame its members' attempts to gain a living. The wider conception of the corporation only emerges when Hegel discusses the role of corporations in the polity. In this context, Hegel suggests that corporations may include the Church (§270R) and local authorities (§288). One's overall view should be that corporations include (any) intermediate associations between the particular, family, member of civil society and the state. In the context of civil society, these associations are predominately those which are formed in pursuit of economic activities. But a corporation is not a firm, nor an association of bosses, nor a league of workers (though Hegel suggests intriguingly in §290A that the 'lower masses' would do better to get organized). Corporations in the narrow sense distinctive of civil society seem to be based on specific industries or trades. They are clearly the descendants of medieval guilds, though Hegel knows well that the old guilds were abolished on the grounds of their operating restraints on trade.

The *model* of a corporation is that of a legally constituted association of persons who work in one particular trade or profession. The task of the corporation is to secure its members' interests, and this it achieves by the following:

1. Maintaining the integrity of the profession by setting out objective qualifications for entry. This is what professions do nowadays when they recognize or set examinations and certify membership by permitting members to cite their qualifications: thus I cite from my university diary Bill Gates BA, MIElectIE, MSERT, TEng, and Gill Bates MB, BCH, BAO, MCH, FRCSI(GEN), not having much clue what these letters mean or even whether they are an accurate transcription of their possessors' credentials. The corporation may also take an active role in training aspirant members, as trades have often done by establishing apprenticeship schemes.

2. Limiting numbers of the profession to protect members from the vicissitudes of the labour market. This restrictive practice is the chief way in which members of corporations evade the threat of poverty. It cannot be seen as a significant contribution to the elimination of poverty in general since necessarily it succeeds by excluding those who may most need work. It is tradesmen and not day labourers who join corporations (§252R). It is not possible to reconcile this feature of corporate activity with the freedom Hegel accords members of civil society to take up the career of their choice (§§206, 262A).

3. Corporations may act more directly to assist members in distress. I don't know exactly what Hegel has in mind here. In §253R, he seems to be advocating transfers from the contingently wealthy to the contingently poor, transfers which contaminate neither the giver with arrogance nor the receiver with humiliation, since they are routed through the corporation of which they are common members. Maybe some element of a membership subscription is diverted into a hardship fund. I can think of some modern examples which might serve.

Perhaps like some trades unions they organize collections for striking members at other factories. Perhaps they operate nursing homes for sick and destitute retired members. Perhaps like some professional groups they arrange for health or unemployment insurance at preferential rates.

In addition to, and in virtue of, the exercise of these enabling and protective functions, corporations promote the social identification and recognition of their members in two distinctive ways. As a member of a proper, legally recognized community, the individual finds himself recognized by others, whose standing he in turn recognizes. The fact of membership means that 'he *is somebody* . . . he has *his honour in his estate*' (§253). This suggests an unwelcome modification to Hegel's account of personhood in Abstract Right. To be a person, in the precise sense of making recognized claims on others (generally, the assertion of rights to person and property) and recognizing the rights that others claim in turn, is no longer sufficient for social standing in the modern world. The moral status of the person is eclipsed by the legal status of the member of the corporation. Recognition is transformed into the rigmaroles of professional accreditation and the respect of one's peers. Pity the poor individual who is not a member of a legally recognized corporation; he is 'without the *honour of belonging to an estate*, his isolation reduces him to the selfish aspect of his trade, and his livelihood and satisfaction lack *stability*' (§253R), notwithstanding presumably the fact that he is working hard and for the moment successfully to support himself and his family. He can't live an honourable and respectable life, if, like the day labourer, there is no 'legally constituted and recognized' estate to which he can belong.

Membership of a corporate body is not merely a matter of acquiring and displaying credentials and perhaps paying a subscription. Corporate membership itself educates members in public service through the administration of its own affairs. Hegel speaks of members as active members, not merely thinking of themselves as having acquired corporate status, but actively serving the common good by taking on a portion of the common task. That said, he disparages the work done by members and officers of corporations. They 'will often be inept', having an incomplete grasp of their business, indulging 'petty passions and imaginings', conducting trivial business inefficiently, foolishly and laboriously (§289R) – all of which underpins the rather sinister duty of the executive, the civil service, to supervise the corporations (§288).

Notwithstanding their clear tendency to incompetence unless partly administered by appointed civil servants, corporations have another task to fulfil in Hegel's scheme. This is the political task of providing representation, of electing deputies to the lower house of a legislature (§§308–11). We shall have more to say about this later. For the moment we should emphasize the role played by the corporation in developing, fostering and sustaining a common (universal) will. Members, and especially officers of corporations, reflect on the service they give to the associations they have voluntarily joined and thereby acquire an ethos of public service which in turn educates them to become model citizens. Family life has taught individuals that they have a universal (though transitory) identity within the family unit. Corporate activity teaches them that the pursuit of personal ends, far from precluding public service, is in fact conducive to the acquisition of a spirit of duty that disposes them to it. This is what Hegel has in mind when he tells us that 'The *family* is the first *ethical* root of the state; the *corporation* is the second' (§255).

Conclusion

Hegel was proud of his distinction of Civil Society and State, although it is a notoriously difficult distinction to rationalize. Civil society is clearly an abstraction from the sum-total of activities within the state: 'only within the state does the family first develop into civil society, and it is the idea of the state that divides into these two moments' (§256R). From the perspective of history, this is obviously true. The state and some variety of political activity is an ancient social formation; civil society, as he describes it, is a modern phenomenon (§182A). This much should have been evident anyway from the detail of civil society as we have explained it. Political institutions, notably a legislature, are necessary for law to be positive. Codification is a legislative task and promulgation is a political activity. The public authority is not a spontaneous outgrowth of market society but an external infrastructural imposition, created and appointed by the state to effect functions necessitated by the contingencies of individual wrongdoing, the need to provide public goods and to protect against and remedy those hazards of economic life which threaten the well-being of citizens. And that is not all. Dubiously, even the corporations, which *are* formed autonomously within the articulated economic sphere, must be protected from the exercise of their own incompetence by the appointment of civil servants to work on their boards. As employed by Hegel (and this is no criticism) the notions of Civil Society and State are not conceptually independent of each other. So it is not possible even to frame coherently such a question as: Why do we need a state if civil society performs its functions effectively?

We can understand Hegel's motivation in constructing his account of civil society by developing two contrasts. We noted, when discussing Part 2, 'Morality', Hegel's hostility to Kant's account of moral motivation. A central feature of this was Hegel's argument that the 'subjective satisfaction of the individual' cannot be ignored or dismissed as being of no moral worth or relevance in the modern world (§124). Furthermore, we recall that personal welfare is accorded a 'right of necessity' which demands not merely food for the starving but also, for example, that debtors be accorded the benefit of competence, that they not be deprived of whatever minimal resources (such as tools) are necessary for them to earn a respectable living (§127). The normative structures of society, its ethical life, must find a place for self-interested behaviour (particularity), and respect its genuinely moral claims. Hegel's insistence is all the more plausible (when modulated to accommodate our contemporary views on capacities and responsibilities within the family) for his integration within the category of self-interest of the father's work to provide for his family. Whatever else we are, we are all of us '*private persons*' (§187) with wider or narrower domains of privacy dependent on our family commitments. Civil society articulates the domain of private life as a branch of ethics.

But privacy ('particularity' in Hegel's terms), as we investigate it, reveals a peculiar logic. It is not to be accorded a specific, isolable, domain of the self-regarding; it is not to be abstracted from the demands of morality widely construed, nor are its interests capable of being advanced without conscious relation to and regard for the interests of others. It 'passes over into *universality*' (§186). Folks cannot pursue a systematic and properly educated concern for their own interests without thereby identifying with and actively pursuing the particular ends of fellow members of civil society. True or false, this is Hegel's thesis: the successful pursuit of self-interested projects requires the phenomenological perspective of the (common, general, universal) social self – the 'I' that is a 'We'. Personal cultivation, self-determination, individual freedom in the modern world: these things turn out to require that persons identify with colleagues and peers in their pursuit of common projects.

The philosophical implication of this thesis of social ontology is that the personal and the social, the private and the public domains, are not to be demarcated, a priori, in thought, although they may well be bounded in practice, as the claims of persons and associations are registered, examined and approved. (Which is not to say that Hegel ignores or derides a concern for civil liberties: that question is to be answered by inspecting the detail of his political prescriptions.) So Civil Society is the ethical domain which articulates, as an abstraction, the private interests of persons concerned to protect and promote the interests of their families, but at the same time charts the patterns of universality, the forms of common life, into which these self-interested members are drawn and through which they express their aspirations and pursue their projects. Its norms, chiefly the ethics of rights, delineate the permissible space within which citizens pursue the not ignoble satisfactions of private life, not, to recall an earlier discussion, because this is productive of happiness, but rather because it is a crucial aspect of personal freedom. The valuable lesson is that the entanglements of sociability do not permit a clear distinction to be drawn between the interests of the self and the interests of others, between self-interested and altruistic behaviour. In Hegel's terms, the particular is mediated by the universal even, or especially, in its pre-eminent domain.

We have seen that the opposition of particular and universal is subsumed in the description of economic activity, as Hegel takes this from the economists and applies his own research, but it would be a mistake to ignore a further implication of Hegel's project. Another of his intentions in introducing a category of civil society is to explore (and in his own terms, explain the contribution to freedom of) institutions which are *intermediate* between those of the family and the state, which mediate particularity and universality in actual social formations.

There is a problem lurking here which is best laid out by drawing a contrast with Rousseau.[6] Rousseau famously operated with a contrast between particular will and general will. We can think of a particular will initially in terms of its content; it is directed to the self-interested ends of the individual person. By contrast, the general will is the will exhibited by persons *qua* members of communities; they identify a common good as the end or purpose of a community and exercise the general will when they self-consciously act in its service. The content of the general will is given by the values of the community to which all members subscribe. Roughly these comprise the preservation of the persons and property of *all* members and, most importantly, the complex social and political values of freedom and equality.

Within a republic, the formation, expression and exercise of the general will necessitates a direct democratic constitution with each citizen a member of the law-making sovereign, and each member of the sovereign equally subject to its laws. The general will is revealed when proposals for legislation are put forward and each citizen asks himself whether the policy which is up for decision promotes the common values shared by the polity. Direct democratic participation issues in laws which express the general will just in case citizens ask themselves the right question – Will this law suit *us*? – as against the wrong question (indicative of a particular will) – Will this law suit *me*? For Rousseau there are two perspectives on decision-making, the particular and the general, and two varieties of will, particular and general, which these perspectives form.

This apparatus gives Rousseau an enormous problem with inter-mediate associations. The particular self-interest of individuals can be contained by a polity which protects the persons and property of all. This end is not intrinsically divisive. But groupings of individuals tend to form a will which is general amongst their members but particular *vis-à-vis* specific other elements of the community as well as against the community at large. This is obviously true of political parties or factions. It is also true of religions which do not tolerate the profes-sion of other faiths. Rousseau bans these sources of dissension from his republic so that social homogeneity and value consensus can be preserved. Family life is (optimistically) not viewed as a threat. The executive arm of the state, the government, clearly is. Rousseau despairs of the problem that members of the government will form a will general amongst themselves but particular against that of the sovereign republic which the government must inevitably suborn.

Rousseau thought like an angel, and Hegel recognized this, but Rousseau's homogeneous utopia was theoretically naïve and utterly impractical. The only society to have approached the severe purity of his prescriptions had issued in the Terror of the French Revolution (§258R). Intermediate associations of the sort Rousseau held responsible for social division are a necessary feature of the modern world. Any attempt to excise them will lead to social disaster. So at least one crucial element of Hegel's agenda is to find a place for intermediate associations that can reveal their essentially constructive role in the modern state. This is what happens in Civil Society. Intermediate associations, of which the corporation is the clearest example, are not corruptive elements of civil society through the exclusive operation of categories of particular and general (universal) will.

Rousseau's opposition of particular and general will is *aufgehoben*, transcended, in Hegel's account of the social world. This is obvious in family life. In Civil Society, we see this process taking shape more generally across the community as estates are formed and corporations instituted. Within these institutions there will be a general will, as Rousseau noticed. His mistake was to deduce that since these associations are limited in range, their particular interests must be antagonistic to the rest of the community. This may turn out to be so, as a matter of fact. In fact something like this underpins Marx's later account of class conflict. But for Hegel there is no necessity that associations, corporations and communities are intrinsically hostile to each other, playing out zero-sum games. His conclusion is the opposite: active membership of civic associations educates members in the ethics of social responsibility in spheres wider than the family. In particular it educates individuals not only to be self-conscious citizens of the widest community of all – the state – it actually grooms them for political activity. For Rousseau, intermediate associations threaten the stability of a general will. For Hegel, the intermediate associations of civil society make it possible for citizens to form that general will which the state expresses as a concrete universal.[7]

I have mentioned several times that Hegel's account of Civil Society is evidently incomplete without supplementation by specifying the forms of political life which make it possible. Wouldn't you have thought that this is the natural point of dialectical transition from civil society to state? Perhaps it is (§256), but Hegel, no doubt influenced by his reading of the political situation in Britain prior to the Reform Bill, also signals as the poles to be transcended, the distinction (opposition?) of town and country – 'these constitute in general the two ideal moments from which the state *emerges* as their true *ground*' (§256R). This is novel and very strange. It is time to consider the state directly.

Chapter 13

The State: §§257–360

Introduction

Once upon a time, in the states of classical antiquity (and contemporaneously, too, 'under the despotic regimes of Asia' (§262A)), subjects identified themselves totally with the state – 'the subjective end was entirely identical with the will of the state' (§261A). Incredibly, Hegel believed that the individual had 'no inner life' under these social conditions, no epistemological stance from which to appraise the demands made on him by masters to whom he unreflectively submitted. As the story proceeds, particularity develops as mankind attains a subjective perspective on its social condition. The narrative varies, but particularity reaches its recognizable modern form with the Protestant Reformation and the political theorists, notably Hobbes and Rousseau, who begin their deliberations from the standpoint of the particular will. Particularity is achieving its due in the economic world, too, as free market capitalism has eliminated feudal and 'old guild' relationships. The apogee of the particular

will was the revolutionary period in France when the demand for equality and liberty reached the point of civic madness. Universality with no social space for particularity is as defunct as Hellas. Particularity which cannot accommodate universality has shown itself to be a failure within Hegel's lifetime. Reason requires that these opposites be melded together.

The political expression of this fundamental demand of reason is the modern state:

> The state is the actuality of concrete freedom. But *concrete freedom* requires that personal individuality [*Einzelheit*] and its particular interests should reach their full *development* and gain *recognition of their right* for itself (within the system of the family and of civil society), and also that they should, on the one hand, *pass over* of their own accord into the interest of the universal, and on the other, knowingly and willingly acknowledge this universal interest even as their own *substantial spirit*, and *actively pursue it* as their *ultimate end*. The effect of this is that the universal does not attain validity or fulfilment without the interest, knowledge, and volition of the particular, and that individuals do not live as private persons merely for these particular interests without at the same time directing their will to a universal end [*in und für das allgemeine Wollen*] and acting in conscious awareness of this end. The principle of modern states has enormous strength and depth because it allows the principle of subjectivity to attain fulfilment in the *self-sufficient extreme* of personal particularity, while at the same time *bringing it back to substantial unity* and preserving this unity in the principle of subjectivity itself.
>
> (§260)

If you understand this passage, you've grasped the drift of Hegel's theory of the state. So let us make it as straightforward as we can manage. The state is an intentional structure, a structure of will, 'the actuality of the substantial will' (§258). As such, it is a structure of freedom. But will might be free only in-itself, in which case the defective state that manifests it has the makings of freedom, but no more than that. The rational modern state, whose social composition Hegel has been describing, 'is the actuality of concrete freedom', which is to say that the persons who compose it are free (for the most part: actuality is not reality, remember) and understand themselves to be free. The institutions which structure the state (domestic institutions and the various domains of civil society, together with the political institutions, still to be described) manifest that freedom in a way that is recognized and endorsed by citizens. In the first place, as family members and/or independent workers in civil society, individuals have reached the point where it is possible for their personal capacities to be fully developed and effectively realized. If one thinks of freedom as opening up at least the *possibility* of self-determination (no social arrangements can cater for the lackadaisical layabout who fails to take available opportunities to develop her talent), then this is achieved in Hegel's state by individuals who are nurtured and educated to fashion a life for themselves.

But this process of self-formation is made possible by social conditions and institutions. Thus the family enables persons to develop their capacity for love and long-term commitment to others, but only for those who recognize themselves, and are in turn recognized, as integral to a substantial domestic unity. The pattern of economic production, the formation of estates within the modern economy, the legal apparatus necessary to protect rights and administer justice, the police and especially the corporations, all entrammel initially self-interested agents within social networks. This is what Hegel means when he says that the particular interests of individuals '*pass over* of their own accord into the interest of the universal'. Furthermore, granted that individuals are socially located within structures which cultivate and express their interests, interests which they couldn't have or couldn't satisfy without these various patterns of social membership, those amongst them who are rational and clearsighted will explicitly endorse and intentionally pursue the ends of the social formations with which they consciously identify; they recognize 'the universal interest even as their own *substantial spirit,* and *actively pursue it* as their *ultimate end*'. Sociability has moulded their goals, initially, through their education, by the back door, but as mature socially fashioned creatures, there is nothing in these processes which is opaque to them and nothing that they will reject.

As a series of claims about the modern social world, these judgements are susceptible to assessment as true or false. If many members of modern societies are alienated from their social condition, if they dissociate themselves from its ethical life, Hegel's description of the modern state will be rejected as false – and of course he sees this. This is why he struggles so hard with the question of poverty. But I see no philosophical objections or difficulties in this conceptualization of the modern social world. What makes it especially interesting is that it is a conceptualization of the modern *state*, and Hegel has said nothing thus far about political institutions. In the crucial account of the state which he gives us in §260, there is nothing with which we are not familiar as a result of the preceding articulation of ethical life, except perhaps the touted completeness of the account. What is the philosophical and practical role of 'the *political* state proper and *its constitution*' (Knox: 'the strictly *political* state': *der eigentlich politische Staat und seine Verfassung*) (§267)?

The Social Contract Theory of the State

We can confect an easy answer. The role of the 'strictly *political* state and its constitution' is *entirely instrumental* to the (socialized, universal) aims of particular individuals. Laws need legislators, private rights need judges to adjudicate disputes and measure effective punishments, regulatory bodies need legitimizing authorities, corporations need governmental board members to ameliorate their tendency to incompetence . . . and so on. All these tasks require a properly constituted political state. We should recognize, too, how close Hegel comes to this conception of the state. Here is another lengthy extract which I cite in full in order that readers can consider carefully whether there is anything in the passage which implies that the state does not have a strong instrumental value for its citizens, an instrumental value that (1) they recognize and (2) accept as the grounds of their allegiance:

> We can see that the moment of particularity is also essential, and that its satisfaction is therefore entirely necessary; in the process of fulfilling his duty, the individual must somehow attain his own interest and satisfaction or settle his own account, and from

his situation within the state, a right must accrue to him whereby the universal cause [*Sache*] becomes *his own particular* cause. Particular interests should certainly not be set aside, let alone suppressed; on the contrary, they should be harmonized with the universal, so that both they themselves and the universal are preserved. *The individual whose duties give him the status of a subject finds that in fulfilling his duties as a citizen, he gains protection for his person and property, consideration for his particular welfare, satisfaction of his substantial essence, and consciousness and self-awareness of being a member of a whole. And through his performance of his duties as services and tasks undertaken on behalf of the state, the state itself is preserved and secured.*

(§261R) (my italics in the final sentences)

What more is Hegel saying here than that the citizen, through the performance of his duties to the state, preserves and secures that social condition which is necessary for the achievement of his particular interests, grants him protection for his person and property and so on?

Nonetheless Hegel is hostile to the theory of the state which takes it to be a mere instrument of the particular will of the citizens. He recognizes two different forms that this theory of the state may take. The first (philosophical) view he associates with Rousseau and more recently, Kant (§29R) and Fichte (§258R).[1] Correctly, he insists, Rousseau 'put forward the *will* as the principle of the state', but Rousseau employed an inadequate conception of the will and hence misunderstood the nature of the state. He thought of the will as an '*individual* [*einzelnen*] will' (§258R), 'as the will of a single person [*des Einzelnen*] in his distinctive arbitrariness' (§29R). To be precise, as we saw in the last chapter, Rousseau adduced the *general* will as the principle of the state. Thus Hegel construes Rousseau's general will as a universal will, but 'not as the will's rationality in and for itself but only as the *common element* arising out of this individual will *as a conscious will*' (§258R).

On this reading of Rousseau, which is mistaken but not idiosyncratic, the general will is what is common to a set of particular wills. Suppose persons *x*, *y* and *z* list their three most important social policy objectives as ABC, BCD, and CDE, respectively. Evidently, the policy which is common to all of these lists is policy C. So on this account there is a general will that C be effected. C might be further denoted as the common good or the public interest, but what we have in truth is a coincidence of particular wills. C can even be described as the will of all. Unfortunately for this interpretation, Rousseau insists that not even the greatest coincidence of particular wills can produce a general will; the will of all does not amount to the general will. The general will differs fundamentally from the particular will in respect of its object, which is not the welfare of the particular individual who expresses it but the welfare of all, consistently with values of liberty and equality shared by all. The general will can neither be reduced to nor constructed out of a consensus concerning prudential goods.[2] In the example given above, it is indeterminate whether the policy goals are perceived as prudential goods or as collective goods, but I think Hegel implies that Rousseau's general will is a construction out of particular wills which pursue prudential, self-interested goals.

Put this misreading of Rousseau to one side. Hegel's fundamental point, which is in fact akin to Rousseau's, is that the universal will manifested as rational in the state cannot be constructed out of the wills of individual persons with their distinctive arbitrariness, their particular ends or idiosyncratic personal values. The way he chooses to make this point is to argue that the conception of social union appropriate to this individualistic approach is that of the state which has its origins in the citizens' consent or in a contract, or which is justified by a social contract argument.[3] This tradition has been dubbed 'voluntarist', because as Hegel sees, the authority of the state is vindicated in terms of the will of the individual citizen. This modulation of the argument into an examination of social contract theory is not arbitrary. It does pick up some authentic historical resonances, notably in Hobbes's writings, but just as important, it brings back into focus Hegel's exemplification of a common will, in the sense of two or more particular wills with an identical object, in contracts (§75). And he argues that this contractarian conception of the state is radically defective.

Before we discuss Hegel's attack on social contract theory, we should notice how attractive some version of that theory should be from within the perspective of civil society. Social contract theory is a deliver-the-goods theory. Contractors identify particular goods and consider how best these goods can be delivered against a background wherein the pursuit of them is taken to generate social conflict. In a simplified Hobbesian version, prudence generates competition which causes strife which motivates a common regimen of self-restraint through universal acceptance of a sovereign authority with coercive legal powers. Basically, this is just what members of civil society can work out that they need. They consent to the state, explaining their voluntary subscription through its protection of personal rights (by the administration of justice) and its promotion of public goods (by the police). They can entrust it with the difficult job of solving the problem of endemic poverty. To return to our initial characterization of the role of the state, they can see it as *instrumental* to private purposes that members of civil society cannot otherwise effect for themselves.

So it is a good question why Hegel does not see this instrumental account of the state as attractive. What exactly are his objections to it? Hegel's major philosophical objection, which has to be constructed from a variety of sources (see Patten 1999: 110–18), is that the social contract argument begs the question. It illegitimately assumes what it sets out to establish: that the contractors are citizens. Who are the contractors? The traditional answer is given by a description of mankind in a state of nature, a condition in which they live independently of society, a pre-social condition (Rousseau in the First Part of *The Discourse on the Origins of Inequality*) or independently of the state, a social but pre- or apolitical condition (Hobbes, Locke, Rousseau in the Second Part of *The Discourse on the Origins of Inequality* and in the *Social Contract*, Kant and Fichte) – the difference between these alternative statements of the argument is important, as in the latter case are the differences between the several theorists as to the specification of the social world.

It is important to specify the social status or otherwise of the contractors because this will determine the goods to be delivered by the state as legitimized in the social contract. Needless to say, such specification differs in both obvious and subtle respects between the different classical sources. Put to one side Rousseau's idiosyncratic description of the state of nature as an entirely pre-social world.[4] We are left with a (number of) portrayal(s) of social creatures (variously described) deliberating how best their social ends can be accomplished and deducing that the state is necessary if they are to be achieved. Hegel's objection can now be stated bluntly: these social purposes cannot be formulated or understood unless we suppose that the contractors are *already* citizens of a state. (Rousseau, in his dotty fashion, says much the same thing of his contractarian predecessors: 'every one of them . . . has transferred to the state of nature ideas which were acquired in society' (Rousseau 1973: 45).) Hegel insists that the citizen 'is not in a position to break away from the state, because he is already by nature a citizen of it. It is the rational destiny [*Bestimmung*] of human beings to live within a state' (§75A).

This is an important passage which I think readers should try to get straight. I read Hegel's statement that citizens cannot 'break away from the state' as the view that citizens cannot so detach themselves in thought that they can deliberate the question of whether or not, on balance, the state is useful to them in light of their personal projects, and whether or not they have, on balance, an obligation to fulfil the duties of citizenship. A more literal reading would have it that Hegel is simply denying that citizens can *leave* the state, that is, emigrate. (These questions are famously interwoven in Hume's criticism of Locke's contract theory in his essay 'Of the Original Contract' (Hume 1963: 462).) I don't think Hegel is addressing the question of whether citizens can or cannot practically emigrate since this issue is not to be settled by an examination of the *nature* of citizens. Citizens can either afford (in the widest sense) to leave or they cannot. The state either permits those who can afford it to leave or it does not. This cannot, then or now, be an a priori argument against the possibility of citizens leaving the state into which they were born.

I read Hegel as arguing directly against the philosophers in the social contract tradition that those who are by nature citizens can no more detachedly consider whether allegiance to the state is in their best interests than can members of families query their familial duties on the basis of a personal cost-benefit appraisal of continuing affiliation. Citizenship is no more a matter of voluntary subscription than the child's finding of her family membership. Her duties to the state as citizen are no more optional or contingent than they are to her parents as their child. None of this implies that Hegel believes that citizens cannot suggest improvements to their regime in the manner of immanent critique, but it does entail that, from Hegel's perspective, a root-and-branch philosophical examination of the credentials of the authority claimed by the state is not possible, given our nature as citizens.

So far as the membership of functional families is concerned, this is surely correct. It may even be true of some citizens that they are blinkered against the light of some deep philosophical questions concerning the basis of their obligations. But Hegel is wrong to find in this empirical phenomenon the Achilles' heel of modern liberalism. For liberals, the question is whether or not, despite the modern citizen's formation (education, *Bildung*) by the interwoven institutions and authorities of society and state, the citizen can sufficiently dissociate herself *in thought* from these formative influences to examine their rational credentials. The evidence (I adduce, maybe self-deceivingly – but that cannot be established a priori) goes against Hegel. The loving parent, the loyal corporate member, the dutiful citizen are not disabled by their love, loyalty or allegiance from conducting a philosophical investigation of the grounds and legitimacy of their respective affiliations. There are, and have been, plenty of truly awful states, but none of them (I speculate) have been so efficient that *all* of their denizens have been benighted in the ideological darkness. There may be, in the modern world, fine (rational?) states. Perhaps that is how I think of mine own – the United Kingdom – but I need not admit the charge that my acquiescence or, indeed, enthusiasm, implies that sort of subservience which attests unthinking (immediate, unreflective) acceptance.

For Hegel's argument to work there has to be some feature of the mindset of the citizen which blocks the possibility of detached appraisal of the institution which is being evaluated. It is important to see that this cannot be the simple fact of social embeddedness. In respect of some institutional affiliations, it is possible that some denizens are blinkered, that some parents, for example, are so devoted to their children that they see no limits to their obligations, that some children are so attached to their parents that they cannot forge an independent life of their own. And no doubt some citizens are like this – 'my state, right or wrong'. But the distinctive spirit of the

Enlightenment, the demand for rational legitimation inherited from Kant's 'age of criticism', cannot be disarmed by telling people what, constitutionally, they cannot think, if that is indeed what they are thinking when they question their allegiance. What Hegel (and his contemporary ally, the communitarian) needs, but what the modern social world will not grant him, is an argument which establishes that the formative influences which culture the modern individual are epistemologically beyond the reach of the enquiring mind.

Hegel does try to explain why this is so, but before we look at his arguments, it is worth saying a little more about his objections to social contract theory. The claim that we cannot examine the philosophical credentials of our citizenship because we are already citizens and cannot, given our natures, be otherwise does not reveal a circularity in the social contract argument. The social contract argument is strongest when it is given a hypothetical formulation. Hegel never sees this, which is not altogether surprising since the classical theorists as one reads them generally thoroughly entangle and confuse arguments from actual (express or tacit) consent, historical and hypothetical contracts. So Hegel thought that contract theorists were committed to the empirical possibility of citizens fixing the terms of the social contract as their arbitrary will and opinions dictate, expressly granting and withdrawing 'their express consent given at their own discretion' (§258R). Once this mindset is established within the community it can 'destroy the divine [element] which has being in and for itself and its [the state's] absolute authority and majesty', it can generate 'the tremendous spectacle . . . of the overthrow of all existing and given conditions within an actual major state . . . the most terrible and drastic event' (§258R, and see §29R). Which is to say that the contract theorist's focus on the individual will can lead, as it did in the Terror, to social calamity. It is as though the theory, once accepted, dissolves all social bonds.

For all I know, this may be a correct historical account of at least one causal factor in the generation of the Terror, but I see no reason intrinsic to hypothetical social contract theorizing which indicates that the dissolution of society must be the outcome. The fundamental confusion behind this way of thinking, a confusion which, to be fair, some contract theorists have encouraged, is to conflate the philosophical stance of the individual who seeks rational legitimation for the institutions which command his allegiance with the self-interested motivation of particular individuals. Social contract theorists can perfectly well include strong social values in their specification of the contractors' position, as Locke and Rousseau do with values of liberty and equality and as Rawls does with his theory of justice as fairness. And furthermore, there is no reason in principle why social goods such as loving family relationships or corporate loyalties cannot be specified as goods to be protected or promoted by the legitimate authority. The socially situated members of civil society could reason their way to an acceptance of the state on the basis of the social goods which they recognize.

This criticism of Hegel can be made even stronger. Whether or not one accepts the hypothetical contract argument as good grounds for accepting the authority of the state (and I certainly find this approach much more promising than Hegel does) its purpose is honourable enough. It is that of displaying the rationality of the state to its members, and doing this in a fashion that will both satisfy the philosophically curious and convince the sceptic or temperamental nay-sayer. This is an ethical perspective which looks very like Hegel's own condition of subjective freedom – 'the right of the subjective will [which] is that whatever it is to recognize as valid should be perceived by it as good' (§132). We've seen already in our study of this passage how Hegel is disposed to take away with one hand what he grants with the other. As we review Hegel's criticism of the social contract argument, we can see how closely his line of criticism approaches the thesis that it doesn't matter what individuals think about the state which demands their obedience so long as the state is objectively rational in accordance with the concept, so long as it exemplifies universality brought together with particularity in a structure of individuality, a concrete universal. 'We should remember', he sternly tells us, 'the fundamental concept according to which the objective will is rational in itself, that is, in its *concept*, whether or not it is recognized by individuals [*Einzelnen*] and willed by them at their discretion' (§258R).

We have reached the same interpretative and evaluational crux that we have encountered before. The final clause of the sentence as quoted suggests that the rationality of an objective state of affairs, in this case the state's imposing duties on its citizens, can be demonstrated quite independently of whether this rationality, as displayed in the logic of the concept, is apparent to citizens. It seems that so long as the state has the necessary structure, is logical in Hegel's special sense of that term, *it doesn't matter* that the citizens fail to recognize this. They are ignorant if they don't see it, and they've just got it wrong if they dispute it. If this is true, we should conclude that Hegel does not sufficiently respect his own principle of subjective freedom, since we have described circumstances in which norms are claimed to be valid which those who are subject to them explicitly *do not* recognize as good.

That is the case for the prosecution. The case for the defence draws our attention to the continuation of the sentence that I last quoted. This does not disparage the individual will. Rather it places its claims in a necessarily limiting context. '[K]nowledge and volition, the subjectivity of freedom (which is the *sole* content of the individual will) embodies only *one* (consequently one-sided) moment of the *Idea of the rational* will, which is rational because it has being both *in itself* and *for itself*' (§258R). The defence advocate will explain that the state must not be rational simply in respect of its formal (logical) structures, rational *in itself* (which the prosecution over-emphasizes). It must be rational *for itself*, too, which is to say that 'knowledge and volition, the subjectivity of freedom' must be given *some* place in the story.

What place is that? The meanest, hardest critic of Hegel will say that the strong, liberal, condition of subjective freedom is not satisfied if the 'correct' story is told to the people whether they understand it or not, and if they understand it, whether they accept it or not. And they will draw the conclusion that, since this story is privileged by the constraints of the Hegelian logic, it is tendentious and question-begging. But this cannot be the end of the matter. I am satisfied, though I readily concede that other readers are not, that Hegel's challenges to contract theory impute metaphysically grounded, epistemological limitations to the pursuit of the liberal agenda: in this context, the individual citizen's search for principles that will amount to a rational legitimation of the state. But I concede further that Hegel will proceed to 'comprehend' the institutions of the state in what follows, and in that respect he attempts to give as much as can ever count as a philosophical justification of the institution. So we have here a crux that looks likely to reveal that the opposing positions are at cross-purposes:

Hegel's critic (perhaps a Kantian – look again at §29R) insists that rational legitimation be offered; Hegel's defender insists that this is what Hegel is doing in his application of philosophical science, not least since he goes on to describe a constitution that exemplifies his categories of universality, particularity and individuality. It may be that the way that these categories are used in the articulation of the elements of the state amounts to a defence of the state that any rational person will accept. In which case the right of subjective freedom is respected in Hegel's doctrine of the state. 'Everything depends on the unity of the universal and the particular within the state', he tells us (§261R). The proof of the pudding will be in the eating, but, as we shall discover, the pudding turns out to be a dismal dish.

Patriotism and Religion

I don't want to develop this criticism at this point, but I will return to it. Instead I wish to examine the *positive* account Hegel develops of the way loyal citizens think about their relationship with the state, as against the negative criticisms of the liberal, social contract approach. 'It is the self-awareness of individuals that constitutes the actuality of the state' (§265A). Remember, Hegel's criticism of the social contract or voluntarist tradition would be cogent if there were some central feature of the mindset of the citizen which foreclosed the possibility of the subject distancing himself from the state to which he owes allegiance for the purposes of examining the philosophical credentials of that allegiance – if, that is, the citizen were effectively blinkered. So we need to characterize the qualities of this distinctive self-awareness.

First, but this takes us no farther than civil society, citizens are aware of the relationships in which they find themselves bound to others through family ties and through their choice of vocation (§§262, 264). Of course they will recognize the role that the state plays in establishing a legal framework for the protection of their domestic and personal activities, but it is hard to see how this framework transforms their self-understanding as they engage in these projects. Yet Hegel insists that something like this happens. Family life and corporate activity are 'the firm foundation of the state and of the trust and disposition of individuals towards it' (§265, also §§255–6). Somehow the daily round, the common task, will generate the sentiment distinctive of the citizen – that of patriotism.

We have noticed as we have covered the ground of ethical life how its various forms give rise not merely to a bloodless collection of rights and duties, but how the members of its various institutions are motivated by distinctive sentiments. Family life is characterized by love, civil society is the sphere of self-interested or self-referentially altruistic behaviour. And corporations educate and express such sentiments as solidarity, loyalty and fraternity. Hegel is quietly reinforcing his criticism of Kant's trichotomy of motives (Chapter 7). (The member of the Actor's Guild is a good example: he pursues his own ends, probably those of his family; he is inclined to look after fellow members, notably those in distress; he performs the duties incumbent on active members. What is motivating him when he pays into a fund established to care for 'aged actors in distress'?) The sentiment particularly appropriate to citizenship is that of patriotism.

Hegel's discussion of patriotism, generally characterized as love of one's country, is particularly interesting. He knows well that it is often the last resort of the scoundrel. Those who 'readily convince themselves that they possess this extraordinary patriotism ["a willingness to perform extraordinary sacrifices"] [may do so] in order to exempt themselves from the genuine disposition, or to excuse their lack of it' (§268R). So what is the genuine article? It is 'certainty based on truth', or, as we might put it, a true conviction that the state is just, together with 'a volition that has become *habitual*' – as we, or Aristotle, might say, a virtuous willingness to perform the duties of one's civic station. The patriot will '*trust*' his state in the absence of more educated insight into the rationality of its institutions (§268). Hegel's thought is that, as citizens go about their daily business in a well-organized state, one that protects their rights and promotes the common good, and supports their collective endeavours, they will settle into a disposition of compliance. They will have the sense that the demands of the state are not an onerous, external, imposition. '[T]his other [the state or its police, maybe] immediately ceases to be an other for me, and in my consciousness of this, I am free' (§268).

What Hegel is seeking to capture is the disposition of generally law-abiding citizens to fulfil their duty to the state 'in the normal conditions and circumstances of life' (§268R). They will not be forever looking over their shoulders in fear of the coercive powers of the state or the violent activities of criminals – 'this habit of [living in] safety has become second nature' (§268). No doubt, when prompted, the uneducated in particular will grumble and find fault, but in truth even conspicuous belly-achers trust the state to maintain the objective conditions in which they can live their lives freely and complain vociferously. The true patriot is one who has confidence in the state, and he has this confidence because it fosters the security and companionship which enable him to carry out his personal projects.

So patriotism is not the spirit of the flag-waver, the ardent royalist, the active politician, or the aged schoolteacher who drives his young pupils to death in the trenches. It is the sense of well-being of those who passively identify with the state, who do not see its demands as onerous or its forces as hostile, who co-operate willingly when asked, and get on with their lives when not. Something like this sense of civic contentment must be familiar to many readers, though it is not easy to characterize since it does have such a dozy, undisturbed feel. Perhaps it is the source of the contempt that ordinary, affable citizens feel for radicals and trouble-makers. It borders on complacency and so is the target, in turn, of those who argue that most of their fellows are engulfed in apathy, miserably subject to a self-serving ruling ideology, servants of the hegemonic powers of the bourgeois capitalist state, and so on. Even Hegel believes that such virtuously dormant citizens need an occasional wake-up call, which incredibly, and not cynically, is one good thing about the occasional war (§§324R, 324A).

Now that we have Hegel's account of patriotism in focus we should notice straightaway that it is exemplary of that conception of freedom which is actualized by the state of 'finding oneself at home in the other'. To repeat, 'this other immediately ceases to be an other for me, and in my consciousness of this, I am free' (§268R). It is clear from this account of the achievement of freedom that freedom does not require the citizen to understand the philosophical provenance of the duties he trustingly, habitually, accepts. And this disposition of law-abidingness is not the product of careful reflection on the part of the citizen. It is not 'something which can originate independently [*für sich*] and arise out of subjective representations [*Vorstellungen*] and thoughts' (§268R), although 'it may pass over into more or less educated insight' (§268).

So we can ask whether or not there is anything in the social psychology of patriotism that prevents the patriotic citizen from examining the authority of the state and scrutinizing the provenance of the duties it imposes on him. The patriotic citizen *habitually* complies with the state's demands, he *trusts* the state as he goes about his business. But there is nothing in this that precludes the citizen asking, in a quiet or reflective moment if that is his temperament, the philosophical question of what is the basis of this trust, just as he can muse with more or less seriousness about whether numbers are objects.

Hegel, I think, the most professional of professional philosophers, the one most determined to pursue the academic life as a vocation despite rotten conditions of service and poor wages, thoroughly misunderstood the nature of a philosophical question when it concerns personal conduct. He clearly believed that one who wishes to work out the grounds of his obligations to the state is one who is actively *challenging* the state to produce its credentials. The voluntarist who maintains a philosophical position is regarded as a radical who will undermine the state, just as poor Rousseau is deemed responsible for the Terror. Of course the patriot, happy or grumbling, does not challenge the state in this fashion. But neither does the political philosopher who asks exactly how the state's demands are validated in accordance with his perception of the good. His is an academic exercise; whatever the result of his enquiry, if he has, *ex hypothesi*, a settled disposition to do his duty, his philosophical deliberations are unlikely to disturb it. He may turn out to be a contented, even conservative, philosophical sceptic concerning the authority of the state and the duties of the citizen. This will not stop him playing backgammon, or paying his taxes.

Of course his philosophical temperament may exacerbate his natural bloody-mindedness. A quick dose of philosophy may turn an intellectual sheep into a critical wolf, or so we philosophers tell the world, so we teachers entice potential students. But so far as I can see, the only serious fools who have believed this self-serving story have been secret policemen in the service of totalitarian states. Their minds move quickly: thought = independent thought = critical thought = subversion of the state. Hence philosophers wishing to study Plato's *Theaetetus* were followed around the streets of Prague by chaps in leather jackets and trilby hats in the later years of the twentieth century. Incredible. And stupid. And, perhaps, not so stupid, given what was later revealed as the fragility of the communist states.

I don't want to locate Hegel in this miserable camp. The old man has suffered too much from anachronistic affiliations – the father of Nazism, the target of Karl Popper's war effort.[5] But I do want to emphasize how far his rejection of liberalism is contaminated by his horror of the Terror. He equates the philosophically-minded examination of the state with the politically-minded challenge to the *ancien régime* and he equates this with the mentality of negative, destructive freedom (§§5R, 5A, 258R) – Terror by association. And he is quite wrong to do so – not least because he identifies himself with that educated elite which *does* have an insight into the rationality of the modern state and can both grasp and disclose the quality of this rationality. The just state, the rational state, has nothing to fear from those who approach its majesty in the spirit of philosophical enquiry.

The second element of the belief system of Hegel's citizen which I wish to examine is religion. This is a subject that needs to be approached carefully, not least since Hegel is famous for ominous remarks he made about the divinity of the state. We have already come across one: the conception of the state as founded in contract and legitimized by the express consent of citizens who are exercising their arbitrary will tends both in thought and practice to 'destroy the divine [element] which has being in and for itself and its absolute authority and majesty' (§258R). In the notes to this paragraph, he claims that 'The state consists in the march of God in the world' (*der Gang Gottes in der Weld*). Later the Idea of the state is described as 'this actual God' (§258A). Worse still, monarchy turns out to have a divine quality – 'the right of the monarch is based on divine authority' (§279R) though Hegel does not like this way of speaking, presumably because of its association with the fundamentally Catholic doctrine of the Divine Right of Kings, which he despised (LPH: 445 / SW 11: 555). From these sources, and others, we conclude that Hegel deifies the state, and draw a sharp breath.

We should not be distracted. It would be just as accurate to say that Hegel drags God down to the level of politics as it would be to say that he elevates the state to the divine.[6] The state is a formation of spirit, it is spirit made objective in persons and the institutions they inhabit. If we then equate spirit and God, objective spirit is identified with the actuality of God. Of course, the metaphysics and the associated philosophy of religion on which these identities are premised are massively controversial, but we can put these issues to one side. We need to know what is the relationship between religion and the state, and helpfully Hegel discusses the matter fully in the long Remark to §270.

Hegel, as we might expect given the political circumstances and his own vulnerability to charges of atheism-as-pantheism, treads delicately. His views are best summarized by first identifying his opponents, then stating his positive doctrine. First he opposes those whose religion operates as consolation in hard times and encourages them 'to treat worldly interests and the course of actual events with indifference'. These are folks who look to the Church as the only authority in matters of conduct. Second he notices that doctrines which emphasize how the oppressed may find consolation in religion may themselves issue from theocratic regimes which lead to 'the harshest servitude within the fetters of superstition and to the debasement of human beings to a level below that of animals'. His lesson is clear: Beware doctrines that tell you to seek consolation for your misery in religion. They may be instrumental in causing that misery in the first place. This advice seems wise to me.

The third variety of error induced by religion is caused by religions that take a correct view as to the form of religious belief, but then license themselves to make awful mistakes as to the content – the requirements of religion concerning how we should behave. In this respect, as Hegel reminds us, the pious are akin to those who are misled by the false promptings of conscience. The content of true religion, as of true conscience (§137) is the truth about the good. But the form in which religion reveals that truth is through the ultimately unsatisfactory sources of 'intuition, feeling and representative cognition'. It cannot attain the standpoint of reason and thus is disposed to error and evil in the same way as conscience. The unexamined voice of the pious can undermine the state, creating 'instability, insecurity and disruption' as it calls its followers to follow such nostrums as 'To the righteous, no law is given.' Worse, it can lead 'to religious *fanaticism* which, like political fanaticism, repudiates all political institutions and legal order as restrictive limitations on the inner emotions'. This fanaticism 'can produce nothing but folly, outrage and the destruction of all ethical relations'. I won't argue with this.

Genuine religion, by contrast, may be necessary within the state, particularly for the uneducated who cannot achieve rational insight and who must rely on religion and faith for their ethical disposition. '[S]ince religion is that moment which integrates the state at the deepest level of the disposition [of its citizens], the state ought even to require all its citizens to belong to such a community – but to any community they please, for the state can have no say in the content [of religious belief] in so far as this relates to the internal dimension of representational thought' (§270R). So Hegel takes the conventional position for the time of tolerating many different religious faiths, but disapproves of atheism. So far as concerns the religious doctrine one professes, this is the 'province of the conscience, and enjoys the right of the subjective freedom of self-consciousness'. So far as acts of worship are concerned, these do concern the state – and rightly, too, though there are borderline cases. The state shouldn't tolerate forms of worship which violate persons' rights (so human sacrifice will be illegal), but if the state is strong it can tolerate small communities, for example, of Quakers and Anabaptists, exempting them from oaths and enabling them to commute or substitute military service. Civil rights, as he reminds those who would continue to exclude and persecute Jews, are based in the humanity of the person. No-one should be denied legal status on the grounds of their religious faith or ethnic origins (fn. to §270R).

Hegel's fundamental commitment to religious freedom puts him in a difficult philosophical position since it portends a liberal approach to the role of the state *vis-à-vis* religion. This is the view he has disso- ciated himself from before, 'that view of the state according to which its sole function is to protect and secure the life, property and arbitrary will of everyone, in so far as the latter does not infringe the life, prop- erty, and arbitrary will of others', the view that treats the state 'simply as a means which should provide for it [life, property, arbitrary will, particular religious belief?] as an end in itself'. The upshot, which is a fudge, but perhaps none the worse for that, is that the state should sustain those varieties of religious belief which subscribe to rules of conduct which are coincident with those of the ethical life of the state. These may be the rules of true religion which express in primitive fashion (through 'representational thought' – religious imagery, parables and the like) the same philosophical principles which rational thought discloses to the initiated. They may be the rules of dotty religions which do no net harm. But the state cannot tolerate, indeed must assert on its own behalf, the 'formal right of self-consciousness to its own insight and conviction' against any 'Church which claims unlimited and unconditional *authority*' – the traditional charge against Catholicism. Interestingly, it turns out to be no bad thing for the state (or the Church) that Christianity has been split into rival faiths. This tendency should dispose its adherents to that humility which, besides being necessary for toleration, is a useful precondition of respect for the authority of the state.[7]

In sum, Hegel's view of Church–state relations is that religion is a valuable resource for inculcating a properly ethical spirit in members of society, although like the misguided conscience, it can also be a threat. For the most part, those who go to church and Sunday school, best of all when young, with their parents, are likely to be patriots in Hegel's sense of that term, committed in the docile, conservative, passive, fashion of the moral majority to the institutions of society and state. So we should ask again, is there anything in this mindset, now bolstered (or tainted) with religious faith, that precludes the citizen from inspecting the credentials of the state to which he affirms his loyalty? I don't see any hindrance. We know (*ex hypothesi*, because Hegel has told us so) that most citizens are too uneducated or unconcerned to bother. But we know, because Hegel has shown us how the philosophical examination can be conducted, that some philosophically-minded souls will do so. To my mind, the only major difference between Hegel's position and that of the archetypal Enlightenment intellectual who seeks the grounds of rational legitimacy is that Hegel imputes to this liberal position a limited framework of ends (life, property, arbitrary will, contingently adopted religious creed) which he rejects as insufficient to the task. Basically this is the same charge that he directed at Rousseau when he analysed the general will as the common element of an aggregation of (egoistic) unprincipled particular wills. But this is not a charge that sophisticated liberals, from Locke to Rawls (and including Rousseau, properly read) should be inclined to accept.

Organicism[8]

We have been trying to pin down exactly why Hegel felt compelled to reject traditional liberal theory. And we have argued that he has been unsuccessful in claiming that the beliefs of the pious patriot foreclose this philosophical project. The final proposal we should examine is that the life of the state has an *organic* quality which precludes this philosophical stance. Hegel unblushingly speaks of 'the inner organism of the state' (§258A). He describes the constitution of the state as 'a self-related organism' (§259). In §263A he employs an extended organic metaphor to illuminate the relation of component elements of the state (family and civil society) to the whole. The subjective contours of patriotism, as expressed in the different ways in which different folk (belonging to different corporations, located in different estates and classes) go about fulfilling the duties of their respective stations, derive their 'particularly derived *content* from the various aspects of the organism of the state' (§269). Citizens are 'not parts, but members', Hegel says (§286R), exploiting the primary sense of *Glied* as a bodily member or limb. Further remarks concerning the organic qualities of the state are scattered about the *Philosophy of Right*, as ever in a variety of contexts which makes the claim that the state is an organism difficult to understand, still less evaluate. A canonical statement is the following: 'This *organism* [the state] is the development of the Idea in its differences and their objective actuality' (§269).

Hegel believes that the (metaphysical, ontological) fact that the state is an organism is incompatible with the claim that the purpose of the state is the service of the particular ends of the individuals who compose it. To review this claim we need to have a clear sense of the statement that the state is an organism, or an organic whole. So let us try to establish the meaning of this difficult thesis. One approach I shall not take is an investigation of the question whether Hegel's statement is literal or metaphorical, since a satisfactory answer to this question requires that we have to hand a non-controversial set of criteria for determining something as a literally living unity. This is a good question, philosophical-cum-biological, and perhaps cum-psychological and cum-sociological, but it is no way to advance the present discussion within a sensible compass, since all we need to know is what Hegel meant by the claim that the state is an organism. It may well be, indeed it will transpire, that Hegel's thesis can be stated without broaching these wider philosophical issues.[9]

Organicism is a thesis to the effect that some social entity is best understood as a self-maintaining, functioning whole. The life of the social organism is in turn to be explained in accordance with the functioning of parts which are directed to the maintenance of the social whole. As stated, and I grant that the statement is extremely vague, social organicism is a variety of social holism which denies that the working of the social entity can be understood as a simple aggregation or mechanical co-ordination of the operation of the parts. Correlatively, the functioning of the social whole cannot be explained by *reducing* it to the operations of the individual parts that compose it. One of the great gifts of Thomas Hobbes to the discipline of political philosophy was his clear statement of the position to which social organicism and social holism are opposed. This has been dubbed 'methodological individualism' and 'social atomism', and it claims that the properties of social entities can be fully understood in terms of the intentional behaviour of the individuals who compose them. Thus the state for Hobbes is analytically, and in some cases practically, a construction out of the intentions of citizens, primarily to preserve their lives and live commodiously. For Hegel, by contrast, 'it is . . . utterly essential that the constitution should not be regarded as something made . . . On the contrary . . . [it should] be regarded as divine and enduring, and exalted above the sphere of all manufactured things' (§273R).

Thus Hegel's espousal of social organicism is designed to block conceptions of the state as aggregations or mechanical constructions of the powers of individual persons. It is also to be contrasted with conceptions of the state as a balance of separate competing *social* powers, whether these separations be the feudal division of ranks (kings, lords and commons, or vassals and pashas (§286R)) or the modern doctrines of the '*necessary division* [*Teilung*] *of powers*' (§272R) associated with Locke, Montesquieu, the Federalists, Kant, and Fichte. Such latter doctrines are 'purely mechanical' (§286R) rather than organic, so it should not be surprising if they perpetuate the social conflict or friction which they are designed to avoid.

We can sidestep a general consideration of these issues by asking directly why Hegel believed that the state should not be understood as a social construction designed to further the projects of individual members of it, whether asserted individually or as represented by competing 'parts' of the state. In other words, we have approached by a different route the question we have been pressing throughout this chapter: Why does Hegel reject the claim that the state is essentially an instrument necessary for serving the purposes of members of families, of institutions and estates within civil society, including as we have mentioned members of various churches? The answer is that the state exhibits a systematicity, a form of organization which blocks reduction. The social properties of the state are *sui generis*. 'The state in and for itself is the ethical whole, the actualization of freedom, and it is the absolute end of reason that freedom should be actual' (§258A). The state uniquely is the social formation which actualizes freedom. This property, the actualization of freedom, cannot be instantiated by citizens severally or as members of subordinate communities, estates or factions, independently of their membership of the ethical whole. Considered in the abstract, they can of course be more or less free, free in-itself, in the ways explored in our discussions of the previous sections of the book. They can exhibit a measure of personal and moral freedom as articulated in Abstract Right and Morality respectively. They can achieve the substantial freedom displayed by family members and the particular freedoms achieved in civil society. But the structures of freedom thus uncovered are limited and probably conflicting. The state, and only the state, 'is the actuality of concrete freedom' (§260).

There are two ways in which Hegel shows this, and they are of course related, and indeed carried forward together as one project. The first way is to give a description of the constitution of the state which portrays it as rational in the sense that its institutions display the logic of the Concept. Thus the state is revealed as a self-sustaining individual, an integrated unity of the categories of universality and particularity. The second way of accomplishing this task is to show how the political institutions of the state manifest in a stable and harmonious fashion all the severally partial elements of freedom hitherto adduced. The obvious way to study Hegel's pursuit of these projects is to follow carefully his description of the constitution of the rational state and his explanation of how rationality is achieved by the workings of the component institutions functioning severally and in harness. We would study the legislature as the manifestation of universality, the executive, including the judiciary, as the manifestation of particularity, and the sovereign power, the constitutional monarchy as the individual, the ethical subject who unites universality and particularity in his social person. We would notice how a full specification of each of these constitutional elements is itself an individual melding of universality and particularity and we would explain the organicism of the social structure as the thorough interpenetration at all levels of the different elements of the Concept. Each power presupposes the others and is in turn presupposed by them (§285). We would pursue this course of study because this is how Hegel introduces his project:

> The constitution is rational in so far as the state *differentiates* and determines its activity within itself *in accordance with the nature of the concept*. It does so in such a way that *each* of the *powers* in question is in itself the *totality*, since each contains the other moments and has them active within it, and since all of them, as expressions of the differentiation [*Unterschied*] of the concept, remain wholly within its ideality, and constitute nothing but a *single individual* whole.
>
> (§272)

This is how Marx studied this section of the *Philosophy of Right* in the manuscript he composed in 1843 (Marx 1970), and a very turgid project he revealed it to be. The major reason for this is the fast-and-loose manner in which Hegel employs the 'logic of the Concept'. It should be clear to all readers that Hegel has worked out, from a mixture of contemporary institutions and respectable proposals for reform, a constitutional blueprint which he believes to incorporate elements of acceptable principle and unquestionable practice. So he rolls out a ramshackle constitutional structure, continuously drawing readers' attention to its 'rational' credentials. Thus, to take a comical example,[10] it is not its utility in preventing the formation of conflicting factions which justifies the practice of hereditary succession to the monarchy – such a consideration would demean the majesty of the monarch (§§281, 281R). Rather it is the fact that the will of the state as expressed in the monarchy is 'simple and therefore an *immediate* individuality [*Einzelheit*], so that the determination of *naturalness* is inherent in its very concept' (§280). 'Logical philosophy' alone (§280R), 'the speculative method of the infinite and self-grounding idea' (§281R), is in a position to explain the nature of constitutional monarchy in such a way that its authoritative power, its majesty, is not undermined by common-or-garden ratiocination. Marx sees through this self-serving nonsense: 'Hegel has demonstrated that the monarch must be born, which no one doubted, but not that birth makes one a monarch. That man becomes monarch by birth can as little be made into a metaphysical truth as can the Immaculate Conception of Mary' (Marx 1970: 33).

I use this example not because I have a taste for comedy or Marx's raucous and generally well-grounded criticism, but rather to disarm a strategy which defenders of Hegel have often employed to deflect straightforward objections to his portrayal of the constitution of the rational state.[11] Thus one might say, speaking from one of the benighted states of contemporary Europe, that all things considered, there's *something* to be said for hereditary monarchy and against elected heads of state. Like students voting for Rectors in the ancient Scottish universities, the electors might go for an attention-seeking celebrity, or they may find themselves in the embarrassing position of having elected an ex-Nazi, as in Austria with Kurt Waldheim. These and other such arguments are good arguments, worthy of consideration, but they are not Hegel's arguments. Even to *endorse* the credentials of a hereditary monarch following free-ranging reflection at a dinner party is to demean the majesty of the institution. *Only* the speculative method will serve – and it serves up a dish so dreadful that it discredits the method.

The Constitution

In what follows I will give a succinct description of the constitution of the rational state so that we might review Hegel's claim that it is the actuality of concrete freedom. The order of exposition of the three substantial elements of the constitution is unusual. There's no nonsense here about the sequence of universal, particular and individual. The powers of the state are discussed in order of importance; the guiding principle seems to be deference rather than the logic of the concept. So he discusses in succession ' a. The Power of the Sovereign' (§§275–86), the moment of individual unity, 'b. The Executive Power' (§§287–97), the power of dealing with particular cases, and 'c. The Legislative Power' (§§298–320), 'the power to determine and establish the universal' (§273), reversing the 'logical' order of exposition.

The sovereign is a constitutional monarch, constitutional monarchy being the culmination of the development of ethical life in universal world history (§273R). Now it's fair to say that constitutional monarchy is an accurate description of the constitution as a whole. Hegel rejects the traditional trichotomy of monarchy, aristocracy and democracy on the grounds that, roughly, this is outdated; the constitution of the rational state, the constitutional monarchy, contains elements of each (§273R). This bears an innocuous reading: modern states require a head of state, with some powers to be specified, an executive civil service widely construed, and a political process to represent the people. By contrast, Hegel's description of the first, pre-eminent power of the state focusses sharply on the monarchical element.

What is the point of the monarchy and what are its powers? Its point, which cannot be stated without equivocation, is that the singularity of the person of the monarch captures the individual aspect of the state. The state could not be a moral substance unless it was conscious of itself 'as *subjectivity*'. The demands of personality could not be met in the state unless the state had the aspect of 'a *person*'. 'This absolutely decisive moment of the whole, therefore, is not individuality in general, but *one* individual, the *monarch*' (§279). Presumably this means we could not recognize the state as a truly ethical whole unless we had a monarch to display subjectivity in his person. The demands of Abstract Right, of personality, will remain abstract no matter how widely or how concretely we construe the quality of personality (accounting families, communities and societies as moral persons). 'The personality of the state has actuality only as a *person*, as *the monarch*' (§279R). Subjectivity will remain a (necessary but dangerous) aspiration until its claims to certainty are actualized in the decision-taking actions of the moral subject-as-monarch who enacts and thereby makes positive the law of the land.

Now it may well be a fact about states that they are unlikely to be harmonious, stable and enduring unless citizens can be brought to identify with them, and it may well be a fact about citizens that they identify more readily with institutions that bear a recognizable human face, and it may also be true that the humanity of the state, as against its property of being a well-armed coercive force, is only recognizable when it is personified in a head of state (I guess these plausible half-truths amount to the best defence of 'the cult of personality'), but this thread of argument does not capture a logical truth of the speculative method. Ditto, as we have seen, for the best defence that can be given for the associated institution of *hereditary* monarchy.

What are the powers of the monarch? They are hard to discern in detail, since the texts and the lecture notes together sustain two very different readings. The 'hard reading' emphasizes the real power in the contingency of the sovereign act of law-making. Certain of itself as superseding all particularities (different points of view) it 'cuts short the weighing of arguments [*Gründe*] and counter-arguments . . . and resolves them by its "I will", thereby initiating all activity and actuality' (§279R). Thus the monarch is the crucial element in 'the legislative power as a whole', having 'the power of ultimate decision' (§300). As against this view of the power of the monarch, the 'soft reading', deriving largely from the lecture notes, emphasizes the monarch's reliance on his expert executive, the fact that 'he often has nothing more to do than to sign his name' (§279A). Likewise, 'in a fully organized state it is only a question of the highest instance of formal decision, and all that is required in a monarch is someone to say "yes" and to dot the "i"' (§280A). The monarch on the hard reading resembles King Friedrich Wilhelm III of Prussia, a suspicious and capricious opponent of reform; the monarch on the soft reading resembles the office of the Doge of Venice or the person of Queen

Elizabeth II of the United Kingdom, a symbol which has significance for some of her subjects.

To continue the contrast, the hard reading points up Hegel's identification of the element of particularity within the sovereign's powers. Thus 'the appointment of individuals for this purpose [the highest executive officers] and their dismissal from office fall within the [competence of the] unrestricted arbitrary will of the monarch' (§283). The soft reading will draw attention to the fact that this arbitrariness is qualified by a policy of appointing executive officers not on the basis of their birth or personal contacts, but on the grounds of their skill. The executive offers a career open to anyone who is genuinely talented and can give proof of his abilities (§291). In the Heidelberg (1817–18) lectures given before Hegel moved to Berlin and before the passing of the Karlsbad decrees in 1819, Hegel says that the monarch is free to dismiss only the most senior executive officers (the ministers), and that all other civil servants have rights of tenure, their dismissal requiring a formal judgement of good cause. He had a particular interest in the employment conditions of university teachers! (VPR17: 258, 265–7 / VNS: 207–8, 214–16). Notwithstanding this element of independence, the hard reader ripostes, the monarch will always have to guard against the formation of a common interest amongst the civil servants which leads them to maintain 'solidarity among themselves in opposition to their subordinates and superiors' (§295R). Rousseau thought this problem was intractable. Hegel thought an active and alert sovereign such as Frederick the Great could tackle the job.

The second power in the constitution is the executive. This includes the judiciary and the police, as well as the governmental administration. And the police, we recall, includes teachers and lamplighters as well as the constabulary. Although together they comprise the universal class, they deal with particular cases – which illustrates nicely the flexibility of the 'logical' categories. Hegel views them as constitutional intermediaries, points of contact with both the monarchy and the people. Again this can be read in hard or soft fashion. The hard reading will stress how far they interpenetrate the spontaneously formed institutions of civil society, fixing prices, making sure that families rear children to be good citizens, and, most sinisterly, regulating and supervising the work of the corporations. The soft reading will note Hegel's emphasis on their sensitivity and responsiveness to the population at large. Their ethos should encompass a (bottom-up) respect for, and civility to, those they administer, as well as a (top-down) commitment to efficiency in pursuit of the objectives of the state. Good ethical training will balance politeness and integrity against the pseudo-scientific rigmaroles of business administration. Exactly how the rights of the corporations will be asserted against over-zealous administrators (§297) must remain a mystery given Hegel's explicit contempt for the ways in which corporations govern their own affairs (§289R).

The final piece in Hegel's constitutional jigsaw is his treatment of the legislative power. In their detail, Hegel's proposals for the constitution of the Estates[12] derive from the various reform proposals charted by Stein, von Humboldt and Hardenberg.[13] The function of the legislative power is to facilitate 'the further evolution of the laws and the progressive character of the universal concerns of government' (§298). It will introduce and amend laws as and when this is required, such changes being envisaged as specifications of the civil rights of persons and communities, which may include alterations of their constitutional status. Such measures are optimistically deemed 'benefits which the state enables them to enjoy' (§299). The legislature will also specify the services which citizens must perform for the state. In the modern world, in contrast to Plato's *Republic*, feudalism and the ancient despotisms of the Orient and Egypt, this will rarely amount to direct personal services – military service is the only such duty that Hegel envisages. The standard universal form of service is the payment of taxes, money being the universal measure of value of persons' skills and resources (§299).

The legislature has a tripartite composition; its three moments are the monarchy, the executive and the Estates. This itself offends against the doctrine of the separation of powers, but Hegel is unconcerned since at all levels the rational state will be an organic unity rather than a forum for competing powers. We already know what the monarch's role in the legislature may be, subject to differences between the hard and soft readings of the text. Put to one side the executive's role for a moment as something of a mystery. (Hegel approves the British model whereby ministers must be Members of Parliament, although he knew full well that the British monarch was constrained in the choice of ministers (§300R).) The function of the Estates is to bring into existence 'the universal interest . . . the moment of subjective *formal freedom* . . . the public consciousness as the *empirical universality* of the views and thoughts of the *many* (§301) – *hoi polloi*.

So the task of the Estates is to express the public view of the universal interest – in Rousseau's terms, it is to voice the general will. The model of the Estates is bicameral, as in Congress with its House and Senate, or Parliament with its Lords and Commons. The first Estate is that of the landed aristocracy, the higher reaches of the substantial estate (§§303–4), whose property is entailed and transmitted by primogeniture, thus offending the basic principles of Abstract Right. Male heads of important rural families, burdened with primogeniture and fated to an existence sustained by their large natural resources, connect the deliberations of the state with nature through their family-based authority ('the patriarchal way of life' (§203A)) and their agricultural source of income. Romantic and sentimental sympathizers with Hegel may describe this as the *ecological* element of the state, but they would be mistaken. Hegel was not one of this misty-eyed species. He was well aware that modern agriculture is an exploitative, agribusiness (§§44, 203, 203A). Members of this Estate are not elected. They must be presumed to speak for small farmers and peasants, who have no political standing at all.

The second Estate represents the commercial estate, 'the estate of trade and industry' (§204), the sphere of town as against the country (§256R). Hegel's contrast between the ethical sources of the two Estates is overblown, since the landed estate must engage in trade (who otherwise will feed the towns?) and the concrete individuals who work in industry and commerce will be for the most part (patriarchal) heads of families. As we noticed in Chapter 11, families don't break down *into* the atomistic units of civil society, they pursue their universal ends as particulars *within* it. That said, we need to examine the representational structure of the second Estate.

Hegel makes much of the fact that not all citizens have a *political* status.

> The idea [*Vorstellung*] that *all* individuals ought to participate in deliberations and decisions on the universal concerns of the

state – on grounds that they are all members of the state and that the concerns of the state are the concerns of *everyone*, so that everyone has a *right* to share in them with his own knowledge and volition – seeks to implant in the state a *democratic* element *devoid of rational form*, although it is only by virtue of its rational form that the state is an organism.

(§308R)[14]

Each citizen has an irreducible moral status as 'a *private person* and at the same time [as] a *thinking* being', but this is an empty '*generic category* [*Gattung*]' with no implications for the person's political standing. Political status is only acquired as a consequence of civic standing, and civic standing is only achieved through the person's activities as a member of 'his corporation, community etc.' (§308R). The thought is simple enough. Folks who are not associated with others through corporate activity of some kind have not developed a conception of how their particular interest both feeds into and is in turn cultivated by the universal interest. (One might have thought this is achieved in family life, and that the domestic formation of this plural ethical perspective is a crucial reason for Hegel's describing the family as 'the first *ethical* root of the state' (§258). Evidently the ethical education of the family member is too limited for children (sons) to be deemed capable of citizenship upon maturity.) To be capable of active citizenship, one needs to be a member of a corporation.

There are three philosophical issues at stake here, and Hegel either confuses them, or brings two to the fore whilst ignoring or concealing the third. The first question, Rousseau's question, is whether a legislative assembly should be a directly and universally constituted body or whether it should be composed of representatives of the sovereign people. Rousseau famously argues for direct democracy, but he is in the minority of democratic theorists. On this question, Hegel sides with those opposed to Rousseau. He favours a second Estate which is a representative institution. So far so good, you might think. The second question concerns the mode of representation. Representative systems need constituencies. Should these be the standard (in Hegel's time, British and US) model of geographically demarcated electorates or should some other system of representing the will of the people be adopted? Hegel favours the second alternative. Representation should be achieved through corporations. There is a metaphysical reason for this: it is the political expression of the organic constitution of civil society 'articulated into its associations, communities and corporations' (§308). But there are practical reasons, too. Representatives from geographical electoral districts may be ignorant and untried advocates of sectional interests (the old Platonic charge of demagoguery, I take it) and moreover, in mass elections, as Rousseau noted in the different context of direct democracy, and as Hegel no doubt learnt from him, the power of the individual elector may be so diluted as to produce apathy and indifference in the electorate (§311R).

This practical response of Hegel's opens up the third question which he explicitly downplays. Granting him his representative system as an answer to the first two questions, we can now ask whether his denial of a universal political status for all citizens implies that some of them will not be fitted to be *members of an electorate*, on the same grounds that he claimed they are not all fitted to be elected deputies.[15] His stated view is that so long as representatives

> are elected by the various corporations, and this simple mode of procedure is not impaired by abstractions and atomistic notions ... it directly fulfils the requirement referred to above [that deputies be familiar with the special needs, frustrations and particular interests of civil society], and the election itself is either completely superfluous or can be reduced to an insignificant play of arbitrary opinion.
>
> (§311)

I don't think Hegel *cares* about how deputies are elected, so long as they are qualified in terms of objectively recognizable knowledge and skills derived from practical experience in positions of authority in private business or political office (§310). And I surmise that it will be those members of the executive whose task it is to supervise the work of the corporations who will validate candidates for office as deputies. As members of trades unions and political parties know well, it is vitally important that the credentials of elected officials be explicit in terms of the composition of the constituency which has elected them. Hegel's prime concern is to guarantee an institutional symmetry, a topological isomorphism between the institutions of civil society and the political constitution of the state, in the belief that this ensures the appropriate organic connection. If his denial that all persons have political status within the state is simply a repudiation of direct democracy many democratically inclined critics will follow him. If it is a denial that all persons can have access to the political process, which I think it is, it is a serious weakness of the constitution of the rational state. It is a serious weakness because it denies an important element of freedom, political freedom, to whole groups of citizens.[16]

The 'virtual representation' of civil society offered through the corporations is itself a sinister and self-serving process on behalf of the political elite who certify the corporations and supervise their activities. I think this constitutional apparatus is also designed to exclude the mass of citizens from the status of being political participators. I think this is explicit in Hegel's contempt for the masses, as it is implied by his contempt for even the officials of corporations. But readers should take their own view.

One final note on these severe criticisms of the institutional structure of the rational state. I insist that they are not anachronistic. Hegel had read Rousseau and was familiar with radical criticism of the British Parliamentary system. In 1835, de Tocqueville, in *Democracy in America*, could confidently announce that the equality of political status distinctive of modern democracy, and witnessed in operation in America, is the fundamental principle of political life. Just ten years after Hegel's death, Marx in his 1843 *Critique* could accurately diagnose his hostility to democracy as the voice of a conservative, if not quite the most reactionary, political elite. Less than thirty years after Hegel's death, a very different political thinker, John Stuart Mill, in *On Liberty* (1859) could announce that we are all democrats nowadays; the problem is to delimit the powers of the democratic sovereign. Hegel stands out in his resistance to the democratic temper.

What is left of Hegel's view that the organic constitution of the state precludes the possibility of political liberalism? It amounts to this claim: that persons who are brought up by their parents to respect the state, educated in civil society to bring skills to the market place and apply those skills successfully to a trade, who join with colleagues in corporate activities which elicit a common social purpose greater than the pursuit of mutual advantage, cannot detach themselves in thought from these affiliations to ask whether the state serves their several and joint purposes, so long as the state is organized in such a way that it does in fact serve these ends.

This seems to me an empirical question in the guise of a philosophical question since, although it asks what citizens can possibly *think* about their social state from an epistemological perspective which is formed within a condition of social life which they habitually approve, it cannot preclude an answer of this shape: I endorse the state and the duties it assigns to me because after careful reflection I understand that it promotes and protects the personal and social goods I recognize, the rights and freedoms I claim, as family member, as worker and active corporate member and as citizen. I say this is an empirical question because if the answer that has been given (which mimics Hegel's own) is true, it is true only contingently. Clearly Hegel believes that the state *does* deliver the goods, *does* manifest freedom, at least in its essentials, so that the citizens he describes are not likely to give a negative answer to it. But to describe a cheerful, pious and patriotic body of citizens who willingly do their duty is not to describe a population that is unable to understand what it is doing and why. The fact that although citizens might grumble and grouse they do not challenge the authority of the state does not show that citizens could not do so if they felt that the state is unjust and its pretensions a fraud. Yet even in Hegel's rational state there are people like this and he has described them. They are the rabble, the contingently, undeservedly, desperately poor, which is why he recognizes that the problem they pose is so deep and why his response to it is philosophically so equivocal. The poor genuinely speak to their rights, yet they speak from a condition of such moral degeneracy that they fail to see the duty incumbent upon them to be contented, peaceful and law-abiding. They attest correctly that the organism is diseased, yet this is not a view that any citizen of the rational organic state can logically take. Philosophically as well as practically it is important that the state be rid of them.

This deep equivocation is not to be seen only in Hegel's treatment of the poor. It raises its head in the final sections of his discussion of the legislative power when he considers the phenomenon of public opinion and the associated issue of freedom of the press. In a nutshell, he tells us that 'Public opinion therefore deserves to be *respected* as well as *despised*' (§318). He cannot alter the fact that public opinion will challenge public policy, whether it is expressed by a deputy to the Estates who has somehow passed through the filters of experience and competence but hasn't yet been thoroughly house-trained (§§315, 315A), or whether it is in the voice of Billy Muggins ('all the contingencies of opinion, with its ignorance and perverseness, its false information and its errors of judgement, come on the scene (§317)'. Fortunately, there is a logical test for whether public opinion is correct or not, for 'the worse the content of an opinion is, the more distinctive it will be' (§318). In other words, any view that diverges from the public wisdom as announced by the sovereign must be wrong, and the wider the divergence, the greater the error. The very fact of the existence of public opinion 'is therefore a manifest self-contradiction' (§316). It attests a range of views although only one of them can be right.

That's the bad news. The good news is that public opinion is containable and educable. The public deliberations of the Estates will reveal 'the functions, abilities, virtues and skills of the official bodies and civil servants' (§315). Where public opinion is recalcitrant it can safely be ignored. Public policy should proceed quite independently of it in the sure knowledge that 'Great achievement may . . . be assured that public opinion will subsequently accept it, recognize it, and adopt it as one of its prejudices' (§318). The state should not concern itself overmuch with interfering with the press since for the most part its functioning is innocuous. If the press reports accurately the wise deliberation of the assemblies of the Estates this leaves 'little of significance for others to say', but if it does express contrary opinions it will bring down 'indifference and scorn' (§319) upon itself. So long as its excesses are prevented or punished by the police, it is a useful safety valve. Again divergence and dissent is to be expected in the nature of things in the modern world, but subjectivity 'has its truth in its own opposite . . . the subjectivity which constitutes the concept of the power of the sovereign' (§320).

We don't need to believe this. We may believe rather that subjectivity has its truth in the power of the citizen to subject the claims of the sovereign to rational scrutiny. In which case we should recognize a feature of Hegel's argument that makes it really peculiar. It is the articulation of a rational structure of thought exhibited in a rational structure of social reality which cannot in principle be appealed to in defence of the institutions which manifest it because this would be to concede powers of rational scrutiny which it explicitly denies. As put it is hard to tell whether this thought is (modestly) self-effacing or (arrogantly) esoteric. It looks to be self-contradictory beyond the power of dialectical redemption.

I think the appearance of self-contradiction can be explained, if not disarmed. Recall that the patriot does not think much about his political status as subject. He trusts the state and habitually conforms to its demands. Religion, too, plays an important role in disposing citizens to comply with what is expected of them. Correct religious doctrine and conventional religious practice tell them a story about how they should behave which nicely fits their political obligations and precludes the necessity of a philosophical examination of which they are likely to be incapable. As organic members of the complexly structured state, they will fulfil the duties of their station, a station which they may have selected or a station, as with the landed aristocracy, into which they have been born. Their freedom does not require that they grasp the correct philosophical account of why they are free. That account is available only to those who have been educated to the point where they do understand the philosophical credentials of their social world, where they do recognize the rational in the actual. But that account tells us why all are free, those who do not comprehend as well as those who do.

I don't think this contrast between the ignorant, uneducated, trustful, pious, incompetent, and sometimes even despicable common folk, on the one hand, and the learned, insightful, and practically wise elite on the other, is a tendentious reading of Hegel's texts. All of the negative characterizations of the psychology of most of Hegel's fellow citizens can be found in the passages I have been discussing. And Hegel's position can be softened by his clear view, akin to that later promulgated by John Stuart Mill, that the political process indirectly, as well as educational practices directly, are a vehicle for improving the comprehension of the ordinary citizen (which is another reason for believing that Hegel's *Lectures on the Philosophy of Education* is one of the great unwritten books).

Moreover, it's not obvious that Hegel was wrong in his estimate of the intellectual capacities of his fellow citizens. There are many folk even nowadays who are concerned that young people are not properly educated for citizenship, that democracy even in the attenuated form of the representative constitution is a demanding personal ideal which imports severe practical problems of political education. Maybe Hegel's disparaging view was the correct view.

So perhaps concrete freedom is attainable by all, if subjective freedom is attainable by some. Perhaps Kant's prescription of rational legitimation can be satisfied even if enlightenment dawns only for those who devote themselves to the task. This raises a vitally important question not only for those who would investigate Hegel's project, but for those who are concerned with the task of political philosophy quite generally. Let me introduce it obliquely with some remarks about Thomas Hobbes. On one anachronistic reading of Hobbes's intellectual ambitions he is a severe reductionist. To understand how men in multitudes may live well together (ethics and politics) we need to understand how mankind acts in light of its characteristic desires and beliefs (psychology). The study of human nature further requires a deeper study of individual persons as themselves but matter in motion (physiology, nowadays neuroscience, notably). This may in principle be reduced to biochemistry, biochemistry to chemistry, and chemistry to physics and maths.

It looks as though we need to uncover the deepest secrets of the universe before we can make any advance in the spheres of ethics and politics. But Hobbes resisted this thought. Mercifully, he believed it was possible to short-cut the physical science by exercises in introspective psychology of the sort at which we are all adept. If we are to live peaceably together, we had better be able to give philosophical arguments which all those who are prone to civil strife and a consequential early death can readily grasp. In the domain of ethics and politics, our reflections must not be conducted at the level of philosophical rocket science. This suggests, although it does not yet justify, the following principle of meta-politics: the principles which are offered in explanation (justification?) of political institutions must be available for philosophical scrutiny by most of those for whom they serve as the basis of their duties as citizens.

The question I raise then concerning Hegel's ethics is this: at what level of comprehension is it pitched? There can be no doubt that it is pitched at a very high level indeed. As we have already noticed, many Hegel scholars have insisted that Hegel's ethics cannot be seriously approached without a careful study of his logic, and Hegel himself encourages this thought. At the very beginning of the *Philosophy of Right* he alerts us to the fact that 'the concept of right, so far as its *coming into being* is concerned, falls outside the science of right; its deduction is presupposed here and is to be taken as *given*' (§2). But even if we don't pitch the study of ethics as high as this, I think the best defence of the doctrines of the *Philosophy of Right* reveals a flaw if it concedes that subjective freedom has two radically different modalities: the first, habitual compliance on the part of most folk; the second, a severe philosophical discipline. Such a state of affairs, I believe, contravenes the Hobbesian principle I suggested above. But then I didn't defend that principle, so, as ever, it looks as though there is more philosophy for me (and you) to do.

War and World History

Hegel completes his discussion of the state in several further sections and subsections, which I shall not discuss in any detail. The next subsection considers *external sovereignty*, roughly, the state as considered from an external perspective, how I might think of states other than mine own. Since the state is the most developed form of self-subsistent individuality, consciousness of its independence constitutes 'the primary freedom and dignity of a nation [*eines Volkes*; Knox: "a people"]' (§322). Hence it is *a priori* impossible for a nation or people to express a coherent wish to give up its sovereignty, as many politicians in Britain state when they consider membership of the European Union, but as many other politicians dispute. It is also incoherent to raise the prospect of perpetual peace between nations as achievable by the constitution of an international world order. Perpetual peace, which was Kant's published aspiration (*Towards Perpetual Peace*, in Kant 1996c: 311–51), would be a recipe for national stagnation.

War is an evil but it is not an 'absolute evil' (§324R); it has its redeeming features. Notably it is conducive to the spiritual health of nations. War brings to consciousness a state's sense of its own integrity. Citizens who in times of peace are rightly preoccupied by their domestic and civil concerns find them a 'nullity' (§323) when the nation is threatened from without. They will be prepared to 'endanger and sacrifice' their own lives and property in order to fulfil 'their duty to preserve this substantial individuality – that is, the independence and sovereignty of the state' (§324). War also provides citizens with the opportunity to display the *formal* virtue of valour – the virtue is formal because it invokes 'the highest abstraction of freedom from all particular ends, possessions, pleasure and life' (as sought by the protagonists in the figure of the life and death struggle in the *Phenomenology* (PS: ¶¶188–9 / SW 2: 151–2)). It is also formal in the sense that it is an *executive* virtue, as Aristotelians describe these things. It can be used in the service of evil or silly ends, by the criminal or the duellist over-concerned with personal honour (§327A). In the service of the state it is noble. These theses cannot be respectably discussed except under the assumption that the war is a just, defensive war. But there is no reason to think that Hegel would dispute this condition. I leave readers to review their plausibility and implications.

The final two sections of Hegel's doctrine of the state concern 'B. International Law' (§§330–40) and 'C. World History' (§§341–60). These comprise the final elements of self-identification in the specification of our full moral address. We are located as citizens of such and such a state, which is recognized by others and recognizes other states in turn, at such and such a time in world history – for Hegel, the Germanic Realm which is its culmination. Hegel's account of international relations is a good illustration of the thesis that Hobbes's state of nature accurately describes the relations between independent nation states.[17] States recognize each other in the way of independent moral persons but inevitably have an adversarial stance since their primary objective is the welfare of their own citizens. Treaty obligations are 'mere' obligations, binding *in foro interno* only, in the necessary absence of a common power or Kantian federation to keep them in peace. So the international state of nature is a condition of endemic war, a product of 'the ceaseless turmoil not just of external contingency, but also of passions, interests, ends, talents and virtues, violence, wrongdoing and vices in their inner particularity' (§340), which is to say, I guess, that states behave no better than their leaders and citizens, as history tells us.

Which takes us on to Hegel's study of world history in less than ten pages. I hope readers of this study of the *Philosophy of Right* will continue their study of Hegel, and I recommend as a further step, attractive because of its accessibility, philosophical interest and historical significance, a reading of Hegel's *Lectures on the Philosophy of History*. These lectures are a massive expansion of the concluding pages of the *Philosophy of Right*, so I intend this recommendation to spare me the effort of exploring his views on the topic. I trust that at the end of my book you will now understand the concluding sentences of Hegel's text:

> The present has cast off its barbarism and unjust [*unrechtliche*] arbitrariness, and truth has cast off its otherwordliness and contingent force, so that the true reconciliation, which reveals the *state* as the image and actuality of reason, has become objective. In the *state*, the self-consciousness finds the actuality of its substantial knowledge and volition in organic development; in *religion*, it finds the feeling and representation [*Vorstellung*] of this truth as ideal essentiality; but in *science*, it finds the free and comprehended cognition of this truth as one and the same in all its complementary manifestations, i.e. in the *state*, in *nature*, and in the *ideal world*.
>
> (§360)

But of course, to understand is not to accept. To comprehend is not to give up on the possibility of deep and continuing philosophical dispute, as I hope my examination of Hegel's doctrines has demonstrated.

Notes

1 Hegel's life, work and influence

1   As Stern argues, 2001: 9–10.
2   Readers may view these judgements as harsh.
     Certainly more sympathetic readings of Hegel have
     been advanced, e.g. Pinkard 2000: 418–68 and Wood
     1990: 11–13, 178–87. These suggest that Hegel was
     foolish to pursue his personal vendetta with Fries in
     this context, since his major complaint was not that
     Fries and his fellow radicals sought to undermine the
     authority of the state (as they did) but that in so doing
     they damaged the cause of genuine constructive reform
     which Hegel favoured. This stance is easily recogniz-
     able. Roughly, and to give a parochial analogy, it is
     the stance of those in the British Labour Party in the
     early 1980s who targeted their venom against
     the radical left wing of the party whose activities
     they believed gifted easy election victories to the
     Conservative Party of Margaret Thatcher. On this
     account, Fries and his radical followers were criticized
     for activities which were the pretext for repression
     and the failure to implement promised reforms. This

picture of Hegel as a proponent of reform who cannot conceal his detestation of the radicals who frustrate his favoured policies may be accurate. But it is not at all obvious that this is his purpose if one makes a judgement solely, or chiefly, on the basis of the Preface to the *Philosophy of Right*.

3   I should clarify one possible implication of my use of the term: I do not regard the term 'conservative' as pejorative; a doctrine may be conservative but none the worse for that. By contrast, I take 'Conservative' to denote the opportunistic and unprincipled promotion of the self-interest of a well-off segment of British society.

4   Robert Stern (private communication).

5   This is the approach defended by Robert Stern in Stern 2001: 15ff.

6   The important texts are translated and collected in Stepelevich 1983, a splendid anthology.

7   Boucher 1997 is a fine anthology of these unfashionable writings.

2   The Introduction to the *Philosophy of Right*

1   This sort of league-table ranking is not worth much, I admit. (How could I argue you out of your view that Kant is *even greater*!?) I say this because (1) I believe it, (2) because I believe anyone who thinks seriously about human freedom can learn something from it, and (3) I cannot emphasize more strongly the importance of studying the Introduction in detail. Unsurprisingly, as we shall see, some of the best modern writing about freedom can be taken as an unwitting (I surmise) recapitulation and elaboration of Hegel's views.

2   See Tunick 1992a: 148ff, for a careful discussion of theory and practice in ethical life.

3   See the remarkable discussion of Brahminism in LPH: Part 1, §2, 144–67; SW 11: 197–226.

4   'Negative freedom' is Hegel's term. It should not be confused with negative freedom as characterized in modern times by Isaiah Berlin in 'Two Concepts of Liberty'. See Berlin 1969.

5   VPR 4: 114: 'der Reformation die Unruhen in Münster'.

6   Hegel's view of the 'Terror' period of the French Revolution is carefully discussed in Stern 2001: 157–68. See also Schmidt 1998.

7   Hobbes 1985: 262 (ch. 21): '*A FREE-MAN, is he, that in those things, which by his strength and wit he is able to do, is not hindered to doe what he has a will to.*'

8   Inwood 1992: 302–5 explains Hegel's use of these terms precisely.

9   See Inwood 1992: 133–6 for further discussion of these terms.

10 See also the *Encyclopaedia*: 'The education and instruction of a child aim at making him actually and for himself [*für sich*] what he is at first potentially [*an sich*] and therefore for others [*für Andere*], viz. for his grown-up friends. The reason, which at first exists in the child only as an inner possibility, is actualized through education: and conversely, the child by these means becomes conscious that the goodness, religion and science which he had at first looked upon as an outward authority, are his own and inward nature' (EL §140A / SW 8: 316).

11 'Self-consciousness, in its immediacy, is a singular . . . in its immediacy [it] has the shape of an external object' (ES §426 / SW 10: 276). 'In the object, the subject beholds its own lack, its own one-sidedness [which it removes by taking possession of the object]' (ES §427Z / SW 10: 278). See also PS ¶¶174–5; SW 2: 145–6.

12 These points are neatly summarized in the *Encyclopaedia*, EL §145A / SW 8:327. Here the *Willkür* is characterized as 'the will in the form of contingency'.

13 A classical source of this view is Moore 1966: ch. 6.

14 Hegel's views on happiness are fully discussed in Wood 1990: 53–71.

15 For further discussion of the importance in Hegel's work of the related notions of individual and cultural education, see Kelly 1969: 341–8.

16 There is now a considerable literature on this subject following Harry Frankfurt's seminal paper: Frankfurt 1971: 5–20. Taylor has developed this view, originally in C. Taylor 1976: 281–99.

17 I borrow this way of putting things from Susan Wolf 1990: ch. 4.

18 Hegel speaks of these as a series of shapes or structures (*eine Reihe von Gestaltungen*) of the Concept (§32), 'these moments of development [of the Concept] attain a distinctive shape of existence' (*zu diesem eigentümlich gestalteten Dasein ihrer Momente gebracht hat*) (§32R).

19 The most sustained modern attempt to understand Hegel's dialectic is found in Rosen 1982. Rosen's conclusions are sceptical. He looks hard, but can't find a clear account of what dialectic amounts to. M. N. Forster, 'Hegel's Dialectical Method', in Beiser 1993: 130–70, is more sympathetic.

20 This notion is particularly hard to accept in the domain of natural science, since it implies a closure of the scientific method around established ways of thinking. But how could we think in ways that are alien to us or genuinely novel in the point of their application of concepts? The quandary is familiar, since it expresses Einstein's well-known bemusement in the face of the results of quantum physics. 'God doesn't play dice?' I add the question mark for mischief.

3   Hegel's Preface

1   For more details on the personal and immediate political context of the
     Preface to the *Philosophy of Right*, see Pinkard 2000: 419–68 and the
     editor's notes to the Cambridge University Press translation (PR).

2   There are thorough discussions of this famous paragraph in Hardimon
     1994: 52–83 and Tunick 1992a: 152–67. See also Wood's editorial notes
     at PR: 389–90.

3   This is what Hegel means when his translators have him say that 'philos-
     ophy paints its grey in grey' (PR: 23). He means philosophy gives us
     the essentials if not the glorious technicolour, the black and white
     picture rather than the colour print, the grisaille rather than the Full
     Monty. It must be said that, in English, 'philosophy paints its grey in
     grey', though literally unintelligible, reads better than 'philosophy
     paints a grisaille picture', not least since this wording (of a genuinely
     poetical conceit) picks up the conceit of the following (even more
     famous) clause: 'the owl of Minerva begins its flight only with the onset
     of dusk' – if dusk is grey, that is. I am grateful to Frau Pender of the
     Goethe Institute in Glasgow for researching the meaning of the term for
     me, in Grimm's *Wörterbuch* and elsewhere, in response to an innocent
     question: What exactly did Hegel mean when he said 'Wenn die
     Philosophie ihr Grau im Grau malt'? Knox's translator's notes and other
     commentaries (Peperzak 1987: 138) claim that Hegel is alluding to a
     famous passage from Goethe's *Faust*, '. . . grey are all theories / And
     green alone life's golden tree', which is odd, since this passage, in the
     voice of Mephistopheles, obviously deprecates theory, whereas Hegel
     does *not* deprecate reason.

4   Readers who wish to continue their investigations could profitably begin
     by reading ch. 3, 'Self-positing Spirit', of C. Taylor 1975.

5   'Sometimes' because at other times he does discuss particular cases,
     and notably the case of Quakers in wartime, with sensitivity. See
     Hegel's footnote to §270R.

6   Hegel makes this point explicitly at §3R where he warns readers against
     confusing 'development from historical grounds . . . with development
     from the concept'. 'To consider the emergence and development of
     determinations of right *as they appear in time* is a *purely historical* task
     [which] . . . bears no relation to the philosophical approach.'

7   The canonical text is ILPWH. For a thorough examination of this subject
     (and an excellent preparation for the study of the *Philosophy of Right*)
     read McCarney 2000.

8   For sentimental reasons, I give Knox's translation.

9   Which is not to say Germany, then or now. The Germanic realm is a confection of North European Protestant states, roughly the Anglo-Saxon nations of Germany, Britain and Scandinavia (LPH: 341–55; SW 11: 437–53). Tantalizingly (what could he have meant?) 'America is therefore the land of the future' (ILPWH: 170; SW 11: 129).

10 I don't take the term 'political correctness' to be pejorative in this context.

11 This difficult point is emphasized in Wood 1990: 21.

12 I think Hegel senses there may be a problem here, but he casts it aside. Read §213 carefully and ask (1) what validates the (majority of) ethical norms of family life which do not concern persons' rights when the family breaks up, and (2) what validates the precepts of morality which 'cannot be the object of positive legislation'. I take it that he is thinking of morality as something close to a virtue ethics, enshrined in such sayings as 'a friend in need is a friend indeed'. I suspect his answer would be that such principles are recognized *customs* (§211R).

4   Abstract Right 1. Persons and their Rights: §§34–43

1   It is remarkable how far Hegel's discussion of Abstract Right antici-pates the moral world of Nozick's *Anarchy, State, and Utopia*. The major sections to follow – 'Property', 'Contract', and 'Wrong' – mirror three elements of Nozick's entitlement theory of justice, the principles of just acquisition, just transfer and, by implication, justice in rectifica-tion of past injustice (Nozick 1974: 150–82). The massive difference, of course, is that, for Hegel, Abstract Right is not the whole of right. It is the first, most primitive, part of it, and the limitations of Abstract Right require a theory of the good which corrects and supplements it, reversing the priority of the right over the good in the order of exposi-tion. So we should read Hegel as, posthumously, putting Nozick in his place. Anachronistically, Hegel's criticism of *Anarchy, State, and Utopia* would be that Nozick never gets beyond Abstract Right – and this criticism is basically correct.

2   For fuller accounts of Fichte's principle of recognition, see R. R. Williams 1992; 1997: 31–8 and Wood 1990: 77–83.

3   Miller translates *Herr* as 'lord' and *Knecht* as 'bondsman'. I use 'master' and 'slave' respectively since these passages are almost universally discussed in English as 'the master–slave dialectic'.

4   I quote Kant (1952), not only as apposite, but to keep alive our sense of what Hegel owed to his predecessors. And Kant, of course, had been reading Rousseau as the source for his account of the dynamically sublime.

5   Which is why, to dispute the interpretation of Leo Strauss (*The Political Philosophy of Thomas Hobbes*, Oxford: Clarendon Press, 1952) Hegel learns nothing from Hobbes in respect of the nature of recognition.

6   The most distinguished modern exponent of this style of argument is Alan Gewirth. See Gewirth 1978, 1996.

7   To my knowledge the only philosophers who recognize the importance of the doctrine of mutual recognition *throughout* the *Philosophy of Right* are Williams (R. R. Williams 1997) and Tunick (Tunick 1994).

5   Abstract Right 2. Property and Contract: §§44–81

1   The phraseology derives from Wenar 1998: 800–1.

2   Kant discusses these questions in §§1–10 of *The Metaphysical Elements of Justice*, Part 1 of *The Metaphysics of Morals*. For a useful discussion, see H. Williams 1983: 77–96.

3   The utilitarian case for institutions of private property is strongly developed by David Hume and comprises the main element of his theory of justice as an artificial virtue. It is first detailed in *A Treatise of Human Nature*, Bk. 3, Part 2 (Hume 1888) and developed in ch. 3 of the *Enquiry Concerning the Principles of Morals* plus Appendix 3 (Hume 1975).

4   I see this ambiguity in Locke alone, but my reading of these authors is (1) idiosyncratic, and (2) cannot be defended here. There is ambiguity in Locke because he is keen to use *any* argument which promises to support his conclusions.

5   Locke's arguments are presented in *The Second Treatise of Government*, ch. 5 (Locke 1960).

6   This point is emphasized by C. Taylor 1975: 87–94.

7   My preferred translation would be an adaptation of Knox, using 'embodiment' for *Dasein* and reading the final sentence as 'The *embodiment* which my willing thereby attains entails its recognizability by others' ('entails' has just the right implication of closure which Hegel's argument uses).

8   In Knowles 1983 I failed to draw this distinction.

9   This is not the most extreme such view that I have encountered. I once met a student who would have loved to study geology but was prevented

from doing so by her moral qualms about hammering away at rocks *in situ*. Quarrying, she believed, was entirely unacceptable!

10   Those who wish to develop a Hegelian account of such a pathology should study the *Phenomenology* (PS ¶570, SW 2: 438–9) and think of the propertyless guru as making a mistake similar to that of Origen who thought he could achieve freedom from the sexual demands of the flesh by castrating himself.

11   For discussion of this idea, and plenty of further references, see Munzer 1990: ch. 3 and Ingram 1994: chs 2–3.

12   Hence note, for an important difference between taking possession of oneself and taking possession of things: 'my *inner* idea and will that something should be *mine* is not enough to constitute property' (§51).

13   'Those goods, or rather substantial determinations, which constitute my own distinct personality and the universal essence of my self-consciousness are therefore *inalienable*, and my right to them is *imprescriptible*. They include my personality in general, my universal freedom of will, ethical life, and religion' (§66).

14   In §66 Hegel makes heavy weather of this point, admitting in the Remark '*the possibility of the alienation of personality*', but insisting that such a process is inherently contradictory. In the background is several centuries' discussion of the legitimacy of slavery (as Hegel acknowledges in discussing 'the alleged justification of *slavery*' at §57R). For an influential contribution, see Rousseau's savage dissection of Grotius in *The Social Contract*, Bk. 1, ch. 4. Hegel's contradiction is speedily resolved. The alienation of personality is possible because slavery, serfdom etc. *happened* and because there are still superstitious people around who are prepared to cede authority to others in matters of religion or conscience (Catholics, presumably). But once a person acknowledges himself truly as a person, he cannot consent to the alienation of the powers of personality, since part of what it is to be a person is to recognize this status as inalienable.

15   Hegel himself does not distinguish collective and common property. For clarification of this distinction, see Waldron 1988: 40–2.

16   In §64R Hegel gives the interesting example of public memorials as national property.

17   Marx himself subjects Hegel's defence of entailment and primogeniture for the land-owning estate to vituperative criticism (Marx 1970: 97–111).

18   To Nozick, valuable to the point that it justifies near-absolute side-constraints against the redistributive activities of others (Nozick 1974: 149–64).

19   For a detailed discussion of needs as an element of distributive justice, see Braybrooke 1987.

20   A distinctive position on this issue is worked out in Burns 1996: 12–66. Burns stresses that Hegel's conception of natural law is not the familiar, universalist, Stoic conception.

21   Mark Tunick, in correspondence, used this terminology, which I appropriate because I think it is apt.

22   I conceal here a very real problem of the modern world concerning policies which might govern the privatization of hitherto common resources. Locke said private property was necessary, otherwise 'man had starved'. I agree. But what principles should constrain the transfer of public resources into private ownership? The question is pressing with respect to the agricultural land of China and rainforests all over the world. Rulers should certainly not give scrips of paper worth, say, two years' income to desperate workers or inhabitants who then sell their capital to national monopolies (as happened in Russia) or global companies.

23   This is a personal allusion. At Birds Green, in Essex, notices were nailed on every tree bounding a water meadow I used to walk through, watching sedge warblers and kingfishers, of the kind 'Keep Out', 'Private Property', 'Trespassers will be Prosecuted', 'Savage Dog'. I never saw the tenants, or their dog, and cared nothing for the rights they announced.

6   Abstract Right 3. Wrongdoing and Punishment: §§82–104

1   This summarizes brutally the discussions in SL, Bk. 2, §2, 479–528; SW 4: 597–661 and EL §§130–41; SW 8: 297–319.

2   He refers us to the *Science of Logic* where he contrasts crime and civil offences. 'But *crime* is the *infinite judgement* which negates not merely the particular right, but the universal sphere as well, negates *right as right*' (SL: 641 / SW 5: 90).

3   Wood 1990: 110 and Tunick 1992b usefully relate this argument to Feinberg's 'expressive theory of punishment'. One element of Feinberg's analysis is the claim that punishment may 'vindicate' the law (Feinberg 1970: 104).

4   Put by Benn and Peters 1959: 177–8, and Wood 1990: 110–12.

5   This reading is confirmed in the *Propaedeutic*: 'It [the principle or law of the criminal's action] is valid only for the one who committed it because he alone recognizes it by his action and no-one else. He himself,

therefore, is essentially subject to this principle or "Law" and it must be carried out against him' (PP: 31; SW 3: 68).

6 I defend this argument in Knowles 1999: 35–47, where I argue that it shores up weaknesses in both forfeiture and consent arguments to the conclusion that the criminal wills his own punishment.

7 Readers who are interested in the range of arguments for punishment which is deemed retributive should look at Cottingham 1979.

8 The terminology is Hart's from Hart 1968: 8–11.

9 A conspicuous example is Duff 1986.

10 W. Cobbett, *Advice to Young Men and Women, Advice to a Citizen*, cited in Waldron 1999: 232.

7 Morality 1. Hegel's Philosophy of Action and Moral Psychology: §§105–28

1 Hegel never met Kant, but readers should be reminded of the chronology. Hegel was born in 1770. Kant's major publications in moral philosophy are dated as follows: *Groundwork of the Metaphysics of Morals* (1785); *Critique of Practical Reason* (1788); *The Metaphysics of Morals* (1797). No doubt, nowadays, he would have met him at a conference.

2 This is not strictly true, as Hegel half-heartedly concedes in §113R, since amongst other things, the analysis of contract and, most conspicuously, the classification of types of wrongdoing, trade on a specification of agents' intentions.

3 For a splendid example of the best modern work which deploys these concepts with due care, see Nagel 1987.

4 Taylor argues the case for the importance of understanding Hegel's philosophy of mind and action in C. Taylor 1985a, 1: 77–96. The 'expressivist' reading of Hegel which underpins this argument is sketched in C. Taylor 1975: ch. 3.

5 Hegel distinguishes *Tat* and *Handlung*. Nisbet scrupulously translates these as 'deed' and 'action' respectively. Knox sometimes translates *Tat* as 'deed', sometimes as 'act'. Hegel is making a philosophical distinction which, to my knowledge, neither the German terms nor the variety of English translations mark. I use the term 'intervention' to translate *Tat*, because to my ear it sounds causal and mechanical. That said, I think that the philosophical points Hegel wants to make could have been advanced more clearly had he spoken of *Tat* as 'initial intervention' in the technical sense of bodily movement in the physical world and then

explained *Handlung* as the expansion of this, taking account of agents' purposes in light of their knowledge of necessary causal consequences.

6   Hegel was enormously interested in the variety of abnormal psychical states which bear on the question of responsibility. See ES §§402–8, especially the very long Remark to §408 where a variety of forms of insanity are (not unsympathetically) discussed.

7   In saying that agents have privileged access to their own intentions, I don't claim that they *always* have knowledge of their intentions or that such knowledge is *always* gained through the route of introspection or self-awareness. I can learn from your critical remarks that I intended to spite another, though I have somehow concealed that from myself. On the other hand, it is generally true that I know what I am doing because I generally act in full light of my intentions. I don't often observe my actions and work out the nature of my actions from my observance of them, but I sometimes do – as when the remarks of others force me to make a review of them. I'm sure Hegel knew these things.

8   In the *Encyclopaedia* this element of normativity is termed 'the "Ought of practical feeling" [*Das praktische Gefühl enthält das Sollen*]' (ES §472).

9   I interpolate 'latter' since both the Knox and Nisbet translations, and the original German, are ambiguous on my reading. Incredibly, this sentence can read as an attack on either egoism or Kantianism as the 'empty assertion', depending on which kind of end (subjective satisfaction / end of absolute worth) one takes Hegel to be referring to. The next sentence compounds the difficulty since it is not clear whether the viewpoint characterized is that of a cynical Kantian or a reductive egoist. The remark clarifies the target of the criticism.

10 I should stress again how far assessment of Hegel's criticism of Kant depends on one's view of the accuracy of Hegel's reading of Kant – and this, of course, will depend on one's own reading of Kant. The difficulties here are immense (which should encourage you to read further). To take the point at issue in the present discussion: I read Kant's discussion of the shopkeeper example to hinge on *the fact that* honesty is the best policy for the shopkeeper, a fact that is known to the shopkeeper and us observers. I take Kant to be considering how far general knowledge of this fact (including the imputation of it to the shopkeeper) affects our judgement of the moral worth of his actions. Allen Wood, by contrast, takes the basic datum of the example to be that the shopkeeper is *motivated* by self-interest, his prime concern being to avoid a bad reputation (Wood 1999: 26–30). I think the example *raises* the

question of the shopkeeper's motivation, and settles the issue of the moral worth of his honest dealings by claiming that the fact of his evident advantage must bespeak his motivation. Thus I see a mistaken inference where Wood sees a postulate of the example – all this on the basis of one paragraph!

11 The quip is Schiller's, inaccurately quoted. For references see Wood's editorial note (PR: 424). Kant resented this imputation, as he would have resented Hegel's recycling of the charge. It is, of course, an open question whether his writings imply this reading or entail this conclusion.

12 'Consequently, effect contains nothing whatever that cause does not contain. Conversely, cause contains nothing which is not in its effect. Cause is cause only in so far as it produces an effect, and cause is nothing but this determination, to have an effect, and effect is nothing but this, to have a cause. Cause as such implies its effect, and effect implies cause; in so far as cause has not yet acted, or if it has ceased to act, then it is not cause, and effect in so far as its cause has vanished, is no longer effect but an indifferent actuality . . . Through this identity of content this causality is an *analytic* proposition. It is the *same fact* which presents itself once as cause and again as effect' (SL: 559–60 / SW 4: 704). I think it is possible to read this passage accurately and to defend every claim in it as true without endorsing the conclusion that cause and effect are identical events.

13 I read the Remark to §126 as making clear reference to the case of de Wette, a theologian at the University of Berlin who was dismissed for sympathizing with Sand, the student who assassinated Kotzbue. For details, see Pinkard 2000: 438–42.

8   Morality 2. The Good: §§129–41

1 'So far, so good', said he optimistically. But now we know that fighter-planes circle our skies with orders to shoot down commercial aircraft which hijackers have converted to armed missiles, notwithstanding the innocent passengers on board.

2 For details, see Beiser 1987: 171–2, 184–5, 190–2, discussing the responses of Tittel and Pistorius to the *Groundwork*.

3 In what follows, I use the account of the application of the categorical imperative as a universalizability test given in O'Neill 1989: 96–103.

4 This example is used by Onora O'Neill 1989: 96. A similar maxim is tested, with similar results, by Wood 1990: 157: 'I will never work, but always live by exploiting the labour of others'.

5   This nice example comes from Blackburn 1998: 218.

6   The principle of humanity: 'So act that you use humanity, whether in
       your own person or in the person of any other, always at the same time
       as an end, never merely as a means' (GMM: 80 / Ak. 4: 429); the prin-
       ciple of autonomy: 'the idea of the will of every rational being as a *will
       giving universal law*' (GMM: 82 / Ak. 4: 432), formulated in a more
       technical fashion as 'act in accordance with the maxims of a member
       giving universal laws for a merely possible kingdom of ends' (GMM:
       88 / Ak. 4: 439).

7   These are reproduced in Rousseau 1997. The conceit of the 'beautiful
       soul' is examined in Norton 1995.

8   Volpone in Molière's play *Volpone*; Holy Willie in Robert Burns's mag-
       nificent eponymous poem; Casaubon in George Eliot's *Middlemarch.*

9   Hegel has opened up a nice question here: I think real hypocrisy always
       adduces an element of self-deception. My wife disagrees. She thinks
       hypocrisy may be adopted as the strategy of an amoral self-interested
       opportunist. I think that's not hypocrisy; that's just self-interested oppor-
       tunism. I invite readers to come between man and wife.

10   Hegel thought irony was the product of the Romantic appropriators of
       Fichte, and had in mind chiefly Friedrich von Schlegel, whom he
       detested from his days in Jena. See Wood's editorial notes in PR for
       further attributions.

11   Here I have in mind Smart 1973: 7–9 and Mackie 1977: chs 1 and 7.

12   Is this what Nietzsche or the post-modernists say? I leave readers to
       pursue the matter.

9   The Concept of Ethical Life: §§142–57

1   The terminology might be clearer. We can think of the State in two
       ways: first, as 'the strictly political state' (Knox's translation in §267),
       the constitutional apparatus of legislative, executive and sovereign
       powers; second, we can think of the Rational State as the structured
       totality of rules and institutions which constitute the Ethical Life of a
       people. As such it will include the Family, Civil Society and the strictly
       political state. It will generally be obvious which conception of the state
       is being employed. (Hegel confuses matters further by referring to Civil
       Society as the (external) state at several points – e.g. §§157, 183, 187.)

2   John Searle has been a conspicuous recent exception in his studies of
       the social world. See Searle 1995 or, for a summary, 1999: 111–34. For
       studies of the nature of law, see, e.g., Hart 1961; Raz 1979.

3   This point is emphasized and helpfully explained in Neuhouser 2000: 37–49.

4   Rawls 1972: 20–1, 48–51. Rawls's exposition is more subtle and nuanced than my use of it suggests. Like many commentators, I find the term 'reflective equilibrium' so useful that I ignore the detail in the work which established the usage.

5   I like the word 'synthesis' in this context and use it despite its association with the old, partly true, partly false, description of the Hegelian and/or Marxist dialectic as a synthesis of thesis and antithesis.

10   The Family: §§158–81

1   This is why Susan Moller Okin is wrong to think Hegel's account of family life is based on an ethics of altruism (Okin 1979: 284–5).

2   Knox's translation of this passage '[marriage] is precisely a contract to transcend the standpoint of contract' makes Hegel's argument look needlessly paradoxical and has possibly misled some critics. Carole Pateman, e.g., asks 'Why should a theorist who declares that it is shameful to see marriage as merely contractual still insist that marriage originates in a contract?' (Pateman 1988: 179). Hegel does not so insist. He speaks of the free consent of parties who stand to each other as individual persons (§162) and in §164 distinguishes the 'solemn declaration of consent to the ethical bond of marriage' from the 'stipulation of a contract', though each have an external embodiment, the first in a public ceremony, the second in the transfer of property. Mutual consent is not always contract, as Hegel knows all lovers know.

3   Dorothea Schlegel and Caroline Schlegel, who married Schelling, are obvious examples. See Pinkard 2000 for details.

4   Neuhouser 2000: 277–8 also draws this conclusion.

5   I think Jeremy Waldron makes this mistake in an otherwise valuable article. See Waldron 1993: 370–3.

6   I know, sadly, this isn't true of, e.g., orphaned or abandoned children brought up in, say, council homes. But I (and Hegel) speak of societal *norms* in a range of senses from the statistical to the ethical. Plato and advocates of the kibbutz would reject what they see as an equivocation.

7   Hardimon makes this point when comparing Hegel's account of social life with that of modern communitarians (Hardimon 1994: 163).

11 Civil Society 1. The System of Needs and the Administration of Justice: §§182–229

1 Which is not to say that it does not have recognizable sources: the term is explicit in Adam Ferguson (1767), *An Essay on the History of Civil Society*; central elements of Hegel's concept were elaborated in Sir James Steuart (1767), *Inquiry into the Principles of Political Oeconomy* and Adam Smith (1776), *An Inquiry into the Nature and Causes of the Wealth of Nations*. Hegel's debt to the great sociologists and economists of the Scottish Enlightenment is barely acknowledged in the text of the *Philosophy of Right*. (He started reading their works as early as 1793/4, and his interest in British current affairs, first stimulated in Berne, continued to his death.) In respect of Hegel's description of the modern economy, Britain at the dawn of the Industrial Revolution is the model of a 'Civil Society'; Germany was backward in these things. The extent and specific details of this important intellectual debt are charted in a lovely book: Waszek 1988. Hegel's originality is challenged in Cohen and Arato 1992: 89.

2 See Riedel 1984: 129–56 for an authoritative discussion.

3 'Need becomes *care for the family*' (§203R). For 'self-interest', 'selfish' and cognate expressions scattered through Hegel's account of Civil Society one could often substitute the barbarous modern coinage 'self-referential altruism' (due, I believe, to C. D. Broad), remembering that the dichotomy of self and other is transcended *within* the family, but is entrenched (though mediated) outside it in Civil Society.

4 These notions are scattered through Rousseau's two Discourses, 'On the Arts and Sciences' and, most conspicuously, 'On the Origin of Inequality'. See Rousseau 1973.

5 For full details, look at Pinkard 2000: Index.

6 The term 'rule of recognition' is due to Hart 1961: 97–107. I intend it to cover whatever sources are appealed to in order to establish the credentials of laws as authoritatively binding. The fact of the enactment of a statute by a properly constituted legislature is a clear example, which can also serve to introduce the difficulties: Does the law introduced by the statute include the preamble to the statute or the legislator's intentions as recorded in Parliamentary debates, and so on? I do not mean to imply that there is but one rule of recognition or that the system of rules which comprise the practice of recognition is susceptible of uncontroversial or uncontestable specification.

7 Curiously, such a defence of Hegel would place him in the camp of Ronald Dworkin in his criticism of modern legal positivism, not least

since Dworkin emphasizes the immanence of rights to the modern mind, i.e. the American constitution. See Dworkin 1977.

8   Interestingly, Hegel evidently has in mind the Napoleonic Code, or a speculative up-to-date Germanicized version of it, rather than the legal system of his contemporary Prussia. Curiously, for historians of ideas, it is possible that his contempt for the lack (of the possibility of) codification in the English legal system comes from his acquaintance with Bentham's trenchant criticisms, as discussed by Romilly in the *Edinburgh Review* (1817). For details, see Petry 1984: 149–50.

9   This principle is stated explicitly in the Preface to the *Phenomenology*: 'Science [must not be so articulated that it] lacks universal intelligibility, and gives the appearance of being the esoteric possession of a few individuals ... Only what is completely determined is at once exoteric, comprehensible and capable of being learned and appropriated by all. The intelligible form of Science is the way open and equally accessible to everyone' (PS: ¶13 / SW 2: 19).

12   Civil Society 2. The Police and the Corporations: §§230–56

1   We should read much of Hegel's description of Civil Society as picking up threads left loose in earlier discussions. Remember the right of distress which posed a conflict between the claims of right and the claims of welfare (§§127–8)? The theory of the good was supposed to resolve this conflict, but of course the Kantian theory of the good was judged a failure. Hegel's attempt to settle the problem is detailed in the following sections, most importantly §§241–6.

2   See the editor's note to §231 at p. 450 for a clear discussion of the unfamiliar and technical terminology and translation.

3   Hegel says in the notes that the rabble are disposed to *eine innere Empörung* (inner rage, anger, indignation, and also rebellion) (VPR 4: 609). He uses the same phrase in the 1819 lectures (VPR 19: 195–6, trans. in Tunick 1992a: 140–1) and argues that the rabble have a *standing* right of distress (whereby the theft of a loaf of bread by a starving person is not to be regarded as common theft) (§§127–8). In his editor's introduction to these lectures, Henrich argues that this amounts to Hegel's unambiguously conceding a right of the poor to rebel. I don't see it. For further discussion of these issues, see Tunick 1992a: 116–20 and Tunick 1998.

4   It is to Hegel's very great credit that he does not say that the allevia-
    tion of poverty is a prudent response on the part of a civil society which
    is anxious to avoid disruption at best, rebellion at worst, that he empha-
    sizes the moral responsibity of society to tackle the problem.

5   Hardimon, whose discussion of civil society and the attendant problem
    of poverty is as good as any in the literature, must be wrong to say that
    'One possible solution that Hegel did not consider but clearly could
    have is colonization'. The promotion and facilitation of colonization
    would not be a function of the police did it not address a problem in
    the civil society of the old country. The only problem I can think of
    which 'drives' nations to colonize is that of over-population, which is
    a problem not of *crowding*, but of poverty.

6   What follows is a very brief and doubtless controversial summary of
    some of Rousseau's key doctrines. Much of Hegel's social theory can
    be read through the lens of Rousseau's sketchy and under-developed
    ideas. This is one of the themes of Neuhouser's excellent recent mono-
    graph (2000).

7   Years ago, at a meeting of the Hegel Society of Great Britain, I heard
    H. S. Harris say something like 'Of course, the *Philosophy of Right* was
    Hegel rewriting Rousseau's doctrine of the general will for the modern
    state realistically described.' It struck me then that there was something
    dead right about this nutshell characterization of Hegel's project and I
    have been trying to work out exactly what that is ever since. The
    nuances required by the project of comparing and contrasting Hegel and
    Rousseau are formidably subtle, not least given the peculiar combina-
    tion of *de haut en bas* commendation, wilful misinterpretation and
    caustic criticism in Hegel's published discussions of Rousseau. Bless
    him for travelling to l'Ermitage when he stayed in Paris, but did he visit
    Rousseau's tomb in the Pantheon? Was it open to visitors? He doesn't
    record the trip in his letters.

13   The State: §§257–360

1   The second target of Hegel's criticism is the theoryless theory of von
    Haller, as Hegel explains it (§258R and fn.), which I shan't discuss.

2   I don't wish to defend this reading of Rousseau in detail. For the gist
    of my account read *The Social Contract*, Bk. 2, chs 3–4, Bk. 4, chs 1–2.

3   For a vigorous recent discussion of Hegel's criticism of contract theory,
    see Patten 1999: 104–38. A shorter version of this chapter is published
    in R. R. Williams 2001: 167–84. The most sustained and thorough

treatment of this question is found in Neuhouser 2000: 175–224 and index. A wider-ranging review of Hegel's hostility to liberal social theory is Smith 1989: 57–97.

4   Which is silly, if Rousseau does indeed believe it to be a (conjectural, historical) description of mankind's origins – which he does – and not so silly, if he takes it as an elaboration of natural values, of mankind's irreducible moral status – which he also does. I hope this note (which I expect those who know Rousseau's work to find controversial) provokes readers to study Rousseau, who in political philosophy would have the same status as Kant is rightly accorded in metaphysics, had he had the same patience in philosophical argument. But, as I have suggested before, he was a philosophical angel, who saw and stated directly truths which need to be advanced by more careful argumentation. Rousseau the philosopher is undone by his *enthusiasm* (in *both* eighteenth- and twenty-first century senses of the word) for philosophy.

5   I refer to a grotesque episode in intellectual history. The curious should read Popper 1945 and the splendid counterblast, Kaufmann 1972. I suspect that one, albeit minor, cause of the wonderful renaissance in Hegel scholarship since the 1960s has been the provocation of Popper's appalling judgements.

6   In the final paragraph of the book Hegel tells us that 'the spiritual realm brings the existence of its heaven down to earth, to the ordinary secularity of actuality and representational thought' (§360).

7   John Rawls draws attention to the importance of this discussion in Rawls 2000: 347–8.

8   The most careful critical study of this aspect of Hegel's theory is Neuhouser 2000, which I commend to readers.

9   I don't want to discourage students who have a deeper interest in Hegel's work on these questions. The canonical texts are *The Science of Logic* (SL: 755–74 / SW 5: 236–61) and the *Encyclopaedia* §§337–76.

10 'Comical': let me explain for non-UK readers. From an insider's point of view, as a subject of HM Queen Elizabeth II, I judge good humour to be the only personal disposition that can accommodate the antics, and the daily dose of reports of the antics, of mine own hereditary monarchy, the British Royal Family.

11 Duncan Forbes takes this tack when defending Hegel against Marx's attack in his Introduction to ILPWH. Against the letter of Hegel's argument, I don't think such sympathetic interpretations can succeed. For a different view see Tunick 1991.

12   I shall capitalize 'Estates' when speaking of the political institutions; 'estates' will refer to the major classes of civil society which feed, in their different fashions, into the deliberations of the Estates.

13   Wood's editorial notes to Hegel (PR) track these sources with care.

14   I said above that Hegel plays fast and loose with his logical categories as he takes us through the detail of the constitution of a rational state. This argument is a good example. The legislative power attests the universal in the state. It issues laws which bind citizens universally in furtherance of the interests of the universal. But would not universality be actualized even more conspicuously were all those subject to laws and taxation granted a measure of political status as participants in public decision-making in *some* capacity? The answer is obviously 'Yes'.

      The harder and more subversive question is this: How could Hegel adjudicate the difference between his use of speculative logic and my modest attempt at the discipline? Notice how he *does* argue for representative institutions and a limited franchise. 'The idea [*Vorstellung*] that *everyone* should participate in the concerns of the state entails the further ["absurd"] assumption that *everyone is an expert on such matters*' (§308R). As Hegel was prone to say of competing positions, this looks to me a merely empirical judgement concerned with issues of efficiency and remedy, a matter for Grub Street practitioners to discuss rather than those entrusted to divine the logic of the concept.

15   The simple answer is that they are not. Thus far we have seen that women, the unemployed poor and members of the agricultural estate who are not members of the landed aristocracy, play no role in the election of representatives. Nor do day-labourers who are unfitted to be members of corporations.

16   For a brief defence of political freedom as an important positive liberty see Knowles 2001b: 105–7, 302–6.

17   The nub of Hobbes's story is to be found in *Leviathan*, ch. 13. The status of laws of nature in the state of nature as obligatory *in foro interno*, binding to 'a desire that they should take place', is given towards the end of ch. 15.

Further reading

The most straightforward brief introduction to Hegel's work as a whole, though necessarily much simplified, is Singer 1983, but if you find Caird 1883 in a second-hand bookshop, buy it, and read it, with pleasure and profit. Still the most comprehensive and stimulating study, though much criticized, is C. Taylor 1975. Plant 1983 is an important study, useful for readers who wish to broach the religious and metaphysical sources of Hegel's ethics. It also contains useful information on the development of Hegel's social philosophy. Beiser 1993 is a first-rate collection of expert but accessible articles covering Hegel's development and the whole range of his philosophy. Readers (*all* readers!) struggling with Hegel's terminology and concepts should keep Inwood's *A Hegel Dictionary* (1992) at their elbow. It is a most valuable resource.

Introductory reading on Hegel's social philosophy might include Walsh 1974; C. Taylor 1979b; Cullen 1979; and Houlgate 1991. K. Westphal's essay in Beiser 1993 is a splendid starting point. More

sophisticated treatments include Reyburn 1921; Forster 1935; Avineri 1972; Ritter 1982; Riedel 1984; Smith 1989; Tunick 1992a; Patten 1999; and Franco 1999. Useful collections include Pelczynski 1971a, 1984; Lamb 1998; and R. R. Williams 2001. Wood 1990 is an outstanding study: insightful, stimulating and provocative in equal measure. Readers will find it contains discussions of all the topics that follow. Theunissen 1991 is an important critical discussion in brief compass. Amongst historians of polical philosophy who deal with Hegel, Plamenatz 1963 and Hampsher-Monk 1992 are surefooted commentators.

For an extended study of Hegel's Preface to the *Philosophy of Right* see Peperzak 1987. Pinkard 2000: 418–68 gives a full account of the political background to, and the initial reception of, the *Philosophy of Right*, which explains the battles Hegel was fighting and the masters he was serving when he wrote the Preface. D'Hondt 1988 is too sympathetic to Hegel's predicament but worth reading as a corrective to hostile accounts. Hardimon 1994: 42–83 gives a splendid account of the implications of Hegel's 'double saying'.

Useful discussions of the Introduction to the *Philosophy of Right* include R. Schacht in MacIntyre 1972: 289–328; G. H. R. Parkinson in Inwood 1985: 153–73; Wood 1990: 36–52; Tunick 1992a: 37–75; R. B. Pippin in Siep 1997: 31–53; D. Knowles in Lamb 1998: 23–47; Patten 1999: 43–81; and Franco 1999: 154–87.

Hegel's account of property in Abstract Right has been widely discussed; his account of personhood less so. R. R. Williams 1997 is a very comprehensive treatment of Hegel's doctrine of recognition in the *Philosophy of Right* and elsewhere. On property, I recommend Stillman 1980a, 1980b and 1991; Ritter 1982: 124–50; Knowles 1983; Waldron 1988: 343–89; Wood 1990: 77–107; and Patten 1999: 139–62.

Hegel's account of punishment is carefully analysed by Cooper in Pelczynski 1971a: 151–67. Cooper's paper is heavily criticized in Wood 1990: 108–26. Lamb 1998 contains a number of fine papers which I do not discuss. The last word on the topic, for the moment (with further references) is Knowles, in R. R. Williams 2001: 125–45.

Careful discussions of the philosophy of action which Hegel broaches in 'Morality' are hard to find in the English literature. Wood

1990: 140–4, as ever, is useful. C. Taylor 1985b, 1: 77–96 is fascinating, though on my reading of Hegel, a curate's egg – mistaken in parts.

Studies of Hegel's criticism of Kant's ethics are legion. Both sides to the dispute have powerful protagonists. Important contributions include Bradley 1927: 142–59; Walsh 1974; T. O'Hagan in Priest 1987: 135–60; Sedgwick 1988; Wood 1989, 1990: 127–73; Siep 1997: 147–66; and Pippin 1997a: 92–128.

Helpful discussions of Hegel's notion of Ethical Life (*Sittlichkeit*) include Walsh 1974: 420–38; C. Taylor 1975: 365–88; Plant 1983: 124–83; Wood 1990: 195–218; Hardimon 1994: 144–73; and Neuhouser 2000.

Further reading on Hegel's discussion of family life includes Westphal 1980, 1984; Hardimon 1994: 175–89, 228–30; and Franco 1999: 234–49.

On Civil Society, useful discussions include Avineri 1972: 87–109, 141–67; Plant 1983: 207–32; Riedel 1984: 107–58; the essays by Ilting, Plant and Walton in Pelczynski 1984; Waszek 1988; Wood 1990: 237–55; Arato 1991; Hardimon 1994: 189–205, 236–50; and Franco 1999: 249–77.

On Hegel's theory of the (political) state, a miserable subject, read Ilting 1984a, a most important study. See also Pelczynski 1971b: 1–29; C. Taylor 1975: 438–61 and 1991; Kelly 1978: 90–152; Hardimon 1994: 205–27; Franco 1999: 278–341; Patten 1999, 2001; and Tunick 2001.

Bibliography

Works by Hegel

Early Theological Writings, trans. T. M. Knox, Chicago: University of Chicago Press, 1948.

Elements of the Philosophy of Right, trans. H. B. Nisbet, ed. A. W. Wood, Cambridge: Cambridge University Press, 1991.

Hegel's Lectures on Natural Right and Political Science: The First Philosophy of Right (Heidelberg 1817–1818), trans. J. M. Stewart and P. C. Hodgson, Berkeley: University of California Press, 1995. A translation of VSN.

Hegel's Logic, Part 1 of *The Encyclopaedia of the Philosophical Sciences*, trans. W. Wallace, Oxford: Clarendon Press, 1975.

Hegel's Phenomenology of Spirit, trans. A. V. Miller, Oxford: Clarendon Press, 1979. Cited by paragraph (¶) number.

Hegel's Philosophy of Mind, Part 3 of the *Encyclopaedia of the Philosophical Sciences*, trans. W. Wallace and A. V. Miller, Oxford: Clarendon Press, 1971.

Hegel's Philosophy of Right, trans. T. M. Knox, Oxford: Clarendon Press, 1952.

Hegel's Science of Logic, trans. A. V. Miller, London: George Allen & Unwin, 1969.

Jenaer Realphilosophie, ed. J. Hoffmeister, Hamburg: Felix Meiner Verlag, 1969. This text is partially translated in Rauch 1983.

Lectures on the Philosophy of World History: Introduction: Reason in History, trans. H. B. Nisbet, Cambridge: Cambridge University Press, 1975.

The Philosophical Propaedeutic, trans. A. V. Miller, ed. M. George and A. Vincent, Oxford: Basil Blackwell, 1986.

Philosophie des Rechts: Die Vorlesung von 1819/20 in einer Nachschrift, ed. D. Henrich, Frankfurt: Suhrkamp Verlag, 1983.

The Philosophy of History, trans. J. Sibree, New York: Dover, 1956.

Political Writings, trans. H. B. Nisbet, ed. L. Dickey and H. B. Nisbet, Cambridge: Cambridge University Press, 1999.

Sämtliche Werke, 22 vols plus *Hegel-Lexikon*, ed. H. Glockner, Stuttgart: Frommann Verlag, 1965. Cited by volume and page number.

Vorlesungen über Naturrecht und Staatswissenschaft, ed. C. Becker et al., Hamburg: Felix Meiner Verlag, 1983.

Vorlesungen über Rechtsphilosophie, 4 vols, ed. K.-H. Ilting, Stuttgart: Frommann Verlag, 1973.

Werke, in 20 vols., ed. E. Moldenhauer and K. M. Michel, Frankfurt: Suhrkamp Verlag, 1970.

Other works

Arato, A. (1991) 'A Reconstruction of Hegel's Theory of Civil Society', in Cornell, Rosenfeld and Carlson 1991: 301–20.

Avineri, S. (1972) *Hegel's Theory of the Modern State*, Cambridge: Cambridge University Press.

Beiser, F. C. (1987) *The Fate of Reason*, Cambridge, Mass.: Harvard University Press.

—— (ed.) (1993) *The Cambridge Companion to Hegel*, Cambridge: Cambridge University Press.

Benn, S. I. and Peters, R. S. (1959) *Social Principles and the Democratic State*, London: George Allen & Unwin.

Bennett, J. (1974) 'The Conscience of Huckleberry Finn', *Philosophy*, 49: 123–34.

Berlin, I. (1969) 'Two Concepts of Liberty', in *Four Essays on Liberty*, Oxford: Oxford University Press, 118–72.

Blackburn, S. (1998) *Ruling Illusions*, Oxford: Clarendon Press.

Boucher, D. (ed.) (1997) *The British Idealists*, Cambridge: Cambridge University Press.

Bradley, F. H. (1927) *Ethical Studies*, Oxford: Clarendon Press.

Braybrooke, D. (1987) *Meeting Needs*, Princeton, N.J.: Princeton University Press.

Burns, T. (1996) *Natural Law and Political Ideology in the Philosophy of Hegel*, Aldershot: Avebury.

Caird, E. (1883) *Hegel*, Edinburgh: Blackwood.

Cohen, J. L. and Arato, A. (1992) *Civil Society and Political Theory*, Cambridge, Mass.: MIT Press.

Cooper, D. E. (1971) 'Hegel's Theory of Punishment', in Pelczynski 1971a: 151–67.

Cornell, D., Rosenfeld, M. and Carlson, D. G. (eds) (1991) *Hegel and Legal Theory*, London: Routledge.

Cottingham, J. (1979) 'Varieties of Retribution', *Philosophical Quarterly*, 29: 238–46.

Cullen, B. (1979) *Hegel's Social and Political Thought*, Dublin: Gill & Macmillan.

Danto, A. (1984) 'Constructing an Epistemology of Human Rights: A Pseudo Problem?' in E. F. Paul, F. D. Miller and J. Paul (eds), *Human Rights*, Oxford: Basil Blackwell, 25–30.

Davidson, D. (1980) 'Actions, Reasons, and Causes', in *Essays on Actions and Events*, Oxford: Clarendon Press, 3–19.

Dennett, D. C. (1984) *Elbow Room*, Oxford: Oxford University Press.

Dent, N. J. H. (1992) *A Rousseau Dictionary*, Oxford: Basil Blackwell.

D'Hondt, J. (1988) *Hegel in his Time*, Peterborough, Ont.: Broadview Press.

Duff, R. A. (1986) *Trials and Punishments*, Cambridge: Cambridge University Press.

Dworkin, R. (1977) *Taking Rights Seriously*, London: Duckworth.

Feinberg, J. (1970) 'The Expressive Function of Punishment', in J. Feinberg, *Doing and Deserving*, Princeton, N.J.: Princeton University Press, 95–118.

Forster, M. B. (1935) *The Political Philosophies of Plato and Hegel*, Oxford: Clarendon Press.

Forster, M. N. (1993) 'Hegel's Dialectical Method', in Beiser 1993: 130–70.

Franco, P. (1999) *Hegel's Philosophy of Freedom*, New Haven: Yale University Press.

Frankfurt, H. (1971) 'Freedom of the Will and the Concept of a Person', *Journal of Philosophy*, 62: 5–20; repr. in Watson 1982: 81–95.

Gewirth, A. (1978) *Reason and Morality*, Chicago: University of Chicago Press.

—— (1996) *The Community of Rights*, Chicago: University of Chicago Press.

Hampsher-Monk, I. (1992) *A History of Modern Political Thought*, Oxford: Basil Blackwell.

Hardimon, M. (1994) *Hegel's Social Philosophy: The Project of Reconciliation*, Cambridge: Cambridge University Press.

Hare, R. M. (1963) *Freedom and Reason*, Oxford: Oxford University Press.

Harris, H. S. (1972) *Hegel's Development: Toward the Sunlight, 1770–1801*, Oxford: Clarendon Press.

Hart, H. L. A. (1961) *The Concept of Law*, Oxford: Clarendon Press.

—— (1968) 'Prolegomenon to the Principles of Punishment', in his *Punishment and Responsibility*, Oxford: Oxford University Press, 1–27.

Hayek, F. A. (1960) *The Constitution of Liberty*, London: Routledge & Kegan Paul.

—— (1976) *Law, Legislation and Liberty*, vol. 2: *The Mirage of Social Justice*, London: Routledge & Kegan Paul.

Hobbes, T. (1985) *Leviathan*, ed. C. B. Macpherson, Harmondsworth: Penguin.

Houlgate, S. (1991) *Freedom, Truth and History*, London: Routledge.

—— (1992) 'Hegel's Ethical Thought', *Bulletin of the Hegel Society of Great Britain*, no. 25, 1–17.

Hume, D. (1888) *A Treatise of Human Nature*, ed. L. A. Selby-Bigge, Oxford: Clarendon Press.

—— (1963) *Essays*, Oxford: Oxford University Press.

—— (1975) *Enquiries*, ed. P. H. Nidditch, Oxford: Clarendon Press.

Ilting, K.-H. (1984a) 'Hegel's Concept of the State and Marx's Early Critique', in Pelczynski 1984: 93–113.

—— (1984b) 'The Dialectic of Civil Society', in Pelczynski 1984: 211–26.

Ingram, A. (1994) *A Political Theory of Rights*, Oxford: Clarendon Press.

Inwood, M. (ed.) (1985) *Hegel*, Oxford: Oxford University Press.

—— (1992) *A Hegel Dictionary*, Oxford: Basil Blackwell.

Kant, I. (1952) *The Critique of Judgement*, trans. J. C. Meredith, Oxford: Clarendon Press, *Akademie* ed., vol. 5.

—— (1996a) 'Groundwork of the Metaphysics of Morals', *Akademie* ed., vol. 4 (Kant 1996c: 41–108).

—— (1996b) 'The Metaphysics of Morals', *Akademie* ed., vol. 6 (Kant 1996c: 353–603).

—— (1996c) *Practical Philosophy*, trans. and ed. M. J. Gregor, Cambridge: Cambridge University Press.

—— (1998) *Critique of Pure Reason*, trans. and ed. P. Guyer and A. Wood, Cambridge: Cambridge University Press.

Kaufmann, W. (1972) 'The Hegel Myth and Its Method', in MacIntyre 1972: 21–60.

Kelly, G. A. (1966) 'Notes on Hegel's "Lordship and Bondage"', *Review of Metaphysics*, 19: 189–217; repr. in Kelly 1978: 29–54.

—— (1969) *Idealism, Politics and History*, Cambridge: Cambridge University Press.

—— (1978) *Hegel's Retreat from Eleusis*, Princeton: Princeton University Press.

Knowles, D. (1979) 'Autonomy and Side-constraints', *Mind*, 88: 263–5.

—— (1983) 'Hegel on Property and Personality', *Philosophical Quarterly*, 33: 45–62; repr. in Stern 1993, 4: 293–311, and Lamb 1998, 1: 405–22.

—— (1998) 'Hegel on Will, Freedom and Right', in Lamb 1998, 1: 23–47.

—— (1999) 'Punishment and Rights', in M. Matravers (ed.), *Punishment and Political Theory*, Oxford: Hart Publishing, 28–47.

—— (2001a) 'Hegel on the Justification of Punishment', in R. R. Williams 2001: 125–45.

—— (2001b) *Political Philosophy*, London: Routledge.

Kojève, A. (1969) *Introduction to the Reading of Hegel*, abridged, trans. J. H. Nichols, New York: Basic Books.

Lamb, D. (1998) *Hegel*, vol. 1, Aldershot: Ashgate/Dartmouth.

Locke, J. (1960) *Two Treatises of Government*, Cambridge: Cambridge University Press.

—— (1975) *Essay Concerning Human Understanding,* ed. P. H. Nidditch, Oxford: Clarendon Press.

McCarney, J. (2000) *Hegel on History*, London: Routledge.

MacIntyre, A. (ed.) (1972) *Hegel: A Collection of Critical Essays*, New York: Doubleday.

—— (1981) *After Virtue*, London: Duckworth.

Mackie, J. L. (1977) *Ethics: Inventing Right and Wrong*, Harmondsworth: Penguin.

Marx, K. (1970) *Critique of Hegel's 'Philosophy of Right'*, ed. J. O'Malley, Cambridge: Cambridge University Press.

—— (1977) *Selected Works*, ed. D. McLellan, Oxford: Oxford University Press.

Mill, J. S. (1910) 'On Liberty', in *Utilitarianism, Liberty, Representative Government*, London: Dent, 61–170.

Moore, G. E. (1966) *Ethics*, Oxford: Oxford University Press.

Munzer, S. R. (1990) *A Theory of Property*, Cambridge: Cambridge University Press.

Nagel, T. (1970) *The Possibility of Altruism*, Oxford: Clarendon Press.

—— (1979) 'Moral Luck', in *Mortal Questions*, Cambridge: Cambridge University Press, 1979: 24–38; originally published in *Proceedings of the Aristotelian Society*, supp. vol. 50, 1976.

—— (1987) *The View from Nowhere*, Oxford: Clarendon Press.

Nash, O. (1985) *Candy is Dandy: The Best of Ogden Nash*, London: Methuen. The poem cited was first published in O. Nash, *I'm a Stranger Here Myself* (1938), Boston Mass.: Little Brown and Company.

Neuhouser, F. (2000) *Foundations of Hegel's Social Theory: Actualizing Freedom*, Cambridge, Mass.: Harvard University Press.

Norton, R. E. (1995) *The Beautiful Soul: Aesthetic Morality in the Eighteenth Century*, Ithaca, N.Y.: Cornell University Press.

Nozick, R. (1974) *Anarchy, State, and Utopia*, New York: Basic Books.

O'Hagan, T. (1987) 'On Hegel's Critique of Kant's Moral and Political Philosophy', in Priest 1987: 135–60.

Okin, S. M. (1979) *Women in Western Political Thought*, Princeton, N.J.: Princeton University Press.

O'Neill, O. (1989) *Constructions of Reason*, Cambridge: Cambridge University Press.

Parkinson, G. H. R. (1972) 'Hegel's Concept of Freedom', in Inwood 1985: 153–73.

Pateman, C. (1988) *The Sexual Contract*, Oxford: Polity Press.

Patten, A. (1999) *Hegel's Idea of Freedom*, Oxford: Oxford University Press.

—— (2001) 'Social Contract Theory and the Politics of Recognition in Hegel's Political Philosophy', in R. R. Williams 2001: 167–84.

Pelczynski, Z. A. (ed.) (1971a) *Hegel's Political Philosophy: Problems and Perspectives*, Cambridge: Cambridge University Press.

—— (1971b) 'The Hegelian Conception of the State', in Pelczynski 1971a: 1–29.

—— (ed.) (1984) *The State and Civil Society: Studies in Hegel's Political Philosophy*, Cambridge: Cambridge University Press.

Peperzak, A. T. (1987) *Philosophy and Politics: A Commentary on the Preface to Hegel's Philosophy of Right*, Dordrecht: Martinus Nijhoff.

Petry, M. J. (1984) 'Propaganda and Analysis: The Background to Hegel's Article on the English Reform Bill', in Pelczynski 1984: 137–58.

Pinkard, T. (2000) *Hegel: A Biography*, Cambridge: Cambridge University Press.

Pippin, R. B. (1997a) *Idealism as Modernism: Hegelian Variations*, Cambridge: Cambridge University Press.

—— (1997b) 'Hegel, Freedom, The Will. *The Philosophy of Right* (§§1–33)', in Siep 1997: 31–54.

Plamenatz, J. (1963) *Man and Society*, 2 vols, London: Longmans.

Plant, R. (1983) *Hegel*, 2nd ed., Oxford: Basil Blackwell.

—— (1984) 'Hegel on Identity and Legitimation', in Pelczynski 1984: 227–43.

Popper, K. (1945) *The Open Society and Its Enemies*, London: Routledge & Kegan Paul.

Priest, S. (ed.) (1987) *Hegel's Critique of Kant*, Oxford: Clarendon Press.

Rauch, L. (1983) *Hegel and the Human Spirit: A Translation of the Jena Lectures on the Philosophy of Spirit (1805–6) with Commentary*, Detroit: Wayne State University Press.

Rawls, J. (1972) *A Theory of Justice*, Oxford: Clarendon Press.

—— (2000) *Lectures on the History of Moral Philosophy*, Cambridge, Mass.: Harvard University Press.

Raz, J. (1979) *The Authority of Law*, Oxford: Clarendon Press.

Reyburn, H. (1921) *The Ethical Theory of Hegel: A Study of the Philosophy of Right*, Oxford: Clarendon Press.

Riedel, M. (ed.) (1975) *Materialien zu Hegels Rechtsphilosophie*, 2 vols, Frankfurt: Suhrkamp Verlag.

—— (1984) *Between Tradition and Revolution: The Hegelian Transformation of Political Philosophy*, trans. W. Wright, Cambridge: Cambridge University Press; a trans. of *Studien zu Hegels Rechtsphilosophie*, Frankfurt: Suhrkamp Verlag, 1972.

Ritter, J. (1982) *Hegel and the French Revolution*, Cambridge, Mass.: MIT Press.

Rorty, A. O. (ed.) (1980) *Essays on Aristotle's Ethics*, London: University of California Press.

Rosen, M. (1982) *Hegel's Dialectic and its Criticism*, Cambridge: Cambridge University Press.

Rousseau, J.-J. (1973) *The Social Contract and Discourses*, ed. G. D. H. Cole; rev. and aug. J. H. Brumfitt and J. C. Hall, London: Dent.

—— (1997) *Julie or the New Heloise*, trans. and annotated by P. Stewart and J. Vaché, vol. 6 of *The Collected Writings of Rousseau*, Hanover, N.H.: Dartmouth College; University Press of New England.

Sandel, M. (1982) *Liberalism and the Limits of Justice*, Cambridge: Cambridge University Press.

Schacht, R. (1972) 'Hegel on Freedom', in MacIntyre 1972: 289–328.

Schmidt, J. (1998) 'Cabbage Heads and Gulps of Water: Hegel on the Terror', *Political Theory*, 26: 4–32.

Scruton, R. (1986) *Sexual Desire*, London: Weidenfeld & Nicolson.

Searle, J. (1995) *The Construction of Social Reality*, Harmondsworth: Allen Lane.

—— (1999) *Mind, Language and Society*, London: Weidenfeld & Nicolson.

Sedgwick, S. (1988) 'Hegel's Critique of the Subjective Idealism of Kant's Ethics', *Journal of the History of Philosophy*, 26: 89–105.

Sidgwick, H. (1907) *The Methods of Ethics*, 7th edn, London: Macmillan.

Siep, L. (1983) 'The "Aufhebung" of Morality in Ethical Life', in Stepelevich and Lamb 1983: 137–56.

—— (ed.) (1997) *G. W. F. Hegel, Grundlinien der Philosophie des Rechts*, Berlin: Akademie Verlag.

Singer, P. (1983) *Hegel*, Oxford: Oxford University Press.

Smart, J. J. C. (1973) 'An Outline of a System of Utilitarian Ethics', in Smart and Williams 1973: 1–74.

Smart, J. J. C. and Williams, B. (1973) *Utilitarianism For and Against*, Cambridge: Cambridge University Press.

Smith, S. V. (1989) *Hegel's Critique of Liberalism*, Chicago: University of Chicago Press.

Steinberger, P. G. (1983) 'Hegel on Crime and Punishment', *American Political Science Review*, 77: 858–70.

Steinkraus, W. E. and Schmitz, K. L. (eds) (1980) *Art and Logic in Hegel's Phenomenology*, Atlantic Highlands, N.J.: Humanities Press.

Stepelevich, L. S. (ed.) (1983) *The Young Hegelians: An Anthology*, Cambridge: Cambridge University Press.

Stepelevich, L. S and Lamb, D. (eds) (1983) *Hegel's Philosophy of Action*, Atlantic Highlands, N.J.: Humanities Press.

Stern, R. (ed.) (1993) *G. W. F. Hegel: Critical Assessments*, 4 vols, London: Routledge.

—— (2002) *Hegel and the Phenomenology of Spirit*, London: Routledge.

Stillman, P. (1980a) 'Person, Property and Civil Society in the Philosophy of Right', in Verene 1980: 103–18.

—— (1980b) 'Property, Freedom and Individuality in Hegel's and Marx's Political Thought', in J. R. Pennock and J. W. Chapman (eds), *NOMOS* 22: *Property*, 130–67.

—— (1991) 'Property, Contract and Ethical Life', in Cornell, Rosenfeld and Carlson 1991: 205–27.

Strauss, L. (1952) *The Political Philosophy of Thomas Hobbes*, Chicago: University of Chicago Press.

Taylor, A. J. P. (1983) *A Personal History*, London: Hamish Hamilton.

Taylor, C. (1975) *Hegel*, Cambridge: Cambridge University Press.

—— (1976) 'Responsibility for Self', in A. O. Rorty (ed.), *The Identities of Persons*, London: University of California Press, 281–99; repr. in Watson 1982: 111–26.

—— (1977) 'What is Human Agency?' in T. Mischel (ed.) (1977), *The Self*, Oxford: Basil Blackwell, 103–35; repr. in C. Taylor 1985a, 1: 15–44.

—— (1979a) 'Atomism', in A. Kontos (ed.), *Powers, Possessions and Freedom*, Toronto: University of Toronto Press; repr. in C. Taylor 1985a, 2: 187–210.

—— (1979b) *Hegel and Modern Society*, Cambridge: Cambridge University Press.

—— (1985a) *Philosophical Papers*, 2 vols, Cambridge: Cambridge University Press.

—— (1985b) 'Hegel's Philosophy of Mind', in C. Taylor 1985a, 1: 77–96.

—— (1989) *Sources of the Self*, Cambridge: Cambridge University Press.

—— (1991) 'Hegel's Ambiguous Legacy for Modern Liberalism', in Cornell, Rosenfeld and Carlson 1991: 64–77.

Theunissen, M. (1991) 'The Repressed Intersubjectivity in Hegel's Philosophy of Right', in Cornell, Rosenfeld and Carlson 1991: 3–63.

Toews, J. E. (1980) *Hegelianism: The Path to Dialectical Humanism, 1805–41*, Cambridge: Cambridge University Press.

—— (1993) 'Transformations of Hegelianism', in Beiser 1993: 378–413.

Tunick, M. (1991) 'Hegel's Justification of Hereditary Monarchy', *History of Political Thought*, 12: 481–96.

—— (1992a) *Hegel's Political Philosophy*, Princeton, N.J.: Princeton University Press.

—— (1992b) *Punishment: Theory and Practice*, Berkeley: University of California Press.

—— (1994) 'Hegel's Non-Foundationalism: A Phenomenological Account of the Structure of the Philosophy of Right', *History of Philosophy Quarterly*, 11: 317–18.

—— (1998) 'Hegel on Justified Disobedience', *Political Theory*, 26: 514–35.

—— (2001) 'Hegel on Political Identity and the Ties that Bind', in R. R. Williams 2001: 67–90.

Verene, D. P. (ed.) (1980) *Hegel's Social and Political Thought: The Philosophy of Objective Spirit*, Atlantic Highlands, N.J.: Harvester Press.

Waldron, J. (1988) *The Right to Private Property*, Oxford: Clarendon Press.

—— (1993) 'The Need for Rights', in his *Liberal Rights*, Cambridge: Cambridge University Press, 370–91.

—— (1999) *Law and Disagreement*, Oxford: Clarendon Press.

Walsh, W. H. (1974) *Hegelian Ethics*, London: Macmillan; repr. in W. D. Hudson (ed.), *New Studies in Ethics*, vol 1.: *Classical Theories*, London: Macmillan, 1974: 379–464.

Walton, A. S. (1984) 'Economy, Utility and Community in Hegel's Theory of Civil Society', in Pelczynski 1984: 244–62.

Walzer, M. (1985) *Spheres of Justice*, Oxford: Basil Blackwell.

Waszek, N. (1988) *The Scottish Enlightenment and Hegel's Account of 'Civil Society'*, Dordrecht: Kluwer.

Watson, G. (1975) 'Free Agency', *Journal of Philosophy*, 72, 8: 205–20; repr. in G. Watson 1982: 96–110.

—— (ed.) (1982) *Free Will*, Oxford: Oxford University Press.

Weil, E. (1985) *Hegel et l'État*, Paris: J. Vrin.

Wenar, L. (1998) 'Original Acquisition of Private Property', *Mind*, vol. 107, no. 428: 799–819.

Westphal, K. (1991) 'Hegel's Critique of Kant's Moral Worldview', *Philosophical Topics*, 19: 133–76.

—— (1993) 'The Basic Context and Structure of Hegel's *Philosophy of Right*', in Beiser 1993: 234–69.

Westphal, M. (1980) 'Hegel's Theory of the Concept', in Steinkraus and Schmitz 1980: 103–20.

—— (1984) 'Hegel's Radical Idealism: Family and State as Ethical Communities', in Pelczynski 1984: 77–92.

Wiggins, D. (1987a) *Needs, Values, Truth*, Oxford: Basil Blackwell.

—— (1987b) 'Weakness of Will, Commensurability, and the Objects of Desire', in Wiggins 1987a: 239–67.

Williams, B. (1981) 'Moral Luck', in his *Moral Luck*, Cambridge: Cambridge University Press, 20–39; originally published in *Proceedings of the Aristotelian Society*, supp. vol. 50, 1976, 115–35.

Williams, H. (1983) *Kant's Political Philosophy*, Oxford: Basil Blackwell.

Williams, R. R. (1992) *Recognition: Fichte and Hegel on the Other*, Albany, N.Y.: SUNY Press.

—— (1997) *Hegel's Ethics of Recognition*, Berkeley: University of California Press.

—— (ed.) (2001) *Beyond Liberalism and Communitarianism: Studies in Hegel's Philosophy of Right*, Albany, N.Y.: SUNY Press.

Wolf, S. (1990) *Freedom within Reason*, Oxford: Oxford University Press.

Wood, A. W. (1989) 'The Emptiness of the Moral Will', *Monist*, 72: 454–83.

—— (1990) *Hegel's Ethical Thought*, Cambridge: Cambridge University Press.

—— (1992) 'Reply', *Bulletin of the Hegel Society of Great Britain*, no. 25, 34–50.

—— (1993) 'Hegel and Marxism', in Beiser 1993: 414–44.

—— (1997) 'Hegel's Critique of Morality', in Siep 1997: 147–66.

—— (1999) *Kant's Ethical Thought*, Cambridge: Cambridge University Press.

Index